THE HUMANITIES · Applied Aesthetics

4 th Edition

THE HUMANITIES

Applied Aesthetics

LOUISE DUDLEY
Professor of Humanities
Stephens College

AUSTIN FARICY
Professor of English
The Osaka (Japan) University of Foreign Studies

McGRAW-HILL BOOK COMPANY
New York   St. Louis   San Francisco
Toronto   London   Sydney

Before the first edition of this text was published in 1940, two experimental versions had been printed for class use; I wrote the first, Mr. Faricy and I the second. For the first and second editions Mr. Faricy contributed the chapters on music. For the third edition I alone was responsible. I made, however, extensive use of the illustrations selected and edited by Mr. Faricy.

For the fourth edition, new areas of subject matter have been introduced: the film, dance, opera, Japanese lyrics. Mr. James Shirky, a member of the Humanities staff of Stephens College, has rewritten entirely the chapters on music. Other important additions are the essays by Dr. James Rice. One essay to the teacher follows this preface; and his "Final Word" makes up Chapter 20 of this text. Mrs. Beverly Sterling and Mrs. Barbara Toalson have almost persuaded me that typing may be an art. Last, but by no means least, I am indebted to all the teachers of Humanities at Stephens College, both present and past, especially to Dr. Alfred Sterling, the present chairman of the department. Everyone has given me something of inspiration and of challenge.

Louise Dudley

CONTENTS

● PART FOUR – STYLE

LIST OF ILLUSTRATIONS

List of Illustrations

List of Illustrations

List of Illustrations

TO THE TEACHER: AN ESSAY ON TEACHING THE HUMANITIES

It used to be possible to define aesthetics as a "philosophy of beauty." In our time, however, "the emphasis has shifted from a definition of beauty as an abstract concept to observation of the arts and the kinds of human activity they involve. . . . It has become primarily a descriptive, empirical subject, aimed at understanding the arts and human activities concerned with them, such as the creation, enjoyment, use, and evaluation of arts."[1] The trend has been away from constructing a metaphysical framework toward a more naturalistic orientation. Psychology, sociology, morphology, and anthropology are seen as having greater relevance to the study of the arts than do ideal constructs. The humanities are thus seen as the expression of that which is most human and, therefore, not apart from the rest of life.

The purpose of the first course in the humanities should be to lead the student to an awareness that he is already an aesthetician, albeit at a very elementary level; that is, that he already reflects about the things he sees and hears and that he compares them and notes differences and similarities among them. It is only as he becomes able to do this that he can begin to appreciate aesthetics as the written record of other people's reflections on their experience with the arts. The first course, therefore, lays the groundwork for later courses in philosophy, aesthetics, history, and the arts themselves. It enables a student to approach these courses in greater perspective as the very human products of the kinds of activity in which he himself has been engaging.

There have been and continue to be two basic approaches to the study of the arts and humanities. The first is the historical approach; the second is sometimes called the "aesthetic-critical judgment" approach. Both types are common, although a recent study of undergraduate courses in the humanities concludes that there is an increasing shift away from the strict historical orientation to one emphasizing the importance of the individual art object and aesthetic-critical response to it.[2]

[1] Thomas Monroe, "Recent Developments in Aesthetics in America," American Council of Learned Societies, Newsletter, 15, 2 (February, 1964), pp. 1–13.

[2] James A. Fisher, (ed.), The Humanities in General Education, William C. Brown Company, Publishers, Dubuque, Iowa, 1960, pp. 237–238.

To the Teacher: An Essay on Teaching the Humanities

THE HISTORICAL APPROACH

In the historical approach examples of the arts are studied chronologically. Even when there is an attempt in the historically oriented courses to focus on the individual art object, the very framework of the course tends to give priority to other sorts of concerns: the date of the work, whether it came before or after another work, whether there are evidences of influence, whether the work is an early or late example of the artist, etc. All these are, of course, important concerns and lead to questions which *can* excite the student and involve him. Nonetheless such as approach may not be the best way of introducing the student to art as something to be responded to and of exercising him in significant ways of response. It tends to overvalue information, facts, and peripheral matters as prerequisite to appreciation, response, or personal experience. It contributes unduly to the student's sense of inadequacy before the art object and thus sets up psychological blocks to appreciation rather than invitations.

There is a further question to be raised about the historical approach in courses introducing the student to the arts. The need of economy in spanning even Western art forces the teacher and textbook writer into generalizations and into the use of a synoptic style. Whether or not the generalizations are accurate and regardless of how much historical fact they hold together, from the very outset they place the student outside the art experience and in a logical construct. They call upon him to operate deductively and tend to limit his response to those aspects of the works which validate the generalization. Because such validation is also a matter of concern to the teacher and the textbook writer, the same limitations predetermine what is included and excluded in the course. Methods of teaching can, of course, ameliorate the distortion presented and can, to some extent, engage the student's sensitivities inductively. There remains, however, a serious question as to whether these are achieved as easily and effectively in a historical framework as in some other approach. The necessity in education of depending predominantly on reproductions and photographs of what have become "the masterpieces" is already a distortion in structuring. It does not seem desirable to interpose willfully other obstacles to the student's moving in the rich and varied stream of artistic expression as he everywhere encounters it.

THE OBSERVING-RESPONDING APPROACH

The approach taken in this book is that of confronting the student with the art objects themselves as the primary content, not to inform him about theories concerning them nor philosophical systems into which they can be placed; it aims, rather, through encouraging experience with art objects themselves to stimulate philosophical thinking about the creative-perceiving process and the world view reflected in the art object.

The primary aim is to guide the student in arriving inductively at a few broad principles and concepts which are applicable to all art creations. This approach is in keeping with

To the Teacher: An Essay on Teaching the Humanities

current curricular design. The advantages of a concept approach are commonly known: concepts have an enduring life in the student after facts, details, and definitions have been forgotten, and they increase the likelihood of transfer from the examples studied to other examples encountered. It should be noted, however, that even this approach is not a complete safeguard against bad teaching nor against learning which is sheer rote or dissociated verbal facility. It, too, can deteriorate into teaching which is no more than the schoolman's game of stating a definition and building a course to support it. The student should be encouraged at every stage to think of the individual art object as unique—to take into account individual differences as well as similarities. Such an approach will permit a wider range of experience to grow out of the works of art instead of their being considered simply as examples of a given set of concepts. The concepts are simply guides to experiencing wherein the uniqueness lies. The aim is firsthand knowledge of the means by which man symbolically formulates the world as he sees it; its approach is to build inductively a reservoir of experiences and a philosophical style of mind which can be developed into more sophisticated formulations in later courses.

DIFFICULTIES

Even the emphasis on primal concepts as course content does not, however, avoid entirely the difficulties in "teaching" the humanities significantly.

> As is true of any learning material, basic concepts can be "taught" so that the student never sees their application or transfer value. An emphasis on rote memorization rather than the involvement of students in the application of ideas to new situations often results in students' comprehending an idea without having the faintest understanding of its significance as an explanatory principle. . . . The tragedy of so much college teaching, especially in broad survey courses, is that the student never comes to see the fundamental significance of what he is learning.[3]

Only the teacher can in the final analysis ensure that a concept remains generative, fertile, "full of seeds, bursting with its own corrections."

Perhaps one of the reasons we do not succeed so well as we would like in developing an appreciation of the humanities in undergraduate students is that we have capitulated too much to the methodologies of the sciences in our teaching of them. It is a little difficult to understand why we have done so. Perhaps it has come about because the sciences currently have an ascendancy on the academic scene and the emulation of them is an attempt to become academically respectable. Perhaps the graduate schools which have prepared our teachers have succeeded so well in becoming scientific that teachers of the humanities are dissociated from primary experience with the objects of their disciplines and no longer respond to them. Perhaps our perceptual apparatus has been so

---

[3] H. Bradley Sagen, "How Do Students Learn?" *North Central News Bulletin*, October, 1965, pp. 56–57.

conditioned, so frozen by education, that we can no longer *see* inductively. We can only deduce from formulations. Whatever the reasons, it is indeed true, as Francis H. Horn points out, that

> The study of the humanities has all too often succumbed to the techniques and objectives of other disciplines. Beginning courses are taught . . . as if every student were a potential major in the subject. Too much humanistic research is marked by the nit-picking characteristics of some scientific research.[4]

It is a purpose of the present text to keep before the student at all times the object of his inquiry and to insist that the object is as much an inquirer of him as he of it.

THE STUDENT

Even when the student is not introduced to the humanities through chronological coverage or survey approaches, he may still be confronted with an assumption that appreciation of a work of art is dependent upon his accurate knowledge of its place in history or his ability to build from bits and pieces of artifacts the world view that produced it and to project himself into it. Although many professors still champion this assumption to justify the kind of scholarship promulgated in graduate schools and operate on it in their own teaching, there is, so far as I can determine, no validity in it.

In the first place, what we now know of human psychology and perception forces us to concede that it is impossible for the student to project himself into another period and thereby to see the world as persons in that period saw it. The student is *himself*, and whatever he engages in involves himself. This *self* in addition to its own psychogenetic development has drawn upon the literary, artistic, scientific, and folk contributions of preceding eras. It is remarkable that professors of the arts who might have been expected to arrive at this insight first are among the last to do so. It was rather the practitioners of the most exact of the physical sciences, physics, who were to discover the solipsistic element in the ambiguous act of human observing and who were to point out that the observer is unable to remove himself from that which is observed and that he, therefore, is an important part of what he "sees."

There is another curious illogicality in the assumption that knowledge of the world in which a work of art was produced is prerequisite to understanding and appreciating it. This is the assumption that the original understanding is the most important—an assumption which discounts completely the concepts of cultural growth and accretion of interpretations. Is a reconstruction of London society in the 1600s more important to an understanding of *Hamlet* than contemporary psychology?

An equally astonishing simplification is the assumption that a "contemporary" *ever* existed. Reflection will reveal that there were at all times and in all places many, many

[4] Francis H. Horn, "Improving Humanistic Education," *Michigan Quarterly Review*, spring, 1965, p. 87.

To the Teacher: An Essay on Teaching the Humanities

variations on the "contemporary" just as there are at present. Who constitutes the contemporary audience which sees Albee's *Who's Afraid of Virginia Woolf?* in some consistent way?

If appreciation is to be developed, therefore, the student must be encouraged to bring to the documents of the past something else, something which historical scholarship cannot provide. That something is, of course, *himself.* The student is concerned with *his* responses to the art object as well as the art object itself. Since each student occupies a different station on the spectrum of cultural experience, he brings different factors to his appreciations, and these are qualitatively unique. He must use his own modes of perception to interpret the past; the most that he can be expected to do beyond this is to formulate a judgment of his own particular values as they relate to a consideration of universals.

In any course which does not take into account the fact that it is the self of the student which is the magnetic nucleus drawing to it whatever it needs for its own growth, extension and fulfillment will fail in developing his appreciative, affective potentials. To the extent that it is exclusively concerned with the knowledge of history and the artificial reconstructions of another world view and that it ignores the intimate personal nature with meaningful experience, it is doomed to produce students who are unable to use the responding sensitivities with which they are endowed.

THE THREE LANGUAGES AND THE ARTS

There is nothing occult or mysterious about the arts. They use two languages. The primary language is built into us as a part of our human heritage. Jacquetta Hawkes, in her introduction to the massive new *History of Mankind,* sponsored by UNESCO, notes that

> While civilizations have come and gone we are still born to the identical equipment of body and limbs already shaped a hundred thousand years or more ago—yes, down to our scratching nails and that tendency to long canine teeth. . . .
>
> What it will prove most important to remember is that our species did not only inherit from the past its bodily equipment, dominated by its subtly elaborated brain, but also highly charged emotional centres and all the strange ancient furniture of the unconscious mind . . . Today some of us believe (while others do not) that among the most elusive and yet the most precious heirlooms of all were shadowy deep-seated memories of the experience of the evolving animal line during the vast stretches of its history; memories which enrich and unite modern men by throwing up from the unconscious the images and ideas that inspire our arts and help to make them universally evocative. Memory of this kind, if it exists, not only unites men at a very profound level of their being through their common response to its

To the Teacher: An Essay on Teaching the Humanities

images, but also can serve to make us aware of their old kinship with all life and all being—that blessed and also truthful sense of one-ness of which our intellect, if granted too much power, quickly deprives us.[5]

This is the language of the arts to which we are all heir and to which we can all respond, given the chance and some reassurance of its validity. It is built into the very center of our humanity, and when it lies uncultivated and becomes "foreign" to us we become less than human:

> The cultivation of the arts is an education of the sensibilities, and if we are not given an education of this kind, if our hands remain empty and our perception of form is unexercised, then in idleness and vacancy we revert to violence and crime. When there is no will to creation, the death instinct takes over and wills endless, gratuitous destruction.[6]

The secondary language of the arts is made up of the conventions, the traditions, the styles, which have accumulated over the ages. The greater the number of art works we come to know intimately, the larger our vocabulary of these conventions.

There is, of course, a third language, which is *about* the arts. It is the language in which this and other books on the arts are written. It is not intended to put obstacles between the student and art, nor is it intended as a substitute for looking. One of the joys that come to us from experiencing the arts comes through our sharing the experience with other people. To do this we need some ability to talk about the arts meaningfully, expressively, and in ways which communicate. A certain amount of terminology, therefore, becomes necessary, not for its own sake but for enhancing our pleasure through sharing.

The distinction between the object as reality and theories, constructs, sciences about it is simple enough on reflection. It is because teachers and students appear to have difficulty in operating on the distinction that it is deserving of mention. Northrop Frye puts the matter neatly:

> Physics is an organized body of knowledge about nature, and a student of it says that he is learning physics, not that he is learning nature. Art, like nature, is the subject of a systematic study and has to be distinguished from the study itself, which is criticism. It is therefore impossible to "learn literature": one learns about it in a certain way, but what one learns, transitively, is the criticism of literature. Similarly, the difficulty often felt in "teaching literature" arises from the fact that it cannot be done: the criticism of literature is all that can be directly taught.[7]

---

[5] Jacquetta Hawkes and Sir Leonard Wooley, *History of Mankind, Volume I; Prehistory and the Beginnings of Civilization,* Harper and Row, Publishers, Incorporated, New York, 1963, p. 4.

[6] Sir Herbert Read, "Art and Life," *Saturday Evening Post,* 232:34–5, Sept. 26, 1959.

[7] Northrop Frye, "The Archetypes of Literature," in James E. Miller (ed.), *Myth and Method: Modern Theories of Fiction,* University of Nebraska Press, Lincoln, Nebraska, 1960, p. 144.

To the Teacher: An Essay on Teaching the Humanities

The student can, however, be invited to place himself in the presence of literature and the arts. He can have his perceptions heightened and his discernment sharpened by guidance. He can be encouraged into a valuing of the experience of perceiving. Further, he can be invited to reflective dialogue and constructive speculation about his responses.

This way of proceeding not only guards and nurtures his wholeness, his potential humaneness; it is the beginning of becoming an aesthetician, a critic. If the process is successfully cultivated it can result in persons who are sensitive yet confident in their authentic responses and who, therefore, will not be timid, awed, nor uncertain when they later meet the grand systems of aesthetics, criticism, and philosophy.

1
THREE BASIC
ASSUMPTIONS

● THE PURPOSE AND PLAN OF THE BOOK

This book has to do with the appreciation of the humanities. It is a subject which concerns everyone, for every day everyone makes decisions that are determined by his knowledge and appreciation of art. A child listens for his favorite radio serial; a teacher waits for a certain program on television; a young couple debate long and seriously about the materials for their living room. Even a hardheaded businessman who would deny emphatically any interest in art will trade in his automobile for one with better lines or will pay an extra hundred dollars for a special paint job! These are not examples of great art, it is true, but they show concern for art values.

Most of these people know that they are not getting all the pleasure they could from art. They know others who are getting greater pleasure than they from concerts, from paintings, from plays, and from poetry. And whether or not they realize it, they themselves would like to be getting more. In the realm of art they feel like the inhabitants of the world before Prometheus brought them the divine fire:

> Though they had eyes to see, they saw to no avail; they had ears, but understood not; but, like to shapes in dreams, throughout their length of days, without purpose they wrought all things in confusion.
>
> —AESCHYLUS (fifth century B.C., Greek dramatist). *Prometheus Bound,* 447–451, trans. Herbert Weir Smyth[1]

This book is written for those people. It cannot teach appreciation and it does not pretend to. Appreciation cannot be taught. Appreciation, like any other pleasure, is an experience, and experience can only be had. A book like this can, however, show some of the bases of appreciation, some of the qualities that others have enjoyed, and some of the basic principles that underlie all the arts. In short, this book tries to open the eyes and ears to art in order that, seeing and hearing, we may understand and enjoy.

The plan of the book is to start with the more nearly obvious principles of art and proceed to the more abstruse. The first two questions asked of any work are usually: What is it about? and What is it for? The first question concerns the *subject,* the second the *function* of a work of art. Accordingly, subject and function are discussed first. Subject and function, however, are not essential to all art, for there are works without subject and works without function. For this reason subject and function are grouped together as background.

The next question asked of a work of art is: What is it made of? The answer is its *medium.* Medium, of course, is essential, since any work of art can be known only as it is presented in some medium.

The fourth question is: How is it put together? This question is important because it has to do with *organization.* The elements of an art, whether they be tones, colors, or words, must be arranged according to some pattern to express meaning; in brief, they must be organized before we can have a work of art.

The two remaining questions are in the nature of a comment on the finished creation. One asks: What is the personality, the individuality of this work? This is the matter of *style.* The other asks: How good is it? This is *judgment.*

If these items are put in order we have the outline of this book:

1. Background.
   A. Subject. What is it about?
   B. Function. What is it for?
2. Medium. What is it made of?
3. Organization. How is it put together?
4. Style. What is its temper? Its mood? Its personality?
5. Judgment. How good is it?

[1]The Loeb Classical Library, published by Harvard University Press.

Before we begin on the formal presentation of these points, however, there are three assumptions about the nature of art which we need to clarify. They will determine our attitudes and our basic premises.

● THE AGE AND IMPORTANCE OF ART

The humanities constitute one of the oldest and most important means of expression developed by man. Even if we go back to those eras called prehistoric because they are older than any periods of which we have written records, we find works to which we give an important place in the roster of the humanities. In 1879 a Spaniard, accompanied by his little daughter, was exploring a cave. Suddenly she began to cry, "Bulls! Bulls!" He turned his lantern so that the light fell on the ceiling of the cave, and there he saw the pictures of wild boar, hind, and bison which we now know as the Altamira cave paintings (Figure 1). Since that time similar paintings have been found in other caves, and the experts have given their judgment that these belong to the Upper Paleolithic Age, ten to twenty thousand years before Christ.

FIGURE 1. GALLOPING WILD BOAR. (Found in the cave of Altamira, Spain. Photograph, courtesy American Museum of Natural History.)

4

Introduction

In almost every country the earliest art goes back to prehistory. The Greek epics the *Iliad* and the *Odyssey* date back to a time before the beginning of recorded history. These poems may have been put together between the twelfth and the ninth centuries B.C., but it is generally believed that they are collections of earlier tales which had been known and sung for many years before that time.

In the eighth century before Christ we hear the prophet Micah giving the essentials of true religion:

> He hath showed thee, O man, what is good;
> And what doth the Lord require of thee,
> But to do justly, and to love mercy,
> And to walk humbly with thy God?
> —Micah 6:8

Music and dancing we cannot find at so early a date because there were no adequate means of notation, but music we know was important at a very early age. In 586 B.C. the Greeks held a festival or competition at which one man played a composition for the aulos—a double-pipe reed instrument; there are also pictures of instruments on Greek vases. On a lekythos from the middle of the fifth century B.C. we have a painting of Apollo holding a kithara (Figure 2). This was the most important of the Greek instruments, the precursor of the modern harp.[2]

FIGURE 2. APOLLO WITH KITHARA, Greek lekythos from the middle of the fifth century B.C. (Red-figured lekythos. Terracotta. Height: 15 inches. New York, courtesy Metropolitan Museum of Art; gift of Mr. and Mrs. Leon Pomerance, 1953.)

[2]Donald J. Grout, *A History of Western Music*, pp. 5–7.

FIGURE 3. *NEFERTITI,* Queen of Egypt, Eighteenth Dynasty (ca. 1375 B.C.). (Plaster cast of a painted limestone original now in Berlin, New Museum. Life-size. New York, courtesy Metropolitan Museum of Art; Rogers Fund, 1925.)

In the Old Testament we have many references to musical instruments. In II Samuel 6:5 we are told that when the ark was brought home, "David and all the house of Israel were dancing lustily before the Eternal and singing with lutes, with lyres, with drums, with rattles, and with cymbals" (Moffatt translation). Moreover, the Hebrews had a song book, the Psalms, which in its present form probably dates from the second century B.C., though many of the songs are older. It is divided into five books, each closing with a doxology. Often there are definite directions as to how the song is to be sung. Psalm 9 is to be sung by a choir of soprano boys. Psalm 12 is for bass voices. Psalms 54 and 67 are with stringed instruments, as is 55. Psalm 5 is to have a flute accompaniment. At times the tune is given; and a favorite tune may be used for several poems, as at the present time. Psalms 57, 58, 59, and 75 are to be sung to the tune "Destroy it not" (Moffatt translation).

Not only is art found in all ages but it is found also in all the countries of the world. Stonehenge (Figure 47) is in England; the beautiful head of Nefertiti (Figure 3) is from Egypt; Aesop's *Fables* are Greek, as is the little song of Sappho:

Mother, I cannot mind my web today
All for a lad who has stolen my heart away.[3]

[3]Translated by Marjorie Carpenter.

The Arabian Nights are of course from Arabia. The *Rubáiyát of Omar Khay-yám* is Persian, though it is known to all of us in the English quatrains of Fitzgerald.

> A Book of Verses underneath the Bough,
> A Jug of Wine, a loaf of Bread—and Thou
>   Beside me singing in the Wilderness—
> Oh, Wilderness were Paradise enow!

It seems very modern, as does this short poem from the Chinese.

> What life can compare with this? Sitting quietly by the window,
> I watch the leaves fall and the flowers bloom, as the seasons come and go.[4]

No matter what age or what country we consider, there is always art. And this art is not good because it is old, but old because it is good! Songs and stories, pictures and statues have been preserved because they are alive, because they meet the needs of people, because they are liked. There is a timelessness and universality about art which makes us feel it is not old; that is, it does not grow old. The girl who says

> Mother, I cannot mind my web today
> All for a lad who has stolen my heart away

is not thinking that she ought to brush up on Sappho and the other Greek lyric poets. The chances are that she is having trouble doing her own work, all for a lad who has stolen her heart away. When we recite the Psalms, "The Lord is my shepherd I shall not want," or "By the rivers of Babylon, there we sat down, yea, we wept, when we remembered Zion," we do so because we find in them something that fits our needs.

A favorite is the tune to which we sing both "We won't go home until morning" and "For he's a jolly good fellow." Early French lyrics of the song began: "Malbrouk s'en va-t-en guerre" ("Marlborough is off to the wars"); it is dated about 1709, when the Duke of Marlborough was fighting in Flanders, and is said to have been a favorite of Marie Antoinette about 1780. It was introduced into the Beaumarchais comedy *Le Mariage de Figaro* in 1784. The tune itself, however, is much older. It was well known in Egypt and the East, and is said to have been sung by the Crusaders. But none of us who sing it today are thinking of these aspects of the song. We sing it because we like the song, because it fits our mood when we want a jolly, rollicking air.

Suppose it is a poem we are thinking about.

---

[4] Quoted from the Chinese of Seccho by Aldous Huxley, *Perennial Philosophy*, p. 63.

FIGURE 4. JACOB EPSTEIN (1880–1959), British sculptor. *Portrait of Oriel Ross* (1931). (Bronze. Height: 26½ inches. New York, Museum of Modern Art; gift of Edward M. M. Warburg. Photograph, courtesy Museum of Modern Art.)

Márgarét, are you gríeving
Over Goldengrove unleaving?
Leáves, líke the things of man, you
With your fresh thoughts care for, can you?
Ah! ás the heart grows older
It will come to such sights colder
By and by, nor spare a sigh
Though worlds of wanwood leafmeal lie;
And yet you wíll weep and know why.
Now no matter, child, the name:
Sórrow's spríngs aré the same.
Nor mouth had, no nor mind, expressed
What heart heard of, ghost guessed:
It ís the blight man was born for,
It is Margaret you mourn for.

        —GERARD MANLEY HOPKINS (1844–1889, British poet),
         "Spring and Fall: To a Young Child" (between 1876 and 1889)[5]

In the final evaluation of any work of art, age and nationality are matters of comparative indifference. Bach, Beethoven, and Brahms lived in different centuries and all composed great music; but the final evaluation depends on the music alone. Epstein's *Portrait of Oriel Ross* (Figure 4) was made in 1931, over three thousand years after the head of Queen Nefertiti of Egypt. There are differences that tell of the country and the date, but our judgment is determined by the works themselves.

[5]From *Collected Poems* by Gerard Manley Hopkins, Oxford University Press.

Introduction

The first point then about the humanities is that art has been created by all people, at all times, in all countries, and it lives because it is liked and enjoyed. A great work of art is never out of date. This point has been stated in many different ways by different people. Some speak of the intrinsic worth of art: its value is in itself. Berenson, the art critic and historian, talks of the "life-enhancing" value of art. Whatever the words used, the fact remains that we like art for itself, and the value of art like all spiritual values is not exhausted. It is used but it is not used up. It does not grow old. A good illustration is found in this quotation from President Kennedy's speech of November, 1962, on behalf of the National Cultural Center in Washington.

> Aeschylus and Plato are remembered today long after the triumphs of imperial Athens are gone. Dante outlived the ambitions of 13th century Florence. Goethe stands serenely above the politics of Germany and I am certain that after the dust of centuries has passed over our cities, we, too, will be remembered not for victories or defeats in battle or in politics, but for our contribution to the human spirit.

● ART AND EXPERIENCE

The second assumption essential to our study has to do with experience. It has been said that art is experience, because all art demands experience, but probably it is clearer to say that all art involves experience, that there can be no appreciation of art without experience.

When we say that art involves experience, we mean by experience just what we always mean by the word: the actual doing of something. If you have talked on television you know what that experience is. If you have never ridden a horse or fallen in love you do not know those experiences. You have always wanted to see the home of Washington at Mount Vernon; you have read much about it and have seen pictures of it, but you do not have the experience until you see it for yourself. It is one experience to sing a song and it is a different experience to hear it. It is an experience to read a story or see a play just as it is an experience to write the story or act in the play. But it is not an experience of the story, the song, or the play just to hear *about* it.

Olga Samaroff Stokowski expresses the idea when she says:

> Someone else can compose music for you.
> Someone else can perform music for you.
> No one on earth can listen to music for you.[6]

[6] Olga Samaroff Stokowski, *The Layman's Music Book*, p. 36.

And of course that statement is true in principle of all the arts. Each one must know a work for himself. The dramatist may write a good play, it may be presented by skillful actors, but it is lost to the critic unless he sees it for himself. The poet and the painter may write their poems and paint their pictures, but you cannot know, you cannot judge them unless you have heard and seen them for yourself, not as fact or information but as experience. On the lowest level, this means that since a work of art is always something to be seen or heard, we must see it or hear it, or see *and* hear it, if we are to know what it is. We must hear the music and see the painting if we are to know them. Years ago, Gertrude Stein was asked why she bought the pictures of the then unknown artist Picasso. "I like to look at them," said Miss Stein. After all, what can you do with a picture except to look at it? A painting is something to be looked at; a poem or a piece of music is to be heard. Many of the people who say they do not like poetry have never heard it; they read a poem as they would a stock market report or a telephone directory.

It is interesting and valuable to learn about any work, to know what the critics have said, or what were the conditions under which it was produced. But unless one knows the work itself, has experience of it, he knows little. The first and last demand of art is *experience.*

It is because of this physical appeal of art that we like to dwell on individual works. We look at a painting or a statue though we have seen it a thousand times. We drive a block out of the way every morning to see a building we admire. We continue to get pleasure from looking at Queen Nefertiti even though we have known this statue for years. In music we wear out a record playing it over and over, and if we are alone or among good friends we hum little bits of the melody. When we have heard Verdi's great aria "Celeste Aïda" ("Heavenly Aïda") the chances are that we will be singing it all the next day. We quote poetry to ourselves and to others:

> If thou didst ever hold me in thy heart,
> Absent thee from felicity a while
> And in this harsh world draw thy breath in pain
> To tell my story.
>
> —WILLIAM SHAKESPEARE (1564–1616, British poet and dramatist), *Hamlet,* V, ii, 356–359
> (ca. 1600)

> It is the blight man was born for,
> It is Margaret you mourn for.
>
> —HOPKINS,
> "Spring and Fall: To a Young Child"

The scientist has no such love for the manner in which a scientific idea is expressed. He does not walk down the street repeating happily to himself, "The square of the hypotenuse is equal to the sum of the squares of the other two sides," or "The distance of the sun from the earth is some ninety millions of miles." Such ideas may be and are just as exciting as those of poetry, but the idea and the words are not the same; to the scientist the physical presentation of an idea is not important. To the poet the idea and the words are the same. Change a word and you have changed the poem. It is this quality of experience that I think MacLeish had in mind when he said:

A poem should not mean
But be.[7]

All of the arts *are* more truly than they *mean*.

Before leaving this discussion we may note two characteristics of experience. First, the experience of art is personal and individual; it depends on what you are, what you have inside you. In the last analysis your experience will not be exactly the same as that of any other person. Do not expect to agree with everyone; all you can do is to be honest and straightforward.

Second, every experience is accompanied by some emotion, or emotional reaction. You like it or you do not like it. As you react, you think it is "wonderful," "frustrating," "fine"; or you say, "Lord, what fools these mortals be!" Your feeling may be changed markedly when you have closer acquaintance with that work or artist, but there is always some feeling that is a part of the experience.

● ART AND NATURE

There have been many books written about art, and there have been many learned theories to explain it. Some of these are good, some are poor; sometimes they agree, often they disagree. But on one point there is universal agreement. Art is *not* nature. Art is made by man. Art and nature are opposites. What is art is not nature; what is nature is not art.

There is a story that a woman looking at a painting by Matisse said, "I never saw a woman look like that!" and Matisse replied, "Madam, that is not a woman,

[7] Concluding lines of "Ars Poetica," from *Poems 1924–1935* by Archibald MacLeish. Used by permission of Houghton Mifflin Company.

that is a painting." A woman must be looked at as a woman, and a painting as a painting. We have just quoted the lines from *Hamlet:*

> If thou didst ever hold me in thy heart,
> Absent thee from felicity a while
> And in this harsh world draw thy breath in pain
> To tell my story.

No dying man ever said that.

Art is made by man, and no matter how close it is to nature, it always shows that it was made by man. Therefore we have a right to ask of any work of art: Why did the artist make it? What did he want to show? What experience was he trying to make clear? What had intrigued him so much that he wanted to share it with others?

As children, probably most of us thought an artist learned how to paint very much as we learned to sew on buttons, to drive a car, or to write on a typewriter. We supposed that when the artist found a scene he wanted to paint, he sat down and painted it. In this view the artist was a kind of human camera to reproduce a scene. Poetry and music seemed as easy, if one "knew how." The artist needed only to find words to rhyme or melodies to write and that was all. Such a view is, of course, nonsense.

The artist sees or learns something that impresses him, he wants to put it into some form so that others may understand it too, and he starts to make a picture, a poem, or a piece of music according to his present inspiration and his previous training. He does not worry much about beauty, but he wants desperately to get it "right," to have it express just the point he has in mind.

Suppose, for instance, a poet is feeling the intoxication and freshness of spring, the very first day of spring, "just spring." The children are all on fire with the new life of the day. They are so eager they can't take time to say Betty and Isabel or Eddie and Bill; instead, the words come rushing out all run together, *bettyandisbel, eddieandbill.* And all this is tied up in the poet's mind with the little old balloon man who is lame, "goat-footed" like a satyr, and whose whistle can be heard "far and wee." To express all that, the poet has only words on paper; he cannot even use voice or hands! No wonder he can't write as people do ordinarily. No wonder his words spill here and there over the page. No wonder he makes up new words—*puddle-wonderful, mud-luscious*—and spaces the words *far and wee* to try to make clear the faint sound of the whistle when it is first heard, and then the way the sound dies away in the distance. And when E. E. Cummings has finished, we feel he has captured the right flavor of the day.

Introduction

in Just-
spring   when the world is mud-
luscious the little
lame balloonman

whistles   far   and wee

and eddieandbill come
running from marbles and
piracies and it's
spring

when the world is puddle-wonderful

the queer
old balloonman whistles
far   and   wee
and bettyandisbel come dancing

from hop-scotch and jump-rope and

it's
spring
and
   the

       goat-footed

balloonMan   whistles
far
and
wee

    —E. E. CUMMINGS (1894–1962, American poet),
     "In Just-spring"[8]

Cézanne painted a landscape which he called *Well and Grinding Wheel in the Forest of the Château Noir* (Figure 5). It looks very much like scenes we have observed, and we would say Cézanne had copied nature. For this painting, however, we have a photograph of the exact scene (Figure 6), and we can compare the actual appearance of the landscape with Cézanne's version. First we notice the amount of detail. Cézanne gains unity by paying no attention to the

[8]From *Poems 1923–1954*, Harcourt, Brace and Company, Inc. Copyright 1923, 1926, 1944, 1951, 1954 by E. E. Cummings.

FIGURE 5. PAUL CÉZANNE (1839–1906), French painter. *Well and Grinding Wheel in the Forest of the Château Noir* (1895–1900). (Oil. Size: 25½ by 31½ inches. Merion, Pa., Barnes Foundation.)

FIGURE 6. Photograph of location of *Well and Grinding Wheel,* Figure 5. (Courtesy of Erle Loran, *Cézanne's Composition,* University of California Press.)

textures of the trees, the grass, or the stones; he paints them all in similar fashion. Next is the arrangement. In the painting the trees on the right are smaller, and there are more of them. The well and the grinding wheel in the center are made larger and more important. The path to the well is left out. And while he has kept the curling branches of the trees on the left, Cézanne has made them into a curved pattern which draws the eye to the trees on the right, and with them makes a circular movement which encloses the entire design. In the painting also he has made the contrasts between light and dark much less pronounced than in the photograph. In the painting we see what Cézanne has done with the landscape, or we see Cézanne's reaction to the landscape. He has changed details from the way they were in nature, and by doing so he has made a design that we want to look at and study. It is not nature, but art.

FIGURE 7. WINGED BULL WITH FIVE LEGS (ninth century B.C.), from the Palace of Ashurnas-irpal II. (Limestone. Height: 11½ feet. New York, courtesy Metropolitan Museum of Art; gift of John D. Rockefeller, Jr., 1932.)

FIGURE 8. Egyptian figure illustrating convention in Egyptian painting. (Drawing by Thad Suits.)

OUR PERCEPTION OF THE WORLD

When we say that art is not nature and that we should not expect to find in art exactly what we find in nature, we assume that all of us see the same things in nature and that our vision is accurate. But only a little study proves the oppo-site. We may look first at the statue of a bull that was found in front of an ancient Assyrian Palace (Figure 7); it is usually referred to as the "Guardian of the Palace." He is an important animal, large and stately, a very realistic bull. He should be capable of guarding anything that needed to be guarded. But if you look carefully, you can see that this bull is not like nature: he has five legs. There are four on the side, as you would see them if you were looking at him from the side. But come around in front; if you meet a quiet bull head-on, you expect to see two legs; one leg would look queer by itself, and so another leg was added.

Or turn to the Egyptians. We are all familiar with the Egyptian paintings of men and women, the thin straight bodies, stiff but graceful (Figure 8). We like them, but they do not follow nature. We notice first the eyes. If you look straight at a person's face, you see his eyes roughly as oval. If you look at a face in profile, the shape is entirely different. But when drawing a face the Egyptians made the head in profile with the eyes as of a full face. Nor was that all. The body was presented facing you, but the arms and legs were in profile. In those cases they were, of course, as were the makers of the Assyrian bull, portraying what they knew, what they thought of as the typical appearance instead of the actual look of things.

The same principles hold true in all aspects of life. The early works of Beethoven were thought to be the ravings of an upstart, and the orchestras of Wagner's time protested that his scores could not be played. We are all inclined to see and hear only what we know is there, what we have been taught to see and hear. The artist opens our eyes and ears so that we can see the world more clearly. Through the artist, we open our eyes and ears to new visions of life. And it is amazing how quickly we do learn to see what the artist is trying to show us. A few years ago, students looking at van Gogh's *Starry Night* (Figure 9) protested they never saw the sky look like that; now they sit back with a general purr of content: "*Ah*, van Gogh's *Starry Night!*"

● SUMMARY

The three basic assumptions of this study of the humanities are:
1. Art has been created by all people at all times; it lives because it is liked and enjoyed.
2. Art involves experience.
3. Art is not nature.

FIGURE 9. VINCENT VAN GOGH (1853–1890), Dutch painter, etcher, and lithographer. *The Starry Night* (1889). (Oil on canvas. Size: 29 by 36¼ inches. New York, Museum of Modern Art; acquired through the Lillie P. Bliss Bequest.)

BACKGROUND

2
SUBJECT

I like to see it lap the miles,
And lick the valleys up,
And stop to feed itself at tanks;
And then, prodigious, step

Around a pile of mountains,
And, supercilious, peer
In shanties by the sides of roads;
And then a quarry pare

To fit its sides, and crawl between,
Complaining all the while
In horrid, hooting stanza;
Then chase itself down hill

And neigh like Boanerges;
Then, punctual as a star,
Stop—docile and omnipotent—
At its own stable door.

      —EMILY DICKINSON (1830–1886, American poet),
        "I Like to See It Lap the Miles"[1]

[1] Martha Dickinson Bianchi and Alfred Lecte Hampson (eds.), *The Poems of Emily Dickinson*, Little, Brown and Company, Boston, 1939. Reprinted by permission.

● WHAT IS SUBJECT?

Subject is the term used for whatever is represented in a work of art. In the painting by Cézanne the subject is the landscape. In the poem at the beginning of this chapter the subject is a railroad train. The same subject is used in Honegger's music called *Pacific 231*. Each of the caryatids on the famous Porch of the Maidens on the Erechtheum (Figure 10) represents a young woman. The short piano composition by Ravel called *The Fountain* shows the rise and fall of the water in a fountain. In brief, the subject of a work of art answers the question: What is it about?

Not all arts have subject. Those arts without subject are called nonobjective; they do not represent anything. They are what they are without reference to anything in the natural world. The caryatids of the Erechtheum represent maidens, but the other columns of the building do not represent anything at all. The columns of the North Porch (Figure 11) are tall and graceful; they are very beautiful, but they do not imitate or represent anything. Bach's cantata

FIGURE 11. ERECHTHEUM, North Porch. (Pentelic marble. Height of columns: 21 feet, 7 inches. Photograph, Clarence Kennedy.)

FIGURE 10. ERECHTHEUM, Porch of the Maidens (420–393 B.C.). (Pentelic marble. Height of each caryatid: 7 feet, 9 inches. Athens, Acropolis. Photograph, courtesy Royal Greek Embassy.)

Christ Lag in Todesbanden has a subject, as the title indicates, *Christ Lay in the Bonds of Death,* but his *Brandenburg Concertos* do not have a subject. Subject is not essential to art.

Not only do some works of art have subject and some not, but in the matter of subject we find characteristic differences between one art and another. Architecture, for example, is essentially an art which is not representational. Occasionally we will see houses built to look like ice-cream freezers or coffeepots, if they are used for selling ice cream or coffee, but they are recognized as freak examples, and fortunately they are rare. A building is constructed for a certain purpose (a home, a factory, an office); and it may be in a definite style (Greek, Gothic, Romanesque); but usually it has no subject. A building may however show details that are representational although the building itself has no subject, as we saw in the Erechtheum.

If architecture is the art with the least use of subject, literature is the one with the most. When we read words we expect them to be *about* something. There are so-called poems and bits of prose which have no subject, but they are rare. So important is subject in literature that we usually name any piece of writing by its content, as, a novel of adventure, a psychological novel, a literary essay, or a poem about nature.

Sculpture and painting usually have subject. In looking at a painting or a statue, we expect to recognize the subject, to know what it is about: a man, a horse, a landscape, etc. And as in literature, painting and sculpture are classified according to the subjects employed. Paintings, for example, are identified as landscapes, seascapes, portraits, figure paintings, paintings of animals, etc. Statues are classified as portraits, single or group figures, animals, etc.

There is, however, a great deal of sculpture and painting without subject. The sculptor or the painter, like the architect, may make a design which is interesting in itself and which expresses his idea though it has no subject. Examples of this type are Henry Moore's *Two Forms* (Figure 12) and Mondriaan's

FIGURE 12. HENRY MOORE (1898–   ), British sculptor. *Two Forms* (1934). (Pynkado wood. Height: 11 inches. New York, Museum of Modern Art; gift of Sir Michael Sadler. Photograph, Soichi Sunami).

FIGURE 13. PIETER MONDRIAAN (1872–1944), Dutch painter. *Composition with Blue and White* (1935). (Oil on canvas. Size: 41 by 38 inches. Hartford, Conn., Wadsworth Atheneum.)

Composition with Blue and White (Figure 13). In these cases the artists do not expect the critic to imagine any specific subject.

Of the combined arts the theater and the opera always have subject; the dance may or may not have subject. The minor arts, such as textiles, metalwork, and pottery, sometimes have subject and sometimes have not. Moreover, in these arts the subject is often a matter of indifference. One may eat with a spoon for months without ever noticing whether the design on the handle represents grapes or roses, or whether it has any subject. Even in wallpaper and dress materials, where the design is more conspicuous, subject is of little importance. Choice is often made on the basis of design and color rather than subject.

● SUBJECT IN MUSIC

Music occupies a position about halfway between literature and architecture. A great deal of music has no subject: sonata, étude, symphony, etc. On the other hand, much music has subject; we have examples in *The Fountain* and the Bach cantata. Music without subject is called *absolute music*, while music with subject is called *program music*.

Sometimes a distinction is made between program music which actually imitates the sounds in question and that which merely sets the mood and suggests the story or picture the composer had in mind. The music in *The Fountain* obviously belongs to the first group: it imitates the motion of the fountain, its ceaseless flow, its constant change, and its monotony. An example of the latter group, on the other hand, is the composition called *Pictures at an Exhibition.* As the

21

title indicates, Moussorgsky represents himself as visiting an art exhibit and looking at one picture after another. There are eleven pictures, with such different subjects as *The Old Castle, Children in the Tuileries Gardens,* and *Two Polish Jews.* There is also a theme which represents the artist walking from one picture to the next. In this composition Moussorgsky tries to give the mood of each picture—romantic or gay, comic or quarrelsome—but he does not imitate the subject itself.

Music is unique among the arts in that it cannot make its subject clear. Even when the music is definitely imitative, as in Rimsky-Korsakov's *The Flight of the Bumblebee,* the subject is not always clear. If the music is played with no clue as to the subject, many people will not recognize what it is about. One person, hearing the piece about the bumblebee, realized that the music had subject, but decided that it represented a blizzard!

● WAYS OF PRESENTING THE SUBJECT

REALISM, ABSTRACTION

REALISM. As we have said, no art is ever like nature. Even when he chooses a subject from nature, the artist changes, selects, and arranges details in order to express the idea he wants to make clear. Often the presentation of details and

the organization of them in the work are so nearly obvious, and seem so natural, that we do not notice that the work is not like nature, as in Cézanne's painting. When this is the case, we say the work is realistic.

ABSTRACTION. Abstraction is another way of presenting a subject. Sometimes an artist gets so interested in one phase of a scene or a situation that he does not show the subject at all as an objective reality, but only his idea of it, or his feeling about it. For example, Brancusi is impressed by the grace of a bird in flight, by the sweep of its body as it flies through the air, so he tries to represent those

FIGURE 14. CONSTANTIN BRANCUSI (1876–1957), Roumanian sculptor. *Bird in Space* (1925). (Polished bronze, marble and oak base. Height: 50¼ inches. Philadelphia, Museum of Art, The Louise and Walter Arensberg Collection. Photograph, A. J. Wyatt, staff photographer.)

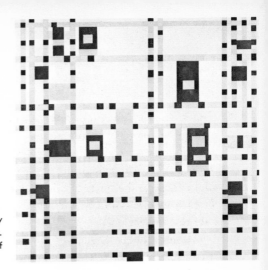

FIGURE 15. PIETER MONDRIAAN. *Broadway Boogie-Woogie* (ca. 1942–1943). (Oil on canvas. Size: 50 by 50 inches. New York, Museum of Modern Art.)

qualities in his statue *Bird in Space* (Figure 14). It does not look like a bird, and it is not supposed to look like a bird. It is supposed only to convey an impression of the bird's grace.

Mondriaan has a painting which he calls *Broadway Boogie-Woogie* (Figure 15). Again, it does not look like Broadway, or boogie-woogie, yet it suggests many of the characteristics we associate with the dance: the perforated roll of the mechanical player piano, monotony of beat, strong accent, improvisation, and the bright lights of the city. Probably no one would recognize the subject by himself, but once it has been suggested, he can see the connection. This painting looks very much like the Mondriaan painting we saw earlier, *Composition with Blue and White.* But that had no subject, and this has; both types are commonly called *abstract.* For the one without subject a more exact term is *nonobjective.*

Between abstraction and realism there are many ways of presenting the subject. Henry Moore's *Reclining Figure* (Figure 16) is fairly close to an abstrac-

FIGURE 16. HENRY MOORE. *Reclining Figure* (ca. 1935). (Elm wood. Dimensions: 19 inches high, 35 inches long, 17¼ inches wide. Buffalo, N.Y., Albright Art Gallery; room of Contemporary Art Collection.)

FIGURE 17. EL GRECO (1541–1614), Spanish painter. *Resurrection* (ca. 1597–1604). (Oil on canvas. Size: 108¼ by 50 inches. Madrid, Prado. Photograph by Anderson.)

tion, whereas El Greco's *Resurrection* (Figure 17) is close to realism. As in many of El Greco's paintings, the bodies are unnaturally long. El Greco was illustrating that part of the Creed which says of Christ that he. . . "was crucified, died and was buried. He descended into hell. The third day he rose again from the dead." In his picture El Greco wanted the body of Christ to rise, and it does seem to rise from the mass of writhing bodies around. A body of normal size would have seemed dumpy, stodgy, and still. For work like the El Greco, which is close to realism, the term *distorted* has been used, and for one that approaches abstraction like the *Reclining Figure* the term *near-abstract* is sometimes used. The use of these or other terms, however, is unimportant. It is important to realize that each artist presents his subject in accordance with his idea of that subject. Often one artist will use different ways of presenting a subject. Picasso's *Old Guitarist* (Figure 18) seems more distorted, when compared with his realistic *Blue Boy* (Figure 19), than when compared with *Fernande* (Figure 20). And *Fernande* seems almost realistic when put by the side of *Ma Jolie* (Figure 21). In that picture the woman has disappeared into a series of straight-edged, transparent planes.

FIGURE 18. PABLO PICASSO (1881–), Spanish painter. *The Old Guitarist* (1903). (Oil on wood. Size: 47¾ by 32½ inches. Chicago, courtesy Art Institute of Chicago; Helen Birch Bartlett Memorial Collection.)

FIGURE 19. PABLO PICASSO. *Blue Boy* (1905). (Gouache. Size: 40 by 22½ inches. New York, courtesy Museum of Modern Art; collection of Mr. and Mrs. Edward M. M. Warburg.)

FIGURE 20. PABLO PICASSO. *Fernande* (1909). (Oil on canvas. Size: 24¼ by 16¾ inches. New York, collection of Mrs. Henry H. Church. Photograph, courtesy Museum of Modern Art.)

FIGURE 21. PABLO PICASSO. *Ma Jolie* (*Woman with a Guitar*) (1911–1912). (Oil on canvas. Size: 39⅜ by 25¾ inches. New York, Museum of Modern Art; acquired through the Lillie P. Bliss Bequest.)

The emphasis on relationship of foreground to background and the use of geometric forms really began with Cézanne. Picasso developed a style which analyzed and broke down the forms or built up shapes into arbitrary patterns. This organization of shapes in space is the major objective of *cubism.*

Since the subject would not be known without the title, the question is often raised about giving a name to a picture or a musical composition if it in no way bears any likeness to the object named. Would it not be better to count all such works nonobjective? Probably not. The title usually helps one to understand what the artist had in mind. In some cases, as in Brancusi's *Bird in Space,* Honegger's *Pacific 231,* or Ravel's *The Fountain,* the name offers a real explanation of the artist's purpose and idea. In others, as in Picasso's *Ma Jolie* or Moussorgsky's *Pictures at an Exhibition,* the title merely gives the source for the original inspiration.

THE SYMBOL

A symbol may be roughly defined as something that stands for or suggests something else. It is a kind of shorthand whereby long or complicated facts or ideas may be expressed in a short time or space. At its simplest it is only a sign which by common agreement has a definite meaning. On the highway red means *stop* and green means *go.* The bands on his sleeve indicate how long a railway conductor has been in the service of the company. Stars, bars, and eagles indicate rank in the army. Words and notes on the printed page are symbols. All such symbols are in reality only signs and can be changed at will. Red could be made to mean *go* and green *stop.* We have in recent years made attempts to change spelling and have succeeded in a few cases.

On the stage signs are often given to tell some detail or some phase of the story. In Ibsen's *A Doll's House* we learn that it is Christmas when men come in with a Christmas tree, and one of the characters announces his coming death by presenting a calling card with a black cross on it.

Time, Father Time, is usually represented as an old man carrying a sickle. In sonnet 116 Shakespeare uses this imagery when he wants to emphasize the triumph of love over time.

> Love's not Time's fool, though rosy lips and cheeks
> Within his bending sickle's compass come.

Mercury (Figure 22), the messenger of the gods, may usually be identified by his winged sandals, his staff entwined with snakes (caduceus), and his flat hat (petasos). The caduceus had magical powers over sleeping, waking, and dream-

FIGURE 22. GIOVANNI DA BOLOGNA (ca. 1524–1608),
Flemish-Florentine sculptor. *Mercury* (ca. 1574). (Bronze.
Height: 5 feet, 9 inches. Washington, D.C., National Gallery of Art; Mellon Collection.)

ing, and as such became identified with healing. It is now the symbol of the
medical profession and of the Army Medical Corps. Bacchus, the god of wine,
is usually portrayed with grapes or grape leaves. In the vase painting by Execias,
Dionysus Sailing the Sea (Figure 23), we recognize Bacchus (Dionysus) by the
grapes and grape leaves which fill the upper part of the picture. The story is
that one day while he was asleep, Bacchus was taken aboard a ship by some
sailors who wished to sell him into slavery. Waking, the god asked them to take
him to Naxos. When they refused, vines laden with grapes grew up around the
mast, and the mariners were changed into dolphins.

FIGURE 23. EXECIAS, (6ᵗʰ cent.) Greek vase painter.
Dionysus Sailing the Sea (550–525 B.C.). (Black on
red pottery. Diameter: 14½ inches. Munich, Antikensammlungen.)

There are many symbols of the Christian Church: Peter is represented with a key because of Christ's saying that he gave Peter the keys of the kingdom of heaven (Matthew 16:19). Paul is often represented as a bald old man carrying a sword. The symbols of the four Evangelists Matthew, Mark, Luke, and John were commonly used in the Middle Ages and are frequently found today. Matthew is symbolized as a winged man, Mark a winged lion, Luke a winged ox, and John an eagle. We see these in a characteristic setting in the tympanum, or curved space above the door, of the cathedral at Chartres (Figure 182).

Even deeper is the private, or art, symbol. In it only the artist knows what the symbol represents. The parables of the New Testament are such symbols.

> Behold, a sower went forth to sow. And when he sowed, some seeds fell by the wayside, and the fowls came and devoured them up: Some fell upon stony places, where they had not much earth: and forthwith they sprung up, because they had no deepness of earth: And when the sun was up, they were scorched; and because they had no root, they withered away. And some fell among thorns; and the thorns sprung up, and choked them. But other fell into good ground, and brought forth fruit, some an hundredfold, some sixtyfold, some thirtyfold.
>
> —Matthew 13:3–8

The disciples often had to ask Jesus to explain his symbols, as in this case. Sometimes one is not certain that a symbol is intended, as in Frost's poem:

Whose woods these are I think I know.
His house is in the village though;
He will not see me stopping here
To watch his woods fill up with snow.

My little horse must think it queer
To stop without a farmhouse near
Between the woods and frozen lake
The darkest evening of the year.

He gives his harness bells a shake
To ask if there is some mistake.
The only other sound's the sweep
Of easy wind and downy flake.

The woods are lovely, dark and deep,
But I have promises to keep,
And miles to go before I sleep,
And miles to go before I sleep.

        —ROBERT FROST (1875–1963, American poet),
          "Stopping by Woods on a Snowy Evening" (1923)[2]

[2]From *Complete Poems of Robert Frost*, 1949. Copyright 1923, 1949, by Henry Holt and Company, Inc.

This poem offers no obvious difficulties; the images are clear-cut, and the sense is clear. The poet stops to admire the scene in the snow, but he does not pause very long because he has made promises he must keep, and he has still a long way to go. But is this all? One wonders if that is all the poem has to say, if there is not a meaning hidden in the seemingly simple lines. When Frost says:

> But I have promises to keep,
> And miles to go before I sleep,

does he have in mind just the trip home? Or does that seemingly simple statement stand for something else? When he says "before I sleep," does he really mean "before I die"? In the "promises to keep," is he thinking of work that he has set out to do? Does he refer to responsibilities that he must meet before he dies? There is nothing in the poem that says Frost has such a meaning, but most of us think that he has. And if we do, we decide that the poem is symbolic.

In Sandburg's "Grass," the grass that covers all is clearly a symbol. The poem means more than that grass grows on battlefields.

> Pile the bodies high at Austerlitz and Waterloo.
> Shovel them under and let me work—
> I am the grass; I cover all.
>
> And pile them high at Gettysburg
> And pile them high at Ypres and Verdun.
> Shovel them under and let me work.
> Two years, ten years, and passengers ask the conductor:
> What place is this?
> Where are we now?
>
> I am the grass,
> Let me work.

>   —CARL SANDBURG (1878–   , American poet),
>   "Grass" (1918)[3]

DREAMS AND THE SUBCONSCIOUS

Recent ways of presenting the subject have to do with dreams and the subconscious. Under the influence of Freudian psychology, the subconscious has come to be recognized as important in human conduct, and naturally it has found expression in art.

Reprinted from *Cornhuskers* by Carl Sandburg, Henry Holt and Company, Inc.

Subjects of this class attempt to show the inside of man's mind as well as th
appearance of his outside world. They try to show thoughts and dreams that ar
not controlled by reason or any conscious order. The work which results is lik
its subject; it may be clear and vivid but it is not necessarily logical. Events an
people are put together in unrelated and therefore irrational combinations. Th
reality of such scenes can best be understood if one remembers his own thought
and dreams; he finds himself taking part in actions under circumstances whic
probably have to do with his ordinary life, but which are combined in form
that are strange and irrational. Paintings of this sort belong to the type calle
surrealism, sur or *super* realism. It gets its name from its attempt to find th
real *behind* the real, and to bring together the inner and outer reality.

Chagall's *I and My Village* (Figure 24) presents a rural scene. The tw
important characters are the man and the cow. Their faces are bound togethe
in a circle and they look at each other with sympathy. The man holds a spra
for the cow to eat. The cow is thinking of being milked, as we can tell from th
small figures painted on her jaw. In the background are the other objects of th
village—a workman with a scythe, a woman, and a row of the village houses—

FIGURE 24. MARC CHAGALL (1887
1911), Russian painter. *I and My Villag*
(1911). (Oil on canvas. Size: 85⅝ t
59⅝ inches. New York, Museum
Modern Art; Mrs. Simon Guggenhe
Fund.)

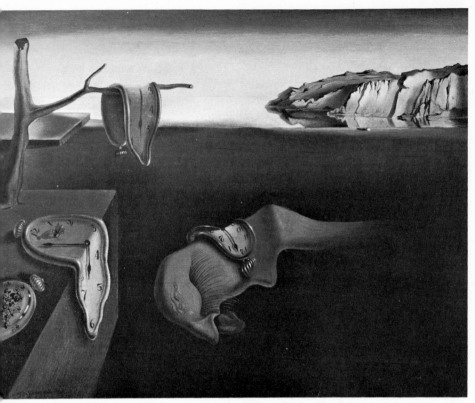

FIGURE 25. SALVADOR DALI (1904–   ). *The Persistence of Memory* (1931). (Oil on canvas. Size: ½ by 13 inches. New York, courtesy Museum of Modern Art.)

ome of them being right side up and some upside down. The cross at the top
f the picture and the ring on the man's hand are symbols we recognize which
elp us to understand the man and the entire situation.

Probably the most famous picture of this school is *The Persistence of Memory*
y Salvador Dali (Figure 25). The four limp watches symbolize the relativity,
lexibility, and destructibility of time.

Several hundred years before the surrealists a Flemish painter by the name
f Hieronymus Bosch (ca. 1450–1516) had been making pictures very like the
urrealists, and like them had created strange creatures, monsters, and demons,
ut with different purpose. Bosch was influenced almost entirely by religious
deas. His demons and devils, his monsters and tempters were those of an imagi-
ation which had fed on visions of hell and its sufferings. One of his most
mportant paintings shows the *Temptations of Saint Anthony*. Anthony was a
elebrated hermit, so good that he became a special target for the schemes of
he Devil. In the paintings of Bosch as in those of the modern surrealists the
etails of a picture are made with startling vividness.

31

Background

The desire to locate and hold the subconscious is found in literature in the stream-of-consciousness novel, in which the author attempts to trap every thought or feeling that passes through the mind of a character. Time, naturally becomes confused in the process. Joyce's *Ulysses* is one of the well-known examples.

Surrealism in poetry can be felt in such a poem as Karl Shapiro's "Love for a Hand." Here the dream world is explicit, and every stanza contains some symbol of the relationship of the man to the woman. The figure of speech and the implications in the last words, "his hand eats hers," is a culmination of the mysterious atmosphere created by the light moving in the room, the ominous references to "little animals that prowl," and the image of drowning.

Two hands lie still, the hairy and the white,
And soon down ladders of reflected light
The sleepers climb in silence. Gradually
They separate on paths of long ago,
Each winding on his arm the unpleasant clew
That leads, live as a nerve, to memory.

But often, when too steep her dream descends,
Perhaps to the grotto where her father bends
To pick her up, the husband wakes as though
He had forgotten something in the house.
Motionless he eyes the room that glows
With the little animals of light that prowl.

This way and that. Soft are the beasts of light
But softer still her hand that drifts so white
Upon the whiteness. How like a water plant
It floats upon the black canal of sleep,
Suspended upward from the distant deep
In pure achievement of its lovely want!

Quietly then he plucks it and it folds
And is again a hand, small as a child's.
He would revive it, but it barely stirs,
And so he carries it off a little way
And breaks it open gently. Now he can see
The sweetness of the fruit, his hand eats hers.

—KARL SHAPIRO (1913–   , American Poet)[4]

[4]Copyright 1952 by Karl Shapiro. Reprinted from *Poems 1940–1953* by Karl Shapiro by permission of Random House, Inc. Originally appeared in The *New Yorker*.

FIGURE 26. EDVARD MUNCH (1863–1944), Norwegian painter and print maker. *The Scream* (1895). (Lithograph. On extended loan to the Museum of Modern Art, New York. Photograph, Museum of Modern Art.)

In Arthur Miller's play *Death of a Salesman*, the scene is sometimes the present and sometimes the past. When the salesman begins thinking about the past, it is acted out before him; then, just as in thought, it shifts back to the present. His two sons are sometimes men of thirty and sometimes boys playing football in high school. The man thinks of his wife as a strong, healthy woman bringing in the clothes from the yard, and so when she appears in those flash-backs she looks about thirty-five and she carries a large hamper of freshly washed clothes. The scenes are not irrational in the sense that they are not internally reasonable, but they are irrational from the point of view of logical stage action in the passage of time.

Similar to the surrealist's attempt in the visual arts to "find the real behind the real" is the intent of the expressionist to ignore naturalistic qualities of external reality in his use of color, shapes, and space. He tries to get at the essential truth which he sees and feels. Such a painter was Edvard Munch, a Norwegian who worked with other expressionists in Germany. His painting *The Scream* (Figure 26) conveys terror through the very omission of realistic details.

FIGURE 27. WASSILJ KANDINSKI (1866–1944), Russian painter. *Improvisation #30* (War-like Theme) (1913). (Oil on canvas. Size: 43¼ by 43¾ inches. Chicago, courtesy Art Institute of Chicago; Arthur Jerome Eddy Memorial Collection.)

A contemporary type of expressionism is known as *abstract expressionism.* It shows no perspective, either linear or aerial. The colors are slapped, dribbled, or sometimes thrown at the canvas. The effects are at times accidental, but the artist feels that the work of art is in itself an event. Kandinski has many of the characteristics of this school (Figure 27).

● BEAUTIFUL AND UGLY SUBJECTS OF ART

The last consideration in this chapter on subject has to do with the artist's choice of subject. What are fit subjects for art? Are there certain subjects that are not allowed in art? Almost instinctively one answers these questions by saying that the noble, the lovely, the beautiful, the distinguished, and the unusual are the proper subjects for art. Subjects such as we found in *The Fountain* or the caryatids of the Erechtheum seem appropriate subjects for art, and usually one has something of this kind in mind when he calls a subject "artistic." By the same impulse subjects that are ugly, undignified, and commonplace do not seem proper subjects for art.

But when one turns from theory to practice, this idea is not borne out. Most of us would turn away in disgust if we met in life the old man with a diseased nose, painted by Ghirlandajo in *Old Man and Boy* (Figure 28). But the old man's concern for the boy and the boy's adoration of the man are so great that we forget the man is old and ugly.

Shakespeare has painted a very clear picture of winter in a short lyric in *Love's Labour's Lost*, but muddy roads, a greasy, sweaty cook, a nose "red and raw" are not beautiful or lovely details.

FIGURE 28. DOMENICO GHIRLANDAJO (1449– 1494), Italian painter. *Old Man and Boy* (ca. 1480). (Oil on wood. Height: 2 feet, ⅜ inches. Paris, Louvre. Photograph by Alinari.)

When icicles hang by the wall
    And Dick the shepherd blows his nail
And Tom bears logs into the hall
    And milk comes frozen home in pail,
When blood is nipp'd and ways be foul,
Then nightly sings the staring owl,
        "Tu-whit; tu-who!"
    A merry note,
While greasy Joan doth keel the pot.

When all aloud the wind doth blow
    And coughing drowns the parson's saw
And birds sit brooding in the snow
    And Marian's nose looks red and raw,
When roasted crabs hiss in the bowl,
Then nightly sings the staring owl,
        "Tu-whit; tu-who!"
    A merry note,
While greasy Joan doth keel the pot.

    —WILLIAM SHAKESPEARE (1564–1616, British poet and dramatist), *Love's Labour's Lost*,
    V, ii, 922–938 (ca. 1590)

Most emphatically, art is not limited to subjects that in themselves are beauti
ful, agreeable, lovely. The beautiful, the agreeable, the lovely, are subjects o
art but they are not the only ones. Any subject may be a subject of art. We lik
in art what we do not like in nature, because we see the subject as it has bee
interpreted for us by the artist.

This last sentence answers the question of the relation of subject to *value* i
a work of art. Does the choice of subject help to determine the final judgmen
as to whether a work may be counted good or bad, great or mediocre? Can w
say that a work of art is good if it has a certain subject, and poor if it ha
another? A "beautiful" subject does not necessarily produce a good work of art
nor an "ugly" subject a poor one; a noble subject does not mean a noble work
of art, nor an ignoble subject an ignoble work. The value of art does not lie i
the subject but in what the artist does with his subject. The greatness of ar
comes not from the subject but from the artist.

3

SOURCES OF
ART SUBJECTS

When I consider how my light is spent
Ere half my days in this dark world and wide,
And that one Talent which is death to hide
Lodged with me useless, though my soul more bent
To serve therewith my Maker, and present
My true account, lest He returning chide,
"Doth God exact day-labour, light denied?"
I fondly ask. But Patience, to prevent
That murmur, soon replies, "God doth not need
Either man's work or his own gifts. Who best
Bear his mild yoke, they serve him best. His state
Is kingly: thousands at his bidding speed,
And post o'er land and ocean without rest;
They also serve who only stand and wait."

  —JOHN MILTON (1608–1674, British poet and essayist),
   "On His Blindness" (ca. 1655)

The subjects used in art are usually clear and obvious. They need no explanation other than the work itself. Rimsky-Korsakov's bumblebee and Emily Dickinson's railroad train are self-explanatory. Cézanne gives the name of the forest in which he found the well and grinding wheel that attracted his attention, but it is of no real importance in our understanding of the picture. On the other hand, there are many works of art which depend for their understanding upon some knowledge of the subject. When Tchaikovsky calls his suite, *Roméo and Juliet,* he takes it for granted that we know the story of Shakespeare's young lovers.

Milton's sonnet "On His Blindness" tells the facts essential for an understanding of the poem: that the poet lost his eyesight when he felt his greatest work lay before him, and that through this experience he learned patience and submission to the will of God. However, one understands the poem better and enjoys it more if he knows, even vaguely, the story of the poet's life. Milton lost his sight in the service of his country before he had written the great poem he had always wanted to write and which he knew he could write, the poem he did write later in spite of his blindness, *Paradise Lost.* Moreover, one's pleasure is increased if he understands the reference to Christ's parable of the talents in the twenty-fifth chapter of Matthew.

> "For it will be as when a man going on a journey called his servants and entrusted to them his property; to one he gave five talents, to another two, to another one, to each according to his ability. Then he went away. He who had received the five talents went at once and traded with them; and he made five talents more. So too, he who had the two talents made two talents more. But he who had received the one talent, went and dug in the ground and hid his master's money." [1]

He praised the man who had been given five talents and the one who had been given two, but he chided the one who had put his talent in the ground, calling him a "wicked and slothful servant," and directed that his talent be taken from him.

Similarly, anyone can tell, with no cause for confusion, that Michelangelo's *David* (Figure 29) is a statue of a young man, a very beautiful young man with a serious, determined expression on his face. He is standing with his left arm raised and his right arm by his side. Anyone can identify the subject to this extent, and he can get a great deal of pleasure from the statue with no other information. But the sculptor has named the young man *David,* and we understand the statue better if we know the story Michelangelo expected us to know. It is told in I Samuel 17 how David, a mere lad, killed the giant Goliath with a pebble from his slingshot.

[1] Revised Standard Version.

FIGURE 29. MICHELANGELO (1475–1564), Italian painter, sculptor, architect, and poet. *David* (1501–1503). (Marble. Height: 18 feet. Florence, Academy. Photograph by Anderson.)

FIGURE 30. SANDRO BOTTICELLI (1444–1510), Italian painter. *Birth of Venus* (ca. 1485). (Tempera on canvas. Height: 5 feet, 3¼ inches. Florence, Uffizi. Photograph by Alinari.)

The examples given so far can all be enjoyed without any knowledge of the subject. But Botticelli's *Birth of Venus* (Figure 30) is very nearly nonsense if one accepts it at its face value. The young woman is very beautiful, but why should she be standing naked on the edge of a shell? Why does not the shell topple over? Who are the people on each side of her? What are they doing? Botticelli assumed that those who looked at his picture would know that Venus, the goddess of love and beauty, was born from the foam of the sea. In the picture, she is being blown to the shore by the winds, while one of the Horae (seasons) is waiting on the bank to receive her.

Background

When we talk about the sources of art subjects, we are thinking primarily of subjects like those just mentioned, those which demand some knowledge on the part of the critic, if he is to get the idea the artist had in mind.

The number of subjects used in this way is limitless. Any artist may use any subject from any source, and it is impossible ever to know all the subjects of art. Even the scholar who has devoted his life to their study never expects to know all of them. There are, however, a few sources which are part of the background of every cultivated person. For convenience they may be grouped under these four headings:

1. History
2. Greek and Roman mythology
3. Christianity
4. Other works of art

● HISTORY

In one sense, all art is conditioned by the historical period in which it is created. The dress, the houses, the manner of living, the thoughts of a period are necessarily reflected in the work of the artist. Such general references, however, may be taken for granted, and we do not call a subject historical unless it refers to specific places, persons, or events.

FIGURE 31. FRANCISCO GOYA (1746–1828), Spanish painter, etcher, and lithographer. *Maria Luisa of Parma* (ca. 1790–1792). (Oil on canvas. Size: 43⅝ by 33⅝ inches. New York, courtesy Metropolitan Museum of Art; bequest of Mrs. H. O. Havemeyer, 1929. H. O. Havemeyer Collection.)

FIGURE 32. HONORÉ DAUMIER (1808–1879), French lithographer and caricaturist. *Rue Transnonain* (1834). (Lithograph. Size: about 11½ by 17½ inches. New York, courtesy Metropolitan Museum of Art; Rogers Fund, 1920.)

Such subjects are numerous. The obvious reason is that rulers like to have themselves and the great deeds of their time perpetuated. And so statues and paintings of the great are found in each civilization. In these the artist often has a double duty in that he is supposed to give a likeness of his subject and at the same time display his skill. An exception to this general rule is found in the portraits of the Spanish court painted by Goya. A first look at the portrait of Maria Luisa of Parma (Figure 31) shows her as a royal person in all her royal finery; a second look, however, gives a telling commentary on her character and disposition. Goya seems to mock her pretentious elegance. The painting tells that she is ugly and vain.

Another reason for the use of historical subjects is that artists are sensitive to the events in the world around them. In *Rue Transnonain* (Figure 32) Daumier was protesting against social injustice. In a street skirmish a shot from one of the windows of No 12, Rue Transnonain, wounded an officer; the soldiers thereupon rushed into the building and killed all its inhabitants. Daumier's

FIGURE 33. PABLO PICASSO. *Guernica* (1937). (Oil on canvas. Mural 11 feet, 6 inches by 25 feet, 3 inches. Collection of the artist, on extended loan to the Museum of Modern Art, New York. Photograph, courtesy Museum of Modern Art.)

lithograph depicts the scene when they had left. A similar protest is found in Picasso's painting *Guernica* (Figure 33) of the unarmed Basque city that was bombed by the fascists in the Spanish Civil War, 1936–1939.

LEGEND AND FOLKLORE

Historical subjects as such can be identified and recognized with little trouble; records are kept, histories are written, and references are usually clear and easy to find. In quite a different class is legend, the elder sister of history. Legend may be defined as history that is not or cannot be authenticated. The facts are not verifiable. We can be sure of few if any facts about King Arthur or King Lear, and those facts do not correspond with the legends about them. Often a legend gets attached to an historical person, Charlemagne for example. Charlemagne is an historical king of France, but the exploits of his nephew Roland are legendary. Till Eulenspiegel, the legendary bad boy of medieval Germany, is the hero of Richard Strauss's tone poem *Till Eulenspiegel's Merry Pranks*.

Wagner used legend for the subject of his great tetralogy *The Ring of the Nibelung*. In it he tells the saga of the Nibelung gold from the time it was stolen until it was restored to the Rhine maidens.

● GREEK AND ROMAN MYTHOLOGY

Greek and Roman mythology has been a very important source for subjects in art. The stream of its influence on Western civilization may be traced primarily to two sources. First are the works of Greece and Rome during the period of Greek and Roman civilization, from the sixth century before Christ to the fifth

42

entury after. Those arts are so well known that they count as a definite part of
ur inheritance: architecture, drama, poetry, sculpture, and painting. Second
re the arts of Europe during the Renaissance, the period of revived interest in
hings Greek and Latin between the twelfth and the seventeenth centuries. Dur-
ng this period, poets, painters, and sculptors drew largely from Greek and Ro-
nan sources for subjects. Of the examples already mentioned, the poems of
Iomer and Sappho, the Erechtheum, and the vase showing *Dionysus Sailing
he Sea* belong to the first period; Botticelli's *Birth of Venus* belongs to the
econd.

Stories from Greek and Roman mythology center around the gods and the
eroes. Each of the gods had his own province and was known by some symbol.
upiter, for example, the king of the gods, was known by his thunderbolt.
Bacchus, god of wine, was shown with grapes and grape leaves.

About each of the gods there clustered many stories. We have already noted
a story about the birth of Venus. Another goddess, Proserpine, the daughter of
Ceres (Demeter) was carried off by Pluto to be queen of the underworld. Ceres
mplored Jupiter for the restoration of her daughter, and at last a compromise
vas made whereby Proserpine would forever spend half her time with her
nother, and half with her husband. It is summer when Ceres has her daughter
vith her.

In addition to the stories of the gods, there are many tales of the heroes, who
vere mortal men in close touch with the gods, and in whose exploits the gods
hemselves assisted. Each of these heroes became the nucleus for a series of
tories to which any author might add additional tales as the fancy struck him.
Among the heroes are Perseus, who killed the Gorgon Medusa and saved the
ife of Andromeda; Oedipus, who was doomed to kill his father and marry his
nother; and Theseus, who killed the Minotaur with the aid of Ariadne and
hen, tiring of her, deserted her on the island of Naxos, where she was met and
oved by Bacchus. Titian's painting *Bacchus and Ariadne* (Figure 34) shows
Bacchus leaping from his chariot to greet Ariadne; she has gathered up her
skirts, preparing to flee, when she looks back at the god.

The greatest of all Greek stories, however, center about the Trojan War,
which was fought over Helen, whose face ". . . launched a thousand ships, and
ourut the topless towers of Ilium." We find many references in art to one or
another story connected with Troy, such as the judgment of Paris when the
shepherd lad had to choose which of the three goddesses was the most beauti-
ul, or the use of a wooden horse by the Greeks to obtain entrance to Troy.
The *Laocoön* (Figure 35) represents the punishment inflicted on the priest when
ne urged the Trojans not to take the Wooden Horse into the city.

The three great classical epics are concerned with the war of Troy. Homer's

FIGURE 34. TITIAN (1477–1576), Italian painter. *Bacchus and Ariadne* (ca. 1520). (Oil on canvas. Size: 69 by 75 inches. London, National Gallery. Reproduced by courtesy of the Trustees.)

FIGURE 35. LAOCOÖN (ca. 40 B.C.), School of Rhodes. (White marble. Height to right hand of Laocoön: 8 feet. Rome, Vatican Museum. Photograph by Alinari.)

Iliad tells of the war itself, beginning with the anger of Achilles and narrating the events through the death of Hector. Homer's *Odyssey* describes the wanderings of Ulysses, and Vergil's *Aeneid* describes the adventures of Aeneas and the founding of Rome.

44

● CHRISTIANITY

Christianity has exerted as great an influence on the art of the Western world as any other single source. When we say Christianity, we mean not only the Bible, but all Jewish and Christian history, legend, and ritual. They may be classified under four headings:

The Bible
The Apocrypha
Legends and lives of the saints
The ritual of the church

THE BIBLE

The Christian Bible, as is commonly recognized, is not a single book but a library. The books of the Bible may be grouped as follows:

I. Old Testament (39 books)
   A. History (Genesis through Esther). The historical books give the story of the Jews from the creation to the Babylonian exile.
   B. Poetry (Job through the Song of Songs). Job is a poetic drama; Proverbs is a collection of wise sayings and epigrams. The Song of Songs and Ecclesiastes are, respectively, a group of marriage songs and a statement of gently cynical philosophy.
   C. Prophecy (Isaiah through Malachi). The Prophets were not soothsayers, but practical men who judged and interpreted the affairs of their own times. They were patriots, reformers, preachers, and teachers.

II. New Testament (27 books)
   A. History. The four Gospels: Matthew, Mark, Luke, and John; The Acts of the Apostles.
   B. Letters. The epistles written by Paul and others to the Christian churches that were just starting in the various parts of the world.
   C. Apocalypse. The Revelation of St. John.

Any consideration of the Bible in relation to art must take into account the fact that the Bible itself is great art. For the English-speaking peoples, the Bible has the additional advantage of being available in the King James version, probably the greatest translation ever made. So the Bible not only is a source of art, but is itself art.

The most frequently used subjects from the Bible are taken from the life of Jesus. And in the life of Jesus the accounts of his birth and death are most often used; the Madonna with the baby Jesus, the Annunciation, the visit of

Background

the Magi and the shepherds, from the stories of his birth; and from his death, the betrayal by Judas, the scourging, the Crucifixion, deposition, and entombment. In the Old Testament, the stories of the creation are probably more important than any others, though reference is frequent to the heroes of the Old Testament: Abraham, Jacob, Moses, Samson, David, Elijah, and others.

Artists of each generation have interpreted the scene or scenes in their own way. T. S. Eliot, for example, in his poem "Journey of the Magi," writes a monologue in which an old man tells of his journey as a young man to find the star, the difficulties and disappointments of his long trip, and at last his finding of the child. Now as an old man he ponders on the meaning.

'A cold coming we had of it,
Just the worst time of the year
For a journey, and such a long journey:
The ways deep and the weather sharp,
The very dead of winter.'
And the camels galled, sore-footed, refractory,
Lying down in the melting snow.
There were times we regretted
The summer palaces on slopes, the terraces,
And the silken girls bringing sherbet.
Then the camel men cursing and grumbling
And running away, and wanting their liquor and women,
And the night-fires going out, and the lack of shelters,
And the cities hostile and the towns unfriendly
And the villages dirty and charging high prices:
A hard time we had of it.
At the end we preferred to travel all night,
Sleeping in snatches,
With the voices singing in our ears, saying
That this was all folly.

Then at dawn we came down to a temperate valley,
Wet, below the snow line, smelling of vegetation;
With a running stream and a water-mill beating the darkness,
And three trees on the low sky,
And an old white horse galloped away in the meadow.
Then we came to a tavern with vine-leaves over the lintel,
Six hands at an open door dicing for pieces of silver,
And feet kicking the empty wine-skins.
But there was no information, and so we continued
And arrived at evening, not a moment too soon
Finding the place; it was (you may say) satisfactory.

All this was a long time ago, I remember,
And I would do it again, but set down
This set down
This: were we led all that way for
Birth or Death? There was a Birth, certainly,
We had evidence and no doubt. I had seen birth and death,
But had thought they were different; this Birth was
Hard and bitter agony for us, like Death, our death.
We returned to our places, these Kingdoms,
But no longer at ease here, in the old dispensation,
With an alien people clutching their gods.
I should be glad of another death.

  —T. S. ELIOT (1888–1965, American poet). "Journey of the Magi."[2]

Another modern artist, the painter Rouault, has painted a head of Christ in which he shows clearly the physical suffering and at the same time the calm of spirit which not only overcomes the suffering but is compassionate (Figure 36).

[2] From *Collected Poems 1909–1962.* Copyright 1936 by Harcourt, Brace & World, Inc.; copyright © 1963, 1964, by T. S. Eliot. Reprinted by permission of the publishers.

FIGURE 36. GEORGES ROUAULT (1871–1958), French painter. *Head of Christ (Christ flagellé)* (1905). (Oil on paper. Size: 45 by 31 inches. From the collection of Walter P. Chrysler, Jr.)

FIGURE 37. WILLIAM BLAKE (1757–1827), English
poet, painter, and engraver. *When the Morning
Stars Sang Together* (ca. 1825). (Engraving. Size:
6 by 7½ inches. Photograph, Don Woolley.)

The influence of the poetry and prophecy of the Old Testament is found
chiefly in music. *The Messiah* by Handel takes its text in part from the
Prophets. The opening tenor recitative uses the words of Isaiah, Chapter 40,
"Comfort ye, comfort ye, my people." An oratorio on King David was written
by Honegger. Haydn's great oratorio is, as the title indicates, on the subject of
the creation. Blake's engraving *When the Morning Stars Sang Together* (Figure 37), is taken from the book of Job. When the Lord answers Job out of the
whirlwind, he asks:

Where wast thou when I laid the foundations of the earth?
Declare, if thou hast understanding.
Who hath laid the measures thereof, if thou knowest?
Or who hath stretched the line upon it?
Whereupon are the foundations thereof fastened?
Or who laid the corner stone thereof;
When the morning stars sang together,
And all the sons of God shouted for joy?
   —Job 38:4–7

THE SISTINE CEILING. It has been a practice not uncommon to tell stories from the Bible in a series of pictures. One of the greatest of these was made by Michelangelo to decorate the ceiling of the Sistine Chapel; it is therefore called the Sistine Ceiling (Figure 38). The chapel is a long, narrow room, about 155 by 45 feet. In painting this space, Michelangelo chose to divide it into a number of small areas.

Down the center of the ceiling is a series of nine rectangles telling the story of the creation through the time of Noah (Figures 39, 40).

Separation of Light and Darkness
Creation of Sun and Moon
Creation of Land and Water
Creation of Adam
Creation of Eve
Temptation and Expulsion
Sacrifice of Noah
The Deluge
The Drunkenness of Noah

FIGURE 38. MICHELANGELO. Ceiling of Sistine Chapel (1508–1512). (Fresco. Length: 132 feet; width: 45 feet. Rome, Vatican. Photograph by Anderson.)

FIGURE 39. MICHELANGELO. *Creation of Adam*, detail of Sistine Chapel Ceiling. (Length of Adam: 10 feet. Photograph by Anderson.)

The pictures given odd numbers in this list are smaller than those with even numbers, and at each corner of these smaller paintings is a figure of a nude man (Figure 41). These figures are primarily decorative, all show splendid physique, and they exhibit different moods.

FIGURE 40. MICHELANGELO. *Temptation and Expulsion*, detail of Sistine Chapel Ceiling. (Photograph by Anderson.)

FIGURE 41. MICHELANGELO. *Decorative Nude,* detail of Sistine Chapel Ceiling. (Photograph by Anderson.)

Forming a border around the entire ceiling is a row of figures representing the Prophets of the Old Testament and the sibyls of classical mythology (Figure 38). Beginning with the one at the bottom of the page and reading clockwise they are as follows:

FIGURE 42. MICHELANGELO. *Libyan Sibyl,* detail of Sistine Chapel Ceiling. (Photograph by Alinari.)

Background

1. Jonah	5. Erythraean sibyl	9. Isaiah
2. Jeremiah	6. Joel	10. Cumaean sibyl
3. Persian sibyl	7. Zachariah	11. Daniel
4. Ezekiel	8. Delphian sibyl	12. Libyan sibyl

In the triangles that separate the Prophets and sibyls are the ancestors of Christ, and in the corners are other scenes from the Old Testament and the Old Testament Apocrypha.

THE APOCRYPHA

The Apocrypha are those books of the Bible which were not accepted in the canons of the Old and the New Testaments. The Apocrypha of the Old Testament include some books found in the Greek Old Testament (the Septuagint) and the Latin version prepared by Jerome (the Vulgate). They are not in the Jewish canon or in the Protestant Bible. In them are found books of wisdom (Ecclesiasticus), history (Maccabees), prophecy (Baruch), and three narratives: Judith, Susanna, and Tobit. Judith is the story of a beautiful young woman who saved her country when it was besieged by Holofernes. She induced Holofernes to enter her tent and persuaded him to go to sleep. Then she cut off his head and carried it back to her home. Inspired by her feat the Israelites fought and drove away their enemies. Botticelli has a picture of her as she goes home, her servant carrying the head of Holofernes in a bag.

The New Testament Apocrypha comprise early stories of the lives of Jesus and Mary. Those that have had the greatest influence on art are the ones that have to do with the birth and death of the Virgin.

> The story is that Joachim and Anna were prosperous and devout, but their childlessness was a source of great affliction to them. On the day when the children of Israel offered their gifts to the Lord, Joachim's offering was refused because he was without child. Joachim was sorely grieved and went off to the country alone. Later in answer to their fasting and prayer, an angel appeared to each of them, foretelling the birth of Mary, declaring her greatness, and bidding them dedicate her in the temple to the service of God. In time Mary was born, and when she was three years old her parents presented her in the temple, where she lived in the greatest piety until she was twelve years old.[3]

In the Arena Chapel at Padua, Giotto has painted a cycle of frescoes depicting the life of the Virgin. The picture of *Joachim Returning to the Sheepfold* (Figure 43) shows the dejection of Joachim after his offering has been refused.

---

[3]From Montague R. James' translation of *The Apocryphal New Testament*, The Book of James or Protevangelium, 38–49, Oxford University Press, 1924.

FIGURE 43. GIOTTO (1266–1336), Italian painter. *Joachim Returning to the Sheepfold* (ca. 1305). (Fresco. Height of figures: 3½ feet. Padua, Arena Chapel. Photograph by Alinari.)

In his sadness he does not even realize that he has reached the sheepfold. The shepherds hold back in doubt and in fear of intruding, but the little dog recognizes his master and runs to meet him.

LEGENDS AND LIVES OF THE SAINTS

The saints are those people formally recognized by the Christian church because of the exceptional holiness and piety of their lives. About them many stories have been told which have found their way into the arts. There is, for instance, the story that one day when St. Jerome was teaching, a lion walked into the room and lifted up its paw. All the students fled, but St. Jerome, noticing that the lion was wounded, pulled a thorn from its paw. After that the lion

FIGURE 44. ALBRECHT DÜRER (1471–1528) German painter, engraver, and wood carver *St. Jerome in His Cell* (1514). (Engraving. Size about 9¾ by 7½ inches. New York, courtesy Metropolitan Museum of Art; Fletcher Fund, 1919.

was Jerome's constant companion. In Dürer's engraving *St. Jerome in His Cell* (Figure 44), the saint is pictured working in his study; the scene is one of scholarly quiet and order, and right in front is a large lion, sleeping peacefully.

The legends and lives of saints present a difficult problem because they are so numerous. Many collections of these stories have been made, one of the most popular being that made in the Middle Ages by Jacobus de Voragine, called *The Golden Legend;* but no account of the lives of the saints can ever be complete, because saints are still being canonized, and new miracles are still being recorded.

RITUAL

The ritual of the church has been of great importance in art. The prayers and the words of the responses are beautiful. Through constant repetition they have become familiar to everyone, and they have had great influence on language and speech patterns. Just as important has been the influence on music; the various rituals were early set to music, and the composers of each generation wrote new·music for the services. The most important of all the rituals of the church is the Mass, which is the celebration of the Holy Communion. It is regularly in five parts (only the opening words are given):

Kyrie: "Lord, have mercy upon us."
Gloria: "Glory be to God on high."
Credo (Creed): "I believe in one God."
Sanctus: "Holy, holy, holy."
Agnus Dei: "O Lamb of God, that takest away the sins of the world."

54

SUBJECTS DERIVED FROM OTHER WORKS OF ART

A last category of subjects may be found in those works that take their subject directly from other works of art.

It is worth observing what the poet adds over and above the description when a painting is the source of information. Anne Sexton gives us vivid images of the power in the revolving constellations in van Gogh's *Starry Night*. The strong verbs, the powerful comparison of the cypress tree to the hair of a drowning woman, the many images of heat and movement all prepare us for the dramatic short lines conveying her personal identification with the powers of nature.

> The town does not exist
> except where one black-haired tree slips
> up like a drowned woman into the hot sky.
> The town is silent. The night boils with eleven stars.
> Oh starry night! This is how
> I want to die.
>
> It moves. They are all alive.
> Even the moon bulges in its orange irons
> To push children, like a god, from its eye.
> The old unseen serpent swallows up the stars.
> Oh starry, starry night! This is how
> I want to die:
>
> Into that rushing beast of the night,
> sucked up by that great dragon, to split
> from my life with no flag,
> no belly,
> no cry.
>
>   —ANNE SEXTON, (1928– , American poet),
>   "The Starry Night," from *All My Pretty Ones*[4]

Brueghel used the subject of Icarus for one of his paintings, and Auden and Madden have been inspired by the painting to write poems. The Greek myth tells that Icarus, the son of Daedalus, the great artisan, was given wings by his father. Since the wings were fastened on by wax, Daedalus warned the boy not to fly too near the sun. But the boy, exulting in his new power, could not restrain himself; soon the wax melted, he fell into the sea, and was drowned.

[4]From *All My Pretty Ones*. Reprinted by permission of Houghton Mifflin Co., 1963.

FIGURE 45. PIETER BRUEGHEL THE ELDER (ca. 1525–1569), Dutch painter. *The Fall of Icarus* (ca. 1554–1555). (Tempera on canvas. Height: ca. 2 feet, 4 inches. Copyright A. C. L. Bruxelles.)

In Brueghel's painting *The Fall of Icarus* (Figure 45) the boy is almost submerged; only one leg is seen as it disappears into the water. Nearby is a luxurious ship, and on a slight rise a farmer is plowing with a horse; below is a shepherd who is looking up at the sky, his sheep all around him.

Auden gives his poem the name of the museum in which the painting is found.

Musée des Beaux Arts

About suffering they were never wrong,
The Old Masters: how well they understood
Its human position; how it takes place
While someone else is eating or opening a window or just walking dully along;
How, when the aged are reverently, passionately waiting
For the miraculous birth, there always must be
Children who did not specially want it to happen, skating
On a pond at the edge of the wood:
They never forgot
That even the dreadful martyrdom must run its course
Anyhow in a corner, some untidy spot
Where the dogs go on with their doggy life and the torturer's horse
Scratches its innocent behind on a tree.

In Brueghel's *Icarus*, for instance: how everything turns away
Quite leisurely from the disaster; the ploughman may
Have heard the splash, the forsaken cry,
But for him it was not an important failure; the sun shone
As it had to on the white legs disappearing into the green
Water; and the expensive delicate ship that must have seen
Something amazing, a boy falling out of the sky,
Had somewhere to get to and sailed calmly on.

     —W. H. AUDEN (1907–   , British poet now living in the United States),
       "Musée des Beaux Arts"[5]

[5]From *The Collected Poetry of W. H. Auden.* Copyright 1940 by W. H. Auden; reprinted by permission of Random House, Inc.

Charles Madden finds a very different emphasis:

The Fall of Icarus

(From Brueghel's painting)

The bulging sails by a riotous wind caught
pull the ships and their rigging nets toward shore
to be emptied. The sailors quickly will calm their floors
and their houses in the evening light will melt into the mountains.

And on the hill with one foot planted in the earth
his plowing almost done, his eyes cast down and fully shielded
from the sun which now is growing shadow, the farmer
turns in soil and toil the final circles of the day.

Below him a quiet pastoral: on lichen-bearing rocks
the feeding sheep, the quiet watching dog, the silent shepherd
so stalking with his eyes the homing flights of birds
that neither he nor the intent fisherman closer to the shore,

none has seen the silent fall of Icarus
through the riotous wind and the shadows of the coming evening light,
nor do they hear his sigh, both of pity and delight
of his remembered waxed and winged flight.

—CHARLES F. MADDEN (1921–   , American poet, teacher),
"The Fall of Icarus"[6]

We have already spoken of Tchaikovsky's suite based on Shakespeare's play *Romeo and Juliet.* Debussy's *Afternoon of a Faun* is based on the poem by Mallarmé, and the ballet is based on both. Rimsky-Korsakov's *Scheherazade* finds its source in the *Arabian Nights.* Browning's poem "Fra Lippo Lippi" was inspired by the painting *The Coronation of the Virgin* by Fra Filippo Lippi. Strauss takes his subject *Don Quixote* from the novel by Cervantes. Maeterlinck's play *Pelléas et Mélisande* was used by Debussy for his opera of the same name.

Dramas are often based on novels, and operas on plays; many cinema plots are taken from dramas or novels. Works that derive from other works of art are always individual and can never be classified or grouped together. Therefore, it is sufficient for our purpose merely to note that works of art often are so derived.

[6]From *Northwest Review*, University of Oregon.

● CONCLUSION

These classifications of the sources of art are by no means exhaustive, but they cover the more important ones. Yet it should never be forgotten that no matter how many classifications are made, no matter how many examples are given, they are never enough. The task, as stated at the beginning, is endless. Artists take their subjects when and where they please, and often they lead us a merry chase before we know and understand what they have referred to. But no matter how difficult the reference, a work of art can never be fully understood until its subject is known.

APPENDIX

SOURCES OF ART SUBJECTS—OUTLINE

I. Norse mythology
    A. Name survivals
           Tuesday, Day of Tyr (Tiu), god of battles
           Wednesday, Day of Woden, king of gods
           Thursday, Day of Thor, god of thunder
           Friday, Day of Freya (Freja), goddess of music, love, and spring
    B. Wagner, *The Ring of the Nibelung*
        1. The operas
           The Rhinegold
           The Valkyrie (*Die Walküre*)
           Siegfried
           The Twilight of the Gods (*Götterdämmerung*)
        2. Main characters
           The gods
               Wotan, king of the gods
               Fricka, wife of Wotan
               Freya, spring
               Loki, fire
           The Valkyrie Brunhild
           The Rhine Maidens
           The Giants
           The Nibelungs
               Alberich
               Mime, the artificer who forged Tarnhelm (helmet), Notung (sword), and the ring
           The Volsungs
               Sieglinde, wife of Hunding
               Siegmund
               Siegfried
           The Gibichungs
               Gunther
               Gutrune
               Hagen, son of Alberich

II. Greek mythology and legend
    A. Important gods and goddesses (The Roman name is given first, then the Greek. After the name
        is the province and the attributes by which the god is recognized.)
           Jupiter, Zeus, supreme ruler of gods; frequently seen with thunderbolt in his hands; eagle
           Juno, Hera, wife of Jupiter; shown with peacock, cow
           Minerva, Athene (Athena), goddess of wisdom; on her breast the aegis, with head of Medusa
              which turns men to stone
           Mars, Ares, god of war
           Vulcan, Hephaestus, god of fire
           Apollo, sun, music, poetry
           Diana, Artemis, moon; usually with bow; often with crescent moon in hair
           Venus, Aphrodite, love and beauty; seen with swan, sparrow, and dove
           Mercury, Hermes, messenger of gods; represented with caduceus (staff), petasos (hat), and
              wings on ankles
           Cupid, Eros, son of Venus; blind; bow and arrows
           Ceres, Demeter, agriculture; represented with sheaves of corn and poppies
           Bacchus, Dionysus, wine; shown with tiger, grape leaves, and grapes
           Pluto, Hades, king of underworld
           Proserpina, Persephone, wife of Pluto; daughter of Ceres
           Neptune, Poseidon, god of sea; shown with trident
    B. Myths of the gods
        1. Jupiter—Danaë
           Europa
           Io
        2. Apollo—Daphne
           Phaethon
         3. Diana—Actaeon
         4. Venus—Adonis
           Cupid and Psyche
           Atalanta's race
    C. Myths of the heroes
        1. Perseus—Medusa
           Andromeda
         2. Theseus—The Minotaur
           Ariadne
         3. Hercules
           The labors
         4. Oedipus—the Sphinx
           The King—Jocasta
         5. Jason—The Golden Fleece
           Medea
    D. The Trojan War
        1. The origin of the war
           Wedding feast of Peleus and Thetis
           Judgment of Paris
           Iphigenia in Aulis
         2. The war (Homer's *Iliad*)
           The wrath of Achilles
           Death of Hector
         3. The fall of Troy
           The Palladium
           The Wooden Horse
           Laocoön

    4. The wanderings of Ulysses (Homer's *Odyssey*)
        The lotus eaters
        The island of Circe
        The meeting with Nausicaä
        The return to Penelope; fate of the suitors
    5. The adventures of Aeneas (Vergil's *Aeneid*)
        Dido
        Visit to hell

III. Christianity
  A. The Bible
    1. The best-known stories from the Old Testament
        The beginnings
          Creation and Fall
          The first murder, Cain and Abel
          The flood, Noah
          The tower of Babel
          The story of Abraham
            Sacrifice of Isaac ·
            Isaac and Rebecca
          Jacob
        Stories of heroes
          Joseph and his brethren
          Moses
          Joshua
          Jephthah
          Samson
          David
          Elijah and Elisha
    2. Most important stories from the New Testament
        The birth of Jesus
          Birth of John the Baptist
          Annunciation, Magnificat
          Birth in Bethlehem, shepherds, Magi, flight into Egypt
          Presentation in temple, Song of Simeon
         Events in life of Christ
          Baptism
          Temptation
          Woman of Samaria
          Calling of disciples
          Rich young ruler
          Mary and Martha
          Mary Magdalene
          Peter walking on sea
          Keys given to St. Peter
         Parables and sermons
          Prodigal Son
          Sermon on Mount
          Sower
          "Can the blind lead the blind?"
          Tribute to Caesar

Trial, death, and resurrection
  Last Supper
  Garden of Gethsemane
  Trial
    Peter's denial
    Scourging
    Barabbas
  Crucifixion
  Burial
    Pietà (pictorial representation of Mary mourning over dead body of Christ)
    Entombment
    Resurrection
B. Legends and lives of the saints
  St. Barbara, patron of buildings; represented with a building
  St. Cecilia, patron saint of music and musicians; usually represented with musical instrument
  St. Christopher, ferryman shown carrying Christ across water
  St. Francis, founder of Franciscan order; represented in monastic habit with hempen cord; usually shown with stigmata in reference to legend that he was transfixed with wounds of Christ
  St. George, patron saint of England; usually represented in full armor conquering dragon
  St. Jerome, a father of Western church in fourth century; translator of the Vulgate; usually represented as an old man studying or writing, often with lion
  St. Patrick, patron saint of Ireland; often shown with snakes because of legend that he drove snakes from Ireland
  St. Sebastian, a young Roman officer killed for being a Christian; usually represented as tied to stake and shot full of arrows

4
FUNCTION

● DEFINITION

Benvenuto Cellini, the famous goldsmith, made an elaborate little bowl for Francis I, King of France (Figure 46). It is of gold on a black ebony base; on it are two figures: a woman representing the land and a man representing the sea. We identify the man by his trident, which is the symbol of Neptune, the god of the sea. As we look at the bowl and marvel at its exquisite workmanship, we ask: What is it for? The answer to this question gives the *function* of an article. Cellini made his bowl as a container for salt, and from its function it is called a saltcellar. As employed in this book the word *function* will be reserved for those arts whose medium is itself directly practical and useful.

Many of the works cited in the last chapter were made primarily for their function. The lekythos on which was represented Apollo with his kithara is primarily a vessel for holding oil. It has a long neck to make it possible to pour the oil slowly.

The painting by Execias showing *Dionysus Sailing the Sea* is in the bottom of a cylix, a shallow drinking cup. The paintings themselves, like the figures on the saltcellar, are decorative but have no other use or function.

Sometimes we do not know the original function of a work. We do not know the purpose of the Altamira cave paintings. They may have had a religious purpose; more probably, they had some connection with hunting. The pictures might be supposed to have ensured the hunters a successful hunt, because the animals depicted are those used for food. The caves may have been set aside as sanctuaries. There may have been some connection with magic, but whatever the purpose, we feel that the paintings were put there for a reason beyond decoration for its own sake.

FIGURE 46. BENVENUTO CELLINI (1500–1572), Italian sculptor and goldsmith. *Saltcellar of Francis I* (ca. 1545). (Gold and enamel. Height: about 8 inches. Vienna, Kunsthistorisches Museum.)

FIGURE 47. STONEHENGE, ca. 1800–1400 B.C. (Diameter of circle: 97 feet; height of stones above ground: 13½ feet. Salisbury Plain, Wiltshire, England. Courtesy Ministry of Works, London. British Crown copyright.)

Stonehenge (Figure 47) is also prehistoric, but of it we have more definite knowledge. Its characteristic feature is a series of circles of huge stones set upright in the ground and capped with lintels. Toward the center are two broken rings of stones and at the center a large slab which may have served as an altar. One long-established fact has seemed most significant. Stonehenge is oriented so that its axis passes through a 35-ton marker stone and points directly to the spot on the northeast horizon where the sun rises at the summer solstice, the longest day of the year. The place may have had some ceremonial or other religious purpose. Certainly it was built with one eye on the calendar. Astronomical calculations prove that Stonehenge was in use about 1500 B.C.

Many works are cherished for themselves after their functions have ceased, and these have the right to be considered as artistic. The Altamira paintings are a case in point. The war speeches of Churchill are now being widely printed and read. The lithographs by Daumier which appeared for forty years in the periodical *Charivari* as cartoons of his day are now collected and reproduced in ours.

● FUNCTIONAL AND NONFUNCTIONAL ARTS

Obviously function plays a larger part in some arts than in others. Architecture is entirely and directly functional: buildings are always built for some special use. The applied arts also are almost entirely functional. In fact, they are called *applied* arts because they have function. Rugs, blankets, clothes, jewelry, cups and saucers, plates, teapots, bowls, baskets—one need only name examples to realize that each is made for some definite and specific use. Moreover, in the applied arts, as in architecture, function is so important that it has usurped the name of the art in the identification of individual works; examples of those arts are ordinarily known by their direct function. Although we speak of a painting, a poem, or a statue, we do not usually speak of a building or a piece of ceramics; we say instead, a school, a church, a plate, a saucer.

If architecture and the applied arts are the most directly functional, literature and painting are probably the least, though there are in them many examples of work with a definite purpose. In *Guernica* and *Rue Transnonain* Picasso and Daumier were protesting against the abuses of their time. *Uncle Tom's Cabin* was written for the definite purpose of fighting slavery, and it did much to arouse antislavery sentiment before the Civil War. Oliver Wendell Holmes's short poem *"Old Ironsides"* was written in protest against a naval order that the frigate *Constitution* be destroyed. This ship, known as "Old Ironsides," was famous for its exploits during the War of 1812. Holmes's poem, which begins with the familiar line, "Aye, tear her tattered ensign down!" aroused so much response that the order to scrap the old ship was countermanded; her "tattered ensign" was not torn down.

Expository and argumentative writings are indirectly functional in so far as they are designed to accomplish some definite end. Newspaper stories and pictures are indirectly functional too; they want to make clear the news. All advertisements, whether in words or in line and color, are functional in that they are designed to influence people.

● FUNCTION IN MUSIC

Music, in its origins, was primarily functional, its two sources being the dance and religion. The earliest peoples invoked their gods by beating the drum and singing, and from that time to the present music has been of primary importance in worship.

Dance music includes the ballet as well as tunes for social and folk dances, such as jigs, waltzes, minuets, fox trots, polonaises, mazurkas, and rumbas. In the dance, music is essential to mark the rhythm and so to keep the dancers together. It also sets the mood of the dance as warlike, gay, courtly, or graceful.

Closely akin to dance music are marches, work songs, and game songs. A march serves the same purpose as a dance in that it marks the time for people walking in a procession, whether it be a military occasion, a wedding, or a funeral. Work songs mark the rhythm of work. Chanteys are sung by sailors when lifting anchor or loading cargo. The popular Russian folk song "The Volga Boatman" helped the sailors in their struggle against the current of the river. Game songs are about halfway between dance and work songs. In "The Farmer in the Dell" or "London Bridge Is Falling Down," the song is sung as the game is played, and the song is an essential part of the game.

Certain compositions become identified with certain specific occasions. One march, "Hail to the Chief," is used for the President of the United States. Another, Handel's "Dead March" from *Saul*, is used for the funerals of the royal family in England. The Wagner and the Mendelssohn marches are so universally used in America for weddings that the wags have wondered if that wedding is legal which does not employ one of them.

With the development of musical instruments, music outgrew its narrow dependence on these two main uses, and we now have much music that has no connection whatever with either the dance or religion, such as symphonies, sonatas, and operas. On the other hand, many musical compositions retain a connection with their functional origin though they are no longer functional. Few of the polonaises and mazurkas of Chopin, for example, could be used as accompaniment for a dance. Bach's great work the Mass in B minor is too long to be used for church services, but it retains the form of the Mass designed for church ritual. Lullabies and serenades also are dissociated from their original use, yet they retain certain connotations: the lullaby, of sweet melody and swaying rhythms; the serenade, of night and love.

● FUNCTION IN SCULPTURE

Sculpture is much more functional than painting or literature. One of the greatest single uses of sculpture is in religion. The bronze doors which Ghiberti made for the Baptistry at Florence (Figure 48) are so faultless that when Michelangelo saw them he exclaimed, "They are so beautiful that they might fittingly stand at the gates of paradise." And they have been called the "Gates of Paradise" ever since.

In the medieval church, sculpture was frequently used for instructional purposes. The panels of the "Gates of Paradise," for example, record scenes from the Old Testament. In the first panel the subject is the Creation. Several different scenes are presented; in the lower left-hand corner God is bringing Adam to life while the angels rejoice; in the center of the panel is the creation of Eve, with a circle of angels surrounding the figures. On the left, behind the creation of Adam, is the temptation: Adam and Eve stand under a tree with the serpent coiled around it. On the right is shown the expulsion: Adam and Eve have

FIGURE 48. LORENZO GHIBERTI (1378–1455), Italian goldsmith, sculptor, and painter. East Door, "Gates of Paradise" (1425–1452). (Bronze. Height of door: 16½ feet. Florence, Baptistry. Photograph by Anderson.)

67

FIGURE 49. LORENZO GHIBERTI. *The Creation*, detail of "Gates of Paradise." (Height of detail: 3 feet, 10 inches. Photograph by Alinari.)

been driven from the gates of Paradise by an angel, while God is seen far back in the heavens (Figure 49).

On the wall of the cathedral at Amiens is a calendar showing the signs of the zodiac. Each of the signs is represented by its symbol, and under it is a relief, of the same size and shape, showing a typical occupation for that sign or month. The first of the three signs in our photograph (Figure 50) pictures a

FIGURE 50. SIGNS OF THE ZODIAC, with corresponding occupations (first half of thirteenth century). Details, basement of west façade. (Stone. Height of each quatrefoil: 2½ feet. Amiens, Cathedral. Photograph, Clarence Ward.)

)at, the sign of Capricorn, which corresponds roughly to the month of Decem-
er. Shown under it is a man putting up meat for the winter. The middle relief
iows a man pouring water, Aquarius, or January. Under him is a table at
hich is seated a man with two heads who, as January (following the Latin
nus), looks both to the new and the old years. February, the last of the three
gns, is represented by two fish, the sign being Pisces, or fish. Under them is
monk trying to keep warm. He has taken off his shoes and is warming his
ands before the blazing fire.

Another important function of sculpture is the commemoration of individ-
als, as in the Lincoln Memorial in Washington. Often a statue records an event
f importance; the *Charioteer* probably commemorates a victory. In sculpture
iat is not connected with architecture, fountains take an important place.
he fountain is frequently used as a medium for telling a mythological or
llegorical story; for example, the fountain by Carl Milles, opposite the Union
tation in St. Louis, represents the union of the Missouri and the Mississippi
vers.

The tombstone is one of the opportunities for sculpture that is too frequently
isregarded. But tombstones can and should be beautiful. In Figures 51 and
2 we have two examples from different ages: one is Greek of the fifth cen-
iry; the other is recent American, the work of Augustus Saint-Gaudens.

GURE 52. AUGUSTUS SAINT-GAUDENS (1848–1907),
merican sculptor. *Adams Memorial* (ca. 1891). (Bronze figure,
ranite setting. Height of figure: 4 feet, 1 inch. Washington,
.C., Rock Creek Cemetery.)

GURE 51. *HEGESO STELE* (late fifth century B.C.). (Pentelic
arble. Height: 4 feet, 10½ inches.
thens, National Museum.
notograph by Alinari.)

Another functional use of sculpture is the coin. Every coin shows a relie the Lincoln penny, the Jefferson nickel, the Franklin Roosevelt dime, and th Washington quarter. In the United States we are now paying more attention the designs on coins than we did fifty years ago. And in a foreign country it interesting to note how the spirit of the country is reflected in the designs o its coins.

● FUNCTION IN ARCHITECTURE

Architecture is the only one of the major arts that is directly functional. It also the art in which the proper performance of function is most importan Buildings are large and expensive and they cannot easily be replaced. If a cha is not comfortable, we can buy another and use this only when we have con pany. But we cannot treat architecture in any such fashion. If a building do not function we have to put up with an inconvenient and inefficient structur Therefore it is in architecture that we see most clearly the influence of fun tional demands. These can be traced to demands that arise from climate an those that come from social conditions.

CLIMATE

With central heating, structural steel, and air conditioning, it is possible t build any kind of house in any climate; nevertheless climate is still a factor c which everyone is acutely conscious. Is the climate wet or dry, hot or col sunny or dark, even or variable, windy or calm? In countries where there strong wind, the house is planned with windbreaks and the living rooms ar put in protected areas away from the wind, whereas in warm climates wit temperate winds, the house is planned to take advantage of the prevailin breeze. In a cold climate, emphasis is placed on building for warmth, in a war climate on the attempt to keep cool. When the climate is mild, the primar function of the wall is to ensure privacy and to keep out the sun and rai hence, it may be of very light material. In China and Japan, for instance, th walls are merely sliding screens.

The size and number of the doors and windows are likewise determine largely by climate. In hot southern countries, where the sun is blinding, th object is to shut out the light; accordingly, in Spain and in Egypt the window are small and few in number. In the northern countries, where there is muc rain and the winters are long and dark, the demand is for more light, and th windows are large and numerous. The shape of the roof depends primarily o the amount of rain and snow. A flat roof is found in warm, dry countries, as i

gypt and Greece, where the roof can be used as an extra sitting room or as a
·droom on warm nights. But a flat roof is practicable only in a dry climate.
'here there is rain it is usually found best to tilt the roof to make it easier for
ιe water to run off. The degree of slope is determined partly by the amount of
.in. In countries where there is much rain the roofs are more steeply pitched
ιan in countries that have only a little rain. The amount of snow is an impor-
.nt factor also. Snow is very heavy; a large quantity will break through a roof;
ɔnce, in mountainous countries where there is a great deal of snow, the roofs
·e very steeply pitched and are left unbroken by windows so that the snow will
ide off. The steeply pitched, broken roofs that are found on the châteaux are
seful in France where there is much rain and little snow, but they would not
ɔ practical in the Alps. In China there are very heavy rains during the mon-
ɔons. Accordingly, the roofs are steeply pitched and project over the house;
: the eaves they are turned up to admit light.

Here in the United States both the Northern and the Southern states have
eautiful examples of the colonial type of architecture. But there are interest-
ιg differences due primarily to differences in climate. In the South there are
ιany more verandas than in the North. And in the South the columns of the
ɔrch often extend to the roof in order to shade the windows of the second
ory. There is a difference, too, in the arrangement of the buildings. In New
.ngland, because of the cold and the snow, the barns and the other outbuild-
ιgs were often attached to the main residence so that the men of the house
ɔuld do the chores without going out in the cold. In the South, with its mild
·inters, the outbuildings were scattered all around the yard as separate struc-
ιres. A very moderate home would have a smoke house (for meat), a hen
ɔuse, a carriage house, probably an ice house (for storing ice), and a cellar
for keeping food cool), as well as the barns.

ɔCIAL FACTORS. The term *social factors* is used here to mean all those elements
ιn architecture that are determined by man, in contrast to those that are gov-
rned by nature. A first consideration in any building is the use to which it is
ɔ be put, its function in the narrower sense of the term. A building is designed
ɔr a special purpose: it may be an office building, a church, a residence, a
arage, and so on. These primary functions are influenced by the physical con-
litions of the land, as we have just seen, but they are even more dependent on
ɔcial forces. In olden times there was always need for protection. Castles and
ɔrtifications were made with very thick, strong walls, as defense against the
·nemy. Palaces had to be strong enough to ward off possible attack. The palace
vhich Michelozzo built for Cosimo de' Medici served both as palace and fortress
Figure 53).

Another example of social influences on architecture can be found by com-

FIGURE 53. MEDICI-RICCARDI PALACE (1444–1452). Michelozzo (1396–1472), Italian architect. (Stone. Length: 300 feet; height: 90 feet. Florence. Photograph by Alinari.)

FIGURE 54. Floor plans showing relative size of Erechtheum, Parthenon, temple at Edfu, and Amiens Cathedral.

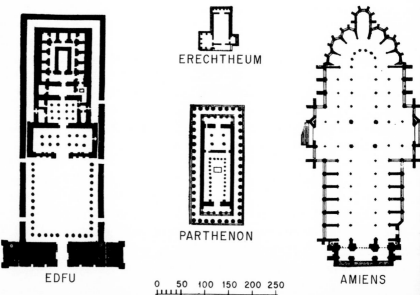

ERECHTHEUM

PARTHENON

EDFU

AMIENS

0   50   100   150   200   250

paring buildings for worship (Figure 54). To Christians a church or a cathedral is primarily a place where large numbers of people can assemble, because corporate worship is an integral part of the Christian faith. Hence the cathedral at Amiens is large, the construction is open, and it will hold many people. The Greeks, on the other hand, had no service in the same sense; their gatherings for religious purposes were infrequent and were held out-of-doors. For them the temple was primarily a shrine for the statue of the god, and in consequence their temples were small, accommodating only a few people at a time. The Parthenon, though large for a temple, is only about one-fourth the size of the cathedral at Amiens. And small as is the Parthenon, it was divided into two rooms: a large room in which the statue of Athena was kept, and a smaller one for the treasures. The Erechtheum, another Greek temple, is even smaller. The Egyptian temple had a different arrangement because the ritual was different. In Egypt the temple was primarily a sanctuary which could be visited only by the Pharaoh and the priest. In front of the sanctuary was a series of rooms to which other people were admitted according to their rank. An Egyptian temple such as that at Edfu consisted of four parts: first, the pylon, a huge gateway covering the entire front of the building; second, a large open court accessible to everyone; third, a hall, or hypostyle, made up of columns. This hall, which was dimly lighted because the columns covered the entire floor, was reserved for dignitaries who occupied a position midway between the people and Pharaoh. And finally, there was a small inner sanctuary for only the priest and the king.

Sometimes the government steps in with laws which affect architecture, though these may not be directly concerned with building as such. A tax on the number of windows, for instance, will result in houses with fewer windows. It is supposed that a tax on the number of stories of a house had much to do with the development of the *mansard roof*, which gave all the space of an extra story though technically it was only an attic.

One of the interesting examples of this type is to be found in the zoning law of New York City. This law was made necessary by the skyscrapers, for if very tall buildings are placed on each side, the street between is left dark, like a very narrow canyon. The purpose of the law is to ensure that a street should always have the proper amount of air and sunshine, and it accomplishes this end by regulating the height of a building in proportion to the width of the street and the size of the lot. An imaginary triangle is drawn with the lot as its base, and the law requires that the building should not project beyond that triangle, except for a tower not to exceed one-fourth the area of the plot. In order to utilize their plots to the best advantage, builders have designed structures in which the upper floors are set *back* of the lower floors. In the McGraw-

FIGURE 55. MCGRAW-HILL BUILDING (completed 1931). Raymond Hood (1881–1934), American architect. (Steel frame construction, 33 stories and basement. New York.)

Hill Building (Figure 55) there are three such setbacks before we reach the central tower, the height of which is not restricted by law.

FORM FOLLOWS FUNCTION

Whenever art has function, the function influences and often determines the form. This is just another way of stating the obvious fact that if an object is made for a certain function it should be made in such a way that it can perform that function. As the function changes, the form changes, and if there are many functions there will be many forms. Take an object of everyday use such as a spoon. There are spoons for babies and spoons for adults, spoons for cooking, spoons for eating, spoons for serving, deep spoons and shallow spoons, spoons with long handles and spoons with short handles. Even a rather small household will have a variety of spoons because there is a variety of functions to be served by them.

Door keys offer another interesting example. Keys are now carried by many individuals, and one person often has to carry more than one; accordingly keys are small. But when gates and doors were in the charge of special porters who were always in attendance, keys were large and massive; they were in fact a visible symbol of the power and importance of the place to be locked.

These examples have all been taken from the industrial arts, but instances may be cited from any art that is functional. A lullaby must have a rocking rhythm to soothe the baby. A march or a jig must keep the time exactly so that one may march or dance in time to it. A coin must be small and flat, and any decoration on it must also be flat.

FUNCTION AND BEAUTY

Some arts are functional and some are not. Is there any relation between function and value as art? Can we say that functional arts are greater or less great than arts that are not functional? The value of any work of art depends on the work itself, not on its being functional or nonfunctional. Architecture, which is always functional, is not superior or inferior to painting or poetry, which are usually nonfunctional. In the evaluation of two works of art, the presence or absence of function, just like the presence or absence of subject, is a matter of no consequence. If one were asked to name the world's greatest works of art he would certainly include the plays of Aeschylus and Shakespeare, the cathedrals at Chartres and Amiens, and the symphonies of Brahms. The plays have subject but no function; the cathedrals have function but no subject; the symphonies have neither subject nor function.

In the evaluation of functional art, however, the problem is different. Obviously the function should be known if the work is to be understood; if it is a birdbath or a saltcellar, it should be known as a bath for birds or as a container for salt when it is judged. It cannot be adequately judged just as shape.

But when the function is understood, is there any relation between the function of a work and its value as art? Yes, in a general way, there is. There has been a great deal of discussion on this point, and any statement may be contradicted by excellent examples to the contrary, but it will usually be granted that a functional object is not beautiful unless it can perform its function adequately and acceptably. If it is desirable for people to see and hear in church, a church should be constructed so that they can see and hear in it. A chair that is uncomfortable is not so good as one that is comfortable. A residence should be so planned that the business of housekeeping may be carried on in it with the maximum of ease and efficiency. A beautiful teapot that is useless is like a beautiful bridge one cannot cross or a beautiful car that will not run.

In this respect we must admit that the saltcellar of Cellini fails if considered as a saltcellar. The figures are well conceived and executed, but the affair is too elaborate for its function. On the other hand, it was a custom at this time to have on the table a large and elaborate saltcellar known as "the salt." The salt was placed before the master of the house, between him and the guest of honor, thus serving to indicate rank. For this social use the Cellini saltcellar was admirably adapted.

In fact, adequate performance of function usually tends to make for beauty of design. Why this should be true we do not know, but it is true. The shapes in nature that are the most beautiful are also the most efficient, as for instance the wings of a bird. Practical design offers many examples; everything is eliminated except what is essential, and the result is beautiful. Examples of such shapes are found in the canoe, the canoe paddle, the handle of an ax or a scythe, the blades of an electric fan.

Nevertheless, it is true that, although efficiency does make for beauty, efficiency and beauty are not the same. An article that adequately performs a function is not necessarily beautiful. Art demands something beyond function, something in addition to efficiency and proper performance of function. The shape of a spoon may be the best possible for its particular function, but the spoon is not for that reason a work of art. In the economy of nature the best shape for an object's use *tends* to be the most beautiful, but it is our pleasure in the shape and not its usefulness that makes it art.

MEDIUM

5

MEDIUM—GENERAL CONSIDERATIONS

● **DEFINITION**

Many widely diverse objects go under the name of art. A song, a sonata, a symphony, a statue, a skyscraper, a tapestry, a tragedy, a teapot, a poem, a painting, a palace, an oratorio, a cathedral, a chest, an etching, an engraving, an epic, a dance, a novel, a lyric—all these and more are classed as art. A single reading of this list, however, is sufficient for certain obvious classifications. The song, the symphony, the sonata, and the oratorio belong to the art of music; the cathedral, the palace, and the skyscraper are examples of architecture; the poem, the tragedy, the epic, the lyric, and the novel are literature. The basis for these classifications is primarily the way the artist has communicated his idea to us, his medium. The word medium, which comes from the Latin word *medium* signifying "means," denotes the means by which an artist communicates his idea; it is the stuff out of which he creates a work of art. Architecture makes use of wood, stone, brick, concrete; sculpture makes use of marble, bronze, wood; painting makes use of colored pigments on wood or canvas.

Medium is essential to art. Subject and function, as we have seen, are not essential. There is art without subject and there is art without function, but there is no art without medium. A work of art could not be known if it did not exist in some medium. And both the art and the artist get their names from the medium. Emily Dickinson and Arthur Honegger were both inspired by the railway train. Because she used words to express her idea she is called a poet, and because he used tones he is called a musician.

On the basis of medium the arts are primarily classified as *visual* and *auditory*. Painting, sculpture, architecture, tapestry, glassware, etc., are visual arts; they are seen. Music and literature are auditory arts; they are heard. Even when one reads silently a musical score or a page of poetry, he hears the sound in his mind. On the basis of medium also the arts are classified as *time arts* and *space arts.* The visual arts are space arts. The auditory arts are time arts. The theater, the opera, and the cinema are known as *combined arts,* being both visual and auditory, existing in both space and time. Though it is largely visual, the dance is classed with the combined arts because it employs both time and space.

By a third classification on the basis of medium the arts are divided into major and minor arts. The five major arts are music, literature, painting, sculpture, and architecture. The minor arts are metalwork, weaving, ceramics, glass, furniture, photography, lettering, bookmaking, etc. The terms *major* and *minor,* however, are of no importance in determining the value of any single work of art. A good piece of glass or porcelain is better than a poor painting; a beautiful Oriental rug is greater than a poor statue; a good saltcellar is greater than a poor building. The five great arts deserve the name *major* not because there is anything necessarily great about them as such, but because more very great works have been made in those mediums than in the other lesser arts. Any work of art is great or not great in itself and should be judged as such regardless of its medium.

● THE ARTIST AND HIS MEDIUM

When an artist uses any medium he chooses the one that can best express what he wants to say. Often an artist will use more than one medium. William Blake, for instance, used words in his poem "The Sick Rose."

> O Rose, thou art sick!
> The invisible worm
> That flies in the night,
> In the howling storm,

Has found out thy bed
Of crimson joy,
And his dark secret love
Does thy life destroy.

  —William Blake, British poet and artist (1757–1827), from *Songs of Experience*
  (1794)

In his print "When the Morning Stars Sang Together" (Figure 37) he used engraving. At other times he used a third medium, watercolor. In each case he chose the medium that seemed right for that particular idea.

In the determination of medium, however, the words *choice* and *selection* give a false impression, for they imply that the artist makes a deliberate choice. The artist does not make a conscious, reasoned choice of his medium; the selection of medium is a part of the artistic inspiration. The idea which Blake put into a poem came to him as an idea for a poem. That for the engraving was for an engraving. He did not have an idea out of which he might make a poem or an engraving. When the unknown Greek sculptor of the fifth century before Christ made the little bronze horse now at the Metropolitan Museum (Figure 56) he chose sculpture because what he wanted to say demanded volume. The poet is a poet rather than a painter because he thinks in terms of words. As one poet said, "When I enjoy a scene, I find myself hunting for words that will exactly express the impression it has made on me."

FIGURE 56. GREEK SCULPTURE. Horse (ca. 480 B.C.). (Bronze. Height: ca. 14 inches. New York, photograph courtesy Metropolitan Museum of Art.)

FIGURE 57. ALBRECHT DÜRER. *The Knight, Death, and the Devil* (ca. 1513). (Engraving. Size: 9¾ by 7¼ inches. New York, courtesy Metropolitan Museum of Art.)

Moreover, the artist thinks in terms of a specific medium. Two of Dürer's great prints are of horsemen; for one the artist has used engraving, for the other woodcut. He chose each medium to express the exact idea he wanted to make clear in that print. The engraving is called *The Knight, Death, and the Devil* (Figure 57). The knight probably represents the Christian who is not led astray by temptations. A very solid and praiseworthy person, he rides across the picture apparently bound for the ideal city shown against the sky. He pays no attention to his companions: Death, who holds an hourglass before him, and the Devil, half pig and half wolf.

The woodcut is called *The Four Horsemen of the Apocalypse* (Figure 58). According to the passage in the New Testament (Revelation 6) the first horse

FIGURE 58. ALBRECHT DÜRER. *The Four Horsemen of the Apocalypse* (ca. 1498). (Woodcut. Size: 15¹³⁄₁₆ by 11½ inches. Boston, courtesy Museum of Fine Arts.)

s white, and its rider who carries a bow "went forth conquering and to con-
quer." Some think Christ is this conquering rider. The second horse is red,
symbolizing war; its rider carrying a sword drives peace from the earth. The
third horse, which is black, represents famine; the scales in the hands of its
rider show that food is scarce and must be weighed. Last is a pale horse, "and
his name that sat on him was Death."

A sculptor plans his statue not for wood in general but for oak or mahogany.
The architect does not plan a house and then decide whether it shall be of
brick, wood, or stone; the demands of brick, wood, and stone are different, and
he must design his house according to his material. The jeweler does not imagine
a design and then say, "Shall I make it in copper or gold?" It is a design for
gold or for copper. The artist thinks and feels in terms of his medium.

Moreover the artist loves and respects his medium for itself; he uses it because
it has certain qualities, and he tries to bring out and emphasize those qualities.
The sculptor gives life to his statue not by denying that it is wood or stone,
but by incorporating the qualities of wood or stone into the meaning of the
sculptured piece. In the statues of Henry Moore, we are always conscious of
the texture of wood as wood, or bronze as bronze. To the poet the words are
the poem. They are not one of many ways he has found to express his idea; they
are the idea. His poem cannot be separated from the words of the poem.

In studying any work of art, therefore, it is always worth while to ask why
the artist chose the particular medium in question. Why did Wagner give the
sword theme to the trumpet? Why did the unknown artist of the horse want it
in bronze? Why did Dürer use engraving for *The Knight, Death, and the Devil*
and woodcut for *The Four Horsemen of the Apocalypse?* How do these works
suit the inherent qualities of the medium chosen?

● THE DISTINCTIVE CHARACTER OF MEDIUM

If what is said in one medium cannot be said in another, it follows that no
work can ever be translated from one medium to another. There is no argument
about this point if it is a question of two different arts. A description of a scene
and a painting of the same scene do not tell the same story; inevitably what
they say is different. And the same is true, though to a lesser degree, when it is
a question of two mediums within a single art. If the artist's intuition demands
a statue of marble, it follows that a copy of the statue in bronze will miss something essential to the original.

It is in music and literature that the problem of translation arises most often.
Music that was written for the orchestra is arranged for piano, and music

written for piano is arranged for orchestra. Works in foreign languages are
translated into English, and English works are translated into foreign languages
In this kind of translation, however, something of the original is always lost or
changed. Every time Stokowski transcribes the music of Bach, the result is
Stokowski as well as Bach. Gilbert Murray's translations of Euripides show us
Euripides plus Gilbert Murray. The orchestral score of *The Afternoon of a Faun*
transcribed for piano has lost something that was essential to the music. Even
when a great artist like Casals plays a Chopin piano prelude on the cello, we
have lost something of Chopin's music.

On this point, however, a caution is necessary. It is better to know a Greek
play in translation than not to know the play. It is better to hear Bach arranged
by Stokowski than not to hear Bach. It is better to know the famous master
pieces of painting and sculpture in reproductions than not to know them at
all. One should strive not to be too much a purist on the one hand, or too
easily pleased on the other; one should not refuse to know Bach's music as
played by the orchestra, but one should hear it on the harpsichord if he has the
opportunity. It is well to study the works of Botticelli in reproductions until
one has a chance to see the originals. One should read translations from the
Greek but remember that one will know Sophocles and Euripides best when
he reads their plays in Greek.

● INFLUENCE OF MEDIUM ON CHOICE OF SUBJECT

SCULPTURE

The nature of the medium inevitably influences the type of subject it can portray. Traditionally sculpture in the round has tended to emphasize mass and
weight, and its subjects are objects of definite form and solidity. Trees and
clouds are not common in sculpture. Moreover, the sculpture of the past has
been limited almost entirely to the bodies of animals and, especially, the bodies
of men. It has emphasized not only the human body but in large measure the
nude human body. We do not really suppose that David was naked when he
fought Goliath, but the body of David is more nearly ideal when it is naked,
and therefore better suited to the meaning and purpose of the statue. When
clothes are used we want them to be simple and straightforward, as in the figures
of the caryatids of the Erechtheum.

Sculpture in relief, unlike sculpture in the round, has a background to which
figures are attached, and because of this it can show more kinds of subjects with
more varied backgrounds. On the background may be carved many subjects
not so appropriate to sculpture in the round: trees, clouds, birds, fish, anything.

FIGURE 59. *LUDOVISI THRONE* (ca. 460 B.C.). (Marble. Height at center: 3 feet, 4½ inches. Rome, Terme Museum. Photograph by Alinari.)

In the famous "Gates of Paradise" Ghiberti seems almost as free as a painter in his choice of subject. In the so-called *Ludovisi Throne* (Figure 59), which is supposed to portray the birth of Venus, the goddess is being lifted from the water by two attendants. The representation of cloth, especially the delineation of the form seen through the cloth, is exceptionally fine.

With the interest in abstract art there have developed new styles, as we have seen in Moore's *Two Forms*. This new sculpture differs from older forms in treatment of medium as well as in subject. Whereas older sculpture is solid, the new sculpture is often hollow, playing up concave as well as convex surfaces. Thin strips of metal are combined with plastic or glass, even with wood and wires, to make interesting arrangements. Often they are suspended where they can move, and one gets various lights and shadows from them. Such sculptures, called *mobiles*, are associated primarily with the name of Alexander Calder. An example is *Lobster Trap and Fish Tail* (Figure 60), which hangs in the stairwell of the Museum of Modern Art in New York City. Of his mobiles Calder said in 1951: ". . . the idea of detached bodies floating in space, of different sizes and densities, perhaps of different colors and temperatures . . . some at rest, while others move in peculiar manners, seems to me the ideal source of form."[1]

[1] Alfred H. Baer, Jr. (ed.), *Masters of Modern Art*, p. 148.

FIGURE 60. ALEXANDER CALDER (1898–   ), American sculptor. *Lobster Trap and Fish Tail* (1939). (Mobile. Steel wire and sheet aluminum. Size: 8½ feet high, 9½ feet in diameter. New York, Museum of Modern Art; gift of the Advisory Committee.)

PAINTING

Painting has a much wider field than sculpture; it may concern itself with anything in space. Whatever can be seen can be painted: lakes, trees, clouds, houses, mountains, fields, anything that has form to the eye either in reality or in the artist's mind.

Painting and sculpture are both limited in time. Each can represent its object only at a single moment of time. In life the running horse or the smiling girl does not stay the same for ten consecutive seconds; the sculptor or the painter chooses one of those seconds and preserves the object at that instant. He may create a feeling or an illusion of movement so that we are conscious of the action that is taking place or is about to take place. In El Greco's *Resurrection*, Christ seems to be really rising out of a mass of bodies. In Botticelli's *Birth of Venus*, the goddess is being blown to the shore. Even in Ghirlandajo's *Old Man and Boy*, we feel that it is just for a moment that they will be in this position, that one or both will move very soon. In each case the artist is showing the characteristic motion or gesture of the person about to move; we feel that the next second there will be movement, but the scene as presented is still, the action does not change.

Some years ago there was a great deal of talk about a painting by Duchamp called *Nude Descending a Staircase* (Figure 61). The artist was trying to picture just what the title indicates, the appearance of forms in motion. He did this by presenting a succession of pictures of the same thing from slightly different points of view. Some modern artists, notably Picasso, have given a sense of movement to a painting by presenting at one time different aspects of a head or figure. Here as in everything connected with art we must admit that all standards are empirical; that is, they are derived from experience. The artist may do anything he can do. In other words, if Duchamp and Picasso can persuade us that we can see action in a painting and that we like to see action portrayed in that way, then painting becomes a medium for the portrayal of action.

FIGURE 61. MARCEL DUCHAMP (1887–), French painter. *Nude Descending a Staircase, No. 2* (1912). (Oil on canvas. Size: 58⅜ by 35⅜ inches. Philadelphia, Museum of Art; collection of Louise and Walter Arensberg.)

LITERATURE

Painting allows a wider range of subjects than sculpture, but literature allows a wider range than painting; while painting can present anything that might be seen, literature can present anything that can be put into words. Moreover, it is not limited to a second of time as are the visual arts. Literature can describe a situation at any given moment and can tell what happened before and after that time. Literature differs from the other arts in another respect. Since the language of literature is the same as the language of abstract thought, it can express abstract thought as the other arts cannot. Shakespeare can have Hamlet say, "There's a divinity that shapes our ends, Rough-hew them how we will— (*Hamlet*, V, ii, 10–11). The sculptor or the painter may portray a thoughtful face; the musician may make one think of immortality; but no one of the three can express the idea as clearly as the poet.

On the other hand, imitation through literature is less exact than imitation through either painting or sculpture. The statue of a dog may conceivably be mistaken for the living dog, but a poem about a dog will never be. And yet the poem may call to mind the characteristics of a dog better than the statue.

MUSIC

As we have seen, music can never portray any subject clearly. And since music can only suggest the subject, it can suggest any subject. Subjects that cannot even be put into words can be expressed in music. Vague ideas, half-formed opinions and emotions, feelings that can never be given tangible form—all these are found in music.

Thus each art is limited in the subjects it can portray, and it is a general rule that the more subjects an art can portray, the less lifelike it is. A statue of an animal is more like the original than the work in any other art, but sculpture can depict fewer subjects. As the medium gets less like the original, the number of subjects it can portray increases until, as in music, any subject is allowed, though the imitation is so little exact that we cannot always be sure what the subject is.

● LIMITATIONS OF MEDIUM

The artist is free to use any medium that seems right to him, but he must work within the limitations of his medium. For each medium has its own possibilities and limitations. What Blake says in words in "The Sick Rose" he cannot say in engraving, and what the Greek artist of the horse says in sculpture could not be said in words or in engraving.

ORPHEUS AND EURYDICE

The limitations and possibilities of medium can be illustrated clearly if we compare the use of a single subject in several mediums. Take, for instance, the myth of Orpheus, the great musician who went to the other world to demand back his wife Eurydice. His request was granted on condition that he should not look back until he had reached the upper world. But just before he arrived he looked back, and his wife was lost.

This legend is the subject of a Greek relief of about the third century before Christ (Figure 62), though the work is known only in a Roman copy. The sculptor had to choose one second and only one from the entire story. He chose the moment just after Orpheus had looked around, when both Orpheus and Eurydice realized that she must return to Hades. In that one instant he has had to show all the love and longing of the lovers. The legend says that when Orpheus turned, Eurydice disappeared. Sculpture could not show a person in the act of disappearing, and hence Hermes, the messenger of the gods, is shown waiting to take Eurydice back to the realm of Pluto.

FIGURE 62. *ORPHEUS and EURY-DICE* (ca. 430 B.C.), Roman copy in Pentelic marble of marble original. (Height: 3 feet, 10½ inches. Naples, National Museum. Photograph by Alinari.)

In this change, however, what seems a limitation of the medium becomes an opportunity, for the sculptor shows the contrast between the mortals and the gods, not in physique but in attitude. The mortals, Orpheus and Eurydice, are pathetic in their fruitless yearning and powerlessness; the god is patient, conscious of the inevitability of the gods' decree, but quite detached from the sufferings of men.

The story is told again by Ovid, a Latin poet who lived about the time of Christ, in his *Metamorphoses*. Since he was using words, Ovid could give minute details of all kinds. He told, for instance, how the wild beasts and even the trees and rocks responded to the playing of Orpheus. He described the bad omen at the wedding when Hymen's torch smoked, and how Eurydice, while running away from the unwelcome advances of a shepherd, was bitten by a snake and died. Orpheus, inconsolable, at last made the desperate resolve to seek her in Hades. Playing on his lyre, he passed all the people being tortured there. Finally, he reached the throne of Pluto and Proserpine, where he declared boldly that if they would not give him back his wife, they would have a new inhabitant of Hades, for he would not leave without Eurydice. They agreed that she might go on condition that he should not look behind to see if she were following. When he had almost reached the entrance, he looked back and she disappeared. Later some Thracian maidens tried to captivate him, but when he refused to have anything to do with them, they tore him to bits and threw the pieces into the river.

Gluck, an eighteenth-century German composer, used this story as the subject of his opera *Orpheus and Eurydice*. The change in medium necessarily involved changes in presentation. In the first place, an opera is limited in time, and singing is much slower than speaking. Therefore, the story had to be shortened; the opera begins after the death of Eurydice and ends with the departure from Hades. Moreover, it would be impossible on the stage to show the various punishments of Hades: Ixion is on a fiery wheel, the daughters of Danaüs are carrying water in a sieve, Tantalus is immersed in water up to his lips. Instead, Gluck introduced bands of Furies who assail Orpheus and challenge his approach.

The most interesting change comes in the return of Orpheus and Eurydice. Ovid says simply that Eurydice followed Orpheus until they were almost out in the world. Orpheus was, of course, playing on his lyre, but there is no other indication as to what was happening on the journey. Such a scene would be difficult if enacted on the stage, a man singing and a woman following in silence. Hence, Eurydice is made to talk. She asks where they are going. Why does Orpheus not look at her? Has he ceased to love her? At last she says in desperation that she would rather be back in Hades if her husband does not love her any more. At this Orpheus can stand it no longer: he turns, and she disappears.

It is not important for our study to notice that in this version the god Amor (love) brings her to life again with the statement that they have suffered enough, and the lovers leave Hades happily. This ending, however, changes the entire tone of the narrative, taking away its tragedy and making it all rather sprightly and sophisticated.

● PRESERVATION OF ART

Since it can be known only as it is expressed in some medium, art is lost if the medium is lost. We cannot study the architecture of Mesopotamia as we can that of Greece, for the houses were made of sun-dried brick and almost all of them have been washed away. The Angles and Saxons, when they settled in England, must have known many stories about the heroes of their native land; but only one of these stories was written down, *Beowulf*; the others have been forgotten.

About some of these lost works of art a great deal is known. The great statue of Athena called the *Athena Parthenos,* for which the Parthenon was a shrine, was described by the historians. It was about forty feet in height, and it was made of gold and ivory. Standing as it did in the Parthenon, lighted by the beams of the early morning sun, it must have been an object of rare beauty. But the statue itself has not been preserved; there are two known copies that are inadequate, and while we may learn various facts about the statue, we cannot experience its beauty. Other examples might be cited almost indefinitely, but the point is clear. If the medium of a work of art is gone, the art is gone. It is therefore extremely important that the medium be preserved.

In this matter of preservation we find a sharp difference between the visual and the auditory arts. The visual arts are material realities and as such can be preserved. A painting, a statue, a building, even a bit of embroidery or lace may be kept; and when we want to study it we can see the original work. It may not be in as good condition as when it was made, but we can see the thing itself. In a painting by Rembrandt we see the actual paint which was put on by the artist; the colors may be darkened by time, but the picture we see is the work of the artist himself. The statues of Michelangelo are the figures made by Michelangelo. In the visual arts, therefore, the problems of preservation are all problems of keeping the medium safe and in good condition: of finding paints that will not fade, of seeing that houses and statues are made of materials that will endure and that they are not destroyed.

● PRESERVATION OF THE AUDITORY ARTS

In the auditory arts the situation is entirely different. Music and literature exist in time, and time once past is gone forever. The only way we can keep the time arts is to reproduce them. We cannot hear the song as it was sung a half-hour ago; we must sing it over again. We cannot listen today to the poem as we heard it yesterday, but we can repeat the poem. The problem of preserving the auditory arts, therefore, is the problem of finding some means of keeping them so that they can be reproduced.

Originally music and literature were kept by memory and by oral transmission. One man taught another; the grandfather told tales to his grandson; the mother sang songs to her child. In most countries, songs and stories were handed down in this way for a long time, often for centuries, before they were put into permanent form. Even today some of our literature and music comes to us by word of mouth. The stories we tell of Santa Claus, the verses and songs we sing in games, and the simple steps to which we dance them are learned from others, not from books. From Maine to California children sing of London bridge and the farmer in the dell, not because the words have any significance for them, but because they have learned the songs from their parents and friends.

The difficulties with this kind of transmission, however, are very great. The song or the story may be forgotten or changed. Moreover, it does not remain the same. When a new singer tells a story or sings a melody, he often changes it, sometimes unconsciously, sometimes consciously. The poet who does not understand one word will substitute another he does know. In the Kentucky mountains songs have been preserved since the time of Shakespeare, but they are not exactly the same: words and music have changed.

A better way to preserve a time art is to convert it into symbols that can be kept. Hence, from the very earliest times, there have been attempts to find such symbols. The symbols for words came first; they are old. In fact, we can almost say that they are as old as history, for we know comparatively little history earlier than the symbols of written language. Moreover, these symbols are accurate and can be accurately interpreted. We know the writings of the Egyptians, the Greeks, and the Hebrews, and we know that we are reading those writings in the main correctly.

The symbols for music were invented much later, and hence we do not know music of as early a date as we do literature. We know that the early peoples had music and musical instruments; the Hebrews talk of the cymbals and the psaltery, and the Egyptians and the Greeks drew pictures of people with musical instruments. We know also that the Greeks had a very elaborate musical system; they have written its laws and principles; much of our present theory derives directly from the Greeks. But none of these people had a precise way of writing the music itself, and very little has been preserved. The earliest music that can be read with any degree of accuracy is that of the Middle Ages. Before that time there were various attempts at musical notation, but either these early examples were not exact or we have not learned how to interpret them accurately. Hence, for us, the history of music is vague until about the year 1000.

More recent devices for preserving the auditory arts are the phonograph record and the tape recorder. These can preserve the exact tone, the exact speed, the intonation, and many other characteristics that are lost in the written symbol. They have not, however, superseded writing; music and literature are still known primarily through written symbols.

For the combined arts there are even yet no very good methods of preservation. In the drama and the opera we have, of course, symbols for words and for music; and we can take photographs of stage sets and actors, of singers and dancers. But for the combination of various effects that make up the theater or the opera, we have now no adequate means of preservation. The film with its sound track would seem to be a perfect means for preserving the combined arts; and it is probably the best we have today. The conditions for the making of a motion picture, however, are so different from the conditions of a stage performance that it is difficult, not to say impossible, to get the same effects. Furthermore, as the film is developing now, it has become a new art rather than a means for reproducing or preserving a stage performance.

It is too soon to know how good television will be for the preservation of the combined arts. It seems to have great possibilities, but if we can judge by present indications it is apt to develop like the film into an independent art.

For the preservation of all the arts there will undoubtedly be improvements in the future. Within the past fifty years we have seen so many changes effected by the film, the phonograph, and television, that we cannot say what the future will hold. Several hundred years from now a library may consist almost entirely of phonograph records and sound films, and it may be that we shall listen to a record of a book or magazine as naturally as we now read it. We have now notation for the dance, and future generations may look on our previous failure to preserve the dance with as great wonderment and lack of comprehension as we have in viewing the period before writing was invented or adequate music notation devised. But whatever may happen in the future, for the present, opera and theater performances are almost entirely lost, and music and literature are preserved primarily through written symbols.

● ADVANTAGES AND DISADVANTAGES OF SYMBOLS

The symbols of music and literature have the disadvantages of all symbols: they are arbitrary, and they must be known to be interpreted correctly. A child or an entirely unlettered person can recognize a picture, but he must know how to read notes or written words before he can get the meaning of written music or literature. Moreover, the symbols themselves are not too exact. The printed page gives only the word; one cannot tell how long it is to be held, in what tone it should be uttered, or how much stress it is to be given, and, unless one knows the language, the symbol does not even give the sound. Printed music is in this respect much more exact, for it can give duration and pitch and can indicate accent. Even so, however, it is far from accurate and, besides, it is so cumbersome that comparatively few can read it and even fewer can write it, whereas the simpler symbols for language can now be read and written almost universally.

The disadvantages of the symbol have, however, a corresponding advantage. In the auditory arts, especially in music, there is often a third person coming between the artist and his audience helping to explain to the audience what the artist is trying to say. We hear the music of the composer and the drama of the author as interpreted by the performer. Under the best circumstances the performer is himself an artist. Reading the lines or playing the music is not to him merely a mechanical performance; it is a new interpretation, a re-creation.

This element of re-creation in the auditory arts is so important that we do not even admit the artist's right to decide on a fixed interpretation. A poet may read one of his poems with a certain emphasis, but anyone has the right to change that emphasis if he desires. A pianist will remember how the music was played by the composer if he was fortunate enough to hear him, but he will not hesitate to change the stress as he thinks best. In both these respects the auditory arts are in marked contrast to the visual. When a painter draws a line or puts on a color, no one has the right to change it, and there is usually no artist-interpreter to make the meaning clear. Hence it may be said that the visual arts, as we know them, are exact and definite; they tend to be finished, complete, and static; and the auditory arts tend to be vague and indefinite; they are always subject to various interpretations, but they are dynamic and creative.

● TECHNIQUE

Technique is the ability to do *what* you want to do, *when* you want to do it, *in the way* you want to do it. Technique, in short, is the artist's control of his medium. It has to do with the way the artist uses his medium in expressing an idea, not with the value of the idea itself.

A musician's technique is his ability to make the music sound as he wants it to sound; a sculptor's technique is his way of handling chisel and hammer to produce the effect he wants from them. In the same way there is a technique of blowing glass, casting bronze, making etchings, laying bricks. And that technique is perfect which enables the artist to do just what he desires with his medium. Browning states this ideal when he makes Andrea del Sarto say,

> I can do with my pencil what I know,
> What I see, what at bottom of my heart
> I wish for. . . .
>
> —Robert Browning, British poet (1812–1889), "Andrea del Sarto" (1855)

Obviously techniques differ not only in the different arts but in various mediums of a single art; a person's technique in one medium will be quite different from his technique in another. A painter may be a good technician in oil but a poor one in watercolor. A musician may have a fine technique with the bassoon but a poor one with the flute.

Technique is the actual doing of something; it is the handling of material; it does not usually apply to mental labor. We speak of the technique of Botticelli in painting the picture but not of his technique in planning the composition. We notice that Michelangelo has used different techniques in *David* (Figure 29) and in the *Entombment* (Figure 210); in the one the surface is smooth, in the other rough. But it was not a matter of technique that made him decide the smooth surface was right in the one case and the rough in the other.

On the basis of technique the distinction is made between an art and a craft. For the artist, the technique is not the end but the means; it is the language of which he is master; through his technique he is able to say what he wants to say. For the craftsman, technique is the end. He is concerned only with techniques, he does not go beyond techniques. He may make an excellent copy of a picture; he may make an engraving or an etching from it. But he will follow the design of the artist; the artist must make the design.

IMPORTANCE OF TECHNIQUE

At various times, however, technique has been considered of great, if not primary, importance, especially in music. It is as though the best singer were the one who could do the most difficult cadenzas and the most amazing trills, as though it were a virtue that the song is hard to sing, not that it is beautiful music. It is interesting, of course, to observe a difficult feat well done, whether it be a player hitting a tennis ball or an acrobat hanging by his teeth. So, likewise, it is interesting to hear a soprano reach a high note or to see a dancer poise on one toe for an inordinately long time. Nevertheless, the real point is not whether the performer is master of a difficult bit of technique but whether that passage expresses the ideas of the music or the dance. Is the dancer merely giving an exhibition of her ability to stand on her toe, or is it an essential part of the dance? Is the high note appropriate, or is it merely difficult? Probably the best commentary on technique is the story told of a critic. After a singer's performance, an admirer said, "Was that not difficult?" and the critic replied, "Would to God it had been impossible!" Technique should always be the means, not the end.

Technique impinges on the question of value in art in yet another way, in the problem of whether an artist's work may be hampered by poor technique. We hear much talk of this kind: "A good artist but poor technique!" "He has good ideas for a landscape, but he cannot paint them!" "He is Milton, but mute and therefore inglorious!" To this problem, as to all other problems in art, no immediate or summary solution may be given that will fit all cases. In the re-creative phases of art, technique is of great importance. A man who speaks with a monotonous voice cannot make as forceful an actor as one who has learned to control his voice. A pianist must know how to play; a singer must be able to sing. In these situations a performer is truly hampered by poor technique.

When, however, it is a matter of creative as against re-creative work, the disparity between technique and artistic ability is much less real. A poet or a musician can write down any words or melodies he can think. Or, if he is illiterate, he can dictate to his friends. The architect is not expected to execute his own designs. Painting and sculpture are more difficult, but in them the artist who knows exactly what effects he wants can usually get them. In general the artist's creative ability and his technique go hand in hand.

This point is of importance in the criticism of art. In judging any work of art it is wise to take it for granted that the artist has done what he wanted to do—in other words, that he has not been hampered by lack of technique. It is easy to look at the distortions and abstractions of Rouault and Picasso and say, "If only he would learn how to draw!" or to hear the dissonances of Hindemith and say, "If only he had had a few lessons in harmony!" But such criticisms are almost always false. The artist who distorts a figure does so because he wants the effect gained through distortion; the composer who puts dissonances in his music does so because he wants the effect of those harmonies.

6
MEDIUMS OF THE VISUAL ARTS

● ARCHITECTURE

Traditionally the material of which a building is made is determined by the materials native to the place where the building is erected. In Greece marble was easily available, and many of the buildings were made of marble. In Rome concrete was used because there were great quantities of an earth called *pozzuolana* which, when mixed with lime, made a hard and enduring cement. Throughout Europe limestone was easily available, and the cathedrals were built of limestone. In most sections of the United States there were heavily wooded forests, and the first houses were built by chopping down trees and putting up log cabins. In some parts of the country clay was to be had for the digging; settlers dug the clay and fired the brick where the house was to be put. In the Southwest the Indians had no stone and no way of firing brick, and so they built their houses of brick dried in the sun, *adobe.* The Eskimos built with blocks of hard snow. In most circumstances buildings have been constructed of the materials at hand.

This condition is changing because new building materials are being made and the architect is less dependent on local materials than he used to be. The most important of the new materials are structural steel and reinforced concrete. But many other new materials have gained wide acceptance. Plate glass makes possible huge expanses of uninterrupted windows. Glass bricks have the advantage of letting in light, i.e., of being translucent, while not being transparent. There are fabricated woods made of thin sheets of wood glued together with grain running in opposite directions in order to obviate the possibility of warping or bending, as in ordinary wood. Under these conditions, wood can take its place with steel and reinforced concrete as a scientific material that lends itself to exact calculation. Aluminum and enameled surfaces are being tried. Linoleum, rubber, and concrete tiles are used for floors. Plastics are being used increasingly, and we can count on other new materials in the future.

The choice of medium determines, or is determined by, the type of construction used in the building. For buildings in wood, the post-and-lintel type is generally used. For stone, post-and-lintel is used if the slabs are large; if the stones are small, the arch is usually employed. The arch is the typical method for stone construction, as post-and-lintel is for wood. Steel and reinforced concrete, which are very strong and relatively light, can be used in any type of construction. The type that is characteristic of them is known as skeleton construction. (See Chapter 14.)

● SCULPTURE

STONE AND BRONZE. The two mediums most commonly used for sculpture are stone and metal. Stone is durable; it resists weather, fire, and all ordinary hazards. On the other hand, it is heavy and expensive. It breaks easily. Of the stones marble is the most beautiful. It takes a high polish and is almost translucent. A noteworthy example is found in the *Hermes and Dionysus* of Praxiteles (Figure 63). The stone is so smooth that one wants to feel it, to run his hand over the surface. So well has the sculptor followed the contours of the body, one almost believes that if he could touch the skin, he would find it soft and pliable.

In medieval cathedrals the figures were carved of the material of which the church was made, usually limestone. Limestone is soft, and for that reason it does not polish well. Even in photographs one can tell the difference between the surface of a marble statue, like the *Hermes and Dionysus* of Praxiteles, and that of softer stones, such as we find in the *King of Judah* (Figure 64) from Chartres. Granite is coarse but hard and is suited for bold effects. In the *Adams*

FIGURE 63. PRAXITELES, Greek sculptor. *Hermes and Dionysus* (ca. 350 B.C.). (Parian marble. Height: 6 feet, 11 inches. Olympia, Museum. Photograph, Saul Weinberg.)

FIGURE 64. *KING OF JUDAH* (twelfth century). (Stone. Above life size. Chartres, Cathedral of Notre Dame. Photograph by Houvet.)

Memorial (Figure 52), Saint-Gaudens has used granite for the background, its hard uncompromising texture and speckled color being used to contrast with the soft clothing of the bronze figure.

Of the metals, the one most commonly used is bronze. The processes used in making stone and bronze statues are exactly opposite. Stone statues are made by cutting away the stone until only the figures are left. For metal sculpture, the sculptor builds up the figure he wants in clay, and then has it cast in bronze.

FIGURE 65. *THE CHARIOTEER* (ca. 475 B.C.). (Bronze with enamel an silver inlay. Height: 5 feet, 11 inches. Delphi, Museum. Photograph Saul Weinberg.)

In small statues the bronze is solid, but in large ones solid metal would be too heavy and too expensive; besides, it has a tendency to crack when it i cooled. Most bronze statues therefore are hollow. The process of casting bronz is a very difficult and intricate one, so difficult that it constitutes one of the disadvantages of the medium. Another disadvantage is that it is easily melted down for other uses; many a bronze statue has been poured into cannons. It rich color, however, and the smooth texture, reflecting lights as they can be reflected only in metal, make it one of the most beautiful of all the mediums for sculpture. Moreover, it is relatively light, and the figure can support itself in many positions that would be impossible in stone. In the *Charioteer* (Figure 65 and the *Hermes and Dionysus* of Praxiteles, we have two original Greek statues the *Charioteer* in bronze, the *Hermes* in marble. The *Charioteer* stands on hi own feet, and though the figure is large, it needs no other support. In the *Hermes*, however, extra support is given by a tree trunk partially covered with a cloak on which the god is leaning his left elbow. The marble would break i the entire weight of the statue were concentrated on the legs.

After the downfall of Greece a large number of Greek statues in bronze were destroyed, but copies in stone were made by the Romans. Since the stone would not support the figure in the position used in the bronze, stone supports often poorly disguised, were added. This is the reason that one often sees a trunk of a tree in a Greek statue where it is not expected.

Because of the differences in method and medium the effects to be gained stone and metal are very different. Stone tends to be heavy, massive, but ·ittle, whereas metal tends to be light, tensile, and graceful.

ᴏᴏᴅ. Besides stone and metal, wood, terra cotta, and ivory are important ediums for sculpture. Wood has an initial advantage in that it is cheap, easily ·ailable, and easy to cut. More important is the fact that it polishes well, has smooth shining surface and a beautiful color. Furthermore it is relatively ·ht and can be made into varied shapes. Often the grain of the wood can be ·en, and if used well, it adds greatly to the effect of the whole, as in Henry [oore's *Reclining Figure* (Figure 16) and *Two Forms* (Figure 12). Wood is ·so useful for relief sculpture. It is of course limited in size, and it burns easily.

ᴏʀʏ. Ivory and terra cotta may almost be counted lost mediums, for they are ·ed very little today, though they have been important. As we have said, the ·eat statue of Athena in the Parthenon was of gold and ivory. In the Boston ·useum is the statuette of ivory called the *Snake Goddess* (Figure 66); it dates ·om the little-known Aegean, or Minoan, civilization, which preceded the ·reek. When excavations were being made in Crete, a woman interested in the ·oston Museum of Fine Arts bought a mass of earth just as it came from the ·ade because it contained fragments of gold and ivory. When the pieces were ·ıt together, this little figure emerged, and it is now counted one of the treas- ·res of the Museum. The snakes and the bands of her skirt are of gold. There ·e holes in her tiara, which would indicate that gold was wound through it

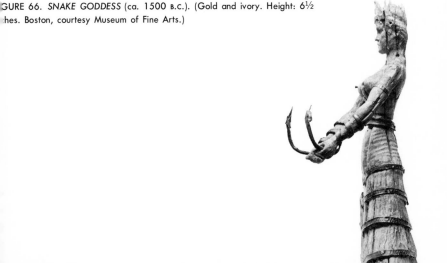

GURE 66. *SNAKE GODDESS* (ca. 1500 B.C.). (Gold and ivory. Height: 6½ ·hes. Boston, courtesy Museum of Fine Arts.)

also. The lady looks very modern with her small waist and full skirts. Probabl
she was a priestess, for she carries snakes in her hands. Certainly she was a
aristocrat; her face and bearing both bear witness to a noble lineage.

From the Middle Ages on, ivory has been much used for small pieces i
which very delicate carving is needed, as for example, crosses, chessmen, an
the backs of books. Usually carvings in ivory are of small size, the reasons bein
the great expense of ivory and the difficulty of securing it in large pieces. Th
color of ivory is a rich, creamy yellow. Like wood, ivory cracks.

TERRA COTTA. The word *terra cotta* means "baked earth." Terra cotta is mad
by firing clay, as in pottery. It is usually painted, and covered with a heav
glaze. The great advantages of terra cotta are: (1) it is very cheap in compariso
with stone or bronze, and (2) brilliant colors are made possible by glazing. Lik
all pottery, terra cotta is easily broken and chipped. As a medium for sculptur
terra cotta has been used at all times. Excellent examples are to be found i
the work of many early peoples, notably the Greeks, the Chinese, and the Etrus
cans. A frequent subject in Chinese art is the lohan, a disciple of the Buddha
Usually, as in the example shown (Figure 67), we find that emphasis on medita
tion which is characteristic of Buddhism. In the Renaissance, terra cotta wa
the favorite medium of the della Robbias.

FIGURE 67. LOHAN. Chinese, T'ang Dynasty (A.
618–906). (Pottery, hard reddish-buff clay, gree
and yellow glazes. Height: 42 inches; base: 7 inche
depth: 35 inches; width: 38 inches. Toronto, Roy
Ontario Museum.)

Artists in all arts at all times have experimented in new mediums, and sculp-
rs of the present day are no exception. Henry Moore's little figure *The Bride*
of cast lead and copper wire. Zorach's *Head of Christ* is of black porphyry
igure 68). Cast stone, wrought iron, aluminum, glass, and steel are other
ediums used today.

PAINTING

ainting may be defined as the application of colored pigments to a flat surface,
ually canvas, paper, wood, or plaster.

GMENTS

igments used in making colors come from different sources: clay, coal tar,
getable matter, etc. Some are manufactured; some are found in nature almost
they are used. Some have been newly discovered; some have been known for
long time. Many of the pigments used today are obtained from natural sources.
he reds and browns now obtained from clay are the same reds and browns
sed by the cave men when they painted on the walls in prehistoric times.
egetables have been the source for many pigments; indigo produces blue and
adder red. Ultramarine, which is the *blue* blue, the most expensive of all
ues, was made by grinding the stone lapis lazuli. Purple, one of the most
mous colors, can be extracted from a shellfish, the murex.

Many pigments also have been made by the chemists. It is generally believed
at the first chemical pigment was Prussian blue, discovered in 1704. About
century later many new pigments were made, and in 1826 Guimet discovered
way to make ultramarine artificially. Since that time there have been an ever
creasing number of pigments made by chemical formulas.[1]

ohn Ives Sewall, *A History of Western Art*, p. 859.

VEHICLES

The sources of color have been pretty much the same throughout the gener
tions, but the way the color is applied to the surface has changed. Since t
colors as procured either from nature or from artificial sources are dry, th
must be mixed with something to be spread on a surface. This substance, usual
a fluid, is called the *vehicle.* In oil paintings the colors are mixed with oil;
other words, oil is the vehicle. In watercolor, water is the vehicle. The vehic
determines the surface on which the paint is spread. Canvas is not a good su
face for watercolor, nor is paper a good surface for oil. Since the pigments a
essentially the same no matter what surface or vehicle is used, a medium
commonly distinguished by the surface and vehicle used. We do not speak
painting in earth colors but of painting in oil on canvas or acrylic. Each mediu
determines its own brush stroke and produces its own effect.

OIL. Probably the most widely used medium for painting at the present time
oil. The vehicle is oil and the surface is usually canvas, though various oth
surfaces may be used. The special advantage of oil is that it stays moist for
long time. The artist can work over what he is doing, and if he wishes he ma
change today what he painted yesterday. The paint may be applied in any wa
that suits the artist, so thinly that the canvas shows through or so thickly as
produce a rough surface. The rough surface of van Gogh's *Self-Portrait in*
Straw Hat may be seen in the photograph (Figure 69); the paint is so thic
that each stroke shows clearly. In contrast, the paint in Gauguin's *The Sulkir*
Woman (Figure 70) is applied smoothly, and individual brush strokes do n
show at all.

There are two methods of painting in oil, the direct and the indirect. In tl
direct method the paints are opaque and are applied to the surface just as the
are desired in the finished picture. In the indirect method the paint is put c
in many thin layers of transparent color; the effect produced in this way is ve
rich and luminous. Unfortunately it cannot be distinguished in a photograp
The direct method is the more flexible medium of expression; the artist ca
use his pigment very freely and express in it any fleeting change in his though
And, if it has not the richness of the transparent colors, it can obtain gre
vitality through the use of colors in high intensity.

The disadvantages of oil have to do with the preservation of the pictur
Because the paint takes a long time to dry, the oil has a tendency to rise to th
surface and form a film over the picture, making the colors dull. Moreover,
tends to become yellow, and in time the paint cracks.

WATERCOLOR. In watercolor the pigments are mixed with water and gum arab
and applied to a fine, white paper. The paper shines through the paint ar

akes the color brilliant. It is difficult to produce warm, rich tones in water-
ɔlor. Once the paint has been applied, changes may be made, but usually a
ɥange tends to make the color less brilliant. In Marin's painting (Figure 71),
ɪe characteristic "watery" look of watercolor can be clearly seen. Watercolor
ɪ best for spontaneous, evanescent expression.

Medium

Opaque watercolor is called *gouache*. Enough white is added to keep th
paper from shining through. As a result the color is lacking in brilliance. Pica
so's *Blue Boy* is done in gouache.

FRESCO. In fresco the pigment is mixed with water and applied to wet plaste
The color dries into the plaster, and the picture thus becomes a part of th
wall. Since fresco must be done quickly it is a very exacting medium; there
no rubbing out and no changing once the design is begun. It is accordingly
medium of broad, bold, direct work, usually with great simplification of for
and freedom in the treatment of the subject. Moreover, because of the chemic
action of the plaster on the paint, only earth pigments may be used, and th
colors lack intensity; there is, however, uniformity of tone with no glaring co
trasts. The disadvantages of fresco are two: first, it is almost impossible to mov
a fresco; second, the painting, being permanently fixed to the wall, is subject t
any of the disasters that may happen to the wall. If the plaster cracks or has
hole punched in it, the picture is hurt to that extent. The Sistine Chapel ceilir
is in fresco; cracks are clearly seen in the decorative nude shown below (Figur
72). For many years fresco was used very little, but in recent times there ha
been a return to fresco painting, notably in the Mexican artists Diego Rivera an

FIGURE 72. MICHELANGELO. *Decorati*
Nude. Detail of Sistine Chapel Ceiling. (Fresc
Photograph by Anderson.)

FIGURE 73. JOSÉ CLEMENTE OROZCO (1883–1949). *Modern Migration of the Spirit* (1932–1934). (Fresco. Baker Library, Dartmouth College, Hanover, N.H.)

osé Clemente Orozco. Orozco's most important work has been on the walls of ne Dartmouth College Library. The theme is the *Modern Migration of the pirit* (Figure 73). The central figure is a very dynamic Christ come back to arth to destroy his cross in a world filled with military equipment.

GG TEMPERA. Tempera and fresco were favorite mediums throughout the Middle Ages and early Renaissance before oil was generally adopted. Tempera ainting is usually done on a wooden panel that has been made very smooth vith a coating of plaster called *gesso*. The colors are mixed with egg yolk (with r without the white). The paint dries almost immediately, and there is in temera painting little blending or fusing of colors; the colors are laid on side by ide or are superimposed. Hence the painting is composed of a large number of uccessive small strokes, and the effect is largely linear. It is hard to obtain ich, deep tones or dark shadows. Because tempera paint dries quickly, the rtist must be precise and exact in his work. It is a medium well designed for areful detail. The advantage of tempera is its great luminosity of tone, the olors being clear and beautiful. On the other hand, the precision needed tends

FIGURE 74. SIMONE MARTINI (ca. 1284–1344), Italian painter. *Annunciation* (1333). (The saints o
either side are probably the work of Lippo Memmi.) (Tempera on wood. Height: 5 feet, 11¼ inches
Florence, Uffizi Gallery. Photograph by Anderson.)

to produce a certain hardness of outline. Botticelli's *Birth of Venus* and Simon
Martini's *Annunciation* (Figure 74) show most of the characteristics of tempera

ENCAUSTIC. Wax was used by the Egyptians for portraits painted on mumm
cases. There were several different ways of preparing the wax, but in genera
the color was mixed with warm wax and burned in. This method was als
used by the Greeks and the Romans, and it was employed to some extent dur
ing the Middle Ages. Paintings with wax have a definite body and a pleasin
sheen which seem to show at their best in portraits. The portrait of a bo
(Figure 75) dating from the second century is an example. In recent year
painting in wax has been revived by some modern painters, notably Dieg
Rivera.

FIGURE 75. PORTRAIT OF A BOY (second century A.D.). Fayum, Lower Egypt. (Encaustic on wood panel. Size: about 10 by 16 inches. New York, courtesy Metropolitan Museum of Art; gift of Edward S. Harkness, 1917–1918.)

PASTEL. In pastel, pigments in the form of powders are compressed lightly into sticks. Its colors are brilliant, and it is a very flexible medium, one in which very rich and varied effects may be produced. As a medium, however, it has never won a high place because no one has yet discovered a way to preserve it in its original freshness. Even if it is covered almost at once with a fixing medium or with a protecting surface such as glass, the chalk rubs and the picture loses some of its brilliance.

ILLUMINATION. In the Middle Ages, when books were lettered by hand, the pages were often decorated with gold, silver, and bright colors. Capital letters, especially, were made large and important. Decorative borders were common, and frequently the artist added miniature paintings of people or scenes. In the page from the *Tickhill Psalter* (Figure 76) shown here, all the capitals are emphasized, but special attention is given the initial letter *B* with which the first Psalm begins, "Beatus qui non abiit in consilio impiorum" ("Blessed is the

FIGURE 76. First page of the Psalms from the *Tickhill Psalter* (ca. 1310). (Illuminated manuscript. Size: 12⅞ by 8⅝ inches. New York, Spencer Collection, New York Public Library.)

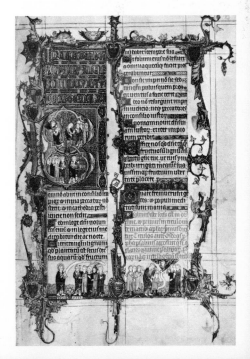

man that walketh not in the counsel of the ungodly"). Each half of the letter is filled with a miniature, and there are further miniatures at the foot of the page. These miniatures tell the story of the anointing of David, the supposed author of the Psalms. The miniatures were made of tempera or pen and ink.

MOSAIC. Mosaic, stained glass, and tapestry are usually classed with painting, though the medium is not pigment. A picture in mosaic is made by putting together small pieces of colored glass or stone, called *tesserae*. These tesserae are often square in shape. They are set in cement to hold them in place, the underside of the tesserae being roughened to make them fast in the cement. The use of stones makes simplification of design necessary. Moreover, the stones can never be set very smoothly in the cement, and hence the surface is always rough, reflecting light in many ways and creating a lively, vibrant effect. The greatest mosaics were made in the Middle Ages before painting became usual in churches. Some of the most famous are found in the church of San Vitale at Ravenna (Figure 77). The enlargement shows the tesserae clearly (Figure 78).

FIGURE 77. THEODORA AND HER ATTENDANTS (ca. A.D. 525). (Mosaic. Figures slightly above life size. Detail from copy of original mosaic in church of San Vitale, Ravenna. New York, photograph courtesy Metropolitan Museum of Art.)

FIGURE 78. "PORTRAIT OF THEODORA," detail of *Theodora and Her Attendants.* (Photograph by Alinari.)

FIGURE 79. *ST. EUSTACE HUNTING* (twelfth century), window, Bay 13. (Stained glass. Height of diamond about 3 feet. Chartres, Cathedral of Notre Dame. Photograph by Houvet.)

STAINED GLASS. Like the mosaic, the stained-glass window is a kind of patch-work. It is made by combining many small pieces of colored glass which are held together by bands of lead. In a large window, the lead is reinforced by heavy iron bars that make very heavy black lines in the picture. In the Middle Ages when many of the peasants were illiterate, the glass of the church windows served as a "picture book" of Biblical scenes. The windows at Chartres are considered among the greatest of a great period. Our illustration shows one section of the window of *St. Eustace* (Figure 79). The saint is shown riding to the hunt, his horn at his lips. At his feet are the dogs, and just before him, the stags; behind him is an attendant urging on the chase.

TAPESTRY. Tapestries are large fabrics in which a design is woven by hand. In the Middle Ages they were hung on the walls of palaces and in the cathedrals on festive occasions, both as decoration and for warmth. Being of very firm texture, they shut out the cold and helped to preserve the heat from the fireplace. In the *Unicorn in Captivity* (Figure 80) we have the famous *mille fleur,* or "thousand flower," background.

FIGURE 80. *THE HUNT OF THE UNICORN: VI, The Unicorn in Captivity* (late fifteenth or early sixteenth century). (French or Flemish tapestry, from Chateau of Verteuil. Silk and wool with silver and gilt threads. Size: about 12 by 8 feet. New York, courtesy Metropolitan Museum of Art; The Cloisters Collection.)

FIGURE 81. JEAN AUGUSTE DOMINIQUE INGRES (1780–1867), French painter and maker of pencil portraits. *Lady and Boy* (1808). (Pencil drawing. Size: 9¾ by 7¼ inches. New York, courtesy Metropolitan Museum of Art; bequest of Mrs. H. O. Havemeyer, 1929. H. O. Havemeyer Collection.)

FIGURE 82. MICHELANGELO. Studies for *Libyan Sibyl* (Fig. 42). (Red chalk. New York, courtesy Metropolitan Museum of Art; Joseph Pulitzer Bequest, 1924.)

DRAWINGS

Drawings and prints are of special interest to the student, both for their intrinsic value and because they are comparatively inexpensive. In them even the person of small means can afford original works of artists.

A drawing may be a finished work, as in Ingres's *Lady and Boy* (Figure 81). Or it may be made as a study for a painting to be completed, like Michelangelo's studies for the *Libyan Sibyl* (Figure 82). Notice in the latter Michelangelo's sketches of the big toe, and his change from the masculine face in the center to the feminine face at the left.

FIGURE 83. LEONARDO DA VINCI (attributed) (1452–1519), Italian painter. Head of a Woman. (Silverpoint with white on bluish paper. New York, courtesy Metropolitan Museum of Art; Hewitt Fund, 1917.)

Drawings are known chiefly by the mediums used, as pencil, pen, silverpoint, and charcoal. *Pencil* is one of the most common because of its general utility, especially for the making of rapid notes. The French artist Ingres made many pencil portraits as one means of support while he was living in Rome. A typical example is the *Lady and Boy*.

Silverpoint, a drawing with a gold or silver wire on a specially prepared paper, is very pale in tone and has little vitality but is very delicate. The difference between the line of the pencil and that of silverpoint can be seen by comparing the Ingres portrait with the *Head of a Woman* attributed to Leonardo (Figure 83).

Ink makes a clear, crisp line; often ink is combined with a wash as in the Rembrandt drawing *St. Peter and St. Paul at the Beautiful Gate of the Temple* (Figure 84).

FIGURE 84. REMBRANDT HARMENSZ VAN RIJN (1606–1669), Dutch painter. *St. Peter and St. Paul at the Beautiful Gate of the Temple*. (Pen and bister, washed. New York, courtesy Metropolitan Museum of Art; Rogers Fund, 1911.)

FIGURE 85. CAMILLE COROT (1795–1875), French painter. *The Forest of Coubron* (1872). (Charcoal. Size: 17 by 11¾ inches. Reproduced by permission of Fogg Art Museum, Harvard University, Cambridge, Mass.; bequest of Grenville L. Winthrop.)

Bister is a brown pigment made by mixing the soot from burning wood with a little binder.

Charcoal is one of the oldest mediums for drawing. It is made by roasting wood in a closed vessel. It is capable of a great variety of tones from the darkest to the very light, as in Corot's *The Forest of Coubron, 1872* (Figure 85).

Chalk is another medium that has been used from the earliest times. It is found in white, black, and red. The red was especially desired for figure sketches as in the Michelangelo sketch for the Libyan Sibyl (Figure 82). *Conté crayon* is one of the chalks; it is less waxy than the schoolboy type of crayon and much more durable than pastel. Seurat used it to produce rich shadows, great brilliancy of light, and strength of tones (Figure 86).

Drawing with a *brush* is characteristic of the Chinese and Japanese, who, it will be remembered, write with a brush instead of a pen. The brush gives very

FIGURE 86. GEORGES PIERRE SEURAT (1859–1891), French painter. *The Artist's Mother* (ca. 1883). (Conté crayon on paper. Size: 12⅞ by 9½ inches. New York, courtesy Metropolitan Museum of Art: Joseph Pulitzer Bequest, 1951, from Museum of Modern Art, Lillie P. Bliss Collection.)

FIGURE 87. KYOSAI (1831–1889), Japanese painter. *Animals, Children, and Men.* (Brush drawing. Height: 10⅞ inches. New York, courtesy Metropolitan Museum of Art; Fletcher Fund, 1937.)

quick results and allows great freedom in handling. See Kyosai's *Animals, Children, and Men* (Figure 87).

PRINTS

A print is something printed; that is, it is the impression left on paper or some other surface from an inked plate. Ordinarily the printing is in black ink on white paper. The plate is made by the artist, and usually he does the printing. For these reasons a print is counted the authentic work of an artist and is signed by him. The number of copies that are made from any plate depends on the design, the kind of print, and the wishes of the artist. Often an artist decides on a certain number—thirty, fifty, one hundred—and destroys the plate when that number has been reached.

There are four major types of prints: *woodcut, engraving, etching,* and *lithograph.* Each print can be distinguished by the way the plate is made. Therefore it is convenient to know both the kind of line characteristic of a print and the way the plate is made.

WOODCUT. The woodcut, as the name implies, is made from a plate of wood. The design stands out in relief, the remaining surface of the block being cut away. A wood block prints just as do the letters of a typewriter. The lines of the

FIGURE 88. ALBRECHT DÜRER. *Christ on the Cross*, from the Small Passion (1511). (Woodcut. Size: 4 by 5 inches. Private Collection.)

design being of wood, they can never be very fine, and woodcuts can be identified by their firm, clear, black lines as we see in Dürer's *Christ on the Cross* (Figure 88), and his *Four Horsemen* (Figure 58). The design is left standing in relief, and any part of the plate that is not cut away will print a solid black. Older makers of the woodcut such as Dürer used solid blacks very sparingly. In more modern prints, as in *The Miraculous Draught of Fishes* by Schmidt-Rottluff (Figure 89), large areas of black are used in the design.

FIGURE 89. KARL SCHMIDT-ROTTLUFF (1884–   ), German painter and print maker. *The Miraculous Draught of Fishes* (1918). (Woodcut. Size: 15½ by 19⅝ inches. From *Kristus*, a portfolio of nine woodcuts, published by Kurt Wolff, Leipzig, 1919. Collection of Mrs. Gertrude A. Mellon, New York. Photograph, Museum of Modern Art.)

The woodcut is made from a plate sawed parallel with the grain of the wood. The print often shows the grain. In recent years prints have been cut from linoleum as well as from wood. Sometimes these prints are called linoleum cuts, but there is so little difference between the two that ordinarily no distinction is made, and both are called woodcuts.

Colored woodcuts are made by preparing a separate block for each color to be used; only the parts to be printed in one color appear on the block of that color. The finished print, however, will show more shades than there are blocks, because one color is printed on top of another and the colors are mixed. The Japanese, especially, have excelled in this type of woodcut, though the technique has been used widely (Figure 90).

ENGRAVING. An engraving is in many ways the opposite of a woodcut. In the woodcut, the parts that are to be black are left standing, and the remainder of the block is cut away. In engraving, the lines of the design are cut into a metal plate; these lines are then filled with ink and transferred from the plate to the paper. The lines of an engraving are cut by hand with an instrument called a *burin,* and since the copper plate is hard to cut, they are very fine, much finer than the lines of a woodcut. For the same reason they are hard and stiff, precise

FIGURE 90. SUZUKI HARUNOBU (1725–1770), Japanese print maker. *Lovers under Umbrella in Snow.* (Wood block. Size: 11 by 8 inches. New York, courtesy Metropolitan Museum of Art; Rogers Fund, 1936.)

FIGURE 91. MARTIN SCHONGAUER (1440–1491), German painter and engraver. *The Annunciation* (undated). (Engraving. Size: 6½ by 4¾ inches. Boston, courtesy Museum of Fine Arts.)

FIGURE 92. PAUL KLEE (1879–1940), Swiss painter and print maker. *Why Does He Run?* (ca. 1932). (Etching. Size: 9⅜ by 11¹³⁄₁₆ inches. New York, Museum of Modern Art.)

and formal. Shadows are made by lines either very close together or crossing at regular angles. Blake's engraving *When the Morning Stars Sang Together* (Figure 37) shows the typical quality of the line. Other engravings are Dürer's *The Knight, Death, and the Devil* (Figure 57) and Schongauer's *The Annunciation* (Figure 91).

ETCHING. Etching differs from engraving in the way the lines are made. In engraving, as we noted, the lines are cut directly in the plate by hand. In etching, the plate is covered with a coating of a thin, waxlike material called a ground. Through it the etcher draws his design. He does not attempt to cut the plate itself; he merely scratches through the wax, leaving the metal uncovered. The plate is then put in an acid bath, and the design is *etched*, or eaten, into the plate. The lines on an etched plate are made much more easily than on an engraved plate, and we see the difference in the finished print. The etched lines have the freedom of a penciled line, go in any direction, and cross at any angle. In *Why Does He Run?* (Figure 92), Klee uses his etching needle almost like a pencil or a pen.

Medium

Obviously neither etching nor engraving can show solid blacks as can the woodcut, and in both prints grays must be made by putting lines close together or by crisscrossing. The etched lines are very clear in Goya's *No Grites Tanta* (Figure 93) and in Rembrandt's *Three Trees* (Figure 94).

FIGURE 93.   FRANCISCO GOYA. *No Grites Tanta* from *Los Caprichos* (*Caprices*) (1793–1798). (Etching and aquatint. Size: 5 by 7⅜ inches. Private collection.)

FIGURE 94.   REMBRANDT HARMENSZ VAN RIJN. *Three Trees* (1643). (Etching. Size: about 8⅜ by 11 inches. New York, courtesy Metropolitan Museum of Art; bequest of Mrs. H. O. Havemeyer, 1929. H. O. Havemeyer Collection.)

FIGURE 95. GEORGE BELLOWS (1882–1925), American painter and print maker. *Dempsey and Firpo* (1924). (Lithograph. Size: 18½ by 22⅜ inches. New York, Museum of Modern Art; Abby Aldrich Rockefeller Purchase Fund. Photograph, Museum of Modern Art.)

FIGURE 96. PAUL SIGNAC (1863–1935), French painter. *Le Port de St. Tropez II* (1897–1898). (Color lithograph. Size: 17¼ by 13⅛ inches. Boston, courtesy Museum of Fine Arts.)

FIGURE 97. PAUL SIGNAC. *St. Tropez: Soleil du Soir* (1894). (Watercolor. Size: 10½ by 8 inches. Los Angeles, County Museum of Art; Mr. and Mrs. William Preston Harrison Collection.)

LITHOGRAPHY. The lithograph is the most recent of the four common types of print. It was discovered just before 1800, whereas woodcuts, engravings, and etchings go back to the fifteenth and sixteenth centuries. In a lithograph the design is drawn with a heavy greasy crayon on a specially prepared stone, and ink impressions are made from it. Every line or shadow made on the stone is transferred to the paper; in fact, a lithograph looks very much like a charcoal or chalk drawing. And it is the only print that can show values shading one into the other as in a drawing or a painting. Daumier's *Strangers in Paris* (Figure 140) and Bellows' *Dempsey and Firpo* (Figure 95), both show the characteristic shading of the lithograph. Signac gives us the same scene in two mediums. One is a lithograph, *Le Port de St. Tropez II* (Figure 96) and the other is a pen and water color drawing, *St. Tropez: Soleil du Soir* (Figure 97).

121

FIGURE 98. FRANCISCO GOYA. *Back to His Grandfather,* from *Los Caprichos.* (Aquatint. New York, courtesy Metropolitan Museum of Art; gift of M. Knoedler and Co., 1918.)

DRYPOINT, MEZZOTINT, AQUATINT. *Drypoint* stands halfway between engraving and etching. It is like engraving in that the lines are cut directly in the metal. It is like etching in that the needle is held as a pencil and is used freely. It merely scratches the metal. As it scratches, it leaves a little ridge at one side like the ridge left by a pin run across a cake of soap. This ridge, called the *burr,* takes the ink and makes a very rich, velvety line. A similar ridge is thrown up in engraving, but it is cleared away before any prints are made. Drypoint can rarely be distinguished from etching in a photograph, but in the original the rough line of the drypoint is clear.

Mezzotint and aquatint are two means of giving a solid tone to a print. *Mezzotint* is made on a copper plate which is artificially roughened by an instrument known as a "rocker" or "cradle." The engraver then scrapes away more or less of the roughness in the parts he wants light. The parts not scraped, or only partially scraped, make a rich, velvety black like the burr of the drypoint. Mezzotint is frequently combined with some other type of print, such as etching or drypoint.

In *aquatint,* powdered resin is sprinkled on the plate and heated so that it adheres to the plate. When the plate is immersed in the acid, the parts not protected by the resin are bitten, and a very fine shadowy gray is produced (Figure 98).

The contemporary print maker uses many combinations of the basic means of producing prints. To obtain color, for example, he may make a basic plate which is inked to give the tone, and then another plate (one for each color) can be superimposed. There is also a tendency to start with a collage in low relief, which is then treated either as relief or as intaglio for the printing. Textures of interest can also be obtained by the use of different materials glued to a plate. A printed collage is called a collagraph.

7
MEDIUMS OF MUSIC

Music and literature are both arts of sound. A word is a sound, and it also has meaning. In music, however, a sound is only a sound; it may be a high sound or a low sound, a long sound or a short sound; still, it is only a sound and has no meaning. A tone is only a tone. It has no other significance. There is a story told of Beethoven, who upon having played one of his piano works for a friend was asked, "But what does it mean?" Whereupon Beethoven, without a word, sat down and played the composition again.

Music has an advantage over literature in that its symbols are understood throughout most of the world. The same musical symbols are used, whether in France, Australia, or Russia.

Music and literature differ also in the way sounds are made. In literature, all the sounds are made by the human voice. In music, the human voice is but one of a number of instruments used. The sound, and hence the music, is quite different when produced by one instrument or another. Therefore, it is important to have some understanding of the physical properties and the kinds of sound produced by the various musical instruments.

Medium

● INSTRUMENTS OF THE ORCHESTRA

There are three main kinds of instruments: those which are bowed, those which are blown, and those which are beaten. These in turn are divided into four traditional groupings often referred to as families or choirs. The instruments which are bowed are called strings and make up the string choir. Those which are blown fall into two choirs: the brasses, so named because they are usually made of brass, and the woodwinds, so named because they were all originally made of wood. The modern flute and piccolo are always made of metal, while clarinets may be of either metal or wood. The fourth choir is made up of those instruments which are beaten. They comprise the percussion choir.

The most common string, woodwind, and brass instruments used in the traditional symphony orchestra are listed here in order of pitch from highest to lowest. Their size corresponds to their pitch, smaller instruments producing higher sounds, and larger instruments lower sounds.

Strings	*Woodwinds*	*Brasses*
violin	piccolo	trumpet
viola	flute	French horn (horn)
violoncello (cello)	clarinet	trombone
double bass (bass)	oboe	tuba
	English horn	
	bass clarinet	
	bassoon	
	double bassoon	

There are two kinds of percussion instruments: those that produce definite pitch or tone, and those that produce indefinite pitch or noise. Here are some of the most commonly used:

Percussion of Definite Pitch	*Percussion of Indefinite Pitch*
tympani (kettledrums)	snare drum (side drum)
xylophone	bass drum
marimba	cymbals
chimes	gong
glockenspiel	tambourine
	castanets
	triangle

There are, in addition to these four choirs, a fifth group of instruments which came into prominence independent of the orchestra. The piano, celesta, harpsichord, and organ may be considered singly, or with the percussion sec- tion when included in orchestral music. These are all keyboard instruments of definite pitch, but each has physical properties quite different from the others. The piano is basically a string instrument but is played by hammers attached to the keys; the celesta, often considered a percussion instrument of definite pitch, has steel plates which are hammered; the harpsichord is a string instru- ment whose strings are plucked by quills or leather or brass tongues attached to the keys; and the organ is a wind instrument, its sounds being made by air forced through pipes. The harp is a string instrument which is always plucked or struck. It too may be considered alone, or grouped with the percussion choir.

● HOW INSTRUMENTS MAKE SOUND

Most instruments have three things in common: a vibrator, a resonator, and a system for producing and regulating fixed pitches.

All sound is caused by vibration, and all musical sound, or sound of definite pitch, is caused by regular vibrations. When vibrations are irregular, noise is the result. Regular vibrations are measurable. When an object such as a string or a bottle vibrates regularly 261 times per second, it produces the pitch, or tone, that we call middle C. The faster the vibration, the higher the pitch. On the piano, the lowest A, when struck, vibrates the A string $27\frac{1}{2}$ times per second, but the highest A on the piano vibrates its string 3,520 times per second.

The resonator is any material used to resound or bounce the vibrations away from the instrument so that they are amplified and can be heard at a distance. The resonator on the piano, for example, is a wooden sounding board placed beneath the strings.

STRING INSTRUMENTS

In string instruments, the vibrator is the string itself, made of gut or wire. The four strings of the bowed instruments are made to vibrate when rubbed by a bow of horsehair made sticky by resin. But the sound of a vibrating string is too small to be heard at a distance, so a resonator is needed. The vibrations of the wooden box along with the vibrating air inside the box act as resonator.

Pitch is determined in string instruments by the length, thickness, and taut- ness of the four strings. When a string is vibrated, at full length, a specific tone is produced. Other tones are made by "stopping," that is, by putting one's finger at a certain point on the string and pressing it to the fingerboard. This shortens the length of string that vibrates and so raises the pitch. A large number of tones can thus be made from each of the four strings.

WOODWIND INSTRUMENTS

In the woodwinds, vibrators are of two kinds, air and reed. In the flute and piccolo, air blown across the opening near the head of the tube is split into two columns, part of the air going over the instrument, and part being forced through the tube. Of course the air blown across the instrument is lost, but its function is to create a steady pressure on the air being forced through the instrument. The same principle is involved in making sounds by blowing across a bottle or jug. In this case air is the vibrator, and the resonator as well. The air passing through the tube, and the tube itself, help to resonate the sound.

A single thin, wooden reed (now sometimes of synthetic material) is the vibrator used in the clarinet, bass clarinet, and saxophone. When air is forced into the mouthpiece, the reed flutters rapidly, and as the air is forced through the tube of the instrument, the tube becomes the resonator.

Double reeds are used by the oboe, English horn, bassoon, and double bassoon. Air forced between the two reeds causes them to vibrate, and again, the tube with the column of air passing through it is the resonator.

Pitch in woodwind instruments is determined by the length of the tube. The very short length of the piccolo makes it capable of playing the highest tones in the orchestra, while the sixteen feet of tubing in the double bassoon make it the lowest pitched of all instruments.

Variety and control of pitch in woodwinds are obtained through the use of a series of holes stopped up by the finger, or by keys which shut the holes. By opening and closing these holes, the length of tube is changed, producing different pitches. When all the holes of the tube are closed, air passes through the entire length of the instrument and produces the lowest pitch.

In addition to the system of holes, pitch can be altered by overblowing. That is, by forcing in more air than can be comfortably responded to by the instrument, the performer produces higher tones. This technique is used chiefly in the flute, where overblowing can raise the pitch one or two octaves.

BRASS INSTRUMENTS

In the brasses, the performer's lips are the vibrators. They are held tightly against the specially shaped mouthpiece, and vibrate when air is forced through them into the instrument. Air passing through the brass walls of the tube is the resonator.

As in the case of the woodwinds, pitch is determined in the brass instruments by the length of tube through which the air must pass. Too, variety and control of pitch are achieved by changing the length of tube. However, in the brass choir, valves and sliding tubes are used in place of holes.

Valves are used in the trumpet, horn, and tuba. When these valves are depressed, air is instantly diverted into different lengths of tube, creating different pitches. The trumpet, for example, can produce seven lengths of tube with its three valves.

The trombone has one tube fitted tightly over another; these can be telescoped in and out to lengthen the tube and change the pitch. It is often popularly called the slide trombone because of this. The trombone player has to rely on his ear to find the right position for the tone wanted.

PERCUSSION INSTRUMENTS

Of the percussion instruments of definite pitch, the tympani are the most important because they are used in most symphonic music. Tympani, or kettledrums, are large copper "kettles" with skin stretched over the top and tightened by taps around the edge. These instruments can be tuned to definite pitch by tightening or loosening the taps. Nowadays some tympani have foot pedals for altering pitch. The vibrator is the skin of the drumhead, which the performer strikes with sticks, some soft, some hard, and the resonator is the disturbed air within the copper walls.

The xylophone is a series of bars of hard wood placed side by side like the keys of a piano, each piece of wood tuned to a different tone. They are made to vibrate when struck with wooden or rubber beaters. The xylophone has no resonator.

The marimba is nothing more than a xylophone with a resonator. Small tubes suspended under the wooden bars resonate the sound of the vibrating wood.

Chimes are tubular bells, metal tubes hung from a frame and struck with a hammer. The vibrating air within the tube acts as resonator.

The glockenspiel is a set of steel bars played with hammers. The sound produced by the vibrations of the bars is adequate, so that no resonator is used.

Among percussion instruments of indefinite pitch, drums and cymbals are the most important. The snare drum, or side drum, is a relatively small military instrument. Parchment is stretched over the top and bottom of a circular wooden frame, making two drumheads. The top drumhead is beaten by two wooden sticks; the bottom drumhead has strings of gut or wire stretched across it, which give a dry, rattling sound when vibrating. Both separate strokes and long, muffled rolls are possible on the snare drum. The air within the drum is the resonator.

The bass drum is relatively large and also has two drumheads (though in English orchestras it often has only one). These are made of skin and are beaten with padded sticks. The performer can make rolls as well as single beats. The resonator is the same as that of the snare drum.

Cymbals are two thin, slightly bowl-shaped plates of brass which can be rubbed together gently, beaten with a soft stick, or banged together violently. Like the glockenspiel, cymbals have no resonator, their initial vibrations being adequately loud.

The gong is a heavy metal disk hit with a padded stick. It has no resonator.

The tambourine is a small wooden hoop over which skin is stretched, with metal disks on the rim. It can be shaken, hit with the hand, or banged on the knee. There is no resonator.

Castanets are two hollowed-out pieces of hard wood which are snapped together by the hand. The two pieces may or may not be connected.

The triangle is a small steel rod bent in the shape of a triangle with one corner left open. It is suspended by a string and hit with a metal rod which is rapidly beaten against two sides. It has no resonator.

● RANGE

The range of an instrument has to do with the total number of tones it can produce, from highest to lowest. Range is determined largely by the size of the instrument, as has already been mentioned. Large objects vibrate more slowly than those which are small, and slower vibrations create lower tones. Small objects produce faster vibrations, hence higher tones. It is understood then that the range of a cello is going to be lower than that of a trumpet. To give an idea of the relative range of the orchestral instruments, here is a chart comparing them, along with the human voice, to the piano keyboard. The overlapping of ranges as seen here becomes dramatically clear. This is one of the reasons that timbre is so very important to the composer.

● TIMBRE

Because of its physical properties, an instrument produces a sound that no other kind of instrument can. For example, the viola, because it is a bit larger than the violin, has a slightly lower range, and thus its sound is mellower, heavier, richer. This is *timbre*, or tone color. It is interesting to note here the

EXAMPLE **1**

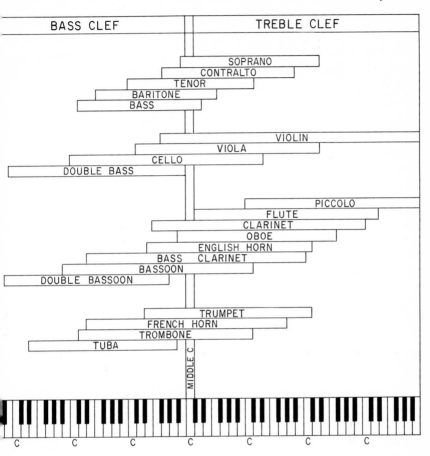

orrelation between painting and music. Varieties of color are vital to both rts. Compare for example the palettes of Renoir or Monet to the tone colors of ᵉebussy or Ravel, or the colors used by Braque in his cubist paintings and travinsky in his *Rite of Spring.*

When an orchestrator thinks a musical idea, aside from the limitations of ᵻnge, he thinks in terms of musical line, tone color, and volume, which means ᵻat he thinks the instrumental sound at the same time. An oboe melody is ᵻst right for the oboe, though the violin, clarinet, or trumpet might play the ᵻme notes. The greatest orchestrators, such as Rimsky-Korsakov, Berlioz, and ᵻichard Strauss, are considered great because they had a genius for using ᵻstruments, either singly or in combination, which could best enhance a musi-al idea.

There is no way to "know" the sound of any instrument other than by ᵻmply listening to it until one can say with accuracy, "That's a bassoon," or

130

Medium

"That's a horn." Still, for those who are learning to recognize the characteristic sound of an instrument, there are a few helpful descriptive adjectives which are agreed upon so generally that they have become clichés. Here follows brief description of the more important instruments, with examples of music listed for each. //

● **THE STRINGS**

The strings form the backbone of the orchestra. They are largest in number and are divided into first and second violins, violas, cellos, and double basses. The leading first violinist is also the concertmaster; he acts as assistant conductor and is in charge of the string choir.

Some of the special effects possible on each of the string instruments are as follows:

Spiccato:	making each note short and crisp by use of the bow
Saltallato:	bouncing the bow on the string to produce light, detached tone
Martellato:	hammering the bow on the string, making each note separate and emphatic
Tremolo:	making the bow quiver on the string to produce a shimmering effect
Sul ponticello:	sound made bowing near the bridge to produce a thin, eerie sound
Pizzicato:	plucking the strings

Besides these effects, double and triple stopping are possible; that is, by playing on two or three strings simultaneously, the performer can produce chords.

VIOLIN. The most important member of the string section, the violin, is so well known as to need no description. Of all the strings, it is the most versatile and expressive. The violin has a wide range of tones which can be sustained indefinitely. It can play very quietly or loudly; it can play very slow passages or be lightning swift. Because of its expressive, voice-like quality, its range, and the special effects it can produce, the violin is a virtuoso instrument. More music has been written for it than for any other orchestral instrument. The second movement of Prokofiev's *Classical Symphony* has some beautiful passages for the violin choir in the upper register. The fourth movement of Brahms's Symphony No. 1 has a broad theme for violins in their lowest register. Mendelssohn's Concerto for Violin shows off the virtuosity of the solo instrument.

VIOLA. Slightly larger than the violin, the viola has thicker strings and a heavier bow; it can be thought of as an alto violin. The viola has never been considered ıs much a solo instrument as the violin, being used more often for harmony han for melody. Nonetheless, it can do everything the violin can do, at a lower ɔitch. But the viola is best suited to passages that reveal its warm, rich tones. Walton's Concerto for Viola demonstrates this admirably.

ʋIOLONCELLO. Called simply the *cello*, this instrument is much larger than either he violin or viola; it has to be held between the knees of a seated performer. Its strings are thicker and heavier than those of the viola, the bow is shorter ınd heavier, and it is tuned an octave lower. The tone of the cello is rich and ʻomantic, deep and full. It is a favorite instrument for solo passages. If the ʋiolin is the soprano of the string choir and the viola the alto, the cello is the ʻenor-baritone. A classic cello line can be found in the second movement of Beethoven's Symphony No. 5.

ɔOUBLE BASS. Known also as the *contrabass* and *bass viol*, the *double bass*, or more simply the *bass*, this is the largest member of the string family. It rests ıpon the floor, and the performer stands to play it. Because of its great size ınd the depth of its tone, it has a limited range of expression. It is most often ısed as a support, supplying the bass tones for the string choir or orchestra, though occasionally it is given a solo part. In the scherzo of Beethoven's Symphony No. 5 it plays a lumbering, almost grotesque role. Berlioz compared this famous passage to "the happy gambols of an elephant."

In dance bands, the double bass is never bowed but is played in a slapping fashion with the hand, not only for its tone but to emphasize the beat.

● **THE WOODWINDS**

FLUTE. The flute is a tube of silver approximately twenty-seven inches long. Its sound is often called silvery, haunting, or liquid. It is very agile and can play rapid, brilliant scale passages. In its lower register the sounds are mellow and rather ethereal, but in its upper register the sound is thinner, more brilliant. One is always aware of its breathy quality. There is a beautiful flute melody in the "Dance of the Blessed Spirits" from Gluck's *Orpheus and Eurydice*.

PICCOLO. This instrument is really a smaller flute. It is constructed like the flute and can be played by all flautists. It is approximately half the length of the flute and produces shrill and piercing tones. Because of its tiny size, it is pitched an octave above the flute and adds a sharp edge of brilliance and bite when it is heard with other instruments.

OBOE. The body of the oboe is a tube of wood which gets wider toward the bell, or end. It is especially good at expressive solos because its sound is reedy and penetrating. The oboe's slightly nasal tone gives it a plaintive or melancholy quality, but it can also be quite lively. A good example is Vivaldi's Concerto in D Minor for Oboe, Strings, and Continuo.

ENGLISH HORN. Despite its name, the English horn is a larger oboe. Its relationship to the oboe is roughly that of the viola to the violin. The oboe and English horn look very much alike except that the English horn has a bulge in its bell. Its range is slightly lower, and its sound is richer and even more plaintive than the oboe's. It is usually given the slower, more expressive line to play. In Franck's Symphony in D Minor, the English horn is heard in the second movement.

CLARINET. Among woodwinds, the B-flat clarinet is perhaps the most versatile instrument. It has a very wide range, within which it produces three distinctive sounds: in its lowest register it makes rich, hollow tones sometimes called barrel tones; in its middle register the sound is smooth and of medium thickness; in its upper range the sound is thin and shrill.

The clarinet is capable of great expression. It can go from a barely audible sound to one quite loud, play lyrical lines with great finesse, or do rapid scale passages. For these reasons it often takes the part of the violin in band music. Mozart's Quintet for Clarinet and Strings is an example.

BASSOON. The bassoon and double bassoon (or contrabassoon) are respectively the tenor and bass of the oboe family. The bassoon has approximately eight feet of wooden tube doubled back upon itself (the contrabassoon has sixteen), and the player supports the instrument by snapping it to a sling worn around the neck. The bassoon produces two distinct sounds: in its upper register, it makes a whining, nasal sound not unlike the saxophone, while in its lower register the tone is gravelly, dry, and gruff. The bassoon's upper register is good for expressive solos, but the lower register, unless for reasons of humor, is not. Rather, this register is used for bass harmony, adding a special edge to the overall effect. In "Dragons D'alcala" from *Carmen* there is a characteristic melody for two bassoons.

● THE BRASSES

TRUMPET. The trumpet has both a bright brassy sound which can ring and pierce, and a soft, muted sound made by inserting a "straight" mute in the bell of the tube. Because of its military history, it is often associated with battle calls and is extremely effective in strident passages where triumph or fury are intended. Purcell's Trumpet Voluntary in D is an example.

FRENCH HORN. Called simply the *horn*, this instrument has been developed from e hunting horn, and its ability to project sound across great distances is still vident. The horn normally has a smooth, mellow tone, but can be made to ound very brassy. By placing a mute or his hand into the bell, the performer n get a muted sound which is both distant and haunting. By pushing his and far into the bell and blowing with greater force, he can produce an xtremely brassy, almost threatening sound.

The horn is a versatile instrument; as a solo instrument it is very satisfactory ecause it can be loud or soft, lyrical or dramatic, and has a wide range. It so has the ability to blend well with every other instrument and is often used r its full, rich tones in harmony. Probably one of the best-loved horn solos is ound in the andante cantabile of the second movement of Tchaikovsky's Symhony No. 5. Mozart's Concertos for Horn are exemplary instances.

ROMBONE. There are two kinds of trombone: tenor and bass. When one speaks f the trombone, he usually means the tenor. The two are alike in construction, ut as would be expected the bass trombone has a lower range. The trombone's ne is rich and mellow. It can play softly, but is more often used for dignified, randiose melodies. When trombones play in unison, they can be overpowerg, as in the overture to Wagner's *Tannhäuser*.

UBA. This instrument is the bass of the brass choir and is therefore most often sed to reinforce the harmony for the orchestra. Its sound is rather like that of e bass trombone, but fuller, richer and more powerful. The overture to Vagner's *Die Meistersinger* has a famous tuba solo.

An invaluable record album which includes text and commentary on each f these instruments is *Instruments of the Orchestra* from Capital Records ducational Series. Concertos for the various instruments are obviously good r hearing timbre.

A number of specific compositions illustrate clearly the timbre of the varius instruments. Some of them are:

The Young Person's Guide to the Orchestra by Benjamin Britten
Bolero by Ravel
Nutcracker Suite by Tchaikovsky
Carnival of the Animals by Saint-Saëns
Peter and the Wolf by Prokofiev

THE ORGAN

'he organ enjoys the distinction of being the only instrument on which a single erformer can produce distinctly different tone colors. In this respect it is a

kind of one-man orchestra, and for this reason is often called the king c
instruments.

The pipes of an organ are arranged in sets, each set with one pipe for eac
note of the keyboard. Each set has its own timbre and all the sets are connecte
mechanically with the keyboard or keyboards. The organ normally has two c
three keyboards, and a set of foot pedals which amounts to another keyboar«
Since each of these can be set to different timbres, organ music when tran
scribed for piano loses its unique quality and seems much less clear.

From his seat, the organist can control all the sets, combining tone color
to create the ensemble he desires. There are usually four kinds of timbre avai.
able on the pipe organ: the organ foundation tone or diapason, flute tone, strin
tone, and reed tone. An example of music for the organ is Bach's Little Fugu
in G Minor, found in Chapter 15. All of the organ music by Bach is recorde«
by a number of artists and is easily obtainable. The tone color will vary accorc
ing to the particular organ being played.

● COMBINATIONS OF INSTRUMENTS

There are certain combinations of instruments that have proved to be satisfyin
and are often used by composers, such as the *piano trio* for violin, cello, an
piano, and the *string orchestra,* which comprises the whole string family. O
the small groups, however, the most important is the string quartet.

THE STRING QUARTET. This group is composed of two violins, a viola, and
cello. The violins are divided into first and second, playing the soprano an
contralto ranges respectively. The viola plays the tenor, and the cello supplie
the bass. Since the sound of four strings is not large, string quartet music fall
into the classification called *chamber music.* The string quartets of Beethove:
are considered among the finest examples of this genre.

THE SYMPHONY ORCHESTRA. By far the most important combination of instru
ments is the symphony orchestra, which is composed of the four choirs dis
cussed earlier in this chapter. It should be pointed out that each of these choir
has an instrument or instruments which fall into the range of soprano, cor
tralto, tenor, and bass.

The number of instruments in any orchestra varies according to the demand
of the music. Bach's orchestra usually had a mere eighteen performers, th
harpsichord and strings being the most important instruments. Haydn's orches
tra had only about forty players. By Wagner's time, more performers had bee
added, so that we have over a hundred required to play the music for *Th
Ring* cycle.

In the score of his Symphony No. 9, Beethoven wrote for this combination
f instruments:

Strings: First and second violins, violas, violoncellos, double basses (the exact
              number determined in terms of balance)
Woodwinds: 1 piccolo, 2 flutes, 2 oboes, 2 clarinets, 2 bassoons, 1 double bassoon
Brasses: 2 trumpets, 4 horns, 3 trombones
Percussion: 2 tympani, triangle, cymbals, bass drum

n *The Ring of the Nibelung,* Wagner composed for this combination:

Strings: 16 first violins, 16 second violins, 12 violas, 12 violoncellos, 8 double
              basses
Woodwinds: 2 piccolos, 3 flutes, 3 oboes, 3 clarinets, 1 English horn, 1 bass clari-
              net, 3 bassoons
Brasses: 3 trumpets, 1 bass trumpet, 8 horns, 4 trombones, 5 tubas
Percussion: 4 tympani, side drum, bass drum, triangle, cymbals, gong, glockenspiel
Harps: 6 harps

At the end of the nineteenth century, composers were writing for orchestras
f enormous size. Berlioz had envisioned an ideal string choir of 240, and
lthough this never became a reality, orchestras after Wagner often had over
00 instruments. The twentieth-century reaction to this has been to experiment
ith much smaller combinations, along with a return to chamber music ensem-
les. Too, the size of today's orchestra has decreased to between 65 and 90
nstruments. There are now also very small orchestras which specialize in per-
orming eighteenth-century music.

THE CONDUCTOR

he conductor's role as we know it today has been in effect for just over 125
ears. Prior to that time, ensemble music was usually conducted by the per-
ormer who sat at the harpsichord or piano. His job was to fill in harmony and
o keep the rhythm and tempo by waving his hand occasionally. This is still
lone with small chamber groups.

However, as orchestras grew in size and as orchestral music grew in expres-
ion, a full-time conductor was needed. From about 1825, conductors were a
egular feature of any large ensemble, and their importance has grown steadily.
Now the conductor is considered to be the most valuable and important man
of the orchestra.

The duties of today's conductor are both demanding and varied. He is
charge of the personnel of the orchestra. It is he who auditions performers ar
decides who will be a member of the orchestra, and what position (first chai
second chair, etc.) that member will have within his own choir.

Of vital importance is the question of what music will be performed. Agai
this is largely the decision of the conductor. The performance of obscure work
the introduction of contemporary works, or the choice of traditional works
his responsibility. Moreover, he must decide what will make a balanced indivi
ual concert. These decisions are of course tempered by the proficiency of th
group, the amount of rehearsal time available, the demands of the music bot
in numbers of performers and in instruments required, the demands of mus
cians' unions, and often the taste of the public which helps to support the grou

Aside from the demands of business, the conductor must be a supermusicia
He must know thoroughly the mechanics of every instrument in the orchestr
Quite often he is able to play a number of them. As it happens, many condu
tors today are quite proficient on the violin or piano.

From the conductor's podium, he reads simultaneously on his score, th
notes for every instrument, and is able to detect and correct any error on th
part of the performer. He must know the score perfectly and also have know
edge of the general style of the composer whose music is being played.

It is in terms of musical performance, however, that the conductor succee
or fails. His most important job is to recreate the music as near to the con
poser's wishes as he is able. Ultimately, the kind of performance given res
upon his interpretation.

The following are what we see the conductor do at a performance: he se
the tempo and controls the rhythm; he adjusts the dynamics from time to tim
asking some players for softer sounds, others for more volume, so that th
audience gets the correct mixture of both volume and tone color; he cues the pe
formers, making sure that each instrument enters precisely when it should; an
most importantly, he indicates the mood of a particular motive, phrase, or se
tion of music. His is the voice that determines the expression of the compositio

● VOCAL TIMBRE

In group singing, voices are commonly divided into four categories whic
describe range. From highest to lowest they are: soprano, contralto (or alto
tenor, and bass. Sometimes a fifth category, the baritone, is added between th
tenor and bass.

In solo singing, however, and especially in art songs and opera, addition
distinctions are made by names which describe timbre. This results in twelv

.inds of singing voice, five women's and seven men's. These voices can be identified by range, by their relative weight (light to heavy), and by the style of he music they sing. From highest to lowest, they are: coloratura soprano, lyric soprano, dramatic soprano, mezzo-soprano (or lyric contralto), dramatic contralto, lyric tenor, lirico spinto tenor, dramatic tenor, lyric baritone, dramatic baritone, basso cantante (lyric bass) and basso profundo (deep bass).

A word of caution is in order here; the vocal timbre of singing voices is not .s exact as that of the orchestral instruments. There are personal qualities which each singer's voice brings to bear on the music. Too, it is sometimes difficult o decide whether or not the music being sung is essentially lyric or dramatic. An opera role, or even a lengthy art song, can demand both. Moreover, some voices are flexible enough to sing in more than one of these categories. For example, some dramatic sopranos can also manage lyric roles, and some baritones can sing either lyric or dramatic music with equal facility. Finally, we should remember that voices can change with study and maturity. Lauritz Melchior made his reputation as a dramatic tenor, yet he began singing as a baritone.

Keeping these remarks in mind, we may look at a description of each kind of voice. The examples are from well-known operas.

COLORATURA SOPRANO. This voice is the lightest in weight and is best suited to music of a florid, technical nature. There is usually an emphasis on the upper reaches of the voice, and the melodies are apt to be highly embellished. The "Indian Bell Song" from *Lakmé* is sung by a coloratura. It could easily be a flute solo.

LYRIC SOPRANO. As the name implies, this voice is one which sings lyrical music. Traditionally, the heroine of the opera is a lyric soprano. Her voice is of medium weight, and she is usually asked to sing a sustained melodic line, often of an emotional nature. The prayer that ends Gounod's *Faust*, "Holy Angels in Heaven Blest," is sung by a lyric soprano.

DRAMATIC SOPRANO. This voice is the heaviest of soprano voices. The dramatic soprano is known for her full, clear tones, and is usually associated with roles of grand passion. The music for this voice is often heroic, with melodies of a tempestuous nature. Brunhilde's immolation scene from Wagner's *Götterdämmerung* is an example; in it Brunhilde greets her steed Grane and prepares to ride him into the fire that will end her life and her lover's.

MEZZO-SOPRANO (lyric contralto). *Mezzo* means middle. This voice is a lyric contralto, but the Italian name is more widely used. The mezzo-soprano has a highly colored timbre, which like the viola's is rich and warm. She sings music of a lyric or animated character. In the opera *Mignon*, she sings the lovely aria, "Hast Thou E'er Seen the Land?"

DRAMATIC CONTRALTO. The dramatic contralto possesses the deepest and riches of women's voices. Her range is much the same as that of the mezzo-soprano, but she is known by her heavier voice and by the dramatic quality of the musi she sings. In vehement passages there is normally a preoccupation with he middle and lower registers. In Wagner's *Lohengrin*, the dramatic contralt Ortrud is a sorceress bent on undoing the hero and heroine.

LYRIC TENOR. This is the lightest in weight of men's voices. The lyric teno produces a pure, relatively thin tone best suited for music of a lyrical nature Outside the field of opera, this voice is sometimes called an "Irish tenor," because it is so well suited to the singing of sentimental ballads and folk songs In *The Magic Flute*, Mozart has written a "Cavatina" requiring both expressio and agility. Here the tenor, a prince, sings rapturous praises upon being show a portrait of the beautiful Pamina.

LIRICO SPINTO TENOR. *Spinto* means "with accent." Just as the lyric tenor i often called Irish, the lirico spinto tenor is thought of as an Italian voice becaus of the emphasis on *bel canto*, or beautiful singing style. His voice is richer an more powerful than that of the lyric tenor and he is most often asked to sing melodies of well turned phrases and emotional content. The lirico spinto teno is traditionally the hero of the opera. In most nineteenth-century operas, hi role calls for an occasional high note usually sustained and adding emphasis t the passage. In Verdi's *Il Trovatore* the hero sings of his imminent death an his love for Leonora in "Let Links Eternal Bind the Vows."

DRAMATIC TENOR. As the name implies, music for this voice is dramatic, eve heroic. Thus the dramatic tenor is often called the heroic tenor as well. His i the heaviest in weight of the three tenor voices. He is known for his large opulent tones, and his voice is even richer and more powerful than that of th lirico spinto. In *Lohengrin* the dramatic tenor, the hero in this opera, reveal his identity for the first time in "Lohengrin's Narrative" as the opera draws t a close.

LYRIC BARITONE. Falling between the range of the tenor and bass, the baritone voice is one of medium weight. The lyric baritone is most easily identified b his rich tones and by the sustained melody he most often sings. In *La Traviata* by Verdi, the baritone, father of the unhappy hero, begs his son to forsake hi love and come home to his family. The aria is entitled "Di Provenza."

DRAMATIC BARITONE. This voice has a wider range than that of the lyric baritone and sings music of a more emotional or dramatic intensity. In the prologue t Verdi's *Simon Boccanegra*, Simon, the hero, is trying to justify seizing powe so that he will be free to marry Maria and give their daughter his name. " hoped to make myself sublime in your eyes."

ASSO CANTANTE (lyric bass). *Cantante* means "singing." This voice then is one
hich is capable of singing a broad melody. His tones are rich and full. One
f the favorite roles of lyric basses is that of Don Giovanni in the opera of the
ame name. "Here with Our Hands Entwining" is a charming duet between
on Giovanni and Zerlina, in which he attempts to lure her away from her
etrothed.

ASSO PROFUNDO (deep bass). Of all voices, this one has the heaviest weight and
e deepest, richest timbre. He sings music of an animated or dramatic char-
cter, but is also capable of sustaining a semilyrical role. Often there is an
mphasis on his lowest tones. The role of Oroveso in Bellini's *Norma* was
ritten expressly for the basso profundo. Here, Oroveso, chief of the druids,
ates that he will annihilate the enemy who has desecrated his temple when he
ngs "Haughty Roman."

Other works which illustrate vocal timbre are:

Coloratura soprano
    "Queen of the Night" from *The Magic Flute* by Mozart
    "Casta diva" from *Norma* by Bellini
Lyric soprano
    "Voi che sapete" from *The Marriage of Figaro* by Mozart
    "Musetta's Waltz" from *La Bohème* by Puccini
Dramatic soprano
    "Vissi d'arte" from *Tosca* by Puccini
    Isolde's "Liebestod" from *Tristan and Isolde* by Wagner
Mezzo-soprano
    "Seguidille" from *Carmen* by Bizet
    "Mon Coeur s'ouvre a ta voix" from *Samson and Delilah* by Saint-Saëns
Dramatic contralto
    "Ah, mon fils" from *The Prophet* by Meyerbeer
    "Erda's Warning" from *The Rhinegold* by Wagner
Lyric tenor
    "Il mio tesoro" from *Don Giovanni* by Mozart
    "Serenade" from *The Barber of Seville* by Rossini
Lirico spinto tenor
    Rodolpho's "Narrative" from *La Bohème* by Puccini
    "Addio alla Madre" from *Cavalleria Rusticana* by Mascagni
Dramatic tenor
    "Forging Song" from *Siegfried* by Wagner
    Tristan's "Nacht der Liebe" (with Isolde) from *Tristan and Isolde* by Wagner
Lyric baritone
    "Il balen" from *Il Trovatore* by Verdi
    "Valentine's Farewell" from *Faust* by Gounod

Medium

Dramatic baritone
"Credo" from *Otello* by Verdi
"To the Evening Star" from *Tannhäuser* by Wagner
Basso cantante
"Mephisto's Serenade" from *Faust* by Gounod
"Some Enchanted Evening" from *South Pacific* by Rogers
Basso profundo
"Hagen's Watch" from *Götterdämmerung* by Wagner
"Finale" of *Der Rosenkavalier* by Strauss

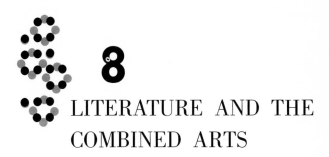

8
LITERATURE AND THE
COMBINED ARTS

● LIMITATIONS OF THE SUBJECT IN LITERATURE

The medium of literature is language, and as we have said, language may deal with anything that can be put into words. Language has a great advantage in that it is the only medium in any art which is used by everyone. Many of us do not try to draw or paint, we cannot play or sing, but we all talk. We may talk much or we may talk little, we may express our ideas easily or with difficulty, but we talk. Furthermore, we use this medium creatively. We make up new sentences to express our ideas.

Against this advantage of literature as a medium is a corresponding disadvantage. Literature is the only art whose medium is not international. A painting in fresco loses its characteristic quality if it is reproduced in oil—there is an essential change; but if one knows it in fresco he recognizes it in oil—he can see that it is the same picture. In the same way, a symphony written for an orchestra loses something that is essential when it is played on the piano, and yet one recognizes it as the same. But if a poem is translated into another language, one has no idea what it is about unless he knows the other language. To the person who knows both languages there is perhaps no greater difference between a poem in French and its translation into English than there is between the symphony played by the orchestra and an arrangement of that symphony for the piano, but unless he knows both languages one version is mere gibberish.

Words are symbols and therefore are incomprehensible to those who do not know them. A symbol is by nature arbitrary. It has a certain meaning because that meaning has been agreed on and for no other reason. In the story of "Ali Baba and the Forty Thieves," there is no intrinsic reason why the door should open if one said, "Open sesame" rather than "Open barley" or "Open wheat," but sesame was the word that had been agreed upon for that purpose, and the door would open for no other word. There is no reason why the symbol "4" should stand for four rather than for three or six. And so it is with most words. With a small group of words, such as *bow-wow, moo-moo, baa*, the sound is supposed to convey the meaning, but the number of such words is negligible, and they do not really convey any meaning. With the vast majority of words the sound has no natural and inevitable relation to the meaning. We are accustomed to associating the sound of the word *dog* with a certain animal, but there is no essential connection between the two. The French word for dog is *chien*, the German, *Hund*, the Latin, *canis*, and there is nothing in any one of the sounds to indicate that particular animal were it not so understood by the people who speak that language.

● THE LANGUAGES OF THE WORLD

The mediums of literature are the various languages of the world: English, French, German, Italian, Russian, Chinese, Japanese, and so on. And as is true of all mediums of all arts, each has its own special characteristics, and what can be said in one cannot be said in another. It is said that the novelist Conrad wrote his novels in English rather than in French, a language he knew much better, because in French he could not say what he wanted to say. A recent writer on the subject of communication has said, "When I read French I need to become as a different person, with different thought; the language change bears with it a change of national character and temperament, a different history and literature."[1] In a small way all of us have experienced this change in assuming a dialect. The man who talks as an American Negro, a Southerner,

[1]Colin Cherry, *On Human Communication*, M.I.T. Press, 1957, p. 70.

r an Irishman assumes the character and personality of that person for that ime.

A delightful account of the difficulties with a foreign language is found in Clarence Day's *Life with Father.*[2]

I got out another Bible that Mother had lent me. This one was in French, and it sometimes shocked me deeply to read it. As my belief was that when God had created the world he had said, "Let there be light," it seemed to me highly irreverent to put French words in His mouth and have Him exclaim, "Que la lumière soit!" Imagine the Lord talking French! Aside from a few odd words in Hebrew, I took it completely for granted that God had never spoken anything but the most dignified English.

Instead of the children of Israel fearing lest the Lord should be wroth, the French said "les enfants d'Israel" were afraid lest "le Seigneur" should be "irrité." This word "irrité" appeared everywhere in the French version. It wasn't only the Lord. Cain was "très irrité." Moise (which seemed to me a very jaunty way of referring to Moses) was "irrité" again and again. Everybody was "irrité." When my regular Bible, the real one, impressively described men as "wroth," their anger seemed to have something stately and solemn about it. If they were full of mere irritation all the time, they were more like the Day family.

● THE QUESTION OF TRANSLATIONS

In a very real sense no translation is ever more than an approximation of the original. The sound of the original is lost completely; only the sense is preserved, and the sense cannot be put into another language with entire accuracy. Sometimes a single translation is made so nearly perfect that it is accepted as an adequate rendering of the original. Such a translation is Longfellow's rendering of Goethe's "Wanderer's Night Song":

Über allen Gipfeln
Ist Ruh,
In allen Wipfeln
Spürest du
Kaum einen Hauch;
Die Vögelein schweigen im Walde.
Warte nur, balde
Ruhest du auch.

— JOHANN WOLFGANG VON GOETHE (1749–1832, German poet, dramatist, and novelist), "Wanderers Nachtlied" (1780)

[2]Clarence Day, *Life with Father.* Copyright 1935 by Clarence Day. Used by permission of Alfred A. Knopf, Inc.

Medium

O'er all the hill-tops
Is quiet now,
In all the tree-tops
Hearest thou
Hardly a breath;
The birds are asleep in the trees:
Wait; soon like these
Thou too shalt rest.

—HENRY WADSWORTH LONGFELLOW (1807–1882, American poet)

But all too often the translations either fail to be good English or they fail to be like the original. If it is necessary to use a translation, the best practice is to compare the versions of several people, for often a different translation gives a new insight into a passage. The Bible is a good book to study in this connection because there are many different translations easily available. Suppose we take the passage in Matthew when Jesus is talking about divorce; it ends with the words we all know: "What therefore God hath joined together, let not man put asunder." The disciples, however, are not satisfied and ask about the law of Moses. "Then why did Moses lay it down that we were to divorce by giving a separation-notice?" is the translation of Moffatt,[3] but Phillips makes it read "Then why did Moses command us to give a written divorce-notice and dismiss the woman?"[4] This question is answered in the King James and Moffatt versions by the statement that it was because of "the hardness of your hearts," whereas the New English Bible gives a different twist: "It was because you were so unteachable."[5] Phillips gives it an entirely new turn: "It was because you knew so little of the meaning of love that Moses allowed you to divorce your wives."

Jesus ends this speech with the statement that adultery is the only ground for divorce, and again the disciples object and the translations differ. The King James reads: "If the case of the man be so with his wife, it is not good to marry." Moffatt ends the discussion: "There is no good in marrying." The New English is more lenient: "If that is the position with husband and wife, it is better to refrain from marriage." And again Phillips differs: "If that is a man's position with his wife, it is not worth getting married."

[3] *The Bible: A New Translation* by James Moffatt, copyrighted in 1935 by Harper & Row, Publishers, New York. Used by permission.
[4] *The Gospels*, translated into Modern English by J. B. Phillips, copyrighted in 1952 by The Macmillan Company, New York. Used by permission.
[5] From *The New English Bible, New Testament.* © The Delegates of the Oxford University Press and The Syndics of the Cambridge University Press, 1961. Reprinted by permission.

● LITERATURE IN ENGLISH

In a text of this kind it is not safe to assume that the readers will know more than one language. Therefore, we are limiting our study of literature to the one medium, English. In doing so we are obviously restricted and are at a disadvantage. In the other arts we can study the work of all countries with equal ease. We can hear the music of Russia, see the sculpture of Greece, and enjoy the architecture of France and the paintings of Italy as clearly and as easily as we can those of England. In literature we are confined to writings in English or to translations from other languages into English.

Fortunately, the English language is a very flexible medium, and a very wide variety of effects can be obtained in it. Fortunately, also, it is a language with a very great literature. But the fact remains that, knowing only English, we are missing other and different types of effect to be obtained in other languages.

● THE COMBINED ARTS

By definition, the combined arts are those which use more than one medium. The special emphasis of a dance is on the movements of the body, but the dancer employs also costume and lighting, usually music, and sometimes stage scenery. The theater presents a story told in dialogue and acted out on the stage; usually it also employs scenery, costumes, furniture, lighting, and at times music. Ideally, the various mediums are combined with just the right emphasis on each to make clear the idea in the mind of the artist. One of the major problems of the artist is the decision as to which of his mediums he will stress at any particular time.

An example is found in *Hamlet,* in the scene in which Hamlet makes his formal renunciation of Ophelia. Hamlet is a young man just returned from the university, and he is sorely perplexed by the condition in which he has found matters at home. His father is dead, and his mother has married again so quickly that Hamlet says, in contempt, she did it to economize on the pies and meats baked for his father's funeral. Shortly afterward he learns from a ghost about his father's murder. Hamlet does not know whether to believe the ghost or not, and he needs help desperately. For a long time he has been in love with Ophelia, and naturally he turns to her now. But, looking in her face, he realizes that she cannot help him; so he shakes his head and leaves the room without saying a word.

Medium

This might seem just the scene to be enacted on the stage. But, instead, Shakespeare uses words only. Ophelia tells her father of Hamlet's coming:

My lord, as I was sewing in my chamber,
Lord Hamlet, with his doublet all unbrac'd,
No hat upon his head, his stockings foul'd,
Ungart'red, and down-gyved to his ankle,
Pale as his shirt, his knees knocking each other,
And with a look so piteous in purport
As if he had been loosed out of hell
To speak of horrors,—he comes before me.

He took me by the wrist and held me hard;
Then goes he to the length of all his arm,
And, with his other hand thus o'er his brow,
He falls to such perusal of my face
As he would draw it. Long stay'd he so.
At last, a little shaking of mine arm,
And thrice his head thus waving up and down,
He rais'd a sigh so piteous and profound
That it did seem to shatter all his bulk
And end his being. That done, he lets me go;
And, with his head over his shoulder turn'd,
He seem'd to find his way without his eyes,
For out o'doors he went without their help,
And, to the last bended their light on me.

> —WILLIAM SHAKESPEARE (1564–1616, British poet and dramatist), *Hamlet*, II, i, 77–84, 87–100

The scene as described by Ophelia is so vivid that most people who read the play remember the event as one that took place on the stage. Why, then, did Shakespeare have Ophelia tell of it? There are many reasons; one is that in this way he kills two birds with one stone: the father is told at the same time that we learn of the action. That is a good but unimportant reason. More important is the fact that a scene of that kind would not be easy to enact. The real reason probably is that Shakespeare wants to be sure that the audience understands the scene as he meant it, and so he must interpret it for them in words.

The mediums used in the combined arts are the mediums used in the separate arts. In this short discussion we shall attempt only to show the mediums that are used in each art and to state some of the possibilities and limitations that arise from their being combined.

DRAMA

Drama is usually listed under literature because the most important part of a play is the dialogue spoken by the characters. As action, however, whether presented on the stage or visualized by the mind, it involves many other mediums. There are of course the actors, for each of whom we have costume, speaking voice, and all his actions. For the story as a whole we have setting and properties. The possibilities in each type of medium are almost limitless. A slight change in costume may be used to indicate that years have passed or that the person has grown richer or poorer. The accent may betray nationality or social status, and the manner of speaking may indicate character. The actor may make use of all the movements of the dancer as well as those of the ordinary person in walking, running, or standing.

In many of the great periods of the theater the setting has been of very little importance. In the Greek theater, for instance, the setting was the same for all plays, a street before a building. In the Elizabethan theater, also, it was very simple, consisting of only a few pieces of furniture to indicate the type of room—for example, a bed for a bedroom. The Greeks and the Elizabethans, moreover, had no control over lighting; both performed their plays in the daytime with natural lighting. Now the producer has full control over the lights and the setting of his play, and he can change them to suit his performance. In his hands the setting and the lighting have become mediums for the artist just as truly as speech, action, or costume.

THE DANCE

"The dance antedates all other forms of art because it employs no instrument but the body itself which everyone has always with him and which, in the final analysis, is the most eloquent and responsive of all the instruments."[6] It is the most personal of all the mediums of art. If we think of a dance as organized movement, we will be interested in the examples given by Curt Sachs in his *World History of the Dance* (p. 988). He cites instances of animals that dance: the stilt birds and anthropoid apes. In them he finds a series of the essential dance motifs: the circle, and ellipse, forward and backward steps, besides hopping, stamping, whirling. Nor can we go into the early history of man without finding the dance. Greek vases show many examples of dancers. The Noh dancing of ancient Japan is six hundred years old.

The movements of the dance may be classified under two headings: (1) movements within the body, such as movement of the head, arms, or torso within a certain space, and (2) movement from one space to another, such as

[6]John Martin, *Introduction to the Dance*, pp. 14–15.

walking, running, jumping. A dance may be performed by a single dancer or by any number.

The dance exists in the three dimensions: time, space, and dynamics. Space of course determines the position of the dancer in relation to his background: in the center, to one side, in front, to the back. It also determines the posture of the body as erect, lying, crouched, stooped, running, still, etc. The time, of course, may be fast or slow, and its dynamics determine the rhythm.

The structure of a dance usually follows that of the music; a two-part tune will have a two-part dance.

In general, dances have been preserved by the dancers, the younger learning from the older. This does not mean, however, that two versions of one dance are the same; each person or each group will find ways to change it.

OPERA

Opera is comprised of three mediums which in order of importance are: music, drama, and spectacle. These serve to make opera one of the most appealing of the arts, but they also make it one of the most complex and difficult. The musical demands alone call for a full symphony orchestra, a conductor, one or more choruses, a choral conductor, and solo singers.

The dramatic demands of opera begin with the *libretto*, or "book of words," upon which the opera is based. A good libretto gives us the essence of character and situation quickly and thoroughly. The composer who finds a librettist with whom he can work well is a man blessed. One of the happiest combinations of composer-librettist is that of Gilbert and Sullivan in the area of operetta.

In opera, a great combination is that of Verdi-Boito. In making Shakespeare's *Othello* into a libretto for Verdi's opera *Otello*, Boito made a number of effective changes. For example, he omitted the entire first act of the play, keeping only Othello's courtship speech, which becomes a duet between Othello and Desdemona. In the opera, Desdemona prays to the Virgin Mary before she is strangled although that scene does not appear in the play.

In the integration of mediums so different as music and drama, compromises must be made. One is in the matter of time. For obvious reasons, singing a script takes longer than speaking it. In opera then, quite often the dramatic action must be either slowed down or stopped altogether while a musical idea progresses. Conversely, while the dramatic action moves forward, we cannot expect to linger over a long, beautiful melody.

Within this perpetual compromise there is no doubt that drama suffers more than music. Since music is the most important medium in opera, it must succeed, no matter what the fate of the dramatic action. Opera stands or falls on the quality of its music. Even an excellent libretto is inadequate if the music to which it is set is inferior. On the other hand, a trite libretto can be sustained by memorable music. Furthermore, one can forgive an opera singer whose acting ability is limited, but no matter how fine the acting, one does not forget or forgive bad singing.

Spectacle involves anything of a visual nature which can be integrated with the opera plot. Dances are found in many operas which are complete works in themselves. Exotic sets and costumes also constitute spectacle, especially when changed often for the visual delight of the audience. Spectacle also occurs when there is an emphasis on the realm of nature such as the use of fire, water, or animals in the production. Verdi's *Aïda* is an example; in the scene of the triumphal march, trumpeters on horseback, camels, chariots, and large numbers of performers can be used when the opera is staged with spectacle in mind.

As he matured, however, Verdi used fewer and fewer extraneous visual effects until in his last two operas, *Otello* and *Falstaf,* there is no spectacle: we have only the bare bones of music and drama. And although his earlier operas are still enjoyed, these two are considered his finest work. Therefore it can be said that spectacle is not necessary to opera.

THE FILM

The film is essentially the art of the moving picture. Just as opera stands or falls upon its music, the film stands or falls upon its visual content. Thus motion photography is its most important medium. The film is a combined art only when aural effects such as dialogue or music are added.

Of course, professional actors, sets, special lighting, costumes, and make-up are a part of the making of most films; still they exist only through photography. Further, they exist as the camera interprets them for us. Actually no one of them is essential. Documentary films such as Robert J. Flaherty's masterpiece *Nanook of the North* are made without their use.

Because the camera is a scientific instrument capable of reproducing exactly what it sees, it is often unjustly dismissed as a mere recorder. But not only can the camera record precisely, it can emphasize or minimize, distort, and create illusion. It can present more than one time and place simultaneously, and it can show all facets of an object from changing viewpoints. It is difficult to remember that the camera is there at all when viewing a film, but it is precisely this quality that helps us gain insight into situation and character. Thus we learn not from being told but from visual revelation.

It follows then that if what is being presented is well presented visually, it matters little what is heard. Theoretically the film should be able to say what it has to say without recourse to sound. This has been done many times of course, but with the judicious addition of dialogue, narration, music, or other sound effects, the film has been enhanced. However, when sound is used in such a way as to become obtrusive, the visual content is damaged to that extent.

Ideally the director of the film is also the editor. It is the editor who selects the best shots and sequences; putting them in an ordered relationship, he creates the pace and mood of the picture by giving it a feeling of continuity or discontinuity as the subject demands. The director is in a very real sense the composer of the film. When he is the editor, then he becomes the conductor as well. Such is the case with most of the distinguished directors.

Among the many fine films of recent years, two of vastly different nature are cited here as models of excellence: *Tom Jones*, directed and edited by Tony Richardson, and *Pather Panchali*, directed and edited by Satyajit Ray.

Based upon Fielding's novel of the same name, *Tom Jones* is high comedy. Essentially it is the story of a young man unjustly turned out of his benefactor's home. Although his spirit is willing, his flesh is weak, and only by chance and the love of a good woman is he saved and welcomed back into society. Although whole portions of the book have been omitted, contracted or altered, this film is visually true to its subject. It is in color and for the most part the pace is quite lively. In some places the scene goes by faster than it can be absorbed, just as in life. The pace and mood are as rollicking as the nature of the hero.

In *Tom Jones* the hunting of the hart begins with an aerial view. Then the camera follows the various horses and riders as they race through the woods behind the yelping hounds. The impressions are as blurred and fleeting as they would be from a participating hunter's point of view.

In another, more lyrical scene, Tom and his sweetheart Sophia are shown as they take turns rowing each other across a pond. Here the pace is as slow as the lovers' gliding boat. We do not have to be told anything about their regard for each other. The camera makes it quite clear.

Pather Panchali is concerned with the plight of the poverty-stricken family of a would-be playwright living in rural India. It is in black and white, and as might be expected, its pace is slow, its mood poetic. There is little dialogue.

In a number of scenes, we see the wife become increasingly lonely and fearful. Her husband has been away for some weeks looking for employment while she is left to care for their two hungry children. Finally she receives a postcard from him saying that he has found work at last and is returning to get his family.

For the first time she relaxes. As she slowly lowers her head to the hard stone of the porch, the camera takes us to the nearby pond. Here we see the first drops of the monsoon rains fall upon the water, and to the sound of a stringed instrument water bugs skim to and fro, abruptly changing course. The rain increases and a breeze lifts up the edges of the lily pads. All of this is done without a word of dialogue, and we have learned as we could learn in no other way what is in the woman's heart; her heavy burden has been lifted. This is a sublime moment in the art of the film.

ORGANIZATION

9
ELEMENTS OF THE
VISUAL ARTS

● MEDIUM AND ELEMENTS

Medium and elements are together the materials the artist uses in creating a work of art. The distinction between them is easy to see but hard to define. Both answer the question: What is it made of? but from different points of view. If, for instance, we say that the building is made of brick and stone, we are talking of the medium; if we say it is made of right angles and vertical lines, we are talking of the elements. If we say that the music is played on the horn, the oboe, or the piano, we are talking of the medium; if we say it is fast or slow, that it has a good tune or a catchy rhythm, we are talking of the elements. If we say that the picture is made of oil or watercolor, we are talking of the medium, but if we say it is made of red and green and blue, we are talking of the elements.

An element can be known only in some medium, but as an element it is independent of medium. If we see a straight line we necessarily see it in some medium such as chalk, pencil, ink, or the corner of a house; but when we think f line we do not necessarily connect it with any medium. And so we talk of ine dissociated from medium. Similarly, if we hear the song "America," we nust hear it sung by some person or played on some instrument, but we think f it as a tune without regard to any instrument. Therefore, when we study lements, we consider them with no attention to the means by which we know hem. The medium is the physical means through which we can come in conact with a work of art; the elements are its qualities or properties. Mediums re concrete; elements are abstract.

The elements of the visual arts are six:

1. Line
2. Value
3. Color
4. Texture
5. Volume
6. Perspective

LINE

Line is the simplest, most primitive, and most universal means for creating visual art. Ask a child to draw an apple, a man, or a house: he will make it first in lines, that is, he will try to outline it. Lines are of many different kinds. They may be broad, or so faint we can hardly see them. They may be ragged, or clear and distinct. Often lines are felt and not seen, as when one object or person points to something we do not see. Often the felt lines are more important than the seen lines.

As a matter of fact, there is no such thing as line. What we see as lines are marks made on paper, or contours of objects. The round vase has no edge, no line, but we see one just as we see the corner of a building as a line. Or we may see shadows as lines.

Lines always have direction. They are always active. They always seem to be moving, and we follow them with our fingers, our gestures, or our eyes. Color has none of this activity. We see a wall of blue or red with no idea of motion of any kind, but whenever we see a line we begin to follow it no matter how long or winding its path.

STRAIGHT LINES. Lines are straight or curved; straight lines are horizontal, vertical, or diagonal. The horizontal line is primarily the line of rest and quiet, relaxation and contemplation; a long horizontal line gives a sense of infinity that is not easily obtained in any other way. Horizontal lines are found in landscapes; the quieter the landscape, the more prominent the horizontals. In

Rembrandt's *Three Trees* the sense of rest and quiet and peace derives largely from the long line of the horizon.

The vertical line is the line of a tree or of a man standing, the line of chimneys and towers. The vertical is a line of rest, but it is not the rest of relaxation we find in the horizontal. The vertical is poised, balanced, forceful, and dynamic. The vertical is a line of potential action, though it is not acting. The early Greek bronze found at Delphi, known as *The Charioteer,* is purely vertical except for the arms which are outstretched to hold the reins. Even a slight deviation from the vertical takes away from its force; in the caryatids of the Erechtheum, for example, each figure is perfectly straight except for one bent knee, but that break from the vertical gives a sense of relaxation. One feels that the load is not too heavy and that the maidens can easily hold up the roof for a few more centuries.

The diagonal is the line of action. A man running makes a diagonal line with his body and leg; a beating rain, trees in a hard wind, almost everything in action assumes a diagonal line. The degree of action is shown in the angle of the diagonal. The diagonal that approaches the vertical shares the force and self-sufficiency of that line; the one that approaches the horizontal shares its abandonment. At an angle of forty-five degrees the diagonal represents the maximum of action, being halfway between the independence of the vertical and the powerlessness of the horizontal. In Daumier's painting *The Uprising* (Figure 99) the forward movement of the mob is shown in the diagonals, especially in the upraised arm of the leader. In Duchamp-Villon's statue (Figure 100) the horse's head is turned to one side and his feet are drawn together for action

FIGURE 99. HONORÉ DAUMIER. *The Uprising* (1860?). (Oil on canvas. Size: 24½ by 44½ inches. Washington, D.C., courtesy Phillips Collection.)

FIGURE 100. RAYMOND DUCHAMP-VILLON (1876–1918), French sculptor. *The Horse* (1914). (Bronze. Size: 40 inches high. New York, Museum of Modern Art; van Gogh Purchase Fund.)

The energy and incipient action of the statue are derived primarily from its diagonals.

Diagonals meeting at sharp angles form jagged lines that are harsh and unpleasant; they connote confusion, disturbance, lightning, battle, war, and sudden death. In El Greco's *Expulsion from the Temple* (Figure 101) the main interest is centered on Christ and the unfortunate tradesmen who are being driven away. The lines made by their arms and bodies are predominantly diagonal, meeting at acute angles. In contrast, the figures to the right of the center are quiet, being formed largely of vertical and curved lines.

FIGURE 101. EL GRECO. *Expulsion from the Temple* (1595–1600). (Oil on canvas. Size: 41⅜ by 50 inches. Copyright Frick Collection, New York.)

CURVED LINES. Curved lines show action and life and energy; they are never harsh or stern. Most of the sights to which we attach the adjective "pleasing" have curved lines: rounded hills, trees bent with fruit, curved arms and cheeks.

Curves may be single or double, slow or quick. A quick curve is an arc of a small circle, the type of curve found on a fat baby. A slow curve is an arc of a large circle, the type of a long, thin face. A single curve is but a single arc; a double curve turns back on itself, an S curve. The double slow curve is the famous "line of grace" or "line of beauty" of Hogarth. The quick curve is more exuberant than the slow curve; when used in great abundance it becomes coarse and gross.

A great deal of the elegance of Harunobu's *Lovers Under Umbrella in Snow* comes from the long single curves. In contrast, van Gogh's *La Berceuse* (Figure 102), in its round curves, is solid and substantial. All the curves are ample; the flowers and other ornaments in the background are circular.

FIGURE 102. VINCENT VAN GOGH. *La Berceuse (Mme. Roulin Rocking the Cradle)* (1889). (Oil on canvas. Size: 36⅝ by 28⅛ inches. Chicago, courtesy Art Institute of Chicago; Helen Birch Bartlett Memorial Collection.)

FIGURE 103. JOAN MIRÓ (1893–   ), Spanish painter and print maker. *Composition* (1933). (Oil on canvas. Size: 68½ by 77¼ inches. New York, Museum of Modern Art; gift of the Advisory Committee. Photograph, Museum of Modern Art.)

Examples of the characteristics of lines are to be found everywhere. In advertisements, the shape of the letter and the quality of the line are frequently used to indicate the character of the thing advertised. For example, the lettering that advertises farm machinery may also try to suggest its product, in solid, heavy, square strokes that sit flatly on the paper. Articles that are supposed to appeal to the dainty or the fastidious will be advertised in thin lines with slow curves.

Lines make shapes, and often we are conscious of line primarily in the shapes made. In Rembrandt's *Three Trees* again we see the line of the horizon but the shape of the trees. Miro's *Composition* (Figure 103) is one of similar shapes. We are not sure what, if anything, they represent. We can distinguish a seated dog in the upper left, and there is a suggestion of horned cattle across

FIGURE 104. GEORGES PIERRE SEURAT. *Sunday on the Island of La Grande Jatte* (ca. 1886). (Oil on canvas. Size: 81 by 120⅜ inches. Chicago, courtesy Art Institute of Chicago; Helen Birch Bartlett Memorial Collection.)

the background. The whole, however, is a scene of quiet and beauty. In hi *Sunday on the Island of La Grande Jatte* (Figure 104) Seurat has united th picture largely through the repetition of the same or similar shapes.

VALUE

Value has to do with the amount and kind of light, or we may say it is th name given to relative degrees of light and dark. In ordinary speech, only th terms *light* and *dark* are employed, but this use is rather vague; we nee greater discrimination. If white is recognized as the highest value and black a the lowest, a point halfway between them is called medium; the point halfwa between white and medium is called light; and the point halfway betwee medium and black is called dark. This makes an exact scale:

White
Light
Medium
Dark
Black

alues that do not fit one of these points may be defined in terms of the nearer alue, as a value halfway between *dark* and *medium,* or a *light* value very close ɔ *white.* The Italian word *chiaroscuro* is commonly used for contrasts of value ɪ painting, especially when they are pronounced.

ALUES IN ARTS OF THREE DIMENSIONS. Values have two sources. The first and bvious source is the value of the object itself, as, for instance, the color of a iece of cloth. This is called its *local color.* The second is the creation of value ɪrough shadows or reflection of light. If a cloth is hung as a curtain, its folds ʻill show many different values. Such values are subtle because they change ʻith every change in the light. If, for instance, a white cloth is held in a dark ʻoset and gradually brought into the light, the hue that seemed black in the ʻarkness appears in all values from black to white as the cloth is brought out ɪto the light. Tooled leather, weaving, chased gold and silver all depend for ʻeir effects on differences in value produced by shadows.

The same is true of architectural design and ornament in general. A mold-ɪg, whether inside or outside a building, can be seen because of the way the ʻifferent surfaces reflect the light. Patterns in shingles or in the arrangement of ʻoards or brick can hardly be seen except for the shadows they cast. A cornice ʻasts a shadow on the wall below and makes a definite change in the design. An ʻrchitect frequently makes a model of the building he is designing in order ʻhat he may learn the exact effects of the shadows. One of the beauties of the ʻathedral of Notre Dame in Paris is found in the varied carvings of the façade, ɪnd in the play of lights and shadows over them.

If the artist has not studied the effects of shadows carefully, he may find the ɪnished work quite different from the one he planned. French's statue of Lin-ʻoln, for example, was made in the studio with an overhead light. When it ʻas placed in the Lincoln Memorial in Washington all the light came from ʻelow (Figure 105). This lighting completely changed the expression on Lin-ʻoln's face, making it little better than a caricature, as seen in the picture on

IGURE 105. DANIEL CHESTER RENCH (1850–1931), American ʻculptor. *Abraham Lincoln* (1920), ʻead before (right) and after (left) ʻhange of lighting. (White marble. ʻize: about three times life size. Wash-ɪgton, D.C., Lincoln Memorial. Photo-ʻraph, courtesy Mrs. Margaret French ʻresson.)

the right. Fortunately the lighting could be and was easily changed, and no
visitors to the Memorial see the statue as French planned it.

RELIEF SCULPTURE. In relief sculpture values are especially important, since th
design can usually be seen only in the shadows cast. In *high relief* the figure
project from the background; they are almost in the round. The shadows a
deep and the lines bold and distinct, as in the metopes of the Partheno
(Figure 106). In *low relief* the figures are only slightly raised from the bac
ground. The shadows are not very deep, and the lines are delicate, as in th
Panathenaic Procession (Figure 107), also from the Parthenon. Therefore
low relief should be in a dimly lighted place where the light shadows mak
clear the outlines of all the figures. A high relief should be in bright ligh

FIGURE 106. LAPITH AND CENTAUR (ca. 447–443 B.C
metope from southwest corner of Parthenon. (Pentelic marbl
Height: 3 feet, 4 inches. Athens. Photograph, Saul Weinberg

FIGURE 107. PANATHENAIC PROCESSION (fifth century B.C.
detail of Parthenon frieze. (Pentelic marble. Height: 40 inche
London, British Museum.)

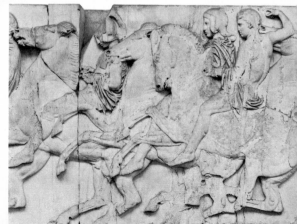

because the higher the relief the deeper the shadows. In high relief, moreover, the design must be very simple; if there are too many figures the shadow of one figure tends to hide its neighbor. In low relief the design may be more complicated. In the reliefs on the Parthenon both these points were observed. The *Panathenaic Procession* is found in the frieze, which was placed on the wall of the building where it was protected from direct sunlight by a row of columns. The metopes were placed above the columns, where they received direct sunlight.

The examples given so far have had to do with rather static effects of value, dealing as they do with the placing of an object with reference to a constant light. But as we all know, natural light changes continuously; it is alive and dynamic, and as Walter Gropius, the designer of the Bauhaus, has said, "Every object seen in the contrast of changing daylight gives a different impression each time".[1] And he continues: "Imagine the surprise and animation experienced when a sunbeam, shining through a stained-glass window in a cathedral, wanders slowly through the twilight of the nave and suddenly hits the altarpiece." This constant change and constant tension has much to do with the charm of stained-glass windows. Not only does each window have its own color and design, but it is constantly shifting in its values.

In modern domestic architecture we have other significant examples. The rooms are built so that they take advantage of the shifts in daylight through the house and in the patio and garden.

VALUES IN PAINTING. In architecture and sculpture values change with the light; in painting values are fixed. When a painter makes an area dark or light, puts in a shadow or leaves it out, it stays that way regardless of the time of year or the source of light. The painting should of course be placed where it can be seen clearly, but its essential values do not change.

In studying the values of a painting we notice first the value tone. Is the picture predominantly light or dark? In Rembrandt's *Old Woman Cutting Her Nails* (Figure 108) the values are dark; in Ingres's *Lady and Boy* they are light. And there are paintings which have an intermediate shade, an overall grayish effect, such as we see in the painting of Jan van Eyck, *The Annunciation* (Figure 109), where the light is diffused.

A second question asks about contrasts in value, are they great or small? We have just mentioned van Eyck's *The Annunciation* as a painting with a diffused light and little contrast. Ordinarily, however, we have greater contrasts of light and dark, as in Titian's *The Young Englishman* (Figure 110), where the white hands and head shine out against the dark background and the chain

[1] Walter Gropius, *The Scope of Total Architecture*, Harper & Row, Publishers, 1955, p. 41.

FIGURE 108. REMBRANDT. *Old Woman Cutting Her Nails* (1658). (Oil on canvas. Size: 49⅝ by 40⅛ inches. New York; courtesy Metropolitan Museum of Art, bequest of Benjamin Altman, 1913.)

FIGURE 109. JAN VAN EYCK (1370?–1440?), Flemish painter. *The Annunciation* (ca. 1425–1430). (Transferred from wood to canvas. Size: 36½ by 14⅜ inches. Washington, D.C., National Gallery of Art; Mellon Collection, 1937.)

FIGURE 110. TITIAN. *The Young Englishman* (ca. 1540–1545). (Oil on canvas. Size: 43½ by 36½ inches. Florence, Palazzo Pitti. Photograph by Anderson.)

occupies a position halfway between them. Often an artist has a particular fondness for one set of values. Rembrandt is outstanding for his contrasts in value, as in the *Old Woman Cutting Her Nails*. In this painting light is concentrated on head, hands, and dress, with some clothes in the background, and indeed seems to emanate from them. Any natural light would of necessity have given greater light to the clothes and the other surfaces.

The next point to notice about values is the way they are separated one from the other. Do they merge one into the other or are they separate? Are the boundary lines blurred or distinct? In the Rembrandt, boundaries are kept clear in the foreground, but in the background all sense of boundary lines is lost.

The last point to consider about values in painting is the character of the dark areas. Is there a single flat surface, or is it subtly varied? This is really a matter of slight variations in value within a single tone, variations so slight as to be almost imperceptible. It is the difference between a wooden box painted sky-blue and the actual blue of the sky. Ruskin complained that the artists before Turner painted hard, flat skies, and it is one of the excellences he finds in Turner that you look *into* and not *at* his skies. The shadows of Rembrandt have this same quality. In the *Old Woman Cutting Her Nails* there is only a little light in the picture; the remainder of the scene is buried in darkness. But this darkness is not hard blackness, against which one might strike his head, but a soft, penetrable shadow; one feels that he can see into the shadow. The effect is much the same as that which is produced by a small light in a large room; only a small space is clearly lighted, and the light fights against the shadows in the remainder of the space.

In emotional connotation light values are, in general, bright, gay, and happy; sometimes they are unsubstantial. Dark values are solid and substantial, sometimes gloomy and melancholy. Sharp contrasts are dramatic, and values that merge hazily one into the other, especially in the darker tones, tend to be mysterious, even mystical. The hazy dark values of Ryder's *Death on a Pale Horse* (Figure 111) are largely responsible for its mood of mystery and doom.

FIGURE 111. ALBERT PINKHAM RYDER (1847–1918), American painter. *The Race Track*, or *Death on a Pale Horse* (ca. 1910). (Oil on canvas. Size: 28¼ by 35¼ inches. Cleveland, courtesy Cleveland Museum of Art; J. H. Wade Collection.)

COLOR

All the effects obtained through line and value alone may be increased by the use of color. Colors may be warm or cold, advancing or retreating, light or heavy, attractive or repulsive, in tension or in suspension.

When we examine color we find three qualities or attributes: hue, value, and intensity. Hue is that quality by which we distinguish one color from another. The three primary hues are red, blue, and yellow. All others can be made from them. The secondary hues are green, violet, and orange, each being halfway between two of the primary colors: orange is halfway between yellow and red, etc. This relation is easily seen on the diagram.

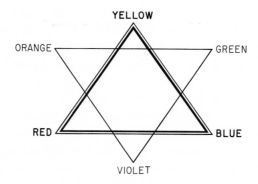

The diagram has another advantage in that each hue is just opposite its complement. Two hues are said to be complementary when they comprise the three primary colors. The complement of yellow is violet. Since violet is made of red and blue the yellow and violet contain all the primary colors. Complementaries intensify each other if placed close together. Red and green mixed make a gray, but a red near a green makes each color seem brighter than when alone.

Colors are either "warm" or "cool." The greens and blues on the right of the palette, from yellow to violet, are cool; the reds and oranges on the left of the palette, from violet to yellow, are warm. Yellow and violet are neither warm nor cool. The cool hues probably seem cool from their association with cool subjects in nature: green grass, green trees, blue sky, and blue or green water. The warm hues are associated with warm objects: yellow sun, red coals, and orange fire. The cool colors are for the most part restful and quiet. The warm colors are more exciting, but we tire of them more quickly. The warm colors always seem closer than the cool colors; therefore, they are called *advancing colors,* and the cool colors are called *retreating colors.* If red, green, and blue ircles are placed one beside the other, the red seems closest to the spectator, and the blue farthest away. For this reason warm colors are usually put in those arts of a picture which are nearest the spectator, and the cool colors are eserved for the shadows.

Colors can of course be known only in values. There are light blues, dark lues, medium blues. Any color may be seen at any degree of darkness, from dark that can hardly be distinguished from black to a light that is almost rhite. In some colors, however, a good deal of confusion is produced by the act that certain values have been given special names, and for that reason they re not recognized as being the same. A light red, for instance, is called pink; nd dark yellows and oranges are called brown. Values above medium are nown as *tints;* those below as *shades.*

The last attribute of color is intensity. Colors differ in intensity or vividness. 'wo colors may both be blue, one just as dark as the other, but one may be nore intense than the other. Powder blue is a dulled blue; old rose is a dulled ed. When a hue is found in its most vivid form, it is said to be in full intensity. he same hue dulled is said to be partly neutralized. A hue completely neutral-zed loses its color and becomes a gray.

But though each color has certain very definite properties, it is almost never een alone. A color is changed by the presence of other colors. It reflects and hanges with all the colors around it. It looks dark beside a lighter color and ght beside a darker color. A blue placed beside a violet makes the violet seem ed, and a red placed beside a violet makes the violet seem blue. Delacroix vas merely stating emphatically the influence of colors on each other when he aid that he could paint a face of the mud from the streets if he were allowed ɔ select the colors that were to go around it.

Painting is predominantly the art of color, but color is also important in culpture and architecture. In terra cotta, the surfaces are colored, and houses nade of wood are painted. In the other mediums of sculpture and architecture he color of the material is itself a factor in the appeal of any work—the rich rown of polished wood or bronze, for instance, or the creamy whiteness of vory or marble.

Colors have very definite psychological and emotional connotations. Black of ourse is death, white innocence and purity; blue is the color of heaven and ruth, the color of the Virgin Mary. Red stands for blood and for both love and ate. Yellow represents divinity, the sacredness of revealed truth as in St. Peter. t also stands for degradation, treason, and deceit. Brown signifies spiritual eath, the renunciation of the world, and for this reason it is the color of the 'ranciscan and Capuchin orders. In modern painting color is often used for tself without regard to the natural color of the object painted.

TEXTURE

Texture has to do primarily with the perception of touch. It is the element that appeals to our sense of the feel of things, whether they are rough or smooth, bumpy or slippery. It is the difference we feel between satin and velvet, between linen and silk, between the roughness of tweed and the smoothness of serge, between marble and bronze. Texture is first known by the actual touch of objects. Later it is interpreted by the eye without physical contact, although there is always the sense of contact; it is as though we had run our hands over the marble or the satin even if we have not touched it.

Texture is found in all the visual arts. In many cases, differences in texture are due primarily to differences in medium. We know the different "feel" of brick and concrete, of shingles and smoothly dressed boards, of rough and polished stone, of wood and bronze. We feel the smooth bronze of the Maillol (Figure 112) and the rough skin of the *King of Judah* (Figure 64). In painting the term *texture* is used for the representation of skin, cloth, metal, jewels, furniture, etc. In van Eyck's *The Annunciation* we are very conscious of the heavy silk and the jewels of the angel's dress, the gold and jewels of her crown, the wood of the footstool, the silk of the cushion on the stool, the tiles of the floor, etc.

FIGURE 112. ARISTIDE MAILLOL (1861–1944), French sculptor. *Île d France* (torso) (1910). (Bronze. Height: 43 inches. New York, courtesy Metropolitan Museum of Art; Edith Percy Chapman Fund, 1953; from Museum of Modern Art, gift of A. Conger Goodyear.)

FIGURE 113. JEAN BAPTISTE SIMÉON CHARDIN (1699–1779), French painter. *Bowl of Plums*. (Canvas. Size: 17¾ by 22½ inches. Washington, D.C., courtesy Phillips Collection.)

FIGURE 114. JEAN BAPTISTE SIMÉON CHARDIN. *The Kitchen Maid* (1738). (Oil on canvas. Size: 18⅛ by 14¾ inches. Washington, D.C., National Gallery of Art; Samuel H. Kress Collection.)

STILL LIFE. In the type of picture known as *still life* the representation of texture may be the primary interest. As the name suggests, still life represents inanimate objects such as flowers, fruits, and vegetables. These subjects offer abundant opportunity for the display of texture, and with them are combined other effects, the play of light on china or glass, the gleam of a knife blade, the color of wine, or even the rich glow of freshly baked bread. One of the greatest painters of still life is the Frenchman Chardin. In the *Bowl of Plums* (Figure 113) he shows us the texture of the plums and that of the pitcher. In a painting such as this there is very slight interest in subject; interest is found entirely in color and texture and in their organization in the design. In Chardin's painting *The Kitchen Maid* (Figure 114) we have the interest of still life in the utensils and vegetables that are scattered around while the figure of the maid remains the center of the picture.

FIGURE 115. MICHELANGELO. *Cumaean Sibyl*, detail of Sistine Chapel Ceiling (1508–1512). (Fresco. About life size. Photograph by Alinari.)

VOLUME

Volume is often called solidity. It is that quality of an object which enables us to know that it has thickness as well as length and breadth. As children we lift and punch, pinch and squeeze objects to find if they are solid, but soon we learn to interpret solidity by sight.

If we use only our eyes we perceive volume primarily in two ways. The first is by contour lines, that is, by outlines or shapes of objects. The second is by surface lights and shadows. When we look at Michelangelo's *Cumaean Sibyl* (Figure 115), we see the figure as rounded and solid. In it both ways of judging volume are found. We see the outlines of the face, the shoulder, the headdress, and we notice the subtle shadows in face and dress.

Usually the artist uses all the means at his disposal, and usually he achieves the effect he desires. They are not all necessary, however. The Japanese give the effect of solidity through the use of line alone, as in the Harunobu print. They leave out shadows because they say that shadows are temporary and that only the permanent should be represented in painting. Their work, however, is done so skillfully that one may look at it a long time without realizing that the colors are flat and the shadows are missing. In Rembrandt's *Old Woman Cutting Her Nails* volume is secured almost entirely through shadows.

Since painting is two-dimensional it can only suggest volume. The shadows and contour lines are painted in and do not change. Sculpture is three-dimensional: the outlines and the shadows change with each shift in the position of the person viewing them. And we obtain not one but many different impressions from a single work, as we see in the two views of the Roman portrait (Figures 116 and 117). In José de Rivera's *Construction #I* (Figure 118), or in Maillol's *Île de France*, the photograph shows the work from a single point of view, but we are aware that it would present a different appearance if the camera were moved. The shadows and the contour lines would both be changed. These statues of José de Rivera and Maillol also illustrate the difference in emphasis referred to earlier. The *Construction* depends almost entirely upon linear effect, whereas the surface modeling in the body of the *Île de France* is all-important. These two statues illustrate another point of importance in sculpture. The Maillol not only is three-dimensional but it is also solid. The José de Rivera is not. The former statue seems to comprise the space within the composition as well as the material of which it is made.

FIGURE 116. ROMAN PORTRAIT (first century B.C.). (Marble. About life size. New York, courtesy Metropolitan Museum of Art; Rogers Fund, 1921.)

FIGURE 117. Profile view of Roman portrait, Fig. 116.

FIGURE 118. JOSÉ DE RIVERA (1904–), American sculptor. *Construction #1: Homage to the World of Minikauski* (1955). (Forged stainless steel. Size: 21½ by 19¼ by 15½ inches. New York, Metropolitan Museum of Art. Photograph, courtesy Mr. de Rivera.)

Organization

Architecture like sculpture exists always in three dimensions. A great building, like a great statue, is seen from many points of view. As we walk around it or through it, the appearance changes with each shift in our position, and each view should be pleasing.

PERSPECTIVE

Perspective has to do with our perception of distance, our ability to see the position of objects in space.

The two arts in which space is of great importance are architecture and painting. Architecture is primarily an art of space. The other arts exist in space; architecture uses space as one of its elements. We can see the exterior of a building only as it appears in space. And if we are within a building we see it as enclosing space. One of the great beauties of a building like the Hagia Sophia (Figure 119) or the church of Sant' Apollinare in Classe (Figure 120) comes

FIGURE 119. HAGIA SOPHIA (A.D. 532–537, restored A.D. 558, 975), interior. Anthemius of Tralles and Isidorus of Miletus, architects. (Width of nave: 108 feet; height of central dome: 180 feet. Istanbul. Photograph, Bettmann Archive.)

FIGURE 120. SANT' APOLLINARE IN CLASSE (second quarter of sixth century). Interior looking toward apse. (Marble, mosaic, and plaster; wooden roofing. Length: 150 feet; width: 98 feet. Ravenna. Photograph by Anderson.)

from the sense of majesty one gets when he enters the building and feels the spaciousness of the interior.

Painting does not deal with space directly as does architecture; it can only represent space on a two-dimensional surface.

Sculpture has in itself little to do with the perception of space or of space relations. Even when it shows a large number of people, as in a frieze, they are usually presented in a single long line, with no other spatial relationship.

With perspective as with volume the act of judging has become instinctive, and most of us do not realize that we are making such judgments, nor do we know on what basis we make them. Briefly, there are two major kinds of perspective; that is, there are two kinds of data on which we form opinions or make judgments about distance. These are known as *linear perspective* and *aerial perspective*.

LINEAR PERSPECTIVE. Linear perspective has to do (1) with the direction of lines, and (2) with the size of objects. Everyone has stood in the middle of a road, or on the track of a railroad, and noticed that the lines seem to rise and to meet in the distance. In the same way parallel lines above the eye seem to meet, but

FIGURE 121. TAJ MAHAL (seventeenth century). (Marble. Length: 186 feet; width: 186 feet; height: 187 feet. Temple built by Shah Jehan in memory of his wife. Agra, courtesy Press Information Bureau, Government of India.)

they fall to the level of the eyes. These facts can be easily demonstrated in the photograph of the Taj Mahal (Figure 121). The lines of the pool, the paving, and the trees rise and tend to meet, whereas the tops of the minarets fall as they approach the center. If the camera is placed at one side, not between the parallel lines, the lines tend to meet just as in the examples studied, but at one side. This can be clearly seen in the picture of the aqueduct at Segovia (Figure 167). Curved lines above the level of the eye seem to drop and those below the eye to rise, as we see in the picture of the *Colosseum* (Figure 122).

FIGURE 122. COLOSSEUM (A.D. 72–82), travertine exterior. (Restorations in brick. Length: 620 feet; width: 513 feet; height: 157 feet. Rome. Photograph, courtesy Trans-World Airlines, Inc.)

In painting of course the lines do not vary with the position of the camera; therefore the artist must paint his lines of perspective, as Raphael has done in the *School of Athens* (Figure 123). Here we notice how the lines of the pavement and of the arches converge on the heads of Plato and Aristotle, the two principals in the scene.

SIZE OF OBJECTS. Objects appear smaller as they recede into the distance. This is a necessary corollary of the facts we have been studying about the direction of lines, and it is illustrated in the examples already given. In the photograph of the Taj Mahal, the minarets are of equal height, but those farther away look smaller. In the *School of Athens* the arches are drawn successively smaller. And if we study the picture we find that Raphael has adapted the height of the men to the distance. Measured in inches, the figures of Plato and Aristotle are shorter than those of the men in front.

FIGURE 123. RAPHAEL (Raffaello Sanzio) (1483–1520), Italian painter. *School of Athens* (1509–1511). (Fresco. Figures about life size. Rome, Vatican, Stanza della Segnatura. Photograph by Anderson.)

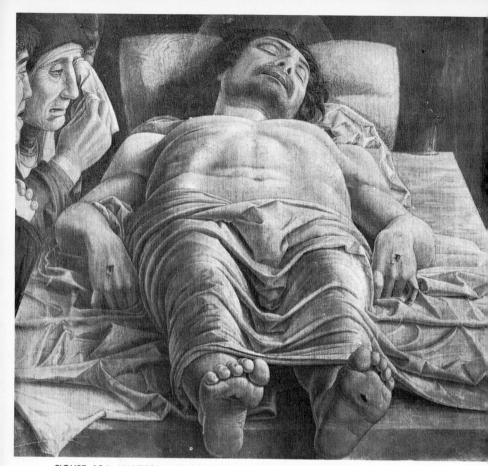

FIGURE 124. MANTEGNA (1431–1506), Italian painter. *Pietà* (1459). (Tempera on canvas. Size: about 32 by 26 inches. Milan, Brera Gallery. Photograph by Anderson.)

FORESHORTENING. This is a term of linear perspective applied primarily to the human figure. An arm held even with the eye and parallel to the line of vision is seen in its entire length. If it is turned slowly, the arm seems to grow shorter until, when it is pointing directly toward one, the arm has disappeared and little more than the end of the fingers can be seen. In Mantegna's *Pietà* (Figure 124) the body of Christ is foreshortened.

Obviously foreshortening is a problem only for the painter. The sculptor makes his figure of normal size. Seen from one point of view an arm appears full-length; from another, it seems foreshortened. The arms of the *Charioteer* are seen in full length if the statue is viewed from the side; if the statue is seen in front the arms are foreshortened. The painter, however, is limited to one point of view and must choose one pose for each figure. Botticelli draws the arms and legs in full length, as though he were trying to avoid the problems of foreshortening. Michelangelo on the other hand likes foreshortened poses for his paintings.

AERIAL PERSPECTIVE. Aerial perspective has to do with changes in appearance due to atmosphere. Objects become lighter in color and hazier in outline as they approach the horizon. In Monet's *Waterloo Bridge* (Figure 125) the buildings on the horizon are so hazy that they can hardly be seen.

Accurate painting of aerial perspective is at its best in landscape painting, and the greatest of landscape painters are the Chinese. With a few blurred outlines they give an impression of a foreground and a background with infinite space in between. A very good example is the landscape scroll of Tung Yuan (Figure 126). In Oriental pictures we find also a diagonal perspective; horizontal and vertical lines appear as diagonals, and a square appears as a diamond.

FIGURE 125. CLAUDE MONET (1840–1926), French painter. *Waterloo Bridge* (1903). (Oil on canvas. Size: 25½ by 36 inches. Worcester, Mass., courtesy Worcester Art Museum.)

FIGURE 126. TUNG YUAN (Sung epoch), Chinese painter. Landscape scroll (late tenth century). (Brush drawing. Size: about 1 foot, 3 inches by 5 feet. Boston, courtesy Museum of Fine Arts.)

FIGURE 127. *KHUSRAU AND HIS COUR-TIERS* (sixteenth-century), Persian minia-ture. King Khusrau seated upon his throne Herat: probably by Mahmud Muzahib or one of his pupils. From MS of Khamsah by Mizami. (Painted. New York, Metro-politan Museum of Art; gift of Alexander Smith Cochran, 1913.)

There is no diminution in size as objects recede in the picture. In the miniature of *Khusrau and his Courtiers* (Figure 127) we see Khusrau near the top of the picture seated on a royal throne which appears as a diagonal. Around him are a group of courtiers. At the bottom of the picture is a similar group. The rugs are shown in full as though they were hanging on the wall, with the courtiers sitting and standing on them.

RENAISSANCE PERSPECTIVE

Perspective as defined in this chapter is primarily an affair of the Renaissance. Artists like Raphael, Perugino, and van Eyck were very careful to make per-spective lines clear and exact. Before that time artists in general did not show realistic perspective. In the paintings of Giotto the buildings and landscapes that form the background for the figures are more nearly symbols than actual presentations. In the *Flight into Egypt* (Figure 128) the mountain and trees are intended only to give the *idea* of mountain and trees.

In more recent years there has been a turning away from exact representation of perspective. There are several reasons. One is the impressionist movement. The impressionists wanted to give the momentary appearance of objects, and the emphasis was on color. "Try to forget what you are seeing," said Monet; "merely think little squares of blue." All parts of a picture were of equal importance, and perspective was minimized or omitted.

Another reason lies in the importance of the camera. Since it can reproduce lines of perspective accurately, there is not much point in doing it in a painting. The ability to draw accurate perspective has therefore become a technique which the artist uses or not as it fits his design. Often an artist will change or falsify exact perspective to bring out more clearly the idea he wants to express. In the first chapter of this book we found Cézanne changing a scene in nature to suit his design. At other times he will tilt a table or change the direction of a

FIGURE 128. GIOTTO. *Flight into Egypt* (ca. 1305). (Fresco. Height of figures: about 3½ feet. Padua, Arena Chapel. Photograph by Alinari.)

wall to give a greater appearance of solidity. Compare one of his still-life pictures (Figure 129) with the one by Chardin (Figure 113). In Chardin we are chiefly conscious of the texture of the objects; in Cézanne the fruit and the table are tilted toward us so that they seem solid.

In the woodcut by Schmidt-Rottluff (Figure 89) the two scenes of the story are juxtaposed, and difference in size is the only indication of a difference in

FIGURE 129. PAUL CÉZANNE. *Still Life with Apples* (ca. 1890–1900). (Oil on canvas. Size: 27 by 36½ inches. New York, Museum of Modern Art; Lillie P. Bliss Collection.)

FIGURE 130. GIORGIO DI CHIRICO (1888–   ), Italian painter and print maker. *Melancholy and Mystery of a Street* (1914). (Oil on canvas. Size: 34⅜ by 28⅛ inches. Collection of Mr. and Mrs. Stanley R. Resor. Photograph, Museum of Modern Art.)

space. In his *Melancholy and Mystery of a Street* (Figure 130) Giorgio di Chirico has changed the perspective lines to give an impression of mystery and melancholy. We see a little girl playing in the street. "At first glance the scene looks solid enough, and yet we feel that the unconcerned little girl with the hoop is endangered by a world that is about to crack along invisible seams or to drift apart in incoherent pieces."[2]

[2] Rudolf Arnheim, *Art and Visual Perception*, p. 242.

10
ELEMENTS OF MUSIC

The elements of music are six: rhythm, melody, harmony, tempo, dynamics, and timbre.

● RHYTHM

Rhythm, the most basic of the elements, is that which gives us a sense of movement. Rhythm pervades all nature; we can sense it in the movement of the tides, in the ordered progression of the seasons, in the beating of a heart. In these instances there is more than repetition; we are conscious of varying degrees of emphasis or accent, which evoke both expectation and tension.

In music, rhythm is the order of movement which gives us the duration of tones and the degree of accent. By tapping out the melody of a song, we become aware of its rhythmic structure.

METER

Meter is a way of measuring rhythm. It is the arrangement of rhythm in a fixed, regular pattern with a uniform number of beats in uniform measures. Meter is confined to the basic underlying pulse; it is always perfectly regular like the ticking of a clock. The pulse of the meter inevitably coincides with rhythmic beats, but the number and placement of beats added to the meter by the rhythm make music so distinctive that we can tell one piece from another merely by hearing the added beats. Here is an example of the rhythm and meter of "Dixie." When the melody is played or sung, we hear the rhythm, whereas we feel the meter.

EXAMPLE 1

There are basically two kinds of meter: *duple,* as in the previous example, in which the accent falls on every other beat (ONE two, ONE two, ONE two, etc.), and *triple,* as in "America," in which the accent falls on every third beat (ONE two three, ONE two three; MY coun—try, 'TIS of thee, SWEET land of, LIB—er—ty). Duple is so named because the beats are felt in groups of two, and triple because the beats are felt in groups of three.

The indication of meter is called the *time signature* and appears at the beginning of every piece of music. The numerator tells us how many basic beats there are in each measure, and the denominator tells the basic duration value of the beat. For example, in $\frac{3}{4}$ meter (triple), which is the time signature for all waltzes, we have three quarter notes or their equivalent for each measure, and in $\frac{4}{4}$ meter (duple), which is the time signature for marches, we have four quarter notes or their equivalent to each measure. Here is a table of duration values and a sampling of time signatures.

EXAMPLE 2

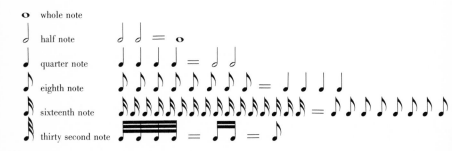

Any note followed by a dot gains half again its value (Example 5, measure 1).

EXAMPLE 3

Time Signatures

When using numerators not divisible by two or three, meter can be felt as a combination of duple and triple. For example, $\frac{5}{4}$ meter can be heard as three plus two or, as the accents indicate in this melody from Tchaikovsky's Symphony No. 6 (the *Pathétique*), two plus three.

EXAMPLE 4

There are also multiplications of triple time called *compound time*. The most used are ⁶⁄₈, ⁹⁄₈, and ¹²⁄₈, and of these three, ⁶⁄₈ is the most widely used. It can be heard as duple or triple, but is considered duple, because the two strong accents in each measure dictate this feeling (ONE two three FOUR five six), the accent falling on beat 4 being weaker than that falling on beat 1.

EXAMPLE 5

Oh! Dear, What Can the Matter Be?

English folk song

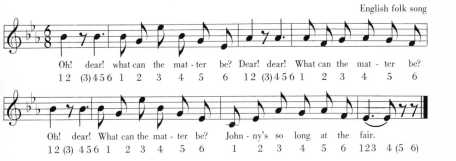

FREE METER

Indefinite or unmeasured meter is the chief characteristic of Gregorian chant, also called *plainsong*. Irregular meter here arises naturally because the vocal melody was written to fit an existing religious text. The plainsong melody was intended to enhance the sound as well as the sense of the words sung, as in Example 6 from the thirteenth century. Notice that the notes of longest duration fall on the word ending a natural phrase.

VARIETY IN RHYTHM

Variety in rhythm is one of the most compelling features of music. There are four ways in which this variety is often shown: (1) by the addition of notes

EXAMPLE 6

Plainsong

Aurelius Clemens Prudentius (348–413)
TR: J. M. Nedle, Henry W. Baker

13th century chant

Of the Fa - ther's love be - got - ten, ere the world be - gan to be

He is al - pha and ·o - me - ga, He the source, the end - ing He,

Of the things that are, that have - - - - - - - been, and that fu - ture years

shall see, Ev - er - 'more and ev - er - more____.

related to what has gone before, (2) by a change in meter, which automatically makes for a change in rhythm, (3) by evolving motives and phrases so that they seem to grow each time they are heard, and (4) by the manipulation of accents so that they become syncopated.

In Haydn's second variation from the second movement of the *Surprise Symphony,* a rhythmic change is made simply by doubling the number of notes heard in the original theme, which gives a hurried, playful feeling.

EXAMPLE 7

original theme

etc.

later statement.

etc.

change in meter, as in this example, produces a rhythmic change.

EXAMPLE 8

Andante Cantabile
from String Quartet in D, Op. 11

Peter Ilich Tchaikovsky
Russian (1840–1893)

and in this example from the second movement of Symphony No. 5 by Beethoven the original melody has been altered by adding other notes and by changing their duration value.

EXAMPLE 9

Perhaps no more famous example of an evolving rhythmic motive could be cited than the following from Beethoven's Symphony No. 5. The opening motive is the heart of the whole first movement. Notice how it has been enlarged upon.

Probably the most distinctive and most used rhythmic variant is *syncopation,* which has to do with the irregular placement of accents. Syncopation is heard in two ways: by having an accent where it is not expected and by not

EXAMPLE 10

having one where it is expected. If we change the accents of "Yankee Doodle," we can easily see the effect of syncopated rhythm.

EXAMPLE 11

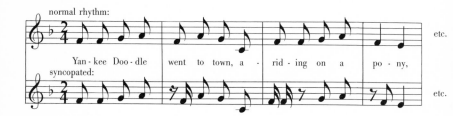

Here is an example of pronounced syncopation in program music.

EXAMPLE 12

Nachtstücke
(Night Visions)
(last four measures)

Robert Schuman
German (1810–1856)

yncopation is one of the obvious features of much twentieth century music in
hich irregular rhythmic motives and phrases result. Much of Stravinsky's
iusic makes a point of changing meter and manipulating accents so that an
most barbarous insistence is put on the shifting rhythms. This is especially
rue in *The Rite of Spring.*

AZZ

specific kind of rhythm is found in jazz, which is African in origin. Jazz is in
uple meter and is characterized by a subtle rhythmic pulsation sometimes
illed swing. Swing is what the performer does with the rhythm, which is a
yncopation so flexible that it cannot be exactly notated.

Jazz then is music which can be studied only by direct listening. It is a per-
rmer's medium. Any sound which can be made by a voice or an instrument
legitimate, and use of counterpoint, variation, ornamentation, and syncopa-
on are up to the performer. This is what gives jazz its special spontaneous
uality.

MELODY

Ielody is any succession of single tones, which by being placed together give a
:nse of pattern and continuity. Melody is heard in terms of duration, and as
itch. Pitch is created by vibrations made by the voice or instrument. Slow
ibrations produce low tones and fast vibrations produce high tones. The higher
le pitch, the more vibrations there are; the lower the pitch, the fewer. We
in think of pitch as having to do with length. A piccolo can play higher
itches than a flute because its tube is shorter. A cello plays lower pitches than
violin because its strings are longer.

Organization

The relationship of one pitch to another is called an *interval,* which is th distance between the two. The first two notes of our National Anthem give th interval of a third; the first two notes of "Reveille" give the interval of a fourt By counting each line and each space of the staff as one, we can discern pattern of intervals visually.

A given piece of music can and often does make use of every kind of inte val, but some pieces are unique because they concentrate on the small, th large, or the scale-wise interval. In Chopin's Prelude in E minor, No. 4, we hav a preoccupation with the small interval. After the initial leap of an eighth, a the intervals shown here are seconds.

EXAMPLE 13

In the following example, the large interval appears in every other measur Notice that the largest interval, the tenth, is the climax of this part of th melody.

EXAMPLE 14

Tales from the Vienna Woods

Johann Strauss J
Austrian (1825–189（

Scale-wise intervals, especially in ascending or descending outlines of a scal are rather common. The hymn "Joy to the World" outlines a descending maj（ scale.

EXAMPLE **15**

the following example, Chopin begins with an ascending major scale, then breaks off with other intervals.

EXAMPLE **16**

When certain patterns of intervals are repeated at a different pitch, we have *sequence.* The sequence embodies melodic and rhythmic repetition. There is sequence in "America" ("Land where our fathers died, land of the Pilgrims' ride"). Here is an example of two sequences following the original interval pattern without pause.

EXAMPLE **17**

Organization

TONALITY

When all the pitches of a melody have been sounded, their total relationsh
establishes a tonality. Tonality is key feeling; there is one central tone call
the *tonic*, toward which all other tones in the melody seem to gravitate. Tonali
is expressed through the use of scale, which is a prescribed pattern giving t
number and relationship of tones. We can think of tonality as a general ide
and of scale as specific facts to sustain the idea. A piece written in D maj
for example, is based upon the major scale and its central tone is the note
Tonal music tends to begin and end with the central tone.

SCALES

There are only a few scales on which most Western music is based. They a
(1) major, (2) minor, (3) pentatonic, (4) chromatic, (5) whole-tone, and (
twelve-tone. Each of these scales is found within the compass of an octave, a
at most only twelve different tones are possible. The chromatic and twelv
tone scales are the only two which make use of all twelve.

The major scale accounts for a vast number of compositions and is famili
to everyone. It is composed of eight tones, the first and last of which are t
tonic. The relationship of intervals for the major scale is as follows:

EXAMPLE 18

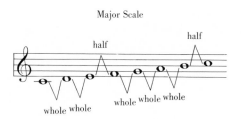

Major Scale

"Joy to the World" and Chopin's Mazurka have been cited to show the outli
of the major scale. Also in this chapter, the Strauss waltz and the second vari
tion of Haydn's *Surprise Symphony* are major.

The minor scale also has eight tones. It too is very widely used. Its interv
pattern is as follows. Again the first and last tones are the tonic.

EXAMPLE 19

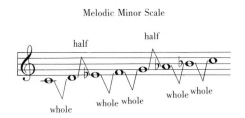

Melodic Minor Scale

examples of the minor scale cited earlier in this chapter are the Chopin Prelude
E minor and the "Agnus Dei" from Bach's B minor Mass. The main difference between major and minor scales is to be found in the third and the sixth
steps of the scale, those in the minor being lowered one half step from their
position in the major. Here is an example by Chopin in which the theme is
quoted in the major and then appears immediately in the minor.

EXAMPLE 20

Valse Brillante

Frédéric Chopin
Polish (1810–1849)

The pentatonic scale is of Oriental origin and very ancient. As its name
implies, it has five tones. Its tone relationships are seen in Example 21.

One of many versions of the ballad "Barbara Allen," is in the pentatonic
scale (Example 22). On the piano keyboard this scale can be played on the five
black keys.

EXAMPLE 21

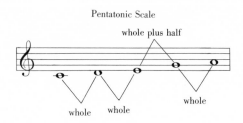

Pentatonic Scale

EXAMPLE 22

Barbara Allen

As she went on the high-way home, She heard the church-bell knell - ing, And

eve - ry stroke it struck her name, "Hard - heart - ed Bar - bara Al - len."

The chromatic scale uses all of the twelve tones, always progressing by h⸤
steps. It is never used as the basis for an entire composition because it seer⸤
to have no real beginning and no real end. Rather, it is used in part to a⸤
interest to music based on other scales, largely the major and minor. Mus⸤
which uses the chromatic scale is harmonically richer because of shifti⸤
tonality.

EXAMPLE 23

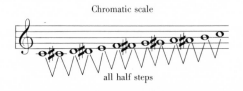

Chromatic scale

all half steps

There are several famous examples of the use of this scale in vocal music:
"My Heart at Thy Sweet Voice" from the opera *Samson and Delilah,* in "To t⸤

vening Star" from *Tannhäuser,* and in the following song from *Carmen.* The
irst two are in the major scale, with chromaticism in the melody; this example
s in the minor.

EXAMPLE 24

Love Will Like a Wild Birdling Fly
(Carmen)

Georges Bizet
French (1838–1875)

Love will like a wild bird-ling fly, Ca - reer - ing whith - er____ he may choose,
L' amour est un oi - seau re- belle Que nul ne peut____ ap - pri - voi - ser,

The whole-tone scale is composed of *seven* tones, each a whole tone from
ts nearest neighbor. It has had rather limited use, and that mostly from the
late nineteenth and early twentieth centuries. This scale has an exotic, rather
noncommittal sound because the feeling of tonality has been weakened.

EXAMPLE 25

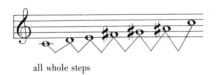

all whole steps

The whole-tone scale, like the chromatic, is used most to enhance melody and
harmony in music based upon other scales. Debussy and Ravel have made
great use of this scale, but within the traditional framework of major or minor
tonalities.

ATONALITY

If the chromatic and whole-tone scales can be considered a breakdown of traditional tonality, then the twelve-tone scale, or twelve-tone row, as it is sometimes called, is the final dissolution of tonality. This scale is an arbitrary place-

ment of the same twelve tones found in the chromatic scale, but the interval relationship is one that avoids any of the traditional tonic feeling.

Arnold Schönberg invented the twelve-tone system in the 1920s. This system forms a basic twelve-tone scale for each composition, but may be presented in different ways. In the Variations for Orchestra, Op. 31, we have the four basic arrangements. First the tone row is presented in its established position, then it is played backward (retrograde), then it is inverted by changing ascending intervals to equivalent descending ones and vice versa. Last we have a retrograde inversion, which plays the intervals of the inversion backward. If each of these four arrangements were used for each of the twelve tones, forty-eight possibilities could be used for each twelve-tone composition.

The tone row, or scale, also forms the basis for the harmony; one chord for example may be made from the first few tones of the row, the next from following ones, etc. Whether in melody or harmony, the use of the twelve tones is often restricted to the order in which they appear in one of the four arrangements of the established position.

In this system there is no tonic, or we might say that every note is the tonic, in which case there is no feeling of gravitation to one key, or even one central tone. For this reason the music is said to be *atonal*.

EXAMPLE 26

Variations for Orchestra
Opus 31

Arnold Schoenberg
Austrian (1874–1951)

(By permission of Mrs. Arnold Schönberg.)

MODES

The modes were the prevalent scales of the Middle Ages. There are seven modes, each corresponding to one of the seven tones of the major scale. The Aeolian mode has become the modern minor scale, and the Ionian mode has become the major scale. The names of the other modes are Dorian, Phrygian, Lydian, Mixolydian, and Locrian.

The use of these modes, excepting the Locrian, was very common in the religious music of the Middle Ages; because of this they are often called the ecclesiastic modes. They survive largely in plainsong and in folk song, as in the following example in the Dorian mode. By playing this example in the key of D major (that is, by putting two sharps in the signature), we may easily hear the difference in the modal quality and in the tonal quality.

EXAMPLE **27**

Henry Martin
(Dorian)

English Folk Song

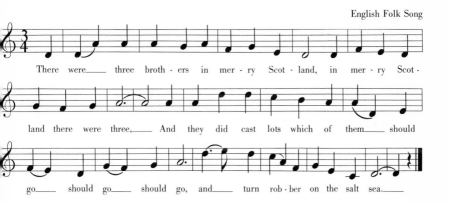

There were___ three broth - ers in mer - ry Scot - land, in mer - ry Scot -
land there were three,___ And they did cast lots which of them___ should
go___ should go___ should go, and___ turn rob - ber on the salt sea.___

COUNTERPOINT

Counterpoint, the earliest kind of harmony, is made by putting together two or more melodies. This is done in two ways. One is shown by playing simultaneously two separate melodies like Dvořák's "Humoresque" and Foster's "Swanee River," or "There's a Long, Long Trail" and "Keep the Home Fires Burning." In the other type of counterpoint a tune makes its own harmony by starting at different times. This is familiar to everyone in rounds. In the round

"White Coral Bells," for instance, the first voice begins with the theme "White coral bells upon a slender stalk," which is two measures in length. As the first voice goes on to measures 3 and 4, "Lilies of the valley in my garden walk," the second voice is singing the first two measures, and so we have the two tunes going at the same time, with one part of the tune accompanying another part.

When one melody is played at the same time as another, it is called the countermelody, since the one is played against (Latin, *counter*, "against") the other; and this kind of writing is called *counterpoint*. (*Point* is an old name for note; hence counterpoint means "point against point," or "note against note.")

EXAMPLE 28

IMITATION AND CANON

When one voice repeats what has just been said by another voice, this is called *imitation*. And when one voice imitates another exactly it is said to be in *canon* (canon means strict rule). A good canon is found in the finale of Franck's Sonata in A major for Violin and Piano (page 199), another in the F major Invention of Bach. All rounds are in canon, each entering voice starting on the same pitch.

Music in canon may be written for any number of voices, usually two, three, or four. The round we were just looking at, "White Coral Bells," is for two

EXAMPLE **29**

Sonata in A major for Violin and Piano
Finale

César Franck
French (1822–1890)

etc.

voices. "White Sands and Gray Sands" is written for three voices, and "Row, Row, Row Your Boat" for four.

TWO SEPARATE MELODIES

The putting together of two separate melodies has long been used in vocal and instrumental music and is found in both serious and popular works. Bach's chorale "Sleepers Wake" from Cantata 140 is an excellent example of the interweaving of two different melodies. Another is the slow movement of Beethoven's Symphony No. 7. The first time the melody is heard, it is alone. The second time it is heard, a new melody has been added to it, just a bit lower in range, which by its chromatic character seems almost to caress the original melody. Finally the two melodies are exchanged, and now the first melody appears beneath, while the melody that was beneath is above.

EXAMPLE 30

Symphony No. 7 in A major
Slow movement

Ludwig van Beethoven
German (1770–1827)

Second appearance.

EXAMPLE 31

EXAMPLE 32

In music since the time of Bach, the tendency has been to put together two melodies that are quite different, as has been done here by Beethoven. In the great period of polyphonic music before Bach, little emphasis is found on the separate melodies as such. Instead, one is conscious only of the way the voices are woven together in a harmonic whole. This can be illustrated in almost any of the polyphonic music of Palestrina, a master of the polyphonic period. A good example is the "Christe eleison" from the Mass *Assumpta est Maria*. In the past fifty years great impetus has been given to counterpoint by the development of jazz, with its emphasis on improvisation, for the jazz player's improvisation is counterpoint on the original theme.

NOTES ABOUT COUNTERPOINT

Not everyone can hear all the melodies that are woven together in polyphonic music, but we can sharpen our ears for polyphony if we listen carefully to the

EXAMPLE **33**

Mass: Assumpta est Maria

Giovanni Pierluigi da Palestrina
Italian (1514 or 1515–1594)

melodies combined, and especially if we notice some of the characteristics which are essential in the making of counterpoint.

CONTRAST IN RHYTHM. The two or more voices contrast in rhythm. In Franck's Sonata for Violin and Piano, one instrument holds a note while the other catches up, as it were. In the Two-part Inventions by Bach there is no waiting of one voice for the other, but when one rests the other tends to move.

CONTRAST IN DIRECTION OF MELODY. Even in a simple round such as "White Coral Bells," when one voice is going up the other is coming down. In "White Sands and Gray Sands" the last two measures have a downward motion, whereas the others are almost horizontal.

CONTRAST IN PITCH. One voice is usually higher than the other. In "Row, Row" the voice gets higher in each of the first three measures. In the Bach Inventions one voice is regularly put in the bass and the other in the treble. In Beethoven's Symphony No. 7 the secondary melody is first lower than the primary and then above it.

● HARMONY

When three or more tones are sounded at the same time, a *chord* is made. The relationship of the tones within the chord, of one chord to another, and the progression of chords, is harmony.

Tonal harmony is based upon tonal scales, such as the major and minor, which divide themselves into certain patterns. The all-important tone is the tonic or basic tone, as has been said before in reference to melody. From the first tone, ascending the scale, the tones are called (1) tonic, (2) supertonic, (3) mediant, (4) subdominant, (5) dominant, (6) submediant, (7) leading tone, and (1) tonic again.

The seventh tone is called a leading tone because it is a half step away from and seems to pull itself or lead toward the conclusive tonic tone. The tonic, dominant, subdominant, and leading tone are the most important tones of the scale, and when chords are based upon them, these chords retain that importance.

The *triad* is the basic kind of chord in tonal music. Its name implies a relationship of three. There are three tones in the triad, and there is an interval of a third between the two lower and two upper tones. In a minor chord, the bottom third is always minor, the top third major. In a major chord, the bottom third is always major, the top minor.

EXAMPLE 34

Triadic chords can be played in three positions, each position having one of the three tones of the triad as its base (CEG, EGC, GCE). The chord remains essentially the same, but its position can weaken or strengthen any musical idea.

EXAMPLE 35

The dominant triad is next in importance to the tonic. It is built on the fifth or dominant tone of the scale. By playing a dominant-tonic progression, we get a sense of stability and completion. This progression is called a *cadence.*

EXAMPLE 36

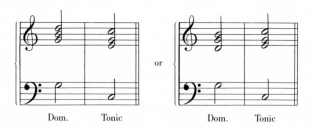

By playing the above examples backward, we get a sense of incompleteness which leads us to expect further chords until we arrive at one which sounds stable and final. This is because the leading tone (B in the above example) is a part of the dominant triad and pulls us toward the tonic.

By using triadic chords built on the tonic, subdominant, and dominant, one can fill in the harmony for almost any simple piece of music, such as hymns or folk songs. Using roman numerals for the chords, here is an example of the use of tonic, subdominant and dominant harmony:

I   IV   I
My Bonnie lies over the ocean,

I   IV   V
My Bonnie lies over the sea,

I   IV or II   I
My Bonnie lies over the ocean,

IV   V   I
Oh bring back my Bonnie to me.

However, diverse chords add a richness to the harmony, and can even make a very dull melody seem beautiful. This is especially true in the Chopin Prelude in E minor (Example 13). In Example 37, which is also by Chopin, notice that the rhythmic pattern is exactly the same in each measure and that the first and last chords in each measure are mostly either tonic or dominant. Between these chords are other kinds which add richness and variety.

CONSONANCE AND DISSONANCE

Consonant harmony is that which we have come to associate with stability, restfulness, accord. Dissonant harmony, however, is thought of as being unstable, and may sound incomplete. It should be pointed out here that dissonance is relative. We tend to think that any fresh combination of tones is dissonant; but this has been so for every generation of music lovers. We have become so used to some nineteenth-century dissonances that we tend to think of them as being rather tame and at times almost consonant.

By adding the interval of a third to any triad, we automatically get a dissonance because the four tones are not in accord with each other, the interval of a seventh (the leading tone) being present. The use of various kinds of seventh chords abounds in music, particularly of the nineteenth century. Example 38 quotes a song beginning on a descending seventh. We do not know the tonality of the music until the end of the second measure when we hear a tonic major chord.

EXAMPLE 37

Prelude No. 20 in C minor

Frédéric Chopin
Polish (1810–1849)

EXAMPLE 38   None But the Lonely Heart

Peter Ilich Tchaikovsky
(1840–1893)

Moving from a dissonance to a consonance, or moving among chords which are sometimes dissonant or consonant, produces variety, suspense, and even tension. This is the crux of harmony. Here is an example of fairly extreme dissonance. The last chord, as we expect, is stable, sounds final, and is therefore consonant.

EXAMPLE 39   Prelude No. 15
(excerpt)

Frédéric Chopin
(1810–1849)

In twentieth-century music our ears have been exposed to more and increasingly dissonant harmonies. In polytonal music (two or more tonalities involved) and in atonal music (no specific tonality) the dissonances are even more pronounced. Here is a polytonal chord from Stravinsky's *Petrouchka* which uses two triads, each belonging to a different key and sounding extremely discordant with the other.

EXAMPLE 40

Petrouchka chord

Other examples of atonal harmony can be found in the works of Schönberg (Example 26), Alban Berg, and Anton von Webern. Here is an atonal chord, the first, from "The Moon Rises" by Ernst Krenek, a short piano piece in the twelve-tone system.

EXAMPLE 41

HEARING HARMONY

Hearing harmonies is primarily a matter of attention. One of the best ways to begin is to listen carefully to a single voice or instrument played with an accompaniment. The solo will sing the melody while the harmonies are heard in the accompaniment. Try to hear what the accompaniment is doing. Sometimes it accompanies the melody step by step; sometimes it anticipates the melody; and sometimes it echoes it. Note what the accompaniment is doing when the solo voice is silent. Does it merely mark the time? Does it repeat the melody? Or does it go off on its own? Note also the direction of the harmony. Does it follow the line of the melody, or does the harmonic line go up when the melodic line goes down?

Are the chords largely consonant, or do you hear dissonances? If there are dissonances, are they resolved? The cry of the Rhine maidens in Wagner's *Rhinegold* is simply a dissonance resolved by a consonance.

EXAMPLE 42

The Rhinegold
(Scene I)

Richard Wagner
German (1813–1883)

How are the chords played? The tones of a chord may be played simultaneously as solid chords, or they may be broken or spread out in *arpeggios*, "harplike figures." The arpeggio always gives a soft, smooth, flowing motion to the music, like that of the harp. In the first movement of Beethoven's *Moonlight Sonata*, the accompaniment is played in arpeggios. The first Prelude in Bach's *Well-tempered Clavier* is in arpeggios.

Ordinarily we listen for the primary melody above the harmony, but it is not always there. In two very popular pieces, Rubenstein's Melody in F and Liszt's "Liebestraum," the melody first appears in the middle of the harmony. In Schumann's "Happy Farmer" the melody is below the harmony, as in Schumann's Romance in F minor. In Chopin's Prelude No. 6 in B minor, the air is entirely below the accompaniment. In his Prelude No. 15 in D-flat major, the music is in three distinct parts: the first and third are calm and peaceful, the second is disturbing. In that section, the melody is below heavy chords, whereas it is above the harmonies in the first and third sections.

Organization

Finally, and in every case, one should try to determine the place of the harmony in the total effect of the composition. Of course, the harmony should fit the melody for which it is designed. A folk song, a hymn, or other simple song, for example, needs a very simple, unpretentious harmony. The beauty is in the tune, and the harmony should not distract from it. In the usual hymn or folk song the accompaniment follows the melody exactly and inconspicuously.

On the other hand, the harmonies can give dignity and grandeur to a melody, as in Chopin's Prelude No. 20 in C minor. The slow movement of Beethoven's *Appassionata Sonata* begins with a theme of the utmost loftiness and grandeur which owes its solemnity to its rich harmonies and to their being placed in the lower register of the piano.

EXAMPLE 43

Sonata Op. 57
Slow movement

Ludwig van Beethoven
German (1770–1827)

● TEMPO

The meter in which a piece of music is written has little to do with the actual speed or *tempo* of the music. Notation for time and rhythm shows the length of each note with reference to the other notes of the piece, but that is all. We can say in general that songs written with half notes as the unit of value are supposed to go more slowly than songs written in quarter notes, and songs written in eighth notes are supposed to go faster, although there is no proof that such is the case.

In general we may say the pace is slow, quick, or moderate, but more commonly we use the traditional Italian terms.

grave   gravely, solemnly, slowly

largo	very slowly and broadly
adagio	very slowly
andante	moderately slowly
andantino	somewhat faster than andante
moderato	at a moderate tempo
allegretto	at a pace between moderato and allegro
allegro	fairly fast
presto	very fast
prestissimo	as fast as possible

These terms are made more exact by the addition of terms that indicate certain qualities of the music.

assai	very
con anima	with life
con moto	with motion
con spirito	with spirit
grazioso	gracefully
maestoso	majestically
dolce	softly or sweetly
con fuoco	with fire
con brio	with vivacity or spirit
molto	much
giusto	in exact tempo
ma non troppo	but not too much
vivace	with vivacity

Generally speaking, the slow tempos mean concentration, reflection, and deep feeling, whereas the quick tempos mean gayety, joy, fun, vigor, excitement. An increasing speed (*accelerando*) means increase in excitement and tension, a decreasing speed (*ritardando*) means loss of life or power; sometimes it shows relaxation and rest, sometimes exhaustion. Sudden tempo changes often show something out of the ordinary.

● DYNAMICS

The word *dynamics* refers to the degree and variations of sonority and force with which music is played, from soft to loud. These gradations of intensity, like the terms for tempo, are traditionally indicated by Italian words, for which there are abbreviations and arbitrary symbols.

pp.	*pianissimo*	as softly as possible
p.	*piano*	softly
mp.	*mezzo piano*	somewhat softly
mf.	*mezzo forte*	somewhat loud
f.	*forte*	loud
ff.	*fortissimo*	as loud as possible
cresc.	*crescendo*	getting louder
decresc.	*decrescendo* ⎫	
dim.	*diminuendo* ⎬	getting softer
sf.	*sforzando*	abruptly loud

● TIMBRE

Tone is produced by musical instruments or by the human voice. Each voice and each instrument has its characteristic quality, called its tone color, or *timbre*. We speak of the timbre of a violin as compared with that of an oboe. Since the timbre of each instrument has been described in the discussion of instruments it will not be repeated here. We should remember, however, that when we have tone, we also have the timbre of the instrument or voice producing the tone.

11
ELEMENTS OF LITERATURE—SENSE

The medium of literature is language, and language, as we know, is composed of words that are combined into sentences to express ideas, emotions, or desires. Words have both sound and meaning. The word *horse,* for instance, stands for the sound *horse* and the animal *horse.* These are usually associated and are separated only by an effort; yet they are distinct. To understand literature we must know both sound and sense. We begin with sense, or meaning.

● MEANING

The first and last rule in knowing literature is that one should know what the words mean. It is always a temptation to guess when one is uncertain, but it is never safe. I remember one time when I was a child seeing the school for retarded children in Frankfort, Kentucky. We called it the "feeble-minded" institute. When I got home I told my mother that there was a big sign in front of the building which said *Eleemosynary Institute.* My mother asked, "Do you know the meaning of eleemosynary?" "Of course," said I, "it means feeble-minded." The word comes from the Latin *eleemosynarius,* "charitable."

Organization

For the student who has studied foreign languages the meaning is often clear without a dictionary, as in the case of *eleemosynary*. This is especially true of Latin because we have taken many of our words from the Latin. Often we have a Latin word and a Germanic (English) word for the same thing, as in the Latin *paternal* and the English *fatherly*, or the Latin *annual* and the English *yearly*. Usually there is a slight difference in meaning, the English being simpler, more explicit, more expressive of the powerful emotions. The prayer which says "almighty and everlasting God" is more powerful than the one which uses the Latin derivatives "omnipotent and eternal God."

The ending of Ernest Hemingway's *A Farewell to Arms* is an example of the simplicity of short native words. There are only three words not of native origin: *statue, hospital,* and *hotel.* The hero's sweetheart has died, and he has driven everyone from the room.

> But after I had got them out and shut the door and turned off the light it wasn't any good. It was like saying good-by to a statue. After a while I went out and left the hospital and walked back to the hotel in the rain.
>
> —ERNEST HEMINGWAY (1899–1961, American novelist), *A Farewell to Arms* (1929)

Some words we do not know, because they are archaic. We do not use them now, or not in the same sense. In the ballad "Sir Patrick Spence" "an *eldern knight*" is an elderly knight, and "a braid letter" is a large letter, one which contains official directions. Hopkins begins his poem "Pied Beauty" as follows:

> Glory be to God for dappled things—
>> For skies of couple-color as a brinded cow . . .
>>> —GERARD MANLEY HOPKINS (1844–1889, British poet),
>>> "Pied Beauty" (between 1876 and 1889)

but we want to be sure we know the meaning of *pied, dappled,* and *brinded.* Some words savor of great learning, as we see in this quotation from Milton.

> Methinks I see in my mind a noble and *puissant* nation rousing herself like a strong man after sleep, and shaking her *invincible* locks; methinks I see her as an eagle *mewing* her mighty youth, and *kindling* her *undazzled* eyes at the full *midday beam; purging* and *unscaling* her *long-abused* sight at the fountain itself of heavenly radiance; while the whole noise of timorous and flocking birds, with those also that love the twilight, flutter about, amazed at what she means, and in their *envious gabble* would *prognosticate* a year of *sects* and *schisms.*
>
> —JOHN MILTON (1608–1674, British poet and essayist), *Areopagitica*, Speech for the Liberty of Unlicensed Printing (1644)

TECHNICAL TERMS. Technical terms belong to the general class of learned words but are distinguished as being the language of a particular profession, business, or trade. Often technical words get into the ordinary language; examples are *tuberculosis, static, carburetor, ignition, wave length.* A great part of this book is devoted to the technical language of the arts. In each art some of the terms have become general knowledge, whereas others have remained terms for the specialist. In architecture, for instance, *cornice, pediment, column,* and *frieze* are universally known, whereas *architrave, entablature, basilica,* and *clerestory* belong to the specialist.

IDIOM. Idiom is the particular expression of a language, as, for instance, *wait for* as against *wait on; need of* as against *need for.* We do not notice an idiom if it is correctly used. Dryden uses an idiom that is now obsolete when he says "those who accuse him to have wanted learning."

DIALECT, PROVINCIALISMS. A dialect is the language of a certain part of a country, as, for instance, the Scottish dialect or the Irish dialect. A provincialism is a word or phrase peculiar to a province or a small section of a country as, for instance, the use of *clever* for *good-natured.*

NEW WORDS. Some words we are conscious of as new: *burglarized, extradited, educationist, tycoon.* Some of these get into the permanent language.

New meanings are constantly being given words, or as we say, the meanings change. Some of these changes have come about very gradually and naturally through a long period of time. The word *treacle,* which now means molasses, comes originally from the Greek θηριον, which means *wild beast.* This change in meaning, though startling at first, has come about very naturally; the word was first used for anything that had to do with a wild animal; then it came to mean the medicine that was good for the bite of a wild animal, and, since that medicine was usually sweet and sticky, it came to mean any such sweet and sticky substance; hence, molasses. In the same way the word *hound,* which originally meant any kind of dog, as it does today in German, came to mean only a certain type.

Modern writers often put two or more words together, as *toycolored, mudguard, posycolored, fatbellied.*

Often one word has several different meanings. A class of students knew only that the word *bar* in Tennyson's "Crossing the Bar" meant some kind of a barrier. One said he knew it was not a saloon bar but it was something like that. Hence Tennyson's lines "And may there be no moaning of the bar When I put out to sea" were meaningless.

Another such word is *macaroni.* In the eighteenth century a macaroni was a dandy, a man who got himself dressed in the very latest fashion. And so it makes sense when we sing of Yankee Doodle that he "stuck a feather in his cap/And called it macaroni."

And we find a similar case when the same thing is called by one name in Great Britain and a different one in the U.S.A. Thus an elevator in England becomes a *lift;* gasoline is *petrol.*

ALLUSIONS. With the words we have been studying, the dictionary is a safe recourse. Even if a single word is used in several different senses, each use is recorded in the dictionary. There is no such speedy help in the case of allusions. An allusion is a reference to some place, person, event, or quotation supposed to be familiar to everyone. In Cummings' "in Just-spring" the old balloon man is said to be *goat-footed.* When we see that, we know that he is a *satyr,* and we connect him with the woods and the joyousness of spring.

In Milton's sonnet "On His Blindness" we have already called attention to the fact that in the beginning of the poem Milton is referring to the parable of the talents in Matthew 25. We did not note the allusion a bit further on when Milton has Patience say:

> "God doth not need
> Either man's work or his own gifts. Who best
> Bear his mild yoke, they serve him best. His state
> Is kingly: thousands at his bidding speed,
> And post o'er land and ocean without rest;
> They also serve who only stand and wait."
>
> —JOHN MILTON,
>   "On His Blindness" (ca. 1655)

This is a clear reference to the saying of Jesus, "For my yoke is easy and my burden is light."

Wordsworth is using Greek mythology when he wishes to

> Have sight of Proteus rising from the sea,
> Or hear old Triton blow his wreathèd horn.
>
> —WILLIAM WORDSWORTH (1770–1850, British poet),
>   "The World Is Too Much with Us" (1807)

CONNOTATIONS. The connotations of a word are the allied meanings or associated ideas that are called to mind when the word is used. The word *father,* for instance, has always had the same meaning, the male parent; its connotations are love, kindliness, protection, greater experience, guidance, wisdom. Not all male parents show these qualities; some fathers are cruel, unkind, foolish; but if one wants to make it clear that a father is of this class he must state the fact clearly and definitely, for the connotations of the word make one suppose just the opposite. The word *spinster* originally meant a person who spins; now it means an unmarried woman and has the same connotations as *old maid*— precise and tidy, fidgety and nervous. The cowboy herds cattle, but the word *cowboy* connotes youth, bravery, adventure, romance, whereas *cattle herder* is merely a person who herds cattle. Oxford is much more than a town or university; it connotes culture, leisure, the gentleman, the future statesman of the British Empire.

Chaucer, in describing the Pardoner, says he "had hair as yellow as wax, but smooth it hung as does a hank of flax." The comparisons leave the impression that his hair was also dirty, full of foreign particles as wax and flax are apt to be, and uncombed, matted together like the threads of flax. When Chaucer says that the Miller had, on the very tip end of his nose, "a wart, and thereon stood a tuft of hairs, red as the bristles of a sow's ears," we know more than the color of those hairs. On the other hand, almost the only good thing Chaucer has to say of the Friar is that "his eyes twinkled in his head aright, as do the stars in the frosty night." That comparison somehow restores a little bit of confidence in the man. It gives him a place in the great out-of-doors, and helps us to understand the confidence people had in him in spite of his worldliness.

These connotations of words frequently cause a poet trouble. In "The Miller's Daughter" Tennyson is describing the boy's first sight of the girl he is to marry. He is looking idly in the millstream when his attention is attracted by something, and he sees the reflection of the miller's daughter in the stream. As first written the lines read:

> A water-rat from off the bank
> Plunged in the stream. With idle care,
> Downlooking through the sedges rank,
> I saw your troubled image there.

But the associations of the water-rat do not harmonize with our thoughts of love and youth and beauty; therefore, Tennyson changed the water-rat to a trout:

> Then leapt a trout. In lazy mood
>   I watch'd the little circles die;
> They past into the level flood,
>   And there a vision caught my eye.

> —ALFRED, LORD TENNYSON (1809–1892, British poet and novelist),
>   "The Miller's Daughter" (1833, 1842)

For the same reason people have objected to the hair of the Blessed Damozel, which was "yellow like ripe corn"; they do not like to think of corn in connection with heaven. Longfellow might better have changed his figure when he says in "The Wreck of the Hesperus":

> Colder and louder blew the wind,
> A gale from the Northeast,
> The snow fell hissing in the brine,
> And the billows frothed like yeast.
>
> —HENRY WADSWORTH LONGFELLOW (1807–1883, American poet),
> "The Wreck of the Hesperus" (1839)

The associations which most people have with yeast call to mind an image of a cup of yeast bubbling placidly on the back of a kitchen stove. Even if one imagines all the yeast in all the bakeries in the world, he still thinks of yeast as a quiet, man-made and man-controlled thing. He does not easily or naturally imagine yeast as going on a rampage and destroying human life. So, when Longfellow says the "billows frothed like yeast," the effect is almost as ludicrous as when Chaucer says many wild beasts were in the forests, even rabbits!

● IMAGERY

> St. Agnes' Eve—Ah, bitter chill it was!
> The owl, for all his feathers, was a-cold;
> The hare limp'd trembling through the frozen grass,
> And silent was the flock in woolly fold:
> Numb were the Beadsman's fingers, while he told
> His rosary, and while his frosted breath,
> Like pious incense from a censer old,
> Seem'd taking flight for heaven, without a death,
> Past the sweet Virgin's picture, while his prayer he saith.
>
> —JOHN KEATS (1795–1821, English poet),
> "The Eve of St. Agnes" (1820)

From this stanza we get a much clearer sense of cold than if we were told the thermometer registered ten below zero. The difference is that Keats has made us conscious of the ways we are conscious of the cold: the owl hunched down in his feathers, the hare limping through the grass, the beadsman's numb fingers, the frosted breath, even the silence of the sheep. To some people these are almost like a real experience, and for everyone they have a certain vividness as they call to mind the sensations described. Sense impressions of this kind are called *images*. *Imagery* is the general name for the functioning of the imagination in the production of images. Or we may say an image is the mental duplication of a sense impression. The most common kind of imagery is visual: we *see* what the author is talking about.

Gerard Manley Hopkins' short poem "Pied Beauty" is just a riot of images of all speckled things:

Glory be to God for dappled things—
    For skies of couple-colour as a brinded cow;
      For rose-moles all in stipple upon trout that swim;
Fresh-firecoal chestnut-falls; finches' wings;
    Landscape plotted and pieced—fold, fallow, and plough;
      And all trades, their gear and tackle and trim.

All things counter, original, spare, strange;
    Whatever is fickle, freckled (who knows how?)
      With swift, slow; sweet, sour; adazzle, dim;
He fathers-forth whose beauty is past change:
          Praise him.
    —GERARD MANLEY HOPKINS (1844–1889, British poet),
      "Pied Beauty" (between 1876 and 1889)[1]

But imagery is not all visual. The other senses may also be duplicated. In the last stanza of Walt Whitman's poem "To a Locomotive in Winter," as in the poem by Emily Dickinson on the same subject, we have vivid auditory and motor images in addition to the visual.

Fierce-throated beauty!
Roll through my chant with all thy lawless music, thy swinging lamps at night,
Thy madly-whistled laughter, echoing, rumbling like an earthquake, rousing all,
Law of thyself complete, thine own track firmly holding,
(No sweetness debonair of tearful harp or glib piano thine,)
Thy trills of shrieks by rocks and hills return'd,
Launch'd o'er the prairies wide, across the lakes,
To the free skies unpent and glad and strong.
    —WALT WHITMAN (1819–1892, American poet),
      "To a Locomotive in Winter" (1876)

[1]From *Poems of Gerard Manley Hopkins*, Third Edition, edited by W. H. Gardner, Copyright 1948 by Oxford University Press, Inc. Reprinted by permission.

Shakespeare's little song from *Love's Labour's Lost* is outstanding for its
clear auditory images as well as images of sight: the shepherd *blows* his nail,
the owl sings *"tu-whit; tu-who,"* Joan *keels* ("stirs") *the pot, coughing drowns*
the parson's sermon, and the roasted crab apples *hiss* in the bowl.

Motor images are important, giving as they do the sensation of motion. The
Psalmist emphasizes the dignity and the majesty of the Eternal when he says:

> Lift up your heads, O ye gates; and be ye lift up, ye ever-
> lasting doors; and the King of glory shall come in.
> > —Psalm 24:7

In "The Eagle" Tennyson gives a clear motor image of the bird's sudden
drop, and the fall is emphasized a hundredfold by the vivid pictures of the
height from which he falls:

> He clasps the crag with crooked hands;
> Close to the sun in lonely lands,
> Ring'd with the azure world, he stands.
>
> The wrinkled sea beneath him crawls;
> He watches from his mountain walls,
> And like a thunderbolt he falls.
> > —TENNYSON,
> > "The Eagle" (1851)

Keats is a poet who is outstanding for both the wealth and the vividness of
his imagery. He has images even of such sensations as touch, taste, smell, and
thermal impressions, not usually counted of first importance. In "The Eve of
St. Agnes" the lover spreads before his sleeping lady a table on which are
heaped all sorts of delicacies. The scene is made vivid by the touch of the smooth
linen and the creamy cheese, the taste of the candied apple and the syrups
flavored with cinnamon, and all are made romantic by the fact that they have
been brought from a distance, "From silken Samarcand to cedared Lebanon."

> And still she slept an azure-lidded sleep;
> In blanched linen, smooth, and lavendered,
> While he from forth the closet brought a heap
> Of candied apple, quince, and plum, and gourd;
> With jellies soother than the creamy curd,

And lucent syrops, tinct with cinnamon;
Manna and dates, in argosy transferr'd
From Fez; and spiced dainties, every one.
From silken Samarcand to cedared Lebanon.

    —KEATS,
       "The Eve of St. Agnes" (1820)

In his "Ode to a Nightingale" Keats wants to get away from the world

. . . where men sit and hear each other groan
    Where palsy shakes a few sad, last, grey hairs, . . .

and he imagines himself in a garden at night; he cannot see the flowers, but he knows they are there by the smells which are much stronger than in the day.

I cannot see what flowers are at my feet,
    Nor what soft incense hangs upon the boughs,
But, in embalmed darkness, guess each sweet
    Wherewith the seasonable month endows
The grass, the thicket, and the fruit-tree wild;
White hawthorn, and the pastoral eglantine;
    Fast-fading violets cover'd up in leaves;
      And mid-May's eldest child,
The coming musk-rose, full of dewy wine,
    The murmurous haunt of flies on summer eves.

    —KEATS,
       "Ode to a Nightingale" (1819)

In fact any sensation can be brought clearly before the mind in imagery. The most common images are listed below in the order of their frequency.

Kinds of Images

1. Images of sight—visual
2. Images of hearing—auditory
3. Images of motion—motor, or kinesthetic
4. Images of touch—tactile
5. Images of heat and cold—thermal
6. Images of taste—gustatory
7. Images of smell—olfactory

● FIGURES OF SPEECH

Words, being symbols, have no meaning in themselves; their only meaning is what is given them by convention. Moreover, a symbol can never be specific; it is always abstract or general. We call words abstract or concrete as they signify abstractions or concrete objects; we say *truth* and *honor* are abstract, *dog* and *lilac* are concrete. But these concrete words are themselves abstractions in that they stand for a whole class of objects. The dog may be any one of a large number of species, of any known color. And when we say *lilac,* we may mean any variety of lilac, in any color, or any one of the other sensations concerned with lilac: its fragrance, the shape of the flower or the leaf, the bush on which the flower grows.

This abstractness of words becomes very clear if it is compared with the necessary concreteness of the other art mediums. Obviously a sculptor cannot carve the abstraction *dog;* he must carve a dog of certain species, age, and size. The painter cannot paint *lilac;* he must paint a white lilac or a purple lilac, a plant in full blossom, beginning to fade, in bud, or without blossoms. He cannot paint what we mean by *lilac,* for that is essentially an abstraction. In the same way, the actor or the musician can make only concrete tones, but in describing his tones the poet can use only abstractions; the poet will speak of "clear, ringing tones," but the actor or the musician must make certain definite tones, just as the sculptor must carve a certain kind of dog or the painter portray a certain species of lilac.

Because of this indefiniteness of words there have grown up certain deviations, or roundabout methods of expression, that attempt to make more clear the exact meaning. If, for instance, Coleridge says the ice is green, he leaves it to us to imagine the shade of green; but he gives the exact shade when he says:

> And ice, mast-high, came floating by,
> As green as emerald.
>
> —SAMUEL TAYLOR COLERIDGE (1772–1834, British poet), *The Rime of the Ancient Mariner* (1798)

He can make us realize more clearly the color of hair, the feeling of fear, and the sound of the departing souls by stating his point indirectly:

> Her lips were red, her looks were free,
> Her locks were yellow as gold:
> Her skin was as white as leprosy,
> The Nightmare Life-in-Death was she,
> Who thicks man's blood with cold.

Fear at my heart, as at a cup,
My life-blood seemed to sip!

The souls did from their bodies fly,—
They fled to bliss or woe!
And every soul, it passed me by,
Like the whizz of my cross-bow!

    —The Ancient Mariner

Such indirect methods of expression are called figures of speech.

SIMILE AND METAPHOR. The most common and therefore the most important of the figures of speech are the simile and the metaphor. Both depend upon the comparison of one thing to another. The simile puts in the word of comparison; the metaphor leaves it out. The simile says: *The ice was as green as emerald;* the metaphor says: *The ice was emerald.* The simile says: *Fear was like a monster which sipped my blood;* the metaphor says: *Fear sipped my blood.* The simile would say: *Thou, Peter, art like a rock;* the metaphor says: *Thou art Peter, and upon this rock I will build my church* (Matthew 16:18).

The simile says:

And he shall be like a Tree planted by the streams of water,
That bringeth forth its fruit in its season,
Whose leaf also doth not wither;
And whatsoever he doeth shall prosper.
The wicked are not so;
But are like the Chaff which the wind driveth away.

    —Psalm 1

The metaphor says:

The Lord is my shepherd;
I shall not want.
He maketh me to lie down in green pastures:
He leadeth me beside the still waters.
He restoreth my soul:
He leadeth me in the paths of righteousness for his name's sake.

    —Psalm 23

Keats uses metaphor in the first eight lines of his sonnet "On First Looking into Chapman's Homer" when he identifies poetry with rich kingdoms. In the last six lines he uses two similes as he tries to tell how he felt when he read

Chapman's translation of Homer: first he felt like an astronomer who discovered a new planet, and second he felt like Cortez when he discovered the Pacific.[2]

> Much have I travell'd in the realms of gold,
> And many goodly states and kingdoms seen;
> Round many western islands have I been
> Which bards in fealty to Apollo hold.
> Oft of one wide expanse had I been told
> That deep-brow'd Homer ruled as his demesne;
> Yet did I never breathe its pure serene
> Till I heard Chapman speak out loud and bold:
> Then felt I like some watcher of the skies
> When a new planet swims into his ken;
> Or like stout Cortez when with eagle eyes
> He stared at the Pacific—and all his men
> Look'd at each other with a wild surmise—
> Silent, upon a peak in Darien.
>
> —KEATS,
>   "On First Looking into Chapman's Homer" (1816)

Many of our most common expressions involve similes or metaphors. We say one person has a "heart of gold" and another is as "slow as molasses in January." Both simile and metaphor are used very commonly by all people at all times. It is hard to find a paragraph of prose or verse that does not contain either a simile or a metaphor. From the nature of the two, the metaphor is used most often in short, vigorous passages, whereas the simile may be expanded to any length.

Both simile and metaphor are based on comparison. In each, comparison is made of one thing to something essentially unlike it for the purpose of showing one point of resemblance. The power of either figure of speech rises of course from the implications and suggestions of the comparison. In "A Song for Simeon" T. S. Eliot has a simile about an old man's life:

> My life is light, waiting for the death wind,
> Like a feather on the back of my hand.[3]

---

[2] A well-known mistake. It was, of course, Balboa, not Cortez, who was the first European to look upon the Pacific Ocean.

[3] From *Collected Poems*, 1909–1962, by T. S. Eliot, copyright, 1936, by Harcourt, Brace and World, Inc.; copyright © 1963, 1964, by T. S. Eliot. Reprinted by permission of the publishers.

By his comparison, Eliot emphasizes the everyday character of the scene, the sense of the nearness of death in everyday life. Another time Eliot compares an evening to a patient on an operating table.

> Let us go then, you and I,
> When the evening is spread out against the sky
> Like a patient etherized upon a table.
>
> —T. S. ELIOT (1888–1965, American poet),
> "The Love Song of J. Alfred Prufrock" (1917)[4]

OTHER FIGURES OF SPEECH. Next to simile and metaphor, synecdoche and metonymy are the most important figures of speech. Synecdoche is a figure in which a part is used for the whole or the whole is used for a part. Metonymy is a figure in which one word is used for another that it suggests. These two figures are very much alike, and often the terms are used interchangeably, though they may always be distinguished. We use synecdoche when we speak of a *fleet of ten sail* instead of a *fleet of ten ships*, or when we say this will *bring my gray hairs in sorrow to the grave*, where a part is used for the whole. The whole is used for the part in expressions such as *Missouri won* when we mean that the football team from the University of Missouri won. Metonymy is used in such phrases as the *crown*, *Shakespeare*, the *bar*, for the man who wears the crown, the works of Shakespeare, and the legal profession.

There are several other ways of writing classed among the figures of speech: personification, apostrophe or address, hyperbole or exaggeration, litotes or understatement, antithesis or statement of contrasts, and irony. Irony is found in an expression which says one thing but really means its opposite, as when a person announces that he has bad news when in reality he has good news. There have been distinguished three different types of irony: irony of statement, irony of situation, and dramatic irony. In irony of statement we have a situation like that one given above of good or bad news. A famous example is found in Job's cry to his so-called comforters: "No doubt but ye are the people, and wisdom shall die with you." Or like Antony in Shakespeare's *Julius Caesar:*

> Brutus is an honorable man;
> So are they all, all honorable men.

Swift is one of the greatest writers of irony. In the essay which he called "A Modest Proposal for Preventing the Children of Poor People from Being a

---

[4]*Ibid.*

Burden to Their Parents," he suggests that the babies of the Irish should b
fattened and sold for meat.

Irony of situation, as the name indicates, makes a contrast between the situa
tion as it is thought to be and as it is. Edwin Arlington Robinson's "Richarc
Cory" makes a contrast between the real situation and the one supposed.

> Whenever Richard Cory went down town,
> We people on the pavement looked at him;
> He was a gentleman from sole to crown,
> Clean favored, and imperially slim.
>
> And he was always quietly arrayed,
> And he was always human when he talked;
> But still he fluttered pulses when he said,
> "Good morning," and he glittered when he walked.
>
> And he was rich—yes, richer than a king—
> And admirably schooled in every grace:
> In fine, we thought that he was everything
> To make us wish that we were in his place.
>
> So on we worked, and waited for the light,
> And went without the meat, and cursed the bread;
> And Richard Cory, one calm summer night,
> Went home and put a bullet through his head.
>
> —EDWIN ARLINGTON ROBINSON (1869–1935, American poet),
>   "Richard Cory"[5]

Dramatic irony is found when the members of the audience have knowledg
not held by the characters on the stage. A characteristic example is found ir
Romeo and Juliet when Romeo tells of his happy dream and assurance that al
will be well.

● GRAMMAR

Knowing a language is not just a matter of knowing words. To get the sense o
a passage we must know how the words fit together as well as the meaning o
each word. The rules which state how words fit together make up grammar

[5]From *The Children of The Night* by Edwin Arlington Robinson. (Charles Scribner's Sons, 1897).

hich is a statement of the accepted sense relationships of words. Each lan-
uage has its own method of expression, its own way of putting words together
) make sense, in short, its own grammar.

Those of us who have always spoken English have no difficulty with the
sual simple arrangements of words. But often an author cannot express his
lea clearly if he uses only the usual, simple arrangements, and so he distorts.
he opening lines of *Paradise Lost* are not easy reading, but through them
lilton has made us realize the magnitude of the task he has set himself, and
1e exalted mood in which he is beginning it.

Of Man's first disobedience, and the fruit
Of that forbidden tree whose mortal taste
Brought death into the World, and all our woe,
With loss of Eden, till one greater Man
Restore us, and regain the blissful Seat,
Sing, Heavenly Muse, that, on the secret top
Of Oreb, or of Sinai, didst inspire
That shepherd who first taught the chosen seed
In the beginning how the heavens and earth
Rose out of Chaos: or, if Sion hill
Delight thee more, and Siloa's brook that flowed
Fast by the oracle of God, I thence
Invoke thy aid to my adventurous song,
That with no middle flight intends to soar
Above the Aonian mount, while it pursues
Things unattempted yet in prose or rhyme.

    —MILTON, *Paradise Lost*, I, 1–16 (1667)

In this and in most older writings the relations between words are always in
ccordance with the established rules of grammar, though it may be hard to
et the sense because of the way words and phrases are piled on each other. In
ome more recent poetry the authors do not write in complete sentences; they
et emphasis by a reference here and an exclamation there, and leave us to put
hem together, as E. E. Cummings does in "here's a little mouse."

here's a little mouse) and
what does he think about, i
wonder as over this
floor (quietly with

bright eyes) drifts (nobody
can tell because
Nobody knows, or why
jerks Here &, here,
gr (oo) ving the room's Silence) this like
a littlest
poem a
(with wee ears and see?

tail frisks)
    (gonE)
''mouse'',
          We are not the same you and

i, since here's a little he
or is
it It
?   (or was something we saw in the mirror)?

therefore we'll kiss; for maybe
what was Disappeared
into ourselves
who   (look).   , startled
      —E. E. CUMMINGS (1894–1962, American poet),
        ''here's a little mouse'' (1926)[6]

In all this discussion of words and grammar there are several points
importance. The first is that it is essential to know the meanings of words an
to understand their relationships. It is not necessary to know the grammatic
name for any relationship. It is only a matter of convenience that we say *Joh*
is the subject and *Henry* is the object when we say *John struck Henry*; but
does matter that we know who got hit! And it does matter that when we sin
that Yankee Doodle called himself a macaroni we do not think of a dish
wheat paste and cheese.

The second point is that when an author varies from the simplest form
words and of sentence structure, he does so for a purpose. The change fro
normal word order in literature is exactly the same as distortion in the visu
arts. The artist does not fail to write simply or to draw realistically because h

[6]From *Poems 1923–1954*, Harcourt, Brace and World, Inc.; Copyright 1923, 1926, 1944, 1951, 1954
E. E. Cummings.

oes not know how, but because he can express what he has to say better in
ae form that is not entirely natural and simple. And our question here is just
ae same as it was in the case of distortions: Why did he do it this way? In the
pening lines of *Paradise Lost* the effect is like that of an organ that begins
uietly and gathers momentum until it finally bursts out into full diapason
ith the rolling "Sing, Heavenly Muse!" And when Keats says "some watcher
f the sky" instead of the more commonplace *astronomer,* he makes us think
f the long, lonely hours the man spends gazing at the stars before his faith is
ewarded and he sees a planet "swim into his ken."

12

ELEMENTS OF
LITERATURE—SOUND

● ELEMENTS OF SOUND

The sound of words is important in making the total sense, for no two word
no two sounds ever have exactly the same meaning. In *The Two Gentlemen*
Verona the host sings a little song that begins:

> Who is Silvia? What is she,
>   That all our swains commend her?
> Holy, fair, and wise is she;
>   The heaven such grace did lend her,
> That she might admired be.
>
>   —WILLIAM SHAKESPEARE (1564–1616, British poet and dramatist), *The Two Gentlem*
>   *of Verona*, IV, ii, 39–43 (ca. 1592)

Here the name *Silvia* means as little as a word could mean; it is a woman
name, and nothing more. But change the name *Silvia* to almost any oth
woman's name—*Alice, Peggy, Margaret, Louise, Phoebe, Laura, Hortense*-
the effect is spoiled; the charm is gone. Or take a single line from Milton:

And I shall shortly be with them that rest.

—JOHN MILTON (1608–1674, British poet and essayist), *Samson Agonistes*, line 598 (1671)

change the sound, keeping as nearly as possible the same sense. *Shortly* means soon; *them* has the same meaning as *those*; and *that* as *who*; in fact, *those who* a more common English idiom than *them that*. Make the substitutions, and the line reads:

And I shall soon be with those who rest.

There is no appreciable difference in sense, but the line is no longer poetry.

It is important, therefore, to know what are the effects that are derived primarily from the sound of words. There are three phases under which we can study the uses of sound in literature.

The sound of letters and words: tone color
The sequence of sounds in a free pattern of accents: rhythm
The sequence of sounds in a fixed pattern of accents: meter

TONE COLOR—DEFINITION

The term *tone color* in literature is borrowed from music because the writer gets effects somewhat comparable to those of different instruments by the sounds of the words or letters he uses. Compare Blake's "Introduction" to *Songs of Innocence* with the opening lines of Vachel Lindsay's "The Congo" for contrast in tone color. The first seems to have the timbre of a high-pitched, sensitive, delicate instrument, such as the flute; this matches the spirit of the piece. The second has the sound of a deep, heavy instrument like a drum or a tuba which can make a great deal of noise but is not precise; the sound alone reminds me of the untutored rhythms of savage men.

Piping down the valleys wild,
　Piping songs of pleasant glee,
On a cloud I saw a child,
　And he laughing said to me:

"Pipe a song about a Lamb!"
　So I piped with merry cheer.
"Piper, pipe that song again;"
　So I piped; he wept to hear.

"Drop thy pipe, thy happy pipe;
    Sing thy songs of happy cheer!"
So I sung the same again,
    While he wept with joy to hear.

"Piper, sit thee down and write
    In a book, that all may read."
So he vanished from my sight,
    And I plucked a hollow reed,

And I made a rural pen,
    And I stained the water clear,
And I wrote my happy songs
    Every child may joy to hear.

—WILLIAM BLAKE (1757–1827, British poet, painter, and engraver),
    "Introduction" to *Songs of Innocence* (1787)

Fat black bucks in a wine-barrel room,
Barrel-house kings, with feet unstable,
Sagged and reeled and pounded on the table,
Pounded on the table,
Beat an empty barrel with the handle of a broom,
Hard as they were able,
Boom, boom, BOOM,
With a silk umbrella and the handle of a broom,
Boomlay, boomlay, boomlay, BOOM.

—VACHEL LINDSAY (1879–1931, American poet),
    "The Congo," opening lines (1914). By permission of The Macmillan Compan
    publishers.

Differences in tone color depend on differences in the sound of letters. Th
consonants and vowels may be grouped as follows:

Consonants: Stops: *p-b; t-d; k-g*
Fricatives: *f-v; s-z; sh-zh; ch-j; wh-w; y* (consonant); *h; th* (thin)–*t*
(their)
Nasals: *m; n; ng*
Liquids: *l; r*

Vowels: Front: *ē* (scene); *ĭ* (begin); *ā* (ate); *â* (rare); *ĕ* (edge); *ă* (cat); *ä* (as
Middle: *ŭ* (cut, above); *û* (burn)
Back: *ōō* (moon); *ȯo* (foot); *ō* (cold); *ô* (all); *ŏ* (stop); *ä* (far)
Diphthongs: *ī* (fly) *ou* (mound); *oi* (coin); *ū* (unit)

The reason for each name becomes clear if one tries to form the sound in question—the sound of the letter, not the name. In the *nasals* the air comes out of the nose. They are used exclusively in humming; therefore, when they are used frequently they produce a sound that suggests humming. The *liquids* are very soft, easy, flowing sounds, hence their name. A *stop* is a sound that does stop: the sound ends abruptly. The sound of a *fricative* is caused by friction; it lingers; it can be carried on for a long time; it may also be called a continuous sound. The two words *stop* and *cease*, for example, have about the same meaning; both begin with fricatives, but the stop sound at the end of the one makes it much more positive than the fricative at the end of the other. The sound of the word *stop* implies a quicker reaction than is conveyed by *cease*, which seems to allow the action to discontinue gradually. If a mother tells her little boy to stop, she wants him to do so at once; but when it is said that the sound of the waves had ceased, a long, gradual dying out is implied.

The vowels are named by the position at which they are formed in the mouth. The front vowels, as in *cat, they, met*, are formed in the front of the mouth. The back vowels, as in *cold* or *far*, are formed in the back of the mouth. The back vowels produce much larger, fuller sounds than do the front vowels, which are lighter and more delicate. In the song by Blake at the beginning of this section the vowels are all at the front of the mouth; hence the light, staccato effect. In the lines from Vachel Lindsay the vowels are at the back of the mouth.

THREE TYPES OF TONE COLOR

All effects of tone color depend on repetition. It may be repetition (1) of words, (2) of sentences or phrases, or (3) of single sounds.

REPETITION OF WORDS. The simplest and clearest example of tone color is the repetition of words. The repetition of a word, though it may become wearisome, is one of the most effective devices in literature. In the "Introduction" to *Songs of Innocence*, for example, the reiteration of the word *pipe* emphasizes the childlike quality of the verse. In the famous passage from Paul's First Epistle to the Corinthians the cumulative effect produced by the repetition of the word *charity* is tremendous. All the emotion in the passage seems to be bound up in that one word.

Though I speak with the tongues of men and of angels, and have not charity, I am become as sounding brass, or a tinkling cymbal. And though I have the gift of prophecy, and understand all mysteries, and all knowledge; and though I have all faith, so that I could remove mountains, and have not charity, I am nothing. And though I bestow all my goods to feed the poor, and though I give my body to be burned, and have not charity, it profiteth me nothing. Charity suffereth long, and is kind; charity envieth not; charity vaunteth not itself, not puffed up, doth not behave itself unseemly, seeketh not her own, is not easily provoke thinketh no evil; rejoiceth not in iniquity, but rejoiceth in the truth; beareth all thing believeth all things, hopeth all things, endureth all things. Charity never faileth; but wheth there be prophecies, they shall fail; whether there be tongues, they shall cease; whether the be knowledge, it shall vanish away. For we know in part, and we prophesy in part. But wh that which is perfect is come, then that which is in part shall be done away. When I was child, I spake as a child, I understood as a child, I thought as a child; but when I became man, I put away childish things. For now we see through a glass, darkly; but then face face; now I know in part; but then shall I know even as also I am known. And now abide faith, hope, charity, these three; but the greatest of these is charity.

—I Corinthians 13

REPETITION OF SENTENCES OR PHRASES. Often a group of words or a sentence repeated. In the last act of *The Merchant of Venice*, Lorenzo and Jessica ha arrived at Belmont and are waiting for the return of Portia and the others. they wait they beguile the time by playing a game in which they picture oth famous lovers. Each speech begins with the words *In such a night*; the phra serves as a musical motive and as a constant reminder of the beauty of the scen

LORENZO. The moon shines bright. In such a night as this,
When the sweet wind did gently kiss the trees
And they did make no noise, in such a night
Troilus methinks mounted the Troyan walls,
And sigh'd his soul toward the Grecian tents,
Where Cressid lay that night.

JESSICA. In such a night
Did Thisbe fearfully o'ertrip the dew,
And saw the lion's shadow ere himself
And ran dismay'd away.

LORENZO. In such a night
Stood Dido with a willow in her hand
Upon the wild sea banks, and waft her love
To come again to Carthage.

JESSICA. In such a night
Medea gathered the enchanted herbs
That did renew old Aeson.

LORENZO.   In such a night
> Did Jessica steal from the wealthy Jew,
> And with an unthrift love did run from Venice
> As far as Belmont.

JESSICA.   In such a night
> Did young Lorenzo swear he lov'd her well,
> Stealing her soul with many vows of faith
> And ne'er a true one.

LORENZO.   In such a night
> Did pretty Jessica, like a little shrew
> Slander her love, and he forgave it her.

JESSICA.   I would out-night you, did no body come;
> But, hark, I hear the footing of a man.

—SHAKESPEARE, *The Merchant of Venice*, V, i, 1–24 (ca. 1595)

In Winston Churchill's famous address to the Commons about Dunkirk, on June 4, 1940, he makes constant use of the phrase *We shall fight.*

> We shall go on to the end, we shall fight in France, we shall fight on the seas and oceans, we shall fight with growing confidence and growing strength in the air, we shall defend our Island, whatever the cost may be, we shall fight on the beaches, we shall fight on the landing grounds, we shall fight in the fields and in the streets, we shall fight in the hills; we shall never surrender, and even if, which I do not for a moment believe, this Island or a large part of it were subjugated and starving, then our Empire beyond the seas, armed and guarded by the British Fleet, would carry on the struggle, until, in God's good time, the New World, with all its power and might, steps forth to the rescue and the liberation of the old.

> —WINSTON CHURCHILL (1874–1965, British statesman), *Dunkirk:* Address to Commons, June 4, 1940.

Ferlinghetti in his poem "I Am Waiting," from the collection *A Coney Island of the Mind*, emphasizes his impatient waiting for a renaissance of wonder by the constant repetition of the words, "I am waiting." The poem has almost the orator's plea in this reiterated phrase.

> and I am waiting
> for the American Eagle
> to really spread its wings
> and straighten up and fly right
> and I am waiting
> for the Age of Anxiety

236

Organization

to drop dead
and I am waiting
for the war to be fought
which will make the world safe
for anarchy
and I am waiting
for the final withering away
of all governments
and I am perpetually awaiting
a rebirth of wonder

—LAWRENCE FERLINGHETTI (1919–   , American poet), "I Am Waiting"[1]

REPETITION OF SINGLE SOUNDS. Subtle examples of tone color are found when single sounds are repeated. These sounds are usually single letters. They are not always the same letters, however, for often two letters have the same sound (*c*orner, *k*ick), and a single letter has two sounds (*c*orner, *c*edar). Besides rhyme there are three types of tone color based on the repetition of single sounds: alliteration, assonance and consonance.

Alliteration is the repetition of accented sounds that begin words: *P*eter *P*iper *p*icked a *p*eck of *p*ickled *p*eppers. When used in extremes, as in the Peter Piper rhyme, alliteration may become obnoxious, but when well used it is pleasing. The use of alliteration is almost universal.

Sigh no more, ladies, sigh no more,
  Men were deceivers ever,
One foot in sea and one on shore,
  To one thing constant never.
Then sigh not so, but let them go,
  And be you blithe and bonny,
Converting all your sounds of woe
  Into Hey nonny nonny.

Sing no more ditties, sing no moe,
  Of dumps so dull and heavy;
The fraud of men was ever so,
  Since summer first was leafy.
Then sigh not so, but let them go,
  And be you blithe and bonny,
Converting all your sounds of woe
  Into Hey nonny nonny.

—SHAKESPEARE, *Much Ado about Nothing*, II, iii, 64ff. (ca. 1599)

[1] 16 lines from *A Coney Island of the Mind*. Reprinted by permission of the publisher, New Directions Publishing Corporation.

n the short poem from *Much Ado* we have alliteration in *s*ea and *s*hore, *b*lithe and *b*onny, and also in *d*itties, *d*umps, *d*ull. Notice the alliteration in the paragraph quoted from Vachel Lindsay's "The Congo:" *b*lack, *b*ucks, *b*arrel, *b*eat, *b*room, *b*oom, *b*oomlay.

Assonance is the effect obtained from the repetition of accented vowel sounds, as in f*oo*lish, cr*oo*ning; r*a*ce, m*a*ke; fr*ee* and *ea*sy; m*a*d as a h*a*tter. The effects to be gained from assonance are delicate and varied.

> Break, break, break,
>   On thy cold gray stones, O Sea!
> And I would that my tongue could utter
>   The thoughts that arise in me.
>   —ALFRED, LORD TENNYSON (1809–1892, British poet),
>   "Break, Break, Break" (1842)

In the second line of this stanza, for example, the words do not themselves express any great grief, yet we have a sense almost of desolation. The explanation is to be found in assonance. *Oh* is universally a cry of grief and mourning; the person who cannot be consoled laments *Oh, oh, oh.* Tennyson uses the exclamation only once, but he repeats the sound two other times in the short line:

> On thy c*o*ld gray st*o*nes, *O* Sea!

In popular speech we use assonance in expressions like *time out of mind, slap-dash.*

Consonance is sometimes called *slant* rhyme. Consonance is a general term for the effects produced by the repetition of accented consonant sounds when one of them is not at the beginning of a word. Often both consonants occur at the ends of the words, as in o*dds* and e*nds*, or bla*ck* and bu*ck*, stru*ts* and fre*ts*.

Consonance is not so nearly obvious as alliteration and is not so common, but it produces many subtle effects. When, for instance, Coriolanus greets his mother,

> My gracious silence, hail!

the repetition of the *s* sounds seems to emphasize her dignity, and his respect for her.

In Emily Dickinson's "I Like to See It Lap the Miles" notice that the second and fourth lines of each stanza are tied together with consonant rhymes: *up-step, peer-pare, while-hill, star-door.* The final consonants rhyme but not the vowels.

RHYME

Two words are said to rhyme when they are identical in sound from the vowel of the accented syllable to the end, provided the sounds that precede the accented vowel are not identical. *Cry, buy; face, place; sorrow, tomorrow; running, cunning*—these words rhyme. *Wright, write, right* do not rhyme because the letters before the accented vowel do not differ in sound. *Romantic* and *chromatic* do not rhyme because they are not identical in the syllables following the accented vowel. A rhyme is said to be "masculine" if the rhyming portion of the words is a single syllable; "feminine" if the rhyming portion is more than one syllable. *Cry, buy; face, place* are masculine rhymes; *sorrow, tomorrow*, and *cunning, running* are feminine rhymes.

Rhyme usually comes at the end of a line and follows a set pattern. Rhyme is indicated by the letters of the alphabet, *a* being used for the first rhyming word, *b* for the second, *c* for the third, etc.

My heart leaps up when I behold	*a*
A rainbow in the sky:	*b*
So was it when my life began;	*c*
So is it now I am a man,	*c*
So be it when I shall grow old	*a*
Or let me die!	*b*
The Child is father of the Man:	*c*
And I could wish my days to be	*d*
Bound each to each by natural piety.	*d*

—WILLIAM WORDSWORTH (1770–1850, British poet),
"My Heart Leaps Up" (1802)

If a poem is divided into stanzas the same rhyme pattern will usually be used in each stanza. In the "Introduction" to *Songs of Innocence* all the stanzas rhyme *abcb* except the first, which rhymes *abab*. In *"Sigh No More Ladies"* the verse rhymes *abab*, and the refrain *cdcd*.

There is no rhyme in the passage from Shakespeare's *Merchant of Venice*.

RHYTHM

Rhythm as defined in *A Prosody Handbook*, by Karl Shapiro and Robert Beum, is "the total quality of a line's motion, and is the product of several elements, not of stress and quantity alone." They say later, "Probably no two lines of poetry, and no two sentences of prose have exactly the same rhythm" (page 60). Rhythm is found in all literature, as in all music; and it is the same in literature as in music.

To a certain extent all speech is rhythmic in that it is grouped in phrases; only a child just learning to read gives the same emphasis to every word. However, some speech is more rhythmic than other speech; the term *rhythmic* is usually reserved for that speech which excites the ear.

Compare these examples for their rhythms. In the first, one has a disagreeable sense of being constantly jerked up; he cannot get into the swing of the sentence; there are no pauses. The other two are in contrast very rhythmic.

Mr. Davies does not let his learning cause him to treat the paintings as material only to be studied by the Egyptologist with a critical and scientific eye.

The young spirit has awakened out of Eternity, and knows not what we mean by Time; as yet Time is no fast-hurrying stream, but a sportful sunlit ocean; years to the child are as ages. . . . Sleep on, thou fair Child, for thy long rough journey is at hand! A little while, and thou too shalt sleep no more, but thy very dreams shall be mimic battles; thou too, with old Arnauld, wilt have to say in stern patience: "Rest? Rest? Shall I not have all Eternity to rest in?"

—THOMAS CARLYLE (1795–1881, English philosopher and essayist), *Sartor Resartus* (1833)

And as we dwell, we living things, in our isle of terror and under the imminent hand of death, God forbid it should be man the erected, the reasoner, the wise in his own eyes—God forbid it should be man that wearies in well-doing, that despairs of unrewarded effort, or utters the language of complaint. Let it be enough for faith, that the whole creation groans in mortal frailty, strives with unconquerable constancy: Surely not all in vain.

—ROBERT LOUIS STEVENSON (1850–1894, Scotch poet, novelist, and essayist), *Pulvis et Umbra*

These examples are all from prose, but rhythm is found in poetry as well as in prose. Often the phrase is practically synonymous with the line.

Shall I, wasting in despair,
Die, because a woman's fair?
Or make pale my cheeks with care,
'Cause another's rosy are?
Be she fairer than the day,
Or the flowery meads in May!
  If she be not so to me,
  What care I how fair she be?

—GEORGE WITHER (1588–1667, British poet),
  "Shall I Wasting in Despair"

Organization

More often the phrase is not synonymous with the line. It may end in the middle of a line, or it may carry over from line to line. In the last lines of "Ulysses" note how Tennyson varies the rhythmic effects:

> Come, my friends.
> 'Tis not too late to seek a newer world.
> Push off, and sitting well in order smite
> The sounding furrows; for my purpose holds
> To sail beyond the sunset, and the baths
> Of all the western stars, until I die.
> It may be that the gulfs will wash us down;
> It may be we shall touch the Happy Isles,
> And see the great Achilles, whom we knew.
> Tho' much is taken, much abides; and tho'
> We are not now that strength which in old days
> Moved earth and heaven, that which we are, we are,—
> One equal temper of heroic hearts,
> Made weak by time and fate, but strong in will
> To strive, to seek, to find, and not to yield.

> —ALFRED, LORD TENNYSON, (1809–1892) British Poet
>   "Ulysses" (1842)

METER

English is a language of pronounced word accent. Words of more than one syllable have at least one accent. Words such as *dismay, avoid, contend* have the accent on the second syllable. Words like *saying, duple, accent* have the accent on the first syllable. A few words of two syllables, such as *baseball,* or *blackbird,* have accents on both syllables. *November, lemonade, vertical, butterfly* have three syllables each. In *November,* the accent is on the second, in *lemonade* on the third, and in *vertical* on the first syllable. *Butterfly* has accents on the first and third syllables. *Commemorate* has four syllables, with a primary accent on the second syllable and a secondary accent on the last syllable.

Sometimes a poet puts words together so that these accents come in a regular order. Take, for instance, the lines quoted from Tennyson's "Ulysses." The accented and unaccented syllables tend to alternate, first an unaccented, then an accented syllable. The last two lines are absolutely regular.

> Made weak by time and fate, but strong in will
> To strive, to seek, to find, and not to yield.

This pattern is not kept with absolute regularity throughout the poem, but it is sufficiently regular for us to recognize it.

Any such regular recurrence of accent is called *meter*. The meter in which an unaccented syllable is followed by an accented syllable is called *iambic*. It is so common as almost to be the universal meter of English poetry, but there are other meters. The accent may come on the first syllable instead of the second.

> Jenny kissed me when we met,
> > Jumping from the chair she sat in;
> Time, you thief, who love to get
> > Sweets into your list, put that in:
> Say I'm weary, say I'm sad,
> > Say that health and wealth have missed me,
> Say I'm growing old, but add,
> > Jenny kissed me.
>
> > —LEIGH HUNT (1784–1859, British journalist, essayist, and poet),
> > "Rondeau" (1838)

Or the accent may fall on every third instead of every second syllable. It may fall on the third, sixth and ninth syllables, as in "Annabel Lee":

> It was many and many a year ago,
> > In a kingdom by the sea,
> That a maiden there lived, whom you may know
> > By the name of Annabel Lee;
> And this maiden she lived with no other thought
> > Than to love and be loved by me.
>
> > —EDGAR ALLAN POE (1809–1849, American poet, short story writer, and critic),
> > "Annabel Lee" (1849)

It may come on the first, fourth, and seventh syllables as in these lines:

> Just for a handful of silver he left us,
> > Just for a riband to stick in his coat—
> Found the one gift of which fortune bereft us,
> > Lost all the others she lets us devote;
>
> > —ROBERT BROWNING (1812–1889, British poet),
> > "The Lost Leader" (1845)

Each of these meters is identified by the pattern of accented and unaccented syllables, and the unit is called a foot.

TYPES OF FOOT. The names and symbols of the meters may be tabulated, with *x* for an unaccented syllable, and *a* for an accented one.

iambic: x a

    x   a   x   a   x   a
    To strive, to seek, to find

trochaic: a x   a   x   a   x
    Jenny kissed me

anapestic: x x a

    x   x   a x x   a x x   a x a
    It was many and many a year ago

dactylic: a x x

    a   x x   a x   x   a x
    Just for a handful of silver

A spondaic foot, called a *spondee,* is composed of two accented syllables. For obvious reasons the spondee cannot be used in an entire poem or even in an entire line. It is one of the important ways of introducing variety. It emphasizes by slowing up the speed of the line. Milton, for instance, uses spondees in *Paradise Lost* to stress the enormous size of Satan:

So stretched out huge in length the Arch-*Fiend lay.*
> —MILTON,
> *Paradise Lost,* I, 209 (1667)

And Tennyson emphasizes the slow passage of time in "Ulysses" by substituting spondees for iambs.

The long *day wanes;* the slow *moon climbs;* the deep
Moans round with many voices.

The length of a line is named according to the number of feet in it.

One foot . . . . monometer
Two feet . . . . dimeter

Three feet	trimeter
Four feet	tetrameter
Five feet	pentameter
Six feet	hexameter
Seven feet	heptameter
Eight feet	octameter

Trimeter, tetrameter, and pentameter are the line lengths most commonly used. The lines just quoted from "Ulysses" are pentameter; "The Lost Leader" is in tetrameter; "Rondeau" is in tetrameter until the last line, which is dimeter; "Annabel Lee" alternates tetrameter and trimeter. Ordinarily a line is designated by the kind of foot and the number of feet in a line, as iambic tetrameter, dactylic dimeter, etc.

● VERSE FORM

A poet usually decides on the kind of meter, the line length, and the rhyme scheme he wishes, and sticks pretty closely to that combination throughout his poem. This is called the verse form. Since the passage we read from "Ulysses" is in iambic pentameter without rhyme, we expect the entire poem to be in that verse form, and it is. And we expect Poe to have stanzas of six lines of anapestic verse alternating tetrameter and trimeter, with the even lines rhyming.

TRADITIONAL FORMS

A poet may make a new verse form, but usually he does not. Some forms have been used so much that they have been given names by which they may be easily identified. The number of named forms is too great for a complete list to be given here, but a few of the more common terms are:

I. General terms
   A. *Couplet:* any stanza of two lines.
   B. *Triplet:* any stanza of three lines.
   C. *Quatrain:* any stanza of four lines.
II. Specific terms
   A. *Heroic couplet:* two lines of iambic pentameter rhymed.
      1. Closed: the two lines express a complete thought.

Hope springs eternal in the human breast:
Man never is, but always to be, blest.

> —ALEXANDER POPE (1688–1744, British poet),
>   *An Essay on Man* (1733)

2. Open: the thought runs on from line to line.

A thing of beauty is a joy for ever:
Its loveliness increases; it will never
Pass into nothingness; but still will keep
A bower quiet for us, and a sleep
Full of sweet dreams, and health, and quiet breathing.

> —JOHN KEATS (1795–1821, British poet),
>   *Endymion* (1818)

B. *Ballad meter:* four lines of iambic verse alternating tetrameter and trimeter. Rhyme *abab*, or *abcb*. Commonly used in ballads. Also called *common meter* from its use in hymns. The most popular of all quatrains.

She dwelt among the untrodden ways
  Beside the springs of Dove,
A Maid whom there were none to praise
  And very few to love:

A violet by a mossy stone
  Half hidden from the eye!
—Fair as a star, when only one
  Is shining in the sky.

She lived unknown, and few could know
  When Lucy ceased to be;
But she is in her grave, and, oh,
  The difference to me!

> —WORDSWORTH,
>   "Lucy" (1800)

C. *Sonnet:* fourteen lines of iambic pentameter. The sonnet is a favorite form for short poems because of its compactness. Ordinarily the poet states an idea in the first eight lines, the octave,

and gives an explanation or an answer in the last six, the sestet.
There are two types of sonnet which are distinguished by their
rhymes.

> 1. Italian, or Petrarchan: *abba abba* (octave); *cde cde* or
> *cdcdcd* (sestet).

The world is too much with us: late and soon,
Getting and spending, we lay waste our powers.
Little we see in Nature that is ours;
We have given our hearts away, a sordid boon!
This Sea that bares her bosom to the moon;
The winds that will be howling at all hours,
And are up-gathered now like sleeping flowers;
For this, for everything, we are out of tune;
It moves us not.—Great God! I'd rather be
A Pagan suckled in a creed outworn;
So might I, standing on this pleasant lea,
Have glimpses that would make me less forlorn;
Have sight of Proteus rising from the sea;
Or hear old Triton blow his wreathèd horn.

> —WORDSWORTH,
> "The World Is Too Much with Us" (1807)

> 2. English, or Shakespearean: three quatrains with alternating
> rhyme and a couplet.

Let me not to the marriage of true minds
Admit impediments. Love is not love
Which alters when it alteration finds,
Or bends with the remover to remove.

O, no! it is an ever-fixèd mark
That looks on tempests and is never shaken;
It is the star to every wand'ring bark,
Whose worth's unknown, although his height be taken.

Love's not Time's fool, though rosy lips and cheeks
Within his bending sickle's compass come;
Love alters not with his brief hours and weeks,
But bears it out even to the edge of doom.

Organization

> If this be error and upon me proved,
> I never writ, nor no man ever loved.
>
>   —SHAKESPEARE,
>   Sonnet 116 (publ. 1609)

Although it is true that poets always conceive of the poem and its idea in the special form in which it appears, it is interesting that the contemporary poet uses less rhyme and more departures from strict meter. Muriel Rukeyser in "Double Dialogue Homage to Robert Frost," does have a regular metrical form, but it is not a sonnet; there are rhymes, but they do not tie together the sections of sixteen lines as a sonnet would. The final couplet presents the gist of the poet's idea; but it retains the conversational tone of the rest of the poem.

> In agony saying: "The last night of his life,
> My son and I in the kitchen: At half-past one
> He said, 'I have failed as a husband. Now my wife
> Is ill again and suffering.' At two
> He said, 'I have failed as a farmer, for the sun
> Is never there, the rain is never there.'
> At three he said, 'I have failed as a poet who
> Has never not once found my listeners.
> There is no sense to my life.' But then he heard me out.
> I argued point by point. Seemed to win. Won.
> He spoke to me once more when I was done
> 'Even in argument, father, I have lost.'
> He went and shot himself. Now tell me this one thing:
> Should I have let him win then? Was I wrong?"

> To answer for the land for love for song
> Arguing life for life even at your life's cost.
>
>   —MURIEL RUKEYSER (1913–   , American poet),
>   "Double Dialogue"[2]

D. *Spenserian stanza:* eight lines of iambic pentameter followed by one of iambic hexameter. Rhyme *abab bcbcc.* A graceful verse invented by Spenser for *The Faerie Queene* and often used for longer narratives.

---

[2] From *The Saturday Review.* Reprinted by permission of Monica. McCall, Inc. Copyright, 1964.

And more to lulle him in his slumber soft,
A trickling streame from high rock tumbling downe,
And ever-drizling raine upon the loft,
Mixt with a murmuring winde, much like the sowne
Of swarming Bees, did cast him in a swowne.
No other noyse, nor peoples troublous cryes,
As still are wont t'annoy the walled towne,
Might there be heard; but carlesse Quiet lyes
Wrapt in eternall silence farre from enimyes.

> —EDMUND SPENSER (1552–1599, British poet), *The Faerie Queene*, I, I, 41 (1590)

E. *Blank verse:* unrhymed iambic pentameter.

When I see birches bend to left and right
Across the line of straighter darker trees,
I like to think some boy's been swinging them.
But swinging doesn't bend them down to stay.

> —ROBERT FROST (1875–1963, American poet), "Birches" (1916)

OTHER TYPES OF VERSE

ACCENTUAL VERSE. This is verse that holds to a fixed number of accents in a line. Old English poetry was of this type; there were usually four accents to each line.

In the second section of "Ash-Wednesday" T. S. Eliot has used this meter successfully, two accents to a line.

Lady of silences
Calm and distressed
Torn and most whole
Rose of memory
Rose of forgetfulness.

> —T. S. ELIOT (1888–1965, American poet), "Ash-Wednesday" (1930)[3]

---

[3] From *Collected Poems 1909–1962* by T. S. Eliot, copyright 1936 by Harcourt, Brace & World, Inc.: copyright © 1963, 1964, by T. S. Eliot. Reprinted by permission of the publishers.

FREE VERSE AND HEBREW METER. Free verse is built on the rhythm of phrase. Its unit is the *strophe,* which is composed of a number of phrases subtly balanced so as to constitute a complete cadence.

> They set the slave free, striking off his chains—
> Then he was as much of a slave as ever.
> He was still chained to servility,
> He was still manacled to indolence and sloth,
> He was still bound by fear and superstition,
> By ignorance, suspicion, and savagery—
> His slavery was not in the chains,
> But in himself—
>
> They can only set free men free—
> And there is no need of that:
> Free men set themselves free.
>> —JAMES OPPENHEIM (1882–1932, American poet),
>>   "The Slave" (1914)[4]

Hebrew meter is often classed with free verse; it is based on parallelism of phrases, one clause or phrase being balanced against another of similar structure. It is, of course, found most conspicuously in the Bible.

> Purge me with hyssop, and I shall be clean;
> Wash me, and I shall be whiter than snow.
> Make me to hear joy and gladness;
> That the bones which thou hast broken may rejoice.
> Hide thy face from my sins,
> And blot out all mine iniquities.
> Create in me a clean heart, O God:
> And renew a right spirit within me.
> Cast me not away from thy presence;
> And take not thy holy spirit from me.
>> —Psalm 51:7–11

THE HAIKU AND THE TANKA

The haiku and the tanka are two Japanese forms that are based on syllable count. The haiku contains 17 syllables in three lines of 5, 7, and 5 syllables.

---

[4]Reprinted from *Songs for the New Age* by permission of Mr. Arthur Spingarn, Executor of the estate of James Oppenheim.

The tanka contains 31 syllables in five lines of 5, 7, 5, 7, and 7 syllables. Naturally they cannot be translated into English of the same count, but often they are very telling. The poet Issa (1763–1828) wrote this haiku after the death of his only child.

> The world of dew
> Is a world of dew and yet,
> And yet.[5]

All the haiku strive like this poem to be concentrated on a single vivid moment. The haiku by Onitsura (1661–1738) is more humorous, as it expresses the eternal desire to write poetry on a beautiful evening.

> Is there, I wonder,
> A man without pen in hand—
> The moon tonight![6]

Bashō (1644–1694), who is generally considered Japan's greatest poet, says that a haiku should have both change and permanence. It should look for the virtues of the old and at the same time express the present, a modern solution. One of his best-known haiku is this:

> The ancient pond
> A frog leaps in
> The sound of the water.[7]

The tanka is similar, though longer. This one is by the Emperor Gotoba (1180–1239).

> When I look far out
> The mountain slopes are hazy
> Minase River—
> Why did I think that only in autumn
> The evenings could be lovely?[8]

---

[5]Donald Keene, *Anthology of Japanese Literature*, p. 21.
[6]*Ibid.*, p. 26.
[7]*Ibid.*, p. 39.
[8]*Ibid.*, p. 36.

13
ORGANIZATION IN
THE VISUAL ARTS

● **WHAT IS ORGANIZATION?**

It has been said that man is most Godlike in his demand for order. He is constantly trying to transform his chaos into a world of order. The mind is confused, if not balked, when it cannot find some order. The "order" in a work of art is its organization. In our study thus far we have been considering the elements found in works of art, but the elements are only the materials used by the artist. Now we begin to study the ways elements are combined to make a whole.

The primary demands made of any organization are two: (1) it must make sense, and (2) it must be interesting. The first of these demands has to do with the arrangement of parts, the overall design or plan of a work. Plan might be called the skeleton of the work of art. Plan covers the entire work—whether it be a symphony that lasts an hour or a song that is over in a minute, whether it be a novel of a thousand pages or a poem of two lines, whether it be the ceiling of a large chapel or the picture on a postage stamp. Whatever the size or the medium, we demand that orderly arrangement of the parts which reflects a plan.

The names by which we identify plans differ in the various arts. In music we usually speak of forms: rondo, sonata, minuet, etc., whereas in literature we talk of types: novel, essay, epic. In the visual arts there are no generally accepted names as such, but we describe plans by obvious names such as pyramidal, symmetrical, etc.

Plan is essential because it holds the work together, but it is not interesting as such. Two works following identical plans may differ widely in interest and value. The sonnet form has been used in very great poems, but the same form is found in poems of no value. The value of a rondo does not come from the rondo form, but from the music written in that form. In any of the arts interest comes from the way the form is used, from the elements of which the plan is made and from their interrelations. This may be called the organic structure of the work. If the plan is compared to the skeleton, the organic structure corresponds to the flesh and blood with which the skeleton is covered. Another analogy for organization is an orchestra. The different elements play with and against each other as do the instruments of an orchestra; and so this organic structure or organic unity of a work of art is sometimes called its orchestration.

For organic structure there is one rule that holds, in all the arts—that of unity and variety, or repetition and contrast. The elements used must be repeated enough to become familiar but varied enough in character to provide contrast. In this way we have the satisfaction of recognizing the familiar coupled with the surprise or tension of the unfamiliar. One of the most beautiful passages in Handel's *Messiah* comes in the singing of the contralto solo "He shall feed His flock," which is followed immediately by the soprano solo "Come unto Him, all ye that labor." The tune is the same, but the soprano sings it a fourth higher. The beauty of the soprano solo is almost unearthly. And yet with the differences in words and in pitch, not only is the song not repetitious, but many hearers do not even know they are hearing the same tune.

● BASIC PLANS IN THE VISUAL ARTS

Plan in the visual arts is simply the arrangement of the parts, with one place given special attention as the center of interest. In the *Sistine Madonna* (Figure 131) the plan is made by the four groups on the canvas, the Madonna and Child at the top in the center, St. Sixtus on the left with the papal crown at his feet to identify him, and St. Barbara on the right; the building which identifies her as the patron of buildings is hardly to be seen above her right shoulder. At the bottom of the picture are two cherubs. The formal arrangement is seen even more clearly in the drawing (Figure 132).

FIGURE 131. RAPHAEL. *Sistine Madonna* (ca. 1515). (Oil on canvas. Height: 8 feet, 8½ inches. Dresden Gallery. Photograph by Stoedtner.)

FIGURE 132. Drawing to show organization of lines and figures in the *Sistine Madonna*, Figure 131. (Drawing by Gordon Gilkey.)

Because plan in the visual arts is obvious, there are no well-established names for types of plan, and hence we do not need any assistance in determining types. There are, however, a few obvious arrangements which are used repeatedly. The two most common are the symmetrical and the pyramidal plans.

SYMMETRICAL PLAN. The two sides of the plan are similar and relatively equal. This is a favorite plan in architecture, where the two sides are identical, as in the Vendramin Palace (Figure 157). It is also a favorite in painting or statues, as in the *Annunciation* by Simone Martini (Figure 74) or the *Ludovisi Throne* (Figure 59).

PYRAMID. The pyramid is almost as great a favorite in painting as is the symmetrical plan in architecture. The broad base gives a sense of solidity, and the apex gives emphasis. It is the natural shape for a painting of a portrait. In the portrait of *Madame Cézanne in the Conservatory* (Figure 133) her skirts make the base of the pyramid and her head the apex. The pyramidal plan is a favorite for representations of the Virgin, as in Giorgione's *Castelfranco Madonna* (Figure 134). The Madonna, though dressed as a simple peasant, is seated on high at the apex of the triangle; St. Liberale and St. Francis are at the corners. In the *Tomb of Giuliano de' Medici* (Figure 135) Michelangelo follows the general shape of a pyramid.

FIGURE 133. PAUL CÉZANNE. *Mme. Cézanne in the Conservatory* (1891). (Oil on canvas. Size: 36½ by 28½ inches. Collection of Stephen C. Clark, New York. Photograph, Museum of Modern Art.)

FIGURE 134. GIORGIONE (ca. 1478–1510), Italian painter. *Castelfranco Madonna* (1504). (Oil on wood. Height: 7 feet, 6 inches. Castelfranco Veneto, Cathedral. Photograph by Alinari.)

FIGURE 135. MICHELANGELO. *Tomb of Giuliano de' Medici* (ca. 1523–1533). (Marble. Height: about 20 feet. Florence, San Lorenzo, New Sacristy. Photograph by Anderson.)

VERTICAL PLAN. Less common plans are the vertical and the radial. The vertical plan shows a single vertical figure or other object. Monuments frequently follow this plan, as do some modern skyscrapers, the Seagram Building in New York (Figure 154), for example. It is used a great deal in sculpture, especially

n statues of a single figure like Michelangelo's *David*. It is not so well liked in
ainting as in sculpture, but it is used for full-length single figures, as in Eakins,
The Thinker (Figure 136).

ADIAL PLAN. In the radial plan the lines of the picture form radii which meet
t a point in the center. In Leonardo's *Last Supper* (Figure 137) all the lines of
he ceiling and walls, as well as the hands and faces of the twelve disciples,
oint to the head of Christ. Leonardo puts his point of focus directly in the

IGURE 137. LEONARDO DA VINCI. *The Last Supper* (1495–1498). (Tempera on plaster. Figures above
fe size. Milan, Santa Maria delle Grazie.)

FIGURE 138. GIOTTO. *Death of St. Francis* (ca. 1325). (Fresco. Figures about life size. Florence, Sant Croce, Bardi Chapel. Photograph by Alinari.)

center of the picture. In the *Death of St. Francis* (Figure 138) Giotto uses a similar organization with the focal point at one side. The lines of the painting— the heads and bodies of the saint's followers, as well as lines of the banner—all converge on the head of St. Francis. The one exception is the soul of St. Francis, which looks ahead as it is being carried through the air.

In abstract and nonobjective art, plan is harder to see because it is not representational. The organization is based entirely on the repetition and variety of the elements. One color is balanced against another color, one line against another.

● BALANCE

As we look at various arrangements or plans in any work, we instinctively demand balance. No matter how the various parts are put together, we want that sense of equilibrium which we call balance. Some people get nervous if they see a picture hanging crooked, and most of us have little satisfaction in looking at the Leaning Tower of Pisa, though we know it has stood for centuries and will probably continue to lean long after we are dead.

Dégas has a painting of two ballet girls, *Dancers Practicing at the Bar* (Figure 139). The two girls are nearly symmetrical; each is poised on one leg, and the raised legs point in opposite directions. The figures are on a diagonal line in the upper right-hand corner of the picture; all the interest points to this one spot. To balance the two dancers, Dégas puts a watering can on the otherwise bare floor. This watering can is essential. If we take out the can or if we narrow the picture, the girls are no longer secure at their bar, the plan becomes unbalanced.

One of the most important ways of getting balance is by control of the direction of lines. One line points in one direction, another in the opposite direction, and from the two we get a sense of balance. In Giotto's *Flight into Egypt* (Figure 128), for example, the entire motion of the picture is left to right until we come to the figure of St. Joseph, which stops us and turns us back. In Daumier's *Strangers in Paris* (Figure 140) the couple in the distance is moving

FIGURE 139. EDGAR DÉGAS (1834–1917), French painter. *Dancers Practicing at the Bar* (1877). (Oil on canvas. Size: about 29½ by 30½ inches. New York, courtesy Metropolitan Museum of Art; H. O. Havemeyer Collection.)

FIGURE 140. HONORE DAUMIER. *Strangers in Paris.* (Lithograph. Size: 8½ by 7 inches. New York, courtesy Metropolitan Museum of Art; Rogers Fund, 1922.)

in one direction; that in the foreground is not moving, but the direction of their heads and umbrella is in the opposite direction. In El Greco's *St. Jerome* (Figure 141) the eyes, head, and beard point to the right, the arms and book to the left. If the picture is cut off just below the shoulders, the beard seems to be blown as by a good breeze or a fan. With the opposing motion of the hands and book, the whole is given living, breathing balance.

Theoretically, every detail is necessary in a well-designed composition; if the balance is perfect, a change in a single detail will upset it. This principle is probably more theory than fact, but at the same time it is interesting to try to

FIGURE 141. EL GRECO. *St. Jerome* (ca. 1596–1600). (Oil on canvas. Size 42½ by 34¼ inches. Copyright Frick Collection, New York.)

FIGURE 142. JAN VAN EYCK. *Jan Arnolfini and His Wife* (1434). (Oil on wood. Height: 2 feet, 9¼ inches. Reproduced by courtesy of the Trustees, the National Gallery, London.)

determine the role played by some detail of a picture. In Jan van Eyck's painting of *Jan Arnolfini and His Wife* (Figure 142) we have an interesting illustration. It is obviously a portrait study. The two figures are placed side by side, the gentleman on the left, the lady on the right. Between them are the mirror on the wall and the chandelier. The light of the window, the man's face, and his hand are balanced by the white of the lady's face, her headdress, and the long cuff on her sleeve. All is regular and as it should be except for some slippers on the floor near the man and the lady. But those slippers are necessary for the balance of the picture. Their irregular line balances the irregular line of the white trim on the lady's skirt. Both lines of white are needed to bring the eye down to the lower half of the picture. The importance of the slippers can be judged in another way also; if we remove the slippers the man seems to fall forward.

259

FIGURE 143. JACOB VAN RUISDAE
(1628–1682), Dutch painter. *The Mil*
(Size: 2 feet, 9 inches by 3 feet, 4 inches
Amsterdam, Rijks Museum.)

FIGURE 144. PIETER BRUEGHEL THI
ELDER. *Parable of the Blind* (1568)
(Tempera on canvas. Height: 2 feet 1
inches. Naples, National Museum. Photc
graph by Anderson.)

FIGURE 145. SASSETTA (Stefano d
Giovanni) (1392–1450), Italian painter
The Journey of the Magi. (Tempera o
wood. Size: 29 by 15¼ inches. Ne
York, Metropolitan Museum of Ar
bequest of Maitland F. Griggs, 1943.

Asymmetrical balance is one of the beauties of landscape paintings. In
van Ruisdael's *The Mill* all the interest is on the right, but it is balanced by
the ship and the view to sea (Figure 143). Another frequent form of balance
is found in the X where two diagonal lines cross, as in Brueghel's *Parable of
the Blind* (Figure 144) or Sassetta's *Journey of the Magi* (Figure 145).

In the *Discus Thrower* (Figure 146) by Myron the body forms a complete

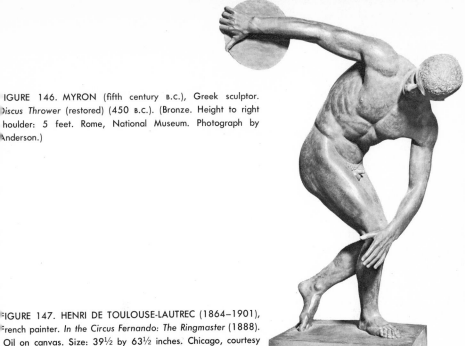

FIGURE 146. MYRON (fifth century B.C.), Greek sculptor. *Discus Thrower* (restored) (450 B.C.). (Bronze. Height to right shoulder: 5 feet. Rome, National Museum. Photograph by Anderson.)

FIGURE 147. HENRI DE TOULOUSE-LAUTREC (1864–1901), French painter. *In the Circus Fernando: The Ringmaster* (1888). Oil on canvas. Size: 39½ by 63½ inches. Chicago, courtesy Art Institute of Chicago; the Joseph Winterbotham Collection.)

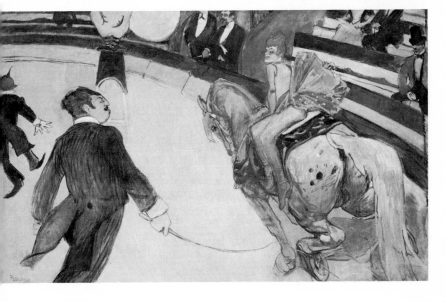

half circle in the long, curved line that begins in the right hand and goes through the right arm and the body to the left foot. In this statue Myron has, as Sir Kenneth Clark puts it, "created the enduring pattern of athletic energy." . . . He shows the athlete "balanced in equilibrium." In Toulouse-Lautrec's *In the Circus Fernando: The Ringmaster* (Figure 147) the lady on the horse starts a movement that is completed in the man on the left with the whip.

● PROPORTION

Proportion is that phase of plan which has to do with the comparative size of the parts of a single work. It is a mathematical concept for relative length or size; it is never an absolute but always a relative matter. A picture is not too large or too small in itself but is too large for this space or too small for that. One side of a rectangle is not too long or too short except in proportion to the other. An inch is very little in computing the distance from New York City to Chicago, but it is a good deal on the end of a nose.

In the visual arts, proportion at its simplest can be seen in the arrangement of objects on an indefinite surface or field, such as wallpaper, carpets, and cloth. A plaid is nothing but a number of straight lines crossing at right angles; the interest of the plaid depends on the arrangement of these lines in relation to one another. In a polka-dotted pattern there are two elements, the size of the dot and the space between dots. Change the size of the dot or the space between them, i.e., change the proportions, and the pattern is changed radically.

Such patterns offer simple problems of proportion, because the elements are judged only by their relation one to the other. But problems in proportion are found wherever there is a question of relative size or length. In dress design proportion determines the length of the sleeve or coat, the space between buttons. In interior decoration it governs the length of curtains, the height of the mantel, the size of the picture over it. Printed pages in books depend for their beauty largely on the proportions used in filling the page: the space at the top and the bottom, the width of the margins, the size of the type, and the space between the lines. Proportion determines also our judgments of the beauty of the human body in life and in art. Is the head too large or too small? Are the legs and arms too long? Are the hips too large? In painting, proportion determines not only the shape of the frame, its height in comparison with its width, but also the placing of the subject in the frame, i.e., whether the center of interest is to be high or low, right or left.

What are good proportions, and what are bad? This is like asking: When is a steak cooked enough? or: What is a long walk? People do not agree. The critic gives the ultimate answer: that is good which seems good, that is in good proportion which we find pleasing. But people have always wanted to know definite rules; accordingly, various people have tried to make exact formulas for pleasing proportions.

Polyclitus, a Greek sculptor of the fifth century B.C., wrote a treatise on the proportions for the ideal human figure, which he called *The Canon*, or *The Rule*. Then he made a statue to illustrate his principles, called also *The Canon*. It is not certain just what this statue was, but it is believed to have been the

FIGURE 148. POLYCLITUS (fifth century B.C.), Greek sculptor. *Doryphorus* (ca. 440 B.C.), Roman copy in marble of bronze original. (Height: 7 feet. Naples, Museum. Photograph by Alinari.)

Doryphorus, or *Spear Bearer* (Figure 148). Unfortunately, the original, probably in bronze, is lost, and the stone copy that is in the museum at Naples is not good; the copyist has had to make certain additions because of the weight of the stone—a tree stump to support the legs, and a bar between the hips and the right arm. Nevertheless, one can see the general proportions of the original. Polyclitus had a mathematical formula for the figure: the head is one-seventh the height of the entire body, and all details are worked out in terms of a fixed ratio.

FIGURE 149. LYSIPPUS (fourth century B.C.), Greek sculptor. *Apoxyomenos* (second half of fourth century B.C.), Roman marble after bronze original. (Height: 6 feet, 8½ inches. Rome, Vatican. Photograph by Alinari.)

A century later Lysippus introduced a new canon with a smaller head and a slimmer body, the head being only one-eighth the height of the body. The statue that has been most commonly associated with these new proportions is the *Apoxyomenos*, or *Strigil Bearer* (Figure 149), a figure of a young athlete holding the strigil, a curved scraper which athletes used to remove oil and dust from the body after exercise.

Often proportions are changed to indicate position and power. The ruler is therefore made larger than his subjects. In *The Palette of King Narmer*, an Egyptian relief of the fourth millennium B.C., we see the king dealing with his subjects (Figure 150). One he has seized by the hair of his head, two others are crouched below, and off to the left is a fourth figure. In all these the king is represented as much larger than any of the others. In the Laocoön the two sons of the priest are represented as much smaller than their father.

FIGURE 150. PALETTE OF KING NARMER. Egyptian, Second Dynasty (ca. 2900–2800 B.C.) Original, found at Hierakonpolis, now in Cairo Museum. (Slate. Height: 25 inches. Photograph, courtesy New York Metropolitan Museum of Art; Dodge Fund, 1931.)

● THE FRAME

In the arrangement of parts, consideration must be given to the frame and the relation of the parts to the frame. Whether we look at the façade of a building, a statue, or a painting, we have a certain area or surface that is to be filled. Within this area the space should seem neither crowded nor empty. The camera offers interesting possibilities for experimentation, for with the finder on the camera, the artist can try different types of content in different relationships to the frame. The stage illustrates another challenge; the proscenium arch offers a frame, and the problem of the director is to fill that frame agreeably with stage set, characters, and lighting. Since the theater and dancing are arts of both time and space, the director deals with a content that is constantly changing; at any moment, however, the stage is supposed to show a scene in which the frame is filled agreeably.

Since the design must fill the shape, the choice of shape partly determines the design of the picture. Moreover, the lines of the enclosing shape strengthen or oppose the lines of the design. In a picture that is rectangular or square all the vertical or horizontal lines are strengthened by the lines of the frame. So powerful are these lines that an artist usually tries to cover them in some way to fill in the corners by the use of trees or shrubbery, or in some other way to change the severe right angle to a more graceful curve. The square is difficult to work with because it is all center and corners; there is no neutral ground, as it were. We have good design in the square in the metopes from the Parthenon and in the panels of the "Gates of Paradise." But because of its difficulty the square is relatively rare in art, and the rectangle is preferred. The rectangle has the advantage of being in straight lines, and yet it has much free space in the middle that is neither exact center nor corner, and in this central space the design is usually placed. If it is standing on its short side it shares something of the strength of the vertical; if it is on its long side it partakes of the peace of the horizontal. Most of the illustrations in this book are rectangular.

Irregular shapes are not always easily filled. An illustration is found in the reliefs made by Brunelleschi and Ghiberti showing the *Sacrifice of Isaac* (Figures 151 and 152). Since these two reliefs were offered in a competition for the north gates of the Baptistry at Florence, they have the same shape, the same general treatment in high relief, as well as the same subject. They have the same figures in the relief: each has Isaac kneeling on the altar, and Abraham arrested by the angel just as he is about to kill his son. In each panel are the servants of Abraham, and the ram which was the actual sacrifice. But the arrangement of the figures in the two compositions is entirely different. Brunelleschi has put Isaac in the center, the other figures are crowded into the corners.

FIGURE 151. FILIPPO BRUNELLESCHI (1377–1446), Italian sculptor and architect. Competition for Gates of Baptistry, Florence. *Sacrifice of Isaac* (1402). (Bronze. Size: about 1½ feet square. Bargello, Florence. Photograph by Alinari.)

FIGURE 152. LORENZO GHIBERTI. Competition for Gates of Baptistry, Florence. *Sacrifice of Isaac* (1402). (Bronze. Size: about 1½ feet square. Bargello, Florence. Photograph by Alinari.)

and the scene is confused. Ghiberti has divided the relief in two by a diagonal line, with Abraham and Isaac on one side and the servants on the other. His plan is clearer, simpler, and better.

The circle is a difficult shape. It is always the same; the eye tends to go around and around it without stopping, and there is a general tendency for a picture to seem to roll over if it is in a circular frame. Some of the best examples may be obtained from Greek vase painting. The cylix, or drinking cup, was ordinarily ornamented on the inside; hence the Greek draftsman had many opportunities to try his hand at filling a circular shape, and he succeeded admirably. A favorite cylix painting shows two women putting away their clothes. It is attributed to Douris (Figure 153).

The lunette, or half moon, is largely associated with architecture and sculpture. It is found most often in the tympanum, or sculptured space over a door. The tympanum at Chartres is an example (Fig. 182). It has the rich curve of the circle but is held steady by its horizontal base.

The shape or enclosing frame of any work is much more important than we usually give it credit for being. The repeated columns of the Parthenon make it seem much taller than it would otherwise, and in the same way the repeated

FIGURE 153. DOURIS (attributed) (fifth century B.C.). *Two Women Putting Away Clothes* (ca. 470). (Red-figured pottery cylix. Ripe archaic style. Size: 5 inches high, 12⅞ inches in diameter. New York, courtesy Metropolitan Museum of Art.)

FIGURE 154. MIES VAN DER ROHE (1886–), and PHILIP JOHNSON (1906–), American architects. Seagram Building (1957). (Bronze. 38 stories. New York.)

FIGURE 155. SKIDMORE, OWINGS, AND MERRILL, contemporary American architects. Inland Steel Building (1958). (Steel and glass. Main building 19 stories, tower 25 stories. Chicago, Illinois. Photograph, Bill Hedrich, Hedrich-Blessing, Chicago.)

FIGURE 156. UNITED NATIONS (1948–1950). General view from the north of permanent headquarters of UN, New York. (Glass panels, marble piers, and aluminum. General Assembly Building in foreground: Auditorium 380 feet long, 160 feet wide.) Marble and glass Secretariat 39 stories. Extreme right, part of the Library. Wallace K. Harrison, Director of Planning. Photograph, United Nations.)

horizontals of Notre Dame (Figure 182) give it a greater sense of calm. Modern office buildings such as the Seagram (Figure 154) are too tall for graceful proportions. The Inland Steel Building (Figure 155) has a frame in two parts, which cuts off part of its height. In the UN Secretariat Building (Figure 156) the side seems a bit wider, and the building is therefore less precarious.

● UNITY AND VARIETY

So far we have said little about unity and variety, but it can be seen in any one of the examples we have used. Take the *Sistine Madonna,* our first painting. It seems simply made, as though anyone could put the various parts together, but it is worthwhile to see what devices Raphael has used. The lines of the painting are predominantly curves, as we see in the small diagram. Then, the figures are also unified by their glances. The Pope looks to the Virgin, who looks to the saint, who looks in turn to the *putti* (cherubs) below, a seemingly obvious and at first glance naïve use of repetition.

The famous old Vendramin Palace on the Grand Canal at Venice is an interesting study in repetition and variety (Figure 157). It was built by the Vendramin family at the end of the fifteenth century. To this palace Wagner retired in 1882, and there he died a year later. One is impressed first by the repetition; the façade of the building shows a single grouping of windows repeated many times. There is, however, no lack of variety; the doorway takes the place of the central window on the first floor, and the place of the two end windows is left blank except for small openings. The first and second stories are separated by a balustrade, the second and third by a cornice. Moreover, the columns

FIGURE 157. PALAZZO VENDRAMIN-CALERGI (1481–1509). Pietro Lombardo (ca. 1435–1515), Italian architect. (Marble. Length: about 80 feet; height: about 65 feet. Venice. Photograph by Alinari.)

FIGURE 158. PARTHENON (447–432 B.C.). Facade seen between columns of the Propylaea. Ictinus and Callicrates (fifth century B.C.), Greek architects. (Pentelic marble. Height of columns: 34 feet. Athens. Photograph, courtesy Trans-World Airlines, Inc.,)

separating the windows are varied; those on the first floor are pilasters, undecorated except for a molding at the side; those of the second story are round and grooved; and those of the third story are round, without grooves. The most important device for securing variety, however, is in the arrangement of the windows. The three central windows are grouped together, but the end window is set off by a narrow panel with two engaged columns. This motive, repeated at the corner of the building, brings a distinct relief in the long line of windows; it is a breathing space, as it were, that makes the façade seem easy and comfortable.

In a cathedral like Modena (Figure 174) we trace the many repetitions and variations of the round arch. In the Egyptian temple (Figure 163) the sequence of rooms one after the other makes a subtle progression in darkness, from the open court at the front through the shadows of the hypostyle hall with its columns to the dark, mysterious chamber of the priest.

These ways of producing variety are fairly obvious. More subtle is the means used in the Parthenon (Figure 158). At first glance the building seems to show nothing but repetition, no variety except in the alternation of triglyphs and metopes in the frieze. In the Parthenon, however, are many subtle variations that do not strike the observer at once. The columns are smaller at the top than at the bottom; about one-third of the way up the shaft of the column there is a slight swell, or convex curve, known as the *entasis* of the column. Moreover, the columns incline at a very slight angle; it has been calculated that the corner columns are slightly larger than the others and are placed closer together. The steps and the entablature both rise in a very slight convex curve.

The idea has been expressed that in such refinements the Greeks were attempting to counteract certain optical illusions. Two long parallel lines tend to look hollow or to approach each other in a concave curve; hence the slight curve outward was introduced in the columns. A column seen against the sky looks slighter than one seen against the background of a building; hence the corner columns were larger and closer together. It cannot be determined, nor does it matter, whether the architects introduced these changes to correct optical illusions, or whether they introduced them merely as a means of giving variety to the building and so of improving its appearance. It is certain, however, that these changes were intentional. Similar refinements have been introduced in many buildings—St. Mark's in Venice, and the old library of Columbia University in New York City, to name only two examples. And it is certain that much of the beauty of the buildings is due to the lack of stiffness, the sense of a unified, almost breathing whole, resulting from these slight variations from the exact rule.

SCULPTURE AND PAINTING. Repetition in sculpture and painting is normally not so exact as repetition that is characteristic of the industrial arts and architecture. In architecture, one half of a building may be, and often is, just like the other half, but in a picture or a statue the two sides cannot be the same. If, for instance, the artist wants to repeat the line of a woman's hair, he may repeat it not as hair but as cloud or tree or scarf. This kind of repetition therefore is not obvious. We see the cloud as cloud and the tree as tree, and we do not see that they are repeating the line of the woman's hair. In the *Annunciation* of Fra Angelico (Figure 159), for example, the curve of the angel's body repeats the curve of the Madonna's body (Figure 160). The round curve of the Virgin's halo is repeated in the neckline of her dress, the stool on which she is seated, and the arches above her head. The arches on the side of the angel are seen in perspective, and they repeat the shape of the angel's wing until the whole place seems alive with the whir of wings. To stabilize the curves and to give variety, Fra Angelico has introduced many straight lines in the columns, the fence, the trees, even the doorway, which has a rectangular picture showing through it.

FIGURE 159. FRA ANGELICO (1387–1455), Italian painter. *Annunciation* (ca. 1440). (Fresco. Figures three fourths life size. Florence, San Marco Dormitory. Photograph by Anderson.)

FIGURE 160. Drawing of *Annunciation*, Figure 159. (Gordon Gilkey.)

FIGURE 161. JAN VERMEER (1632–1675), Dutch painter. *Young Woman with a Water Jug.* (Oil on canvas. Height: 18 inches. New York, courtesy Metropolitan Museum of Art; gift of Henry G. Marquand, 1889.)

In Vermeer's *Young Woman with a Water Jug* (Figure 161) the composition is worked out primarily in terms of the straight lines of the map and the slow curve which we find in the young woman's cape. In the Medici Tomb (Figure 135) we find repetition of lines in the bodies of the three figures. In the figure of Night the arm and the head make a complete half circle, and this curve is repeated in the curves of the body.

In *The Young Englishman* (Figure 110) Titian has made his design primarily in the three white spots of the head and two hands. It is, however, united in repeated circles of head, beard, and chain, with circular lines in the lace at neck and hands. There is also an interesting study in values.

274

14
ORGANIZATION IN ARCHITECTURE

Because of its size and complexity architecture needs separate treatment for the study of its design and organization. In this chapter the historical approach is used as the one best suited to make clear the various designs or styles of building.

● EGYPTIAN ARCHITECTURE (4000–2280 B.C.)

Egyptian architecture is closely bound up with religion. The *ka*, or "vital force," was dependent upon the body for its life; if the body was destroyed, the ka ceased to exist. Hence pyramids were built to preserve the body, that the ka might be safe. The most striking group of pyramids is at Giza, where there are the great pyramids of Khufu, Khafre, and Menkure (Figure 162).

FIGURE 162. PYRAMIDS OF GIZA seen from the air (ca. 2700–2200 B.C.). Photograph, courtesy Trans-World Airlines, Inc.)

Great as were the pyramids, however, they did not protect their dead from robbers and marauders, and later tombs were cut in rocky cliffs. A temple adjoined each tomb, and, as the tombs were made more inaccessible, these temples developed independently. The great temples are those at Karnak, Edfu, and Luxor. They followed the same basic plan. First was the *pylon*, a huge gateway covering the entire front of the building. The temple itself, as we have said when discussing the adaptation of plan to function, was composed of a series of halls. In one of these halls the roof was supported by rows of columns (*hypostyle*). In the temple at Karnak and in some of the other temples, the center columns are higher than those next to the wall, thus making a *clerestory* for the light to enter (Figure 164).

FIGURE 163. TEMPLE OF HORUS, pylon seen from first court (started by Ptolemy III, third century B.C.). (Sandstone. Height: about 100 feet. Edfu, Egypt. Photograph by Stoedtner.)

FIGURE 164. TEMPLE OF AMON (ca. 1300 B.C.). Hypostyle hall. (Red-brown sandstone. Height of columns in middle aisle: 69 feet; width of capital at top: 22 feet; height of columns in side aisles: 42½ feet. Karnak, Egypt. Model in Metropolitan Museum of Art, New York. Photograph, courtesy Metropolitan Museum of Art.)

Egyptian columns are primarily of two types, the flower and the bud. In the flower columns the flower makes a wide, bell-shaped capital. In the bud columns the uppermost part of the capital is smaller than the lower, like the bud of a flower. The model of the hypostyle hall at Karnak shows the clerestory and the columns; the central columns have flower capitals, the aisle columns, bud.

An outstanding characteristic of Egyptian art is its size. This is probably due to the nature of the country, for in the desert everything is swallowed up, and only the very large stands out in the wide stretches of sand. But even with this warning one can hardly grasp the enormous size of Egyptian buildings. The columns of the Great Hall at Karnak are large enough for a hundred men to stand on top of each capital.[1] The Great Hall at Karnak is 338 feet wide and 170 feet deep, furnishing a floor area about equal to that of the cathedral of Notre Dame in Paris, although this is only a single hall of the temple.[2] The pyramid of Khufu at Giza is 480 feet in length and covers about 13 acres.[3]

● MESOPOTAMIAN ARCHITECTURE

Of all the great palaces and temples of the Mesopotamians, Chaldeans, Babylonians, and Assyrians, very few examples are left; the brick, either unbaked or only partially baked, has crumbled away. The distinguishing characteristic is the *ziggurat,* or tower, built at successive levels, with ramps leading from one platform to the next. In many respects the ziggurat is like the modern building with setbacks.

[1] James Henry Breasted, *The Conquest of Civilization,* Harper & Row, Publishers, 1926, Plate IX, p. 98.
[2] *Ibid.,* Fig. 61, p. 96.
[3] *Ibid.,* p. 64.

● GREEK ARCHITECTURE (1100–100 B.C.)

Greek architecture in its most characteristic form is found in the temple, a low building in post-and-lintel construction as was the Egyptian temple. In this type of construction, two upright pieces, *posts*, are surmounted by a horizontal piece, *lintel*, long enough to reach from one to the other. This is the simplest and earliest type of construction, and it is more commonly used than any other. Barns are good examples, since the beams are exposed and can be seen. Post-and-lintel construction is well adapted to wood, because wooden beams are strong and are able to uphold the weight of a roof; at the same time they are long, so that a large building may be erected. However, wooden beams are not permanent; they burn, they rot, and they are eaten by insects. Stone lintels, in comparison, are enduring; but they cannot be obtained in as great lengths, and they stand much less weight than wood; therefore, in stone buildings the distance between posts must be small. A typical example of post-and-lintel construction is found in the ruins of the Temple of Apollo at Old Corinth (Figure 165).

The typical Greek temple had columns in front and often at the back also. Sometimes the entire building was surrounded by a row of columns, making a double row of columns in the front and back of the building and a single row at the side. The Parthenon belongs to this class. In the pure Greek style all columns are fluted.

FIGURE 165. TEMPLE OF APOLLO (sixth century B.C.). (Porous limestone, originally covered with stucco. Height of columns: 23⅔ feet. Old Corinth. Photograph, courtesy Royal Greek Embassy.)

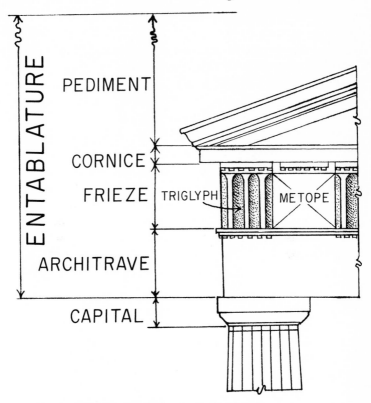

FIGURE 166. THE DORIC ORDER. (Drawing by Thad Suits.)

There are three styles of Greek architecture, Doric, Ionic, and Corinthian. The Doric (Figure 166) is seen in the Temple of Apollo at Old Corinth, and in the Parthenon, one of the greatest temples ever built. The Doric column has no base; the bottom of the column rests on the top step. The capital is very plain; a flat block, or slab, is joined to the column by a simple curve looking something like a cushion. The frieze is divided into *triglyphs* and *metopes;* the triglyph is a square slab having two vertical grooves (or glyphs) in the middle and a half groove at each end; the metope, which alternates with the triglyph, is also square. Metopes are often carved, as in the Parthenon (Figure 106).

The Ionic column is taller and slenderer than the Doric. It has a base, and the capital is ornamented with scrolls, or volutes, on each side. In the Ionic order the frieze is continuous instead of being divided into triglyphs and metopes. The architrave below the frieze is stepped; that is, it is divided horizontally into three parts, each being set in slightly. The greatest example of the Ionic order is the Erechtheum, which is unfinished and, unlike most Greek

FIGURE 167. CALLICRATES? Temple of Athena Niké (ca. 435 B.C.). (Pentelic marble. Size: 18½ by 27 feet. Athens. Photograph, courtesy Royal Greek Embassy.)

FIGURE 168. TEMPLE OF OLYMPIAN ZEUS (174 B.C.–A.D. 130). (Pentelic marble. Height of column: 56½ feet. Athens. Photograph, courtesy Royal Greek Embassy.)

temples, is irregular in shape; but, like all examples of the Ionic order in general, it is characterized by great elegance and grace. The Ionic column is found also in the little temple of Athena Niké at Athens (Figure 167).

The Corinthian column is distinguished from the Ionic by still greater height and by its capital, which shows two rows of acanthus leaves with volutes rising from them. The Corinthian, although an authentic Greek order, was last in point of development and was not so much used as the Doric and the Ionic. The late second-century Temple of Zeus at Athens has Corinthian capitals (Figure 168).

● ROMAN ARCHITECTURE (1000 B.C.–400 A.D.)

Roman architecture follows the general lines of the Greek with significant changes. The temple is no longer the typical building; equally important are civic buildings, baths, law courts, amphitheaters, aqueducts, and bridges.

Structurally the most important innovation of the Romans is the arch, which was widely used, though it was not invented by them. Next to the post-and-lintel, arch construction is historically of greatest importance. An arch is made of wedge-shaped stones that are arranged with the small side of the wedge turned down toward the opening. When the stones have been put in place by means of scaffolding or centering, their shape keeps them from falling, as we can see in the aqueduct of Segovia (Figure 169). Each stone of the arch, by its weight, exerts constant pressure on the stones on each side, and the arch is held in position only by an exact balancing of these pressures. If that balance is upset, the arch collapses. As the old Arabic proverb has it, "An arch never sleeps."

FIGURE 169. SEGOVIA AQUEDUCT (first century A.D.). (Granite. Length: 2,700 feet; height: 102 feet. Segovia. Photograph, courtesy Spanish National Tourist Office.)

FIGURE 170. PANTHEON (A.D. 120–124; portico A.D. 202). (Brick, mortar, and concrete, originally faced on the exterior with Pentelic marble and stucco. Height of columns: 46½ feet. Rome. Photograph, courtesy Italian State Tourist Office.)

Another characteristic of Roman architecture is the flat round dome that covers an entire building, as in the Pantheon (Figures 170 and 171).

When the Romans used the same designs as the Greeks, they did not use them in just the same way. The columns are taller and thinner, and often, as in the Pantheon, the columns are not fluted. The Corinthian column is used extensively, as is the composite column, an invention of the Romans made by combining the Ionic volutes with the Corinthian acanthus-circled bell. The orders are not kept separate, but are stacked, or superimposed, as in the Colosseum (Figure 122). Those on the first floor are Doric, on the second Ionic, and on the

FIGURE 171. PANTHEON (A.D. 120–124), interior. (Cement dome; wall decoration and pavement of marble and porphyry. Diameter of rotunda: 142 feet. Rome. Photograph by Alinari.)

third Corinthian. Moreover, the elements borrowed from the Greeks are sometimes used only as ornaments, whereas with the Greeks they were used structurally. In the Colosseum, again, the columns between the arches and the entablature above them are not essential to the structure of the building; this is seen in that part of the building from which the outer layer of concrete has been torn away; the columns are missing, but the arches stand as before.

● BYZANTINE ARCHITECTURE
(200–1453 A.D.; GOLDEN AGE—SIXTH CENTURY A.D.)

During the Middle Ages, religion again took an important place; the most important buildings were the church and the cathedral. But architecture developed on different lines in the East and in the West.

Eastern, or Byzantine, architecture takes its name from Byzantium, later called Constantinople and now called Istanbul. Byzantine architecture is characterized by a great central dome with half domes grouped around it. The dome, which is rather flat, reminds one of the Pantheon but is fitted to the building in a different way. In the Pantheon the round dome just covers the round building. In the Byzantine building the dome has to be fitted to a square area, and the space between the arches and the dome is filled by curved triangles (pendentives) on which the dome rests. This gives greater height and makes the interior more spacious and inspiring. A dome supported in this way is called a *dome on pendentives*.

The greatest example of Byzantine architecture is the Hagia Sophia, or Church of the Divine Wisdom, in Istanbul. The Byzantine type has been widely used for the national church of Russia, for Mohammedan mosques, and for Jewish synagogues (Figure 119).

● WESTERN ARCHITECTURE IN THE MIDDLE AGES
(200–700 A.D.)

During the medieval period Western architecture passed through three stages of development in the three styles known as early Christian, Romanesque, and Gothic. These developed one out of the other; the Romanesque was an outgrowth of the early Christian, and the Gothic of the Romanesque. As in all such cases, there is never any sharp line to be drawn between one style and the other; there is never a time when one can say definitely that all buildings before that time are one style and after that time they are another. Accordingly we shall attempt to trace the development of the styles in their prominent characteristics.

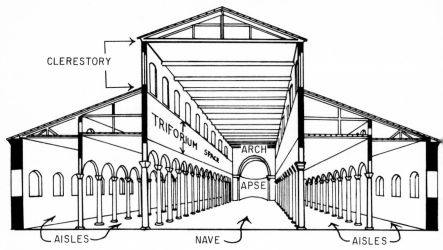

FIGURE 172. BASILICA. Perspective cross section of early Christian basilica. (Drawing by Thad Suits after Dorothy Shea in John Ives Sewall, *A History of Western Art*, p. 281. Henry Holt and Company, Inc.)

THE BASILICA. In basic plan the three Western styles follow the general type of the Roman basilica, a long rectangular building divided by pillars into a central nave and aisles (Figure 172). Sometimes there is one aisle on each side of the nave; sometimes there are two. Often the nave is higher than the aisles, and, therefore, there is opportunity for clerestory lighting. Between the clerestory windows and the columns there is necessarily a space in which there can be no windows because of the roof over the aisles. This space, which was later used for the *triforium*, was decorated differently in different periods and is one of the significant features in determining the style of a building. At one end was a semicircular *apse*, which was used for the high altar. It was traditionally at the east, and that part of the church was known as the choir.

In the early churches the building was the one simple rectangle with apse. Later the plan was adapted to the shape of a cross by the addition of cross aisles between the nave and the choir. The arms thus made are known as *transepts*. Directly opposite the high altar, i.e., at the west, was the main entrance.

EARLY CHRISTIAN ARCHITECTURE

The early Christian church, of which Sant' Apollinare in Classe at Ravenna (Figure 120) is an example, does not have transepts; the clerestory is heavy and the windows are small. The columns separating the nave from the aisles follow the Roman orders with flat lintels or round arches between them. The interiors are often decorated with elaborate mosaics, as in Sant' Apollinare.

● **ROMANESQUE ARCHITECTURE** (Eleventh and twelfth centuries)

Romanesque architecture differs from early Christian in many ways. One of the most important is its use of the arch. In shape it was the round arch employed by the Romans, but when it was introduced into Romanesque building, it took on several different forms. First is the *recessed arch*. An opening, especially if it be a door, is made of a series of arches, each slightly farther back than the preceding, so that the door or window is deeply recessed. Often, as in the door at Aulnay (Figure 173), each recess is decorated with carvings. In this way the opening gains greatly in weight and massiveness. The arch, also, is combined with one or two other arches under one large arch and becomes a *compound*

FIGURE 173. ST. PIERRE, AULNAY, portal of south transept (twelfth century). (Stone Foto Marburg.)

FIGURE 174. MODENA CATHEDRAL (1099–1106).
(Photograph by Anderson.)

arch. In the cathedral at Modena (Figure 174) we have three small arches combined under one large arch which is recessed. Between the small arches is a small column, or *colonnette*. The colonnette is very light and unsubstantial, largely ornamental. In the doorway at Aulnay we notice that each of the recesses ends with a colonnette. Often the small arches are combined to form an arcade, as in the cathedral at Pisa (Figure 175). In the façade at Modena we see a round window above the main doorway. Such a window, called a *rose window*, becomes usual in the Gothic adaptation of this style. Towers are another feature that made a first appearance in Romanesque architecture.

In the interior of the Abbaye-aux-Dames at Caen (Figure 176) the triforium space is no longer empty but is filled with small arches. There are recessed

FIGURE 175. CATHEDRAL AND LEANING TOWER, PISA (1063–1100). (Busketus and Rainaldus, architects.) (White, black, and colored marbles and some stone. Length: 312 feet; width: 106 feet. Photograph, courtesy of Italian State Tourist Office.)

arches between the pillars of the nave. Most important is the ceiling. When the principle of the arch was used in the covering of large buildings, the first result was the barrel vault. It was simply a succession of arches. The groin vault was next made by cutting the barrel vault at right angles (Figure 177). Later it was discovered that diagonal arches or ribs could be built that would support the entire weight of the roof. The space between the ribs could then be filled in with lighter material. This system, known as "ribbed vaulting," is the chief characteristic of Romanesque and Gothic architecture. This construction also made a change in the columns; the ribs of the ceiling had to be supported at the base and were, therefore, carried down to the floor. A number of these ribs made a pier or column.

FIGURE 177. Groin vault. (Drawing by Thad Suits.)

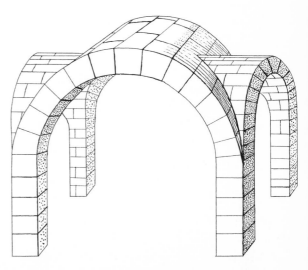

● GOTHIC ARCHITECTURE (1194–1600)

As the Gothic developed from the Romanesque, the buildings became larger and taller, the change having been made possible by the use of the pointed arch. The thrust of an arch changes with its shape (Figure 178). In general, the flatter the arch the greater the thrust, and the steeper the arch the more nearly the thrust is absorbed in the vertical wall. With the pointed arch, therefore, the buildings could be made higher than with the round arch.

With the higher buildings came a new type of buttress. The general shape of the exterior of a cathedral can be clearly seen in the cathedral of Pisa, with its central nave rising above the aisles on each side. In the early churches, as at Pisa, no extra support was needed for the central section, but as the churches grew larger and taller, it was found necessary to reinforce this part of the building. If a solid buttress were put up, it would cut off the aisles below. Accordingly the plan was devised of making a buttress at the aisle wall from which a half

FIGURE 178. Direction of thrust in round and pointed arch. (W. D. Richmond, from Sewall, *A History of Western Art*, p. 191. Drawing by Thad Suits.)

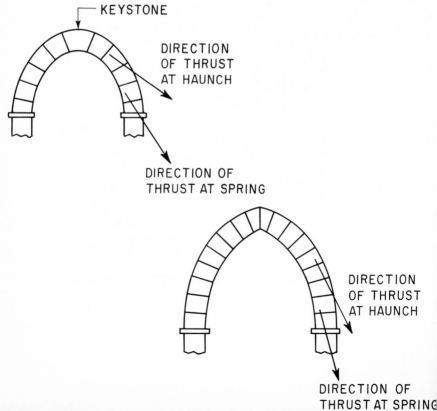

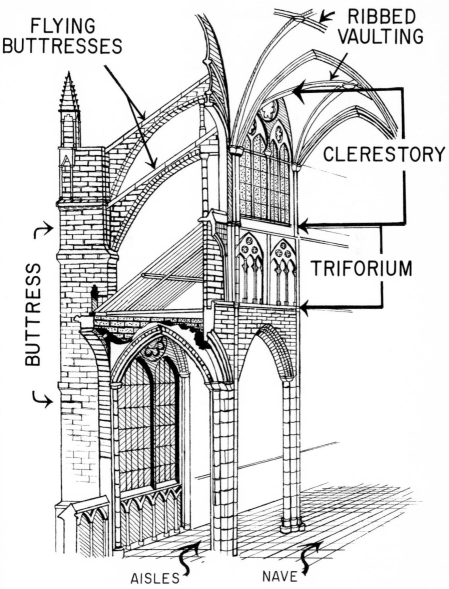

FIGURE 179. AMIENS CATHEDRAL (begun 1220), perspective cross section. (Drawing by Thad Suits after Viollet-le-Duc.)

arch was stretched out over the aisle to support the roof of the nave (Figure 179). Sometimes just one such arch was sufficient; sometimes, as at Amiens (Figure 180) two were used, one above the other. These are called *flying buttresses*.

FIGURE 180.   AMIENS CATHEDRAL,
interior. (Stone. Height: 147 feet; width
of middle aisle: 43 feet. Photograph,
Clarence Ward.)

The photograph of Notre Dame at Paris (Figure 181) shows the flying buttresses as they are actually seen. More than any other characteristic of Gothic architecture, they seem to create its mood of soaring aspiration.

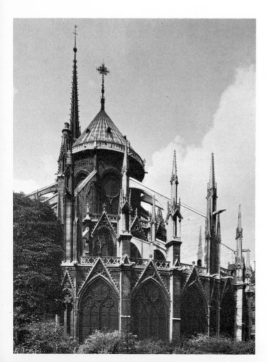

FIGURE 181. CATHEDRAL OF NOTRE DAME, PARIS
(twelfth and thirteenth centuries). View of apse, showing the flying buttresses. (Length: about 415 feet;
height of flèche: about 310 feet. Photograph,
Clarence Ward.)

In the Romanesque cathedral, several small windows were combined in a compound arch; in the Gothic, this process was continued until the arches appeared only as stone tracery. Eventually the windows became so large that the walls ceased to have any function as walls; the roof was supported by the huge buttresses and the entire wall space filled with stained-glass windows. The triforium space was regularly filled with small arches, and the rose window became large and important. The doorways changed too. In the Romanesque church the façade sometimes had one doorway, sometimes three. The Gothic façade regularly had three doorways. Each was made with multiple orders, like the Romanesque, though the arch, of course, was pointed. The decorations, also, were much more elaborate. In the Romanesque they were relatively simple moldings, with or without carvings of conventional designs, figures, animals, or fruit. In the Gothic the human figure became the characteristic decoration, a recessed doorway being filled with rows of saints or kings.

The west, or "Royal," portal of Chartres Cathedral (Figure 182) is an excellent example of early Gothic. It was finished in the middle of the twelfth century and is generally recognized as transitional work, though by common consent it is classed as Gothic. As is usual in Gothic there are three doorways with a lintel and a tympanum over each. Sculpture forms the only decoration. The three portals are treated as a single unit proclaiming the majesty and omnipotence of Christ.

FIGURE 182. CHARTRES CATHEDRAL (twelfth and thirteenth centuries), West, or "Royal," Portal. (Stone. Height of royal ancestors: 20 feet, 6 inches; width of west portal: ca. 50 feet. Photograph by Houvet.)

In the tympanum above the central doorway is shown the second coming of Christ when he is to judge the quick and the dead. His right hand is raised in blessing; in his left hand he holds a book. Around him the four evangelists are represented by their symbols. On the lintel below are the twelve Apostles.

The tympanum and the lintels over the right door celebrate the birth of Christ. In the first (lower) are represented the Annunciation, the Visitation, and the birth of Jesus. Mary is lying on a couch and the child is above her in a manger. Joseph stands at Mary's head, and on beyond are angels and shepherds. The second lintel shows the presentation in the temple. In the tympanum Mary is seen in her glory, the Infant in her arms. On each side is an angel swinging a censer.

In the tympanum to the doorway on the left is shown the Ascension. Christ on a cloud is being supported by two angels. On the lower lintel are the Apostles, while between them and Christ are four angels who look as though they might be leaning toward the Apostles while they say:

> Ye men of Galilee, why stand ye gazing up into heaven? this same Jesus, which is taken up from you into heaven, shall so come in like manner as ye have seen him go into heaven
>
> —Acts 1:11

On either side of the doorways are rows of kings and queens. They are commonly supposed to be the ancestors of Christ, as told in the first chapter of Genesis; hence the name "Royal" for this portal. They are richly clad in embroidered robes befitting royalty, and each carries in his hand some index to his work or character—a book, a scepter, a scroll; many wear crowns.

These kings and queens are, however, remarkably elongated. Each stands by a column, and is stiffly posed with arms close to the body and never projecting beyond that contour. As Helen Gardner says: "They grow from the columns they rest on—this is what the artist was striving for—to use the human figure to adorn a column and yet not lose the feeling of the column."[4]

In general shape the façade of a Gothic cathedral is a rectangle resting on the short side, and the great height is emphasized by the two towers that usually complete the design. In Notre Dame at Paris (Figure 183) the towers are square and relatively short, but in many other cathedrals, such as Chartres (Figure 184), the towers are tall and pointed.

The Gothic cathedral often took centuries to build, with the result that the same style was not used throughout a building. Part of a building may be in

[4] Helen Gardner, *Art Through the Ages,* p. 314.

FIGURE 183. CATHEDRAL OF NOTRE DAME, PARIS.
(Diameter of rose window: 42 feet; height of towers: 223
feet. Photograph, courtesy Trans-World Airlines, Inc.)

FIGURE 184. CHARTRES CATHEDRAL. (Width of façade:
156 feet; height of north tower: 378 feet. Photograph by
Houvet.)

Romanesque, part in early Gothic, and another part in late Gothic. As the
ideas of architecture changed, the building itself changed. In Chartres Cathedral, one of the greatest of all cathedrals, the towers are not the same; the
older tower is shorter, more solid, and more substantial than its younger brother.

293

FIGURE 185.   CA' D'ORO (1422—ca. 1440). Italian Gothic (Venice. Courtesy Italian State Tourist Office. Photograph by Alinari.)

The Gothic style in architecture is known, and rightly known, primarily for its cathedrals and churches. There are also, however, many beautiful palaces, especially in Venice, where the light tracery is reflected in the water of the canals. One of the favorite examples is known as the Ca d'Oro (Figure 185). It was built in the fifteenth century.

● RENAISSANCE ARCHITECTURE (Fifteenth and Sixteenth Centuries)

In Renaissance architecture the cathedral, or temple, is no longer the typical building; secular architecture comes to the fore as in Roman times. Although Renaissance architecture is a return to the ideals of the Greeks and Romans, it is not a slavish imitation, but rather a free use of the materials found in classic architecture. The designers got their ideas from Greece and Rome, but they used these suggestions freely, according to their own tastes, in a way that was original. For example, in the Medici-Riccardi Palace at Florence designed by Michelozzo, we find the round arches of the Romans. On the first floor a single arch occupies the space of two arches on the second and third floors. In the upper floors, moreover, the window space is filled with the compound arch of the Romanesque. At the top of this building there is a large cornice, heavy enough to crown the whole mass of the building. There is also a molding, or *stringcourse*, that separates one story from the other.

In the Palace of the Senate at Rome (Figure 186), designed by Michelangelo, we find the stringcourse and the cornice, this time surmounted by a balustrade. In addition, each large window has its own post-and-lintel system. The windows are decorated with pediments; some are triangular, some are rounded. The classical rule would have been one pediment, one building, and the pediment would have been in scale with the building. Between the windows are flat columns called *pilasters*.

The overhanging cornice, the stringcourse, the pilaster, and the ornamental pediment are characteristic features of the Renaissance style. Another is the dome on a drum. The Roman dome was so low that it could hardly be seen from the outside. In Renaissance architecture the dome was made small, and

FIGURE 186. MICHELANGELO. Palace of the Senate (begun 1538). (Rome. Photograph by Anderson.)

FIGURE 187. MICHELANGELO. St. Peter's Cathedral, apse and dome (1547–1564). (Stone. Height of dome: 435 feet. Rome. Photograph by Stoedtner.)

it was raised high on a circular drum and surmounted with a lantern. The curve of the dome was changed, too; it was made much steeper, and its sides were ribbed, as we see in the dome of St. Peter's (Figure 187).

In the smaller building, whether residence, church, or store, the Renaissance produced a type of symmetrical structure of great simplicity and beauty. In England it is known as the Georgian style, and in the United States as the American colonial.

● BAROQUE ARCHITECTURE (1600–1750)

Baroque architecture flourished in the seventeenth century and in the opening years of the eighteenth. It is characterized primarily as a period of excessive ornamentation. The architectural framework remained close to that of the Renaissance, but it was overburdened with a profusion of carved decoration. Columns and entablatures were decorated with garlands of flowers and fruit, shells and waves. Often alcoves were built into the wall to receive statues, thus making a pattern in light and dark. Surfaces were frequently curved. The churches of this period no longer use the Gothic nave and aisles; the area is filled with chapels which take the place of the aisles. They often have domes or cupolas, and they may or may not have spires. The church of San Carlo alle Quattro Fontane (Figure 188) is an excellent example of the love for ornament, the movement, restlessness, and excitement of the style.

Comparison of the apse and the façade of St. Peter's offers interesting differences in style. The apse, which was designed by Michelangelo, is a solid, unified whole, an appropriate symbol of the power of the church. The façade built by Maderna after the death of Michelangelo is too crowded. It covers the drum, and the dome does not look at home with it as it did with the apse. In the façade itself we see the spirit of the Baroque in the massed columns which are doubled for the sake of ornament, the decorative pediments, the pilasters, and the heavy stringcourse (Figure 189).

The Palace of the Senate, which was named as an example of Renaissance style, has definite leanings toward the Baroque in the stairway and elaborate doorway with ornamental carvings on each side.

FIGURE 188. SAN CARLO ALLE QUATTRO FONTANE (begun 1635, façade 1667). Francesco Borromini (1599–1667), Italian architect. (Rome. Photograph by Anderson.)

FIGURE 189. MADERNA. St. Peter's Cathedral, façade. (Stone. Photograph courtesy Italian State Tourist Office.)

● NINETEENTH–CENTURY ARCHITECTURE

The nineteenth century in architecture is known as a period of *eclecticism.* Eclecticism means freedom of choice; in architecture it means the freedom to choose from the styles of the past. In former times architects had used the style of the period because that was the way things were being done. But in the nineteenth century both architects and clients became style-conscious, and they deliberately chose to make a building in one style or another. Hence it happens that we have in almost any American city examples of all the historical styles from the Greek down. This self-consciousness about choice of style has produced some good and some bad results. The Gothic motive in the Brooklyn Bridge is well suited to the tall pillars of that bridge. On the other hand it is love for the Gothic that is responsible for the "gingerbread" and scroll decorations on many houses.

The interest in various styles has resulted in the adoption of certain styles as suitable for certain types of building: Gothic for churches, Baroque for theaters, Renaissance for government buildings, and so on.

The real objection to eclecticism is philosophical. In the course of historical development, each of the major styles has been evolved to meet the needs of its own age and to express its philosophy. To go back to the style of a previous age is essentially false.

● MODERN ARCHITECTURE

SKELETON CONSTRUCTION

Skeleton construction is a development of modern times, and on it most of our great modern structures depend. But skeleton construction in its turn was made possible by the development of two new materials: structural steel and reinforced concrete.

Structural steel dates back to 1855, when Bessemer invented his process for the mass production of steel. As the advantages of steel became apparent, it gradually superseded cast iron. These advantages are primarily that it is resilient, strong, and reliable.

Concrete is composed of sand, crushed stone or gravel, water, and cement. When mixed, it is a semifluid which, owing to the cement, dries into a hard, stonelike substance. Forms are made just the size and shape desired. The fluid concrete is poured into them; when dry it forms a solid substance of just that form and shape. Concrete is very strong, and it will stand great weight, but it will not stand strain or tension. At the end of the last century, some French engineers discovered that by adding steel rods to concrete they could give it the lacking tensile strength; in other words, it would withstand strain. Reinforced concrete, as the new material is called, is thus the combination of concrete and steel. It has the strength of concrete, and like concrete it can readily be made into any shape. At the same time it will withstand strain as steel does. It also has the advantage of being much cheaper than steel and lighter in weight.

In skeleton construction, strong but slender beams of steel or reinforced concrete make the framework of a building, and on it all the other parts are placed or hung. This type of construction has opened many new possibilities in building. First, it has made possible tall buildings, because the skeletons are strong but light. The walls which are hung from the skeleton are merely curtains to keep out cold and air. They may be made entirely of glass. They have no weight to speak of, and they are not essential to the strength of the building. A modern skyscraper, if built of masonry in the old fashion, would need to have the first floors of solid stone to support the weight of the upper stories. In the building of the Inland Steel Company in Chicago, the columns which carry the weight of the building are on the outside. As a result, the entire space on any floor is free of posts or pillars and, if it is desired, can be used as a single room (Figure 155).

Moreover, with skeleton construction the building may be set up off the ground on posts so that the ground floor may be used for outdoor living or for garage and driveway. Another important result of this type of construction is the fact that an opening of any size may be spanned. Lintels of stone are necessarily short, since stone cannot be cut in great lengths and will not bear strain. Lintels of wood are longer, but they are obviously limited. Since steel may be made of any length and strength, a door or a window may be of any desired size.

Skeleton construction also allows freedom in the shape of the house. Concrete is a fluid material and can take any shape. Buildings of wood, brick, or stone tend to be rectangular, partly because of the difficulty of putting a roof on any but a rectangular building. Now, buildings may be made of any shape: circular, round, or square. In the Guggenheim Museum in New York City the galleries mount in a continuous spiral. In the State Fair Arena (Figure 190) at Raleigh, North Carolina, the walls are two opposing parabolas of glass and concrete, with their open ends joined on the ground and their arches rising outward from each other. The arena measures eight hundred feet across in all directions, and there is not a single column to obstruct the view. It seats about nine thousand.

FIGURE 190. STATE FAIR ARENA (1953). Matthew Nowicki (1910–1950) and William Henley Deitrick (1895–   ), American architects. (Width of interior: 300 feet. Raleigh, N.C. Photograph, State Advertising Division, Raleigh, N.C.)

CANTILEVER CONSTRUCTION

Cantilever is a special form of steel and reinforced concrete construction. The term *cantilever* has reference to any member or unit of an architectural design which projects beyond its support. The cantilever principle is often seen in bridges, where each half of the bridge is supported on one side only. The two halves meet in the center to form the bridge, but each half is entirely independent of the other. In most airplanes the wings are attached to the body in a cantilever construction. We see the principle in buildings when the upper story juts out beyond the lower. The two essentials of cantilever construction are, first, that the material used be able to stand the strain (i.e., have the tensile strength), and second, that it be fastened securely at the side where it is supported. This principle, which is very old, has been much used in recent years, because the piece that projects can be larger in steel and reinforced concrete than in older materials.

The cantilever was used rather widely by the American architect Frank Lloyd Wright. In a number of houses he used the cantilever in a veranda, so that the roof projects over the porch with no columns or pillars to hold it up.

300

In one case he had a house projecting over a waterfall by means of cantilevered balconies. For the research building of the Johnson Wax Company (Figure 191), Mr. Wright erected a tall building in which all the floors are cantilevered from one central column. The floors are alternately square and round. The whole is enclosed in glass. The central column contains elevators and tubes for air conditioning, besides all the passages for the machinery of the building, electric controls, etc.

INTERNATIONAL STYLE. The buildings of the twentieth century fall in general into two different styles known as the international and the organic. Both use the new materials but they differ in their aims and techniques. The international style is recognized as a modern style by its severe horizontal and vertical lines, its reinforced concrete, its white walls and flat roofs. There is directness and simplicity in its use of materials and avoidance of ornament. The design is planned very carefully, usually with a *module*, or measure, to determine the

FIGURE 191. FRANK LLOYD WRIGHT (1869–1959), American architect. Research and Development Tower of S. C. Johnson and Son, Inc. (1947–1950). (Brick and concrete with walls of glass tubing. Height of tower: 156 feet [50 feet underground]; each floor 40 feet square; each alternate floor 38 feet in diameter. Racine, Wis. Photograph, courtesy Johnson Wax.

FIGURE 192. FRANK LLOYD WRIGHT. Interior, Administration Building of S. C. Johnson and Son, Inc. (1936–1939). 400 foot area. Racine, Wis. Photograph, courtesy Johnson Wax.

exact proportions. The "Seagram Building in New York City is a bronze and glass shaft with every dimension, from total height to smallest bevel, determined by an arbitrary modular system."[5]

Adjectives often applied to buildings in this style are "spare," "aristocratic," "chilly," and this character explains why many people find it cold and forbidding. Moreover, it is a design that can be imitated easily. Anyone can understand and use the structural elements. There are in this book three examples of this style: the Seagram Building, the UN Secretariat Building, and the Inland Steel Building. Of these the Seagram has generally been accounted superior to the other two.

ORGANIC STYLE. The organic architecture of the twentieth century is identified primarily with the work of Frank Lloyd Wright. With Mr. Wright architecture is organic when there is organic unity in planning structure, materials, and site. As Wright said, "I build a home for myself in southern Wisconsin: a stone, wood, and plaster building, make it as much a part of my grandfather's ground as the rocks and trees and hills there are."[6] And again: "Modern architecture, let us now say organic architecture, is a natural architecture: the architecture of nature, for nature."[7]

It is generally recognized now that next to his residences Wright's ability showed itself best in the various buildings he designed for the Johnson Wax Company of Racine, Wisconsin. The tower of that group of buildings has been discussed (Figure 191). The Administration Building (Figure 192) should be studied for the skill and beauty with which the various buildings are harmonized.

[5] John Cannady in Sewall, *A History of Western Art*, p. 925.
[6] Frederick Gutheim (ed.), *Frank Lloyd Wright on Architecture: Selected Writings* (1894–1940).
[7] *Ibid.*, p. 248.

In the administration building interior the columns are made to flare at the top, and some do not reach to the ceiling. They have a decorative effect and give a sense of gaiety and freshness to the room, like sunlight falling through the leaves of trees.

The boast of modern architecture is that it is organic. Eclectic architecture, as we saw, was primarily decorative. The architect and his client chose a certain façade or a certain treatment of the material because they liked the looks of it, and often it had little if any relation to the actual structure of the house. House plans were frequently presented as floor plans with the exterior to be finished in Gothic, classic, American colonial, or what have you. But when we say modern architecture is organic, we mean that there is organic unity in planning, structure, materials, and site; all are designed to meet exact needs. The needs of the age are many and various: factories, office buildings, laboratories, railroad stations, schools, hospitals, mass housing, airports, broadcasting stations, theaters, churches, homes, dormitories. The demands of each must be studied and met if the building is to be good.

To study in detail one example of a building designed for a special need, we will take the chapel at Stephens College, designed by Eero Saarinen (Figure 193).

FIGURE 193. EERO SAARINEN (1910–1961), American architect. Stephens College Chapel (finished 1956). (Brick. Size: 70 feet by 70 feet. Columbia, Mo. Photograph, Stephens College.)

The chapel was intended primarily as a place for private worship. It was presumed that small functions might be held there, such as a wedding, a baptism, or an occasional concert, but such occasions were not to be frequent enough to interfere with private devotions. Moreover, the chapel was dedicated to the One God, the one maker and ruler of the universe, whether the form of worship were that of Jew, Mohammedan, Buddhist, or Christian. No one was to feel a stranger or unwelcome. Therefore, there were to be no symbols of any one faith, such as the cross, or the star of David: all symbols were to be large and general.

The building as designed by Mr. Saarinen is square, foursquare, close to the earth; walls and roof make one unit, clinging to the ground and at the same time pointing up and ending in the central steeple. The walls are not interrupted by any windows, but at the entrance in the center of each side is a portico of stained glass, serving, as Mr. Saarinen said, as a small lantern leading to the chapel (Figure 194).

FIGURE 194. STEPHENS COLLEGE CHAPEL, interior.

The interior is simple and direct. If one were to draw diagonals from the four corners of the building, he would obtain four equal triangles. One of these is designed for the organ and choir, the other three for the audience. In the exact center of the room is the altar, a plain square block. The chief light comes from the base of the spire and falls directly on the altar.

An ambulatory around the entire auditorium is separated from the main chapel by a screen of interlaced brick, which makes a division but at the same time gives a view of the interior and the stained-glass doors beyond. The organ and choir are set behind a screen of wooden pieces, light brown and black. The ceiling is of wood in a square design.

The general effect is of simplicity and greatness. The place is small, but one has vistas of vast spaces; the room is intimate, but its many vistas are conducive to thoughts of the distant and the far away. It is the kind of place where one can get away from the perplexities of the everyday in the contemplation of the infinite.

15
FORM IN MUSIC

Since music is an auditory art, it can exist only in time. Therefore, it must be formed into patterns which give it substance and clarity. Form solves this problem; it makes music last and gives it a coherent design.

The word *form* can be used to mean both the structural design of a piece of music and the type of music. A distinction of these two meanings will be kept here, the term *form* being reserved for structural design and the term *genre* for the type. The mass, for example, is a genre within which we sometimes find the form of a fugue.

The listener should be made aware at the outset that form is not a fixed mold, or that not all forms having the same name will be exactly alike. The composer creates the form as he creates the music, which may mean that the form arising from the music fits no prescribed mold. Nevertheless, there are a few major forms in which most examples show such marked similarity that their design can be said to be standard. These are the forms to be discussed in this chapter.

● SONG FORM

Vocal music was the first music to develop standard forms. But although vocal forms were often dependent upon the form of the text being sung, some of them, like song form, have been carried over into instrumental music as well.

In any case, the most important element in song form, as in most tonal music, is the melody. By listening to what happens to the melody, we can identify the form.

There are two types of song form which are widely used: binary and ternary. Binary song form (AB), as its name implies, is of two parts. The second part of binary form is both a contrast and a complement to the first. In binary form some balance of design and some related musical idea are usually present. It is somewhat like a question and answer; that is, part A presents a musical idea which is resolved in part B. The two parts are usually divided by a significant pause such as a dominant or tonic cadence. Brahms's famous "Lullaby" is binary, and part B is exactly as long as part A, each being eight measures.

EXAMPLE 1

Lullaby

Johannes Brahms
German (1833–1897)

In this example, part A could stand alone because it ends on a tonic cadence, but part B sounds like a natural extension of it. Part A is primarily tonic, part B dominant, but ending on the tonic.

Not all binary forms are exactly balanced in length. In Handel's "Harmonious Blacksmith" part B is twice the length of part A. Here part A cannot stand alone, because it ends on a dominant cadence. Part B begins with the tonic and after going through the dominant ends on the tonic.

EXAMPLE 2 Harpsichord Suite in E major
(Harmonious Blacksmith)

Georg Friedrich Handel
German (1685–1759)

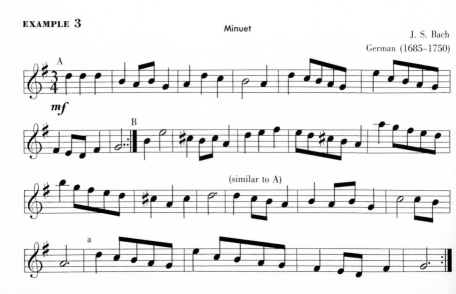

Sometimes part B quotes, either at the beginning or end, a section of part A. In the majority of Domenico Scarlatti's sonatas, part B ends with a quotation from part A. In this Bach Minuet we have an exact quotation of part A at the end of part B, which gives us a rounded, or ABa binary.

EXAMPLE 3 Minuet

J. S. Bach
German (1685–1750)

Ternary form (ABA), or three-part form, like the binary, depends on two distinct thematic sections; but in ternary form there is a full restatement of part A after part B, creating a pleasing symmetrical balance. In some music of this form, the composer will at the end of section B write Da Capo or merely D.C., which means to go back to "the head," or beginning, to repeat part A. This saves repeating it in the score. Here is an example of ternary form.

EXAMPLE 4

Plaisir d'amour
(The Joy of Love)

Jean Paul Martini
French (1706–1784)

allegretto, con moto

Perhaps the most widely used song form is an extended kind of ternary which is sometimes called quatrain form (AABA). The extension, the second A, is either an exact repetition of the first A or of such obvious similarity that we call it a second A. Ordinarily the repetition of a section of music is not of any importance, since it does not alter the form, which is true in this case. Here is a well-known example of the extended ternary.

EXAMPLE 5 Drink to Me Only with Thine Eyes

Ben Jonson, "To Celia"
Music traditional

Other examples of AABA form are:

Beautiful Dreamer   Deck the Halls
Au Claire de la Lune   Down by the Salley Gardens
Blue Bells of Scotland   The Rose of Tralee
Swanee River   The Last Rose of Summer

● THEME AND VARIATION

One of the most popular and enduring forms in music is the theme and varia-tion form (A, A1, A2, A3, etc.). In this form there is a constant interplay between repetition and variation, and it is the delight of both composer and listener to see how many ways there are of saying essentially the same thing.

Variations tend to progress by contrast or by increasing virtuosity. In either case the variations show more use of ornamentation than the original theme. For the most part, therefore, this form is confined to a light, even witty manner of presenting the theme in several guises. As a result there are perhaps only a few sets of variations that could be called monumental, two of them being the *Goldberg Variations* by Bach and the *Diabelli Variations* by Beethoven.

Theme and variation form is often based on a binary or ternary song form because the themes are concise and show contrast. Handel's "Harmonious Blacksmith," quoted earlier as an example of binary song form, is followed by five variations, which progress by increasing virtuosity. In the following example we have a theme and variation form by Mozart. These variations progress by contrast. The theme is binary but only the first half of the theme is quoted.

EXAMPLE 6

Theme & Variations from the 1st movement
(Sonata K331)

Wolfgang Amadeus Mozart
German (1756–1791)

In variation I the melody is greatly changed by the use of syncopation and chromatic intervals. Notice that the duration of the notes is half that of the theme, making twice as many.

VARIATION IV

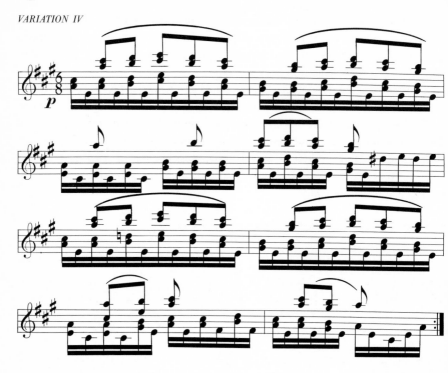

In variation IV the greatest change is in the texture which is thicker, and in the range which is higher. Here the melody flows serenely because of the stepwise rise and fall of the melodic line.

In variation VI changes occur in the meter, which becomes 4/4 and in the tempo, which is speeded up to allegro. The last half of the melody is treated quite differently from the first and acts as a finale, or grand flourish, to end the variations.

VARIATION VI (allegro)

In some variations, particularly those of the nineteenth century, greater freedom is taken. In Schumann's Symphonic Studies there are incomplete and irregular references to the theme throughout a set of short pieces that follow.

A particular kind of variation treatment is the *passacaglia*. This is a short, simple bass theme which is repeated again and again with little or no change in the bass, while in the upper voices a different variation is presented for each repetition of the bass theme. The passacaglia is in a minor key, has a triple meter, and the theme is usually eight measures long. In the following example for organ, the passacaglia theme is stated. It is followed by twenty variations and by a fugue.

EXAMPLE 7   Passacaglia and Fugue in C minor

J. S. Bach
German (1685–1750)

● FUGUE

The fugue is not really a form. Rather, it is a kind of imitative contrapuntal treatment of a relatively short theme. This theme is called the subject because it is the melodic idea on which the whole fugue is based. Although no two fugues have specifically the same design, they all have two parts in common: an exposition and a development section.

In the exposition, the fugue subject is presented in the tonic by one "voice" and then imitated exactly or very closely at the interval of a fourth or fifth by one or more voices which follow one at a time. If the imitation is exact, we say that it is *real:* if only very close, it is called *tonal.* When each of the voices has stated the subject, the exposition is complete. A fugue requires at least two voices, but most fugues are written for three, four, or five, rarely six or two. However many voices appear in the exposition, that number then remains constant for the duration of the fugue.

Sometimes a countersubject is used in addition to the subject. This is the continuation of the melodic line following the subject, and is considered a countersubject only if each of the voices states it. Otherwise, whatever music follows the subject is incidental counterpoint.

In the development section the subject is quoted in its entirety or in abbreviated form at various intervals until the end. It may also go faster (diminution), slower (augmentation), or be inverted (inversion).

Organization

Many fugues make use of the episode, which is any musical interlude not based primarily on the subject, or at least not referring to the entire subject. The purpose of the episode is to provide relief from the theme and often to lighten the texture. Episodes are commonly used at the end of the exposition as a transition to the development section, and within the development section between entrances of the complete subject.

Stretto is another commonly used device. In stretto, the subject is announced in one voice, and before it has been completed other voices enter one at a time in quick succession imitating it. This creates an effect of overlapping. Stretto may occur at several places in the fugue, but is most commonly used at points of climax, especially near the end, where it is effective in creating tension.

Pedal point is also commonly used in fugal writing. It gets its name from music literature for the organ in which a pedal is held down while melodic and harmonic changes take place in the voices above. By common usage, however, any tone which is held for a significant length of time is called pedal point. Like the stretto, pedal point is effective for creating tension at points of climax. In the fugue, pedal point tones are usually dominant or tonic.

EXAMPLE 8

Little Fugue in G minor

J. S. Bach
(1685–1750)

● MINUET AND TRIO

The minuet-trio form makes an easy introduction to the group of larger forms
that use the ternary, or ABA, pattern. The first section, which is a minuet, is
followed by a second, called the trio, and then the minuet is heard again. Both
the minuet and trio are in 3/4 meter and are binary. The trio is used as a
bridge between the two minuets; its function is to give a sense of contrast, and
so it is in a key different from the minuet (often the dominant) with melodies
of contrasting character. Traditionally the first minuet is repeated and so is the
trio, but in the restatement the minuet is heard only once. This is true of the
following example from Mozart's *Eine kleine Nachtmusik;* in outline the form
looks like this:

A—Minuet—AABaBa (binary, repeated)
B—Trio—CCDCDC (binary, repeated)
A—Minuet—ABa (binary, once only)

EXAMPLE 9

Serenade in G major
Eine kleine Nachtmusik
Minuet

Wolfgang Amadeus Mozart
German (1756–1791)

The minuet-trio form is regularly used for the third movement of a sonata or symphony having four movements. However, Beethoven, in his later symphonies, substituted a *scherzo* or "jest," for the minuet. The minuet-trio form can be found in the works of eighteenth-century classical composers such as Haydn and Mozart.

● RONDO

The rondo is also an outgrowth of the ABA form, but is extended. The main theme, or refrain, which is usually a full binary or ternary form, alternates with other themes, called *episodes*. The episodes provide relief from the refrain and contrast in range, texture, and character between restatements of the refrain, and are most often in different keys. The rondo always begins and ends with the main theme.

The shortest possible rondo would be ABABA, or more commonly ABACA. There are numerous rondo designs, the most often used being ABACA or ABACABA, which is exactly balanced like an arch. Within these designs, the treatment may vary. In some rondos, the episodes are developments of musical ideas found in the refrain. In others the reappearance of the refrain is varied, much as it would be in variation form, and in still others, when the refrain occurs in restatement it may be in abbreviated form.

For some obscure reason, many rondos which comprise the second movements of sonatas or symphonies are not labeled as rondos, but merely given mood and tempo markings. Here is the rondo of the second movement of Mozart's *Eine kleine Nachtmusik.* The main theme is binary.

EXAMPLE 10

Serenade in G major
Eine kleine Nachtmusik
Slow movement

Wolfgang Amadeus Mozart
German (1756–1791)

Main theme–A
Andante

A2

Episode–B

after which theme A is repeated

Episode–C

after which theme A is repeated, leading to the Coda

● FIRST MOVEMENT FORM

First movement form is also known as sonata form or sonata allegro form, but we shall use *first movement* since it is more widely accepted and is more specific. Perhaps more great instrumental music has been composed in this form than in any other, because it has such a satisfying organic quality. The whole form is based on two themes which appear in three large sections called exposition, development, and recapitulation. First movement form is ternary in its broadest outline because the recapitulation is a restatement of the themes heard in the exposition.

The exposition contains two contrasting themes. Themes A and B are always in different keys. These themes are usually binary and are connected by extra-thematic music called a transition. If the transition links two themes based on different keys, it is called a modulation, or modulating passage. After the two themes have been stated, there is usually a transition to the development.

In the development the two themes are developed in any way the composer chooses. They may appear in new keys, be quoted only in part, be extended, or be in any way varied. Often theme A gets preferential treatment, since it is the theme that introduces the form. At the end of this section there is normally another transition to the recapitulation.

The recapitulation is a restatement of the exposition with one change; theme B is now heard in the same key as theme A, which allows the piece to end on the tonic as it began.

There may or may not be a *coda* after the recapitulation. The coda is used as a flourish to put a conclusive feeling to the end, and when used often explores some phrase or rhythmic idea from one of the two themes. The coda is always in the tonic. The plan may be mapped as follows:

Exposition
    Theme A, in tonic (if binary—A1, A2)
        Transition to theme B
    Theme B in key of dominant or other related key (if binary—B1, B2)
        Transition
Development
    Varied use of themes A and B in new keys
Recapitulation
    Theme A in original key (tonic)
        Transition to theme B
    Theme B in key of theme A (tonic)

Mozart's *Eine kleine Nachtmusik* illustrates first movement form admirably. The development section, however, is much abbreviated.

EXAMPLE 11

Serenade in G major
Eine kleine Nachtmusik
First movement

Wolfgang Amadeus Mozart
German (1756–1791)

The first movement of Beethoven's Symphony No. 5 is another clear example of the form. In the exposition, the first theme is built on the famous "knocking" motive (p. 188). This theme is primarily rhythmic, with little interest in melody

The second theme therefore offers great contrast, since it is primarily melodic. The development uses chiefly the knocking theme, and the recapitulation repeats the two themes. The coda uses both themes, with emphasis on the first.

● THE SUITE

One of the earliest efforts in the attempt to make music of stature was the *suite,* a collection of dances. In the seventeenth and eighteenth centuries there were usually five dances known collectively as the classical suite: (1) the *allemande,* a rather slow dance in duple meter, (2) the *courante,* a dance of simple rhythm and running passages in triple meter, (3) the *saraband,* a slow, stately, ceremonial dance in triple meter, (4) an optional dance whose character and meter were not predetermined, and (5) the *gigue,* a fast, lively dance, kin to the English jig, in duple meter. These dances were held together as a unit by two things: they were all binary and were all in the same key.

Not all suites follow the organization of the classical suite, however. In Bach's Suite No. 2 in B minor for flute and strings, there are a rondo, a saraband, a bourrée, a polonaise, and a minuet. Furthermore, the suite opens with an overture, and ends with a *badinerie,* a playful bit of music.

The modern suite has no necessary connection with dance forms. It is a collection of separate pieces which have been put together because of some unifying idea, not necessarily musical. Bizet, for instance, puts together excerpts from the opera in his *Carmen* suite; Ravel tries to evoke the spirit of former times in his suite *Le Tombeau de Couperin* (*The Tomb of Couperin*). Rimsky-Korsakov based his symphonic suite *Scheherazade* on the *Arabian Nights*. Prokofiev has written a suite on the adventures of the imaginary hero Lieutenant Kijé.

● SONATA

The sonata was developed after the suite. It is like the suite in that it is a series of independent compositions, each one of which may be played without any of the others. However, these are not all in the same key as are the dances in a suite. Traditionally the sonata is made up of three or four *movements*, and there are very definite traditions about each. The first, which is the longest and most important, is usually a bright, gay piece; ordinarily it is marked allegro. In contrast, the second movement is slow and tuneful, and is marked andante, adagio, or even lento. The third is a dance; in the earlier sonatas the minuet was used, but in Beethoven's time the scherzo replaced the minuet. It is usually the shortest of the four movements, and when a sonata has only three movements, it is the third which is omitted. The fourth movement is again a bright, gay, fast movement, marked allegro, or presto. Thus we have in the four movements of a sonata the contrasts in mood and speed which were characteristic of the suite, the sonata being successively fast, slow, dance, fast.

There are definite traditions, also, about the form of each movement. The first is usually in first movement form; in fact, that form gets its name because it is the first movement of a sonata. It is sometimes called sonata form because it is the characteristic movement of a sonata. The third, or dance movement, if there be one, is always in the minuet-trio or scherzo-trio form. For the second and fourth movements, the composer may use any form he wishes. Since the second movement is slow and melodious, the variation form is a favorite; and the rondo is often found in the last movement.

Sonata form is the form most widely used for long, serious compositions. When it is played on different instruments and with different combinations of instruments, it is given different names, according to the instruments used. The word *sonata* is used when one or two instruments are involved. The symphony, written for and played by a symphony orchestra, is a sonata which calls for all the varied timbres and dynamics of the orchestra. The terms *trio, quartet,* and *quintet* designate combinations of three, four, or five instruments. The strings usually form the backbone of the group, and such groups are always designated as string quartet, piano quintet (for strings and piano), etc. The *concerto* is played by a solo instrument with an orchestra, and is designated by the name of the solo instrument, as violin concerto, etc. In the concerto the music is designed to show off the solo instrument, and hence it is usually music that demands technical dexterity. Sometimes the concerto is thought of primarily as a means for the exhibition of the brilliant technique of the solo performer, but that is hardly fair. The essential contrast is between the timbre, and even more the volume, of the solo instrument and the orchestra.

● FREE FORMS

There are also musical compositions without standard form, music with no set design. This is not to say that they are free of form. On the contrary they are as carefully structured as the more formal designs. The more usual of these are listed here.

The *prelude* originally meant something designed to be played before something else, as in the preludes and fugues of Bach, the Prelude to *Lohengrin,* etc. But the word has become less definite; the twenty-four preludes of Chopin are not preludes to anything; they are pieces complete in themselves. The word now enjoys both meanings: a piece to be played before something else, and a separate piece.

The *ballade* is an extended piece professing to be narrative. The only formal characteristic that can be discerned is that the ballades of Chopin are all in compound time.

The *impromptu* is a contradiction in terms, for it purports to be extemporaneous, which it obviously cannot be, being written down and published. However, it has connotations of spontaneity and of rather slight organization.

The *nocturne* professes that its atmosphere is suggested by the night. The nocturnes of Chopin are usually meditative or elegiac.

The *capriccio* is a capricious piece, and the *intermezzo* should be an interval in some larger whole. Brahms uses these two titles in his piano works for lively or reflective pieces respectively.

The *symphonic poem,* or *tone poem,* is an orchestral work based upon a story taken from literature. It is of the length and complexity of a symphony but has no prescribed form.

The *étude,* a technical study, became important in music at the time of Chopin and Liszt. The *toccata* is earlier; its name conveys a display of keyboard skill.

● PROGRAM MUSIC

Program music may use any kind of form that seems fitting to the subject which it attempts to express. Often the music has its own unique form.

In Chapter 2 program music was defined as music with subject, and little needs to be added to that discussion. However, we may note that program music generally falls into three classes: the imitative, the descriptive, and the narrative.

Imitative music imitates the actual sound of the subject, as in Rimsky-Korsakov's *Flight of the Bumblebee.*

Descriptive music is typified in Beethoven's Symphony No. 6, the *Pastoral.* It describes a day in the country, with a festive gathering of country people. Their pleasure is interrupted by a storm which soon subsides, and the festivities are resumed. Beethoven's own notes, usually printed with the symphony, are as follows:

Pastoral Symphony, or a recollection of country life (more an expression of feeling than a portrayal):

1. *Allegro ma non troppo*—The cheerful feelings aroused by arrival in the country
2. *Andante molte moto*—Scene by the brook
3. *Allegro*—Peasants' merrymaking
4. *Allegro*—Storm
5. *Allegretto*—Shepherds' song: glad and thankful feelings after the storm

In this class too belong compositions which try to distill the feeling or essence of a scene, for example, the moonlight evoked in Debussy's "Clair de Lune."

Narrative music tells a story. Dukas in *The Sorcerer's Apprentice* tells the old story of the person who starts a magic charm going and cannot stop it. His immediate source is a ballad by Goethe, "Der Zauberlehrling" ("The Sorcerer's Apprentice"). The apprentice has often heard his master utter a charm and order a broomstick to do his work. Left alone one day, he tries his hand, repeats the charm, and tells the broomstick to draw water for him. But when he has all the water he wants, he realizes that he has forgotten the word to stop the broom from bringing water. In desperation he seizes an axe, cuts the broomstick in two, only to have each half hauling water! Just when the flood is getting out of control the master returns and speaks the correct formula. To the great relief of the apprentice, the broomstick retires to its corner, and the deluge ceases.

● GENRE

FOLK SONG AND ART SONG

A song in the broadest sense is anything sung. Songs are easily divided into two classes: folk song and art song. Folk songs are the songs of the folk. They are communal in that they are the property of the community and express the life of the community. Everybody knows them and everybody sings them. No one knows, and no one cares, who wrote them. They show no trace of individual authorship, or if they ever did, these traces have been lost throughout long ages of singing.

An *art song* is the work of an individual composer and as such shows his individuality. Some of the greatest writers of art songs are Schubert, Schumann, Brahms, Wolff, and Grieg. Each composer tries to make the music of his song fit the words, but his song is nevertheless characteristic of himself. One of Schumann's songs is not like one of Schubert's. On the other hand, certain songs by known composers have so much of the simplicity and spontaneity of folk songs that they are accepted and sung by the people as their songs. Such songs are classed as folk songs and are usually found in volumes of folk songs. Examples are the American "Dixie" and "Swanee River," and the Bohemian *Songs My Mother Taught Me.* The person who sings one of Schubert's songs is usually conscious that the song is by Schubert; at any rate he thinks of it as an art song, and could look up the composer if he wished. But the Southerner who applauds "Dixie" almost certainly never heard of its composer Dan Emmett; and he might dispute the point if he were told it was written by a Northerner. Or, if he did know these facts, he would be indifferent to them. "Dixie," to him, is not a song like Schubert's "Serenade." It is the expression of community spirit; it is the song of the South.

Folk songs are often classified according to subject as hunting songs ("John Peel"), cowboy songs ("Home on the Range"), spirituals ("Nobody Knows de Trouble I See"), etc. They are also classified according to the country from which they come: The "Volga Boatman" is Russian, "Auld Lang Syne" is Scottish, etc.

The Christmas carol is the folk song of the Christmas season. Many are very old. The "Angelic Hymn," with the refrain "Gloria, in excelsis Deo," is supposed to be the one referred to by the Bishop of Rome in A.D. 129, the first Christian hymn as well as the first carol. The melody of "Adeste Fideles" (*O Come, All Ye Faithful*) is attributed to St. Bonaventura (thirteenth century). It is thought to be an old Latin carol. The "Coventry Carol" ("Lullaby, thou little tiny child") originated in the fifteenth-century Coventry play, probably around 1591. Composed carols include: "O Little Town of Bethlehem" by Lewis Redner, and "Silent Night," by Franz Gruber.

STROPHIC FORM AND CONTINUOUS FORM

Folk songs and art songs follow one of two kinds of treatment. In strophic form the same music is repeated exactly for each stanza. In "Barbara Allen," for example, the same music is used no matter whether one is singing of the "Merry month of May," Barbara's scorn of her lover, or her death. The only differences that can be introduced are in tempo, dynamics, and general expressiveness.

In continuous form, new music is adapted to each stanza of words. However, repetition of musical phrases or motives may be and often are used in continuous form. Schubert's "Erl-King" is a classic example.

Wer reitet so spät durch Nacht und Wind?
Es ist der Vater mit seinem Kind.
Er hat den Knaben wohl in dem Arm,
Er fasst ihn sicher, er hält ihn warm.

Mein Sohn, was birgst du so bang dein Gesicht?
Siehst, Vater, du den Erlkönig nicht?
Den Erlenkönig mit Kron' und Schweif?
Mein Sohn, es ist ein Nebelstreif.

"Du liebes Kind, komm, geh mit mir!
Gar schöne Spiele spiel' ich mit dir.
Manch' bunte Blumen sind an dem Strand,
Meine Mutter hat manch gülden Gewand."

Mein Vater, mein Vater, und hörest du nicht,
Was Erlenkönig mir leise verspricht?—
Sei ruhig, bleibe ruhig, mein Kind:
In dürren Blättern säuselt der Wind.—

"Willst, feiner Knabe, du mit mir gehn?
Meine Töchter sollen dich warten schön;
Meine Töchter führen den nächtlichen Reihn
Und wiegen und tanzen und singen dich ein."

Organization

Mein Vater, mein Vater, und siehst du nicht dort
Erlkönigs Töchter am düstern Ort?—
Mein Sohn, mein Sohn, ich seh' es genau:
Es scheinen die alten Weiden so grau.—

"Ich liebe dich, mich reizt deine schöne Gestalt;
Und bist du nicht willig, so brauch' ich Gewalt."
Mein Vater, mein Vater, jetzt fasst er mich an!
Erlkönig hat mir ein Leids getan!—

Dem Vater grauset's, er reitet geschwind,
Er hält in den Armen das ächzende Kind,
Erreicht den Hof mit Mühe und Not—
In seinen Armen das Kind war tot.

> —JOHANN WOLFGANG VON GOETHE (1749–1832, German poet, dramatist, and novelist),
> "Der Erlkönig"

Who gallops so late through wind and night?
A father bearing his son in flight;
He holds him tightly, breasting the storm,
To bear him safely and keep him warm.

"My son, why bury your face thus in fear?"
"Don't you see, father, the Erl-King draw near,
The king of spirits, with crown and with shroud?"
"My son, it is a wisp of cloud."

"My darling child, come, go with me!
I'll play the finest games with thee.
The brightest flowers grow on the shore;
My mother has clothes of gold in store."

"My father, my father, but surely you heard
The Erl-King's whisp'ring, promising word?"
"Be quiet; there is nothing to fear:
The wind is rustling through thickets sere."

"Wilt thou come with me, my boy, away
Where my daughters play with thee night and day?
For my daughters shall come in the night if thou weep
And rock thee and dance thee and sing thee to sleep."

"My father, my father, but do you not see
His daughters lurking by yon dark tree?"
"My son, my son, it is only the light
Of old willows gleaming gray through the night."

"I love thee so, thy beauty leaves no other course,
And if thou'rt not willing, I'll take thee by force."
"My father, my father, he drags me from you;
Erl-King has seized me, and hurts me too."

The father shudders; he spurs through the wild.
His arms strain closer the weak, moaning child.
He gains his home with toil and dread—
Clasped in his arms there, the child was dead.

    —Translated by Calvin Brown[1]

In Schubert's music we hear the galloping of the horse, and the thunder of the storm. The voices of the three characters are carefully differentiated. The father's voice is low, calm, assured; that of the child is high-pitched, afraid, curious, wondering; the erl-king's voice is pleading and ingratiating, until he announces he will take the child by force, when it becomes brusque and harsh. At the end of the song the galloping and thunder, which have been continued throughout, suddenly cease as the father stops at his home and finds that the boy is dead.

    Another song in continuous form is Schubert's "Gretchen at the Spinning Wheel." Gretchen is singing a sad song that begins "Meine Ruh' ist hin, mein Herz ist schwer" ("My peace is gone, my heart is heavy"), as she mentally passes in review all the hours she has spent with her lover. Throughout, the song is accompanied by the ceaseless turning of the spinning wheel until she recalls the time of his kiss; then she stops work and the spinning sound is broken off abruptly. Later it is resumed slowly, but finally it gets back to its usual swift speed.

    All folk songs are in strophic form, frequently though not always in the AABA quatrain. Art songs may be in either strophic or continuous form. We have cited two of Schubert's songs as examples of continuous form. His "Serenade" and "Hedgeroses" are in strophic form.

    The *aria* is a set piece for solo voice from an opera, oratorio, or cantata; usually it has the association of technical difficulty, although this is not essential. However, in many ways the aria is only a song. It is not usually in strophic form.

[1]Calvin Brown, *Music and Literature*, pp. 71–72. Courtesy of Mr. Brown and the University of Georgia Press.

● MADRIGAL, MOTET, ANTHEM, HYMN

The *madrigal* and the *motet* are part songs and are generally considered to be a product of the fifteenth, sixteenth, and seventeenth centuries. The madrigal and the motet are alike in that they are designed for unaccompanied voices and are usually polyphonic, though they may contain homophonic sections. They differ in that the madrigal is secular and the motet is sacred. The English madrigal school (Byrd, Morley, Gibbons, Weelkes, Wilbye) is the glory of English music and, indeed, one of the peaks in the whole history of the art. An example is Gibbons' "The Silver Swan."

The *anthem* is the Protestant successor to the motet, though as time goes on, it is losing all the distinguishing characteristics of its predecessor. Anthems may be accompanied; they are not necessarily polyphonic, and they are being written today. But in the anthem we can still see vestiges of its polyphonic origin in the motet.

The *hymn* is a sacred strophic song; it is most often of four related phrases and is usually several stanzas in length, intended for community singing. The hymns of the German Lutheran church, especially those dating from the period between the Reformation and the time of Bach, have the special name of *chorals,* or *chorales.* In these is to be found what is probably the highest level of hymn tunes. Examples are Luther's "A Mighty Fortress," and the "Passion Chorale," harmonized by Bach, and usually sung to the words "O Sacred Head Now Wounded."

● OPERA

Opera began (ca. 1600) as an attempt to reproduce the effect of the Greek drama in a kind of musical speech called *recitative.* The voices followed the accents of speech, but in musical tones. This recitative is more like chant than any other form of music today. The first operas, which were largely composed of recitatives, must have been very tedious. Accordingly, songs or arias were added to break the monotony: solos, duets, trios, quartets, choruses, etc. For a time the drama lost its importance, and the music was everything. At this time Gluck (1714–1787), known as the first great reformer of opera, brought the drama back into prominence and insisted that the singers be subordinate to the plot. At the same time he continued to stress recitative and had many set and separable songs and choruses. This concept of opera is to be seen in the great operas of Verdi and Mozart. Drama is emphasized, but the music still contains recitative; and the great arias, duets, and choruses are set pieces which can be detached from the drama. We can cite the arias "Caro nome" from *Rigoletto*, "Celeste Aïda" from *Aïda,* as well as the "Soldier's Chorus" from *Faust* and the sextette from *Lucia.*

A new and different type of opera was inaugurated by Wagner. He attempted to make a more unified work, with music and drama of equal importance, and therefore he called his works *music dramas.* The voices and the music combine to tell the story. In this way the orchestra is made important, and the music is continuous. In short, the music is not interrupted for set arias and ensembles by the singers; the vocal line is treated like the orchestral lines, and often the voices are subordinated to the orchestra. The action, too, is continuous; there is no pause from the beginning of an act to the fall of the curtain.

In addition, Wagner devised a new type of musical development based on themes. Each character and many of the important objects and places in the drama have a musical motive called a *leitmotiv:* the "sword," the "rainbow," the "ring," the "Rhine," and even such abstractions as "fate." The entrance of a character is announced by his theme in the orchestra, and often the music tells us what the characters do not know. In *The Valkyrie,* for instance, when Siegmund is lying in Hunding's house, desolate because he has no sword, the music fairly shouts the sword theme, calling our attention, if not his, to the sword in the tree beside him.

There are a number of distinct types of opera, three of which are basic: *grand opera* always has a serious subject, is usually tragic, and has no spoken dialogue (example: *Aïda*). *Comic opera* is any opera having spoken dialogue, whether comic or not (*Carmen*). Originally the term derives from French comic opera having spoken dialogue (*opéra comique*). The third type is *operetta,* which is synonymous with *musical comedy* or *light opera.* The subject may be tragic or comic, and there is spoken dialogue. Generally speaking, the music is not as ambitious as in serious opera, and the demands made on the musicians are much lighter (*South Pacific*).

● ORATORIO

Oratorio, like grand opera, is an extended piece of music employing the resources of orchestra, chorus, and solo singers. It differs from opera in many ways.

SUBJECT. In oratorio, the subject is usually biblical, and in many of the great oratorios the words are taken directly from the Bible. Handel's *Messiah* and Mendelssohn's *Elijah* are outstanding examples.

PERFORMANCE. Operas are enacted on the stage, and oratorios are sung in a concert without costume, stage sets, or lighting. The oratorio chorus and soloists are on the stage, each rises when he is to perform, but there is no acting out of the music sung.

USE OF RECITATIVE. In oratorios the recitative is of greater importance than in contemporary opera. Each aria is preceded by its recitative. We may cite from *The Messiah* the recitative "Then shall the eyes of the blind be opened," preceding the aria "He shall feed His flock like a shepherd."

CHORUSES. The choruses of an oratorio tend to be polyphonic in structure and, as befitting the subject, are solemn and powerful, like the "Hallelujah Chorus" from *The Messiah,* or "The Heavens are telling" from Haydn's *The Creation.* The usual opera, probably telling a love story, has no like occasion. Accordingly, the choruses from opera are apt to sound less sublime in comparison with the choruses of oratorio. We can see this in the "Soldier's Chorus" from *Faust,* the "Anvil Chorus" from *Il Trovatore,* and even the "Triumphal March" from *Aïda.*

Cantata and *passion* are special forms of the oratorio. A cantata is a small oratorio. It may also be secular in subject. The subject of a passion, as the word implies, is the agony and death of Jesus. The words follow the text as found in one of the Gospels. Passions are not numerous. Two of the greatest are Bach's *The Passion According to St. John,* and *The Passion According to St. Matthew.* A passion introduces singing by the audience from time to time. Otherwise a passion corresponds closely to an oratorio.

● MASS

The *Mass* has been discussed earlier as an essential part of the liturgy of the Catholic Church, and its five parts were named in Chapter 3. From very early times the Mass has been set to music, and some of the greatest music of the world has been that composed for the Mass. In its music we find illustrations of the three great periods in music history. From the earliest period before the time of harmony or counterpoint, we have the Gregorian chant, which is simple, unaccompanied melody. Disembodied, aspiring, and unworldly, these Masses are absolutely cut off from any secular consideration. In the polyphonic period we have the great Masses of Josquin and Palestrina. In the later periods we have the Masses of Beethoven and Mozart.

The *Requiem* is celebrated for the repose of the dead. It gets its name from the first words of the text: "Requiem aeternam dona eis, Domine" (Give to them, O Lord, eternal rest). Among Requiems we may mention those of Brahms, Verdi, and Mozart.

16

ORGANIZATION IN
LITERATURE AND
THE DANCE

● THE BASIS OF PLAN IN LITERATURE

Organization in music and literature is largely a matter of memory and anticipation. We remember what we have heard, and on the basis of that, we anticipate what is to come. In music, we know when we hear a theme that we have or have not heard that theme, but we can rarely be very definite about it. We do not recall the themes and arrangements of music easily. Hence our memories and anticipations are not very clearly formulated. In literature, on the other hand, we remember the events and the ideas of a work clearly and exactly, and we retain the entire organization in our minds with very little difficulty. Therefore we know the organization of literature much better than we do that of music. And we demand in literature a logical organization. Take, for instance, this sonnet of Shakespeare's:

Organization

When, in disgrace with Fortune and men's eyes,
I all alone beweep my outcast state,
And trouble deaf heaven with my bootless cries,
And look upon myself and curse my fate,
Wishing me like to one more rich in hope,
Featur'd like him, like him with friends possess'd,
Desiring this man's art, and that man's scope,
With what I most enjoy contented least;

Yet in these thoughts myself almost despising,
Haply I think on thee; and then my state,
Like to the lark at break of day arising
From sullen earth, sings hymns at heaven's gate;
For thy sweet love rememb'red such wealth brings
That then I scorn to change my state with kings.

> —WILLIAM SHAKESPEARE (1564–1616, British poet and dramatist),
> Sonnet 29 (publ. 1609)

There is a big break between the octave and the sestet. The octave, the first eight lines, says that the poet is in a bad mood, discouraged, and blue. The sestet, the last six lines, says that he cheers up when he thinks of his lady-love. Nor is that all; the two quatrains of the octave are clearly differentiated. The first states the trouble in general, the second gives details. In the sestet the quatrain relates his change of spirit when he thinks of the lady, and the couplet at the end sums up the whole matter.

There are as many logical ways of ordering the content of a work of literature as there are of thinking. Sometimes a writer begins with the least important and goes on to the more important. Sometimes he begins with the simple and goes on to the difficult or complicated. Cause usually precedes effect. In Milton's sonnet "On His Blindness," the octave asks a question and the sestet gives the answer. In the Shakespearean sonnet just quoted, there is the statement of a difficulty and its solution. The writer arranges his ideas in the manner that will make them say what he wants them to say. It is not necessary that the author follow any one particular plan; it is only necessary that there be a logical plan and that it be clear.

● ARGUMENTATION AND EXPOSITION

Argumentation includes all forms of writing that are made with the express purpose of influencing others to do or say or think as the writer wishes. In older times arguments were usually spoken, and the sermon, the oration, and the debate were the usual forms. Since the spread of printing, editorials and articles in newspapers and magazines have largely superseded the spoken word, but the address is still a vital way of reaching people and, with the use of the radio and television, is rapidly regaining its lost prestige.

Argumentation must move people; otherwise it has no reason for being. It is, therefore, one of the most vital and interesting forms of writing, as we see in the ending of one of Garibaldi's speeches to his soldiers.

> I am going out from Rome . . . I offer neither pay, nor quarters, nor provisions; I offer hunger, thirst, forced marches, battles and death. Let him who loves his country in his heart and not with his lips only, follow me.[1]

Exposition expounds, or explains. Thus it is the fundamental form for all scientific writing. In pure literature it is found chiefly in the treatise and the essay. The treatise is a longer, more thorough, and more finished study than the essay.

The word *essay* was first used by Montaigne, who called his writings *essais,* or trials. An essay is an incomplete or partial treatment of a subject. Essays are classified according to the subject as familiar, historical, literary, philosophical, etc.

The *familiar essay* is the only one that calls for any discussion. It was made popular by Lamb and has kept to this day many of the characteristics he gave it. It is always short and always personal. It is frequently humorous, sometimes sad or pathetic. The subjects chosen are often trivial or fantastic; the interest lies in the presentation of a point of view that is not the usual common-sense, commonplace one. Cowper, for instance, tells of the characteristics of the card table that had grown old in the service of his house; Lamb writes of the children he never had; and Stevenson makes a defense of idlers. Always the writer takes a philosophic point of view; he is calm and enjoys the pleasures of the moment; or, if there are difficulties, his attitude toward them is one of acceptance and calm, not of protest.

Many books do not fit in the category of either essay or treatise, though they are usually expository in nature. Among them are books of political ideas, such as *The Republic* of Plato or *The Prince* of Machiavelli; statements of philosophy, such as the *Noble Truths* of Buddha or the dialogues of Plato; or statements of practical wisdom, such as the *Meditations* of Marcus Aurelius and the sayings of Epictetus. To this class also belong books of devotion such as the *Confessions* of St. Augustine or *The Imitation of Christ* by Thomas à Kempis.

[1] G. M. Trevelyan, *Garibaldi's Defence of the Roman Republic*, pp. 231–232.

Organization

● THE LYRIC

The lyric is a poem which expresses a single emotion. It is frequently short, like Landor's four-line poem "On Death":

Death stands above me, whispering low
  I know not what into my ear:
Of his strange language all I know
  Is, there is not a word of fear.

     —WALTER SAVAGE LANDOR (1775–1864, British poet, literary critic, and prose writer)

Or it may be a poem of several pages like Wordsworth's "Ode on Intimations of Immortality."

Sometimes the emotional quality is preserved in what is only a fragment, not a complete poem at all, as in these lines from Sappho:

Before the lovely queen each night
The stars in shyness hide their face
As all the earth swims soft and bright
And the full moon rides in her place.

    —SAPPHO (about 600 B.C., Greek lyric poet)[2]

Love and death are the two favorite subjects, though any subject may be used. Dylan Thomas tells of his reasons for writing poetry:

In my craft or sullen art
Exercised in the still night
When only the moon rages
And the lovers lie abed
With all their griefs in their arms,
I labour by singing light
Not for ambition or bread
Or the strut and trade of charms
On the ivory stages
But for the common wages
Of their most secret heart.

[2] Translated by Marjorie Carpenter.

Not for the proud man apart
From the raging moon I write
On these spindrift pages
Nor for the towering dead
With their nightingales and psalms
But for the lovers, their arms
Round the griefs of the ages,
Who pay no praise or wages
Nor heed my craft or art.

> —DYLAN THOMAS (1914–1953, British poet),
> "In My Craft or Sullen Art" (1945)[3]

And Hopkins writes of the grandeur of God:

The world is charged with the Grandeur of God.
   It will flame out, like shining from shook foil;
   It gathers to a greatness, like the ooze of oil
Crushed. Why do men then now not reck his rod?
Generations have trod, have trod;
   And all is seared with trade; bleared, smeared with toil;
   And wears man's smudge and shares man's smell: the soil
Is bare now, nor can foot feel, being shod.

And for all this, nature is never spent;
   There lives the dearest freshness deep down things;
And though the last lights off the black West went
   Oh, morning, at the brown brink eastward, springs—
Because the Holy Ghost over the bent
   World broods with warm breast and with ah! bright wings.

> —GERARD MANLEY HOPKINS (1844–1889, British poet),
> "God's Grandeur" (between 1876 and 1889)[4]

In the lyric we have the most pronounced use of the various devices of literature, such as assonance, alliteration, meter, rhythm, rhyme, simile, imagery, metaphor, and all the figures of speech. The reason why lyric poetry draws so heavily on these devices, says Suzanne Langer, is that it has so little content in itself. It is "usually nothing more than a thought, a vision, a word, or some

---

[3] From *The Collected Poems of Dylan Thomas*, copyright 1953, by Dylan Thomas, and reprinted by permission of the publisher, New Directions, and J. M. Dent & Sons, Ltd.

[4] From *Poems of Gerard Manley Hopkins*, Oxford University Press, Copyright 1948.

other poignant emotion."[5] But because of all these devices it becomes the form in which exact wording is most important. We want to repeat and sing to ourselves separate lines such as these:

> It is the blight man was born for,
> It is Margaret you mourn for.

> Of his strange language all I know
> Is, there is not a word of fear.

> Fair as a star, when only one
> Is shining in the sky.

In drama and the novel one may forget *how* an event was told in the interest of the event itself, but not in the lyric.

A lyric is usually written in the first person: "Death stands above *me*," "Oh the difference to *me*," "In *my* craft or sullen art." And yet it is not in itself personal. We do not feel that we are intruding on the writer. Once the song is written it is a song for everyone, it acquires a certain timelessness, it lives in a "sort of eternal present."[6]

> I'm going out to clean the pasture spring;
> I'll only stop to rake the leaves away
> (And wait to watch the water clear, I may):
> I sha'n't be gone long.—You come too.

> I'm going out to fetch the little calf
> That's standing by the mother. It's so young,
> It totters when she licks it with her tongue.
> I sha'n't be gone long.—You come too.
>   —ROBERT FROST (1875–1963, American poet),
>   "The Pasture"[7]

Even when Miss Moore writes about her father, as in "Silence," it is not, strictly speaking, personal but universal.

[5] Suzanne Langer, *Feeling and Form*, p. 259.
[6] *Ibid.*, p. 268.
[7] From *Complete Poems of Robert Frost*. Copyright 1930, 1939 by Holt, Rinehart and Winston, Inc. Copyright 1958 by Robert Frost. Reprinted by permission of Holt, Rinehart and Winston, Inc.

My father used to say,
"Superior people never make long visits,"
have to be shown Longfellow's grave
or the glass flowers at Harvard.
Self-reliant like the cat—
that takes its prey to privacy,
the mouse's limp tail hanging like a shoelace from its mouth—
they sometimes enjoy solitude,
and can be robbed of speech
by speech which has delighted them.
The deepest feeling always shows itself in silence;
not in silence, but restraint.
Nor was he insincere in saying, 'Make my house your inn.'
Inns are not residences.

  —MARIANNE MOORE (1887– , American poet),
   "Silence"[8]

● NARRATIVE

The narrative probably comprises more examples of pure literature than all the other types put together, and with good reason. All the world loves a lover, and it is equally true that all the world loves a story. The formula "once upon a time" still has magic to lure us all, young and old.

PLOT. The essentials of a narrative are the essentials of every story. First is action, or conflict. The narrative begins with the emergence of a situation that demands solution. Something has happened to disrupt the established order. And there will be anxiety, tension, frustration, until the problem is solved. The problem itself may be of any kind—finding a dead body, as in a detective story, falling in love, or spending the night in an open boat. The occasion is not limited. It may be serious or frivolous. Chaucer tells the story of the three rioters who went out to hunt death, and found it. Cervantes tells of the adventures of an old knight who fought windmills.

Whatever the story, it is related in a series of incidents each of which has some relation to the solution of the main problem, and each of which must be credible in terms of that problem. Each of these incidents will bring new knowledge and help reach the solution. This is the *plot*.

Sometimes there are two plots that run side by side; we find this often in Shakespeare's plays like *King Lear*. In this play the two plots are bound together

---

[8] From *Collected Poems* by Marianne Moore. Reprinted with permission of the Macmillan Company. Copyright 1953, Marianne Moore. Copyright renewed 1963 by Marianne Moore and T. S. Eliot.

so that each helps the other; but in addition one is definitely more important than the other. In Tolstoi's *Anna Karenina* the main plot is concerned with the unhappy love of Anna and Vronsky, but counter to them runs the contented life of Levin and Kitty.

CHARACTERS. There could be no plot without people, and so the second requirement of a narrative is *characters*. There must be people who are concerned in the main plot; they are the characters of the story. They answer the question: Why do people do what they do? And every incident should throw light on the characters. Why did the three rioters set out to find death? And how did the old man know where they would find it? Why did Don Quixote charge the windmill?

Moreover, the characters must talk and act like the persons they are. The characters of a narrative usually are human beings, because they are the animals we know best. When the characters are animals, the animal names are fundamentally disguises for human beings, as the hen and the rooster in Chaucer's *Tale of the Nun's Priest*. The hen and the rooster, although essentially true to what we know of fowls, nevertheless talk and act as do men and women. Chanticleer shows all the characteristics in which a man is most like a cock, and Pertelote is the eternal feminine.

SETTING. The setting gives the time and place of the action. The time is always past. It is always "once upon a time." It may be any time in the past, provided it is past. The place may be any place at any time. Jules Verne writes of what happens twenty thousand leagues under the sea; Butler in *Erewhon* tells of people who live in a land that is as logical as ours is illogical. Writers of all ages have told of the land of the dead.

In the setting we count not only the physical character of the place—country, city, lake, etc.—but also all the beliefs, customs, moral and social values that make up what we usually call the environment. And no matter where it is placed, the setting should fit the action; it should be a place in which those events might take place. Ivanhoe does not belong in *Tom Jones*, and Elizabeth Bennet of *Pride and Prejudice* would not be happy on *Main Street*.

THEME. Plot, characters, setting are found in every narrative, but they are not of equal importance. Any one of the three may in some narrative be of greatest importance. In Theodore Dreiser's *An American Tragedy* the boy is the victim of his environment. In Stevenson's *Treasure Island* the action is most important, and in Thackeray's *Vanity Fair* the characterization is most important.

All depends on the author's *theme*. This is his point of view, his idea about the tale, what he is trying to say in the story—in short, his understanding of life. This of course is the basis by which action, characters, and setting have been determined. The author decides what kind of a character belongs in *Main Street* and he draws the picture that way.

NARRATOR. A last question has to do with the *narrator*. Who is telling the story? There are two favorite devices. One is the omniscient person who knows everything about each character, all he says, does, or thinks; but there is never any indication as to who he is or how he gets his information. The other favorite device is to have the story told in the first person by some character in the tale.

In the early days of prose fiction the letter or journal was much liked as a way of telling the tale. In Richardson's *Pamela* the heroine tells the tale in a series of letters to her friend.

Many good suggestions for the story may be brought in by means of the narrator or narrators. A writer need not keep the same narrator throughout the story. In Faulkner's *The Sound and the Fury* the first chapter is told by a half-wit. Later material is narrated by the Negro nurse and cook. In the end Faulkner uses the omniscient narrator.

WAYS OF TELLING A STORY

Within the general framework of the narrative there are many ways of telling a story and hence of changing the plan. Ordinarily a narrative starts at the beginning and goes through to the end. *Pride and Prejudice* begins when strangers move into the community and Elizabeth and Darcy have a chance to meet each other, and it continues through many different events until they are safely married at the end. *Vanity Fair* begins when Becky Sharp leaves boarding school as a young girl, and it carries her through all her adventures until she is an old woman.

This is the method followed in the ballad "Sir Patrick Spence." The story is presented in three scenes: The first is at the court when the king and the old knight are discussing plans for the trip; the second is on the seashore when Sir Patrick hears the message and suspects foul play; the third jumps to the ending after the lords and their ship have gone down. Except for the third stanza, however, there are no connecting links between one part and the other; the reader must guess from the context what has happened.

> The king sits in Dumferling toune,
>   Drinking the blude-reid wine:
> "O whar will I get guid sailor,
>   To sail this schip of mine?"

Organization

Up and spake an eldern knicht,
   Sat at the kings richt kne:
"Sir Patrick Spence is the best sailor,
   That sails upon the se."

The king has written a braid letter,
   And signd it wi his hand,
And sent it to Sir Patrick Spence,
   Was walking on the sand.

The first line that Sir Patrick red,
   A loud lauch lauched he;
The next line that Sir Patrick red,
   The teir blinded his ee.

"O wha is this has don this deid,
   This ill deid don to me,
To send me out this time o' the yeir,
   To sail upon the se!

"Mak hast, mak hast, my mirry men all,
   Our guid schip sails the morne:"
"O say na sae, my master deir,
   For I feir a deadlie storme.

"Late late yestreen I saw the new moone,
   Wi the auld moone in her arme,
And I feir, I feir, my deir master,
   That we will cum to harme."

O our Scots nobles wer richt laith
   To weet their cork-heild schoone;
But lang owre a' the play wer playd,
   Thair hats they swam aboone.

O lang, lang may their ladies sit,
   Wi thair fans into their hand,
Or eir they se Sir Patrick Spence
   Cum sailing to the land.

O lang, lang may the ladies stand,
   Wi thair gold kems in their hair,
Waiting for thair ain deir lords,
   For they'll se thame na mair.

Haf owre, haf owre to Aberdour,
  It's fiftie fadom deip,
And thair lies guid Sir Patrick Spence,
  Wi the Scots lords at his feit.

      —ANON.,
        "Sir Patrick Spence"

Sometimes we see one character through the eyes of another, and our understanding of that character changes as our informant learns to know him. In Henry James's *Portrait of a Lady* we see one of the main characters, Madame Merle, through the eyes of the heroine, Isabel Archer. At first Madame Merle is glamorous; then as Isabel begins to see her more clearly, we learn of her faults and shortcomings.

Another device is to present the story as it was known to different people. This method is used by Browning in *The Ring and the Book*. An old count is tried for the murder of his young wife who had fled to the home of her foster parents in company with a young priest just before the birth of her son. In the twelve books of the poem Browning tells the story as it appears to many different people—the casual bystander, the girl wife, the priest who helped her escape, the husband when he appears in court for the trial, the husband just before he is executed for the murder, the Pope before whom the case is tried, and others.

Again, the story may be related a long time after the events have taken place. This is the method followed by Conrad in *Youth*. Marlowe, an old man, tells about the experiences of his youth. This method is used by T. S. Eliot in "The Journey of the Magi," when one of the wise men remembers his trip to Bethlehem. One of the advantages of this plan is that the narrator can intersperse comments and explanations, criticism and evaluations.

In recent years there has been much emphasis on a new type of narrative—the "stream of consciousness" method—in which all matters are presented in an uninterrupted flow of ideas, sensations, memories, and associations, as they would be presented to the consciousness of any one individual. James Joyce and Virginia Woolf are but two of a large number of contemporary writers who have used this method of writing.

In another recent type of narrative, there is not one sequence of events; instead events are presented in a kaleidoscopic series of pictures focusing on different occurrences of the story. In *John Brown's Body*, for instance, Stephen Vincent Benét paints a picture of the Civil War by giving short scenes that tell what was happening to various people at various times. There is no attempt to make a connection between one of these scenes and another, but they all fit together into a clear composite of the whole.

Organization

TYPES OF NARRATIVE POETRY

EPIC. Of all the types of narrative, the *epic* is one of the most distinct as well as the rarest. An epic is a long, dignified poem in lofty style; its hero is of more than ordinary strength, and his deeds are of consequence to the entire nation. The authentic, or natural, epic is the product of an age of heroes, of a people just emerging from barbarism, when the individual, as an individual, performed deeds that were or seemed to be superhuman. In the *Iliad,* Achilles and Hector fight side by side with the gods, and are by no means inferior to them. Beowulf, in a foreign country, hears of the damage being done by the monster Grendel and goes across the sea to fight him.

The authentic epic probably originated as a series of songs in praise of the hero, which were later joined into one poem. The author or authors are not known, or, if a name such as Homer is given, it is merely a name, for the poetry does not reflect the personality of the poet. Because it is the product of a stage of civilization that lasted for only a short time, the authentic epic is extremely rare. The *Iliad,* the *Odyssey, Beowulf,* the *Song of Roland, Le Cid,* and the *Songs of the Nibelung* almost complete the list for Western literature.

The literary, or artificial, epic is the work of a single, conscious literary artist. We would expect it to be more common than the authentic epic, but it is not. The *Aeneid* of Vergil and *Paradise Lost* of Milton are two that are given the title without dispute. The literary epic also has a conscious purpose. Vergil is trying to arouse in the people a greater reverence for the gods, the country, and the family. Milton is trying to "justify the ways of God to man."

ROMANCE. The medieval romance is, as the name implies, a product of the Middle Ages, being, par excellence, the literary expression of chivalry. It has been defined as a story of love and adventure, or of adventure for the sake of love. Spenser chooses a typical romance subject for *The Faerie Queene.* A lady appears at the court of Arthur asking redress for the great wrongs done to her father and mother; a knight springs up, volunteering for the expedition. He and the lady have many adventures, and in the end the parents are released, and the knight and the lady are married. The medieval romance is usually in verse, though it is sometimes in prose. The fifteenth-century collection made by Malory, *Morte d'Arthur,* is in prose.

In the age of romanticism the romance was revived, and many authors— Keats, Byron, Swinburne, Tennyson, and others—began to write romantic tales of knights and ladies or other faraway, strange, and unknown people.

The term *romance,* as distinguished from the medieval romance or its modern revival, is used for any work of fiction in which the emphasis is on plot, such as Stevenson's *Treasure Island.* A romance may be either in prose or in verse.

THE BALLAD. The ballad is a story told in song. The folk ballad is the story of an important event, told dramatically for popular singing. The subject may be any conspicuous event: the death of a suitor, the betrayal of a sister, the hunting of the cheviot, or the adventure of a hero. As in all folk songs, the author is of no importance, and hence he is not usually known.

"O where ha'e ye been, Lord Randal, my son?
O where ha'e ye been, my handsome young man?"
"I ha'e been to the wildwood; mother, make my bed soon,
For I'm weary wi' hunting, and fain would lie down."

"Where gat ye your dinner, Lord Randal, my son?
Where gat ye your dinner, my handsome young man?"
"I dined wi' my true-love; mother, make my bed soon,
For I'm weary wi' hunting, and fain would lie down."

"What gat ye to your dinner, Lord Randal, my son?
What gat ye to your dinner, my handsome young man?"
"I gat eels boiled in brew; mother, make my bed soon,
For I'm weary wi' hunting, and fain would lie down."

"What became of your bloodhounds, Lord Randal, my son?
What became of your bloodhounds, my handsome young man?"
"O they swelled and they died; mother, make my bed soon,
For I'm weary wi' hunting, and fain would lie down."

"O I fear ye are poisoned, Lord Randal, my son!
O I fear ye are poisoned, my handsome young man!"
"O yes, I am poisoned; mother, make my bed soon,
For I'm sick at the heart, and I fain would lie down."

  —ANON.,
   "Lord Randal"

In most ballads, as in this one, there is a great deal of repetition, probably because it made the singing easier. This repetition is not exact; each recurrence of a phrase carries the story forward a little. Each question adds to our knowledge of Lord Randal's day until we know the truth in the last stanza. The ballad seldom tells a story directly from beginning to end. In "Lord Randal" we begin at the end and learn by degrees what had happened earlier. The ballad form is also used by literary artists; with them it approximates the folk song more or less closely, as in Coleridge's *The Rime of the Ancient Mariner.*

PROSE FICTION

THE NOVEL. In contrast to the romance, which deals with the strange and un-usual, the spectacular and the aristocratic, the novel has to do with the relations of people to each other. It is not so much concerned with how things are done as with why they are done. It supposes a series of actions which show why a character does a certain thing, and accomplishes this largely through the choices he makes. We learn his deliberations, his assertions, arguments, demonstrations, the conclusions that determine thought—deliberate reflections. A story so conceived and made alive is often more vivid than actual experience. Often life seems "stale, flat, and unprofitable," but the interest in a novel must not fall. The people of the book may be dull but not the book itself. It must have what Henry James called "felt life." The excellence of the novel lies in its life, in its seeming truth, its unity. If it seems to be a true picture of life, if the characters move and work and make the decisions that are true of those characters at those times, we say it is true and good.

The novel is a recent form; the earliest examples that belong strictly to the type are those of Richardson and Fielding in the eighteenth century. And as Mrs. Langer says: "The novel is peculiarly suited to formulate our modern life by taking our most pervasive interest for its theme—the evaluation and the hazards of personality." Our interest in personality is what makes our world different and most of its problems relatively new.

SHORT STORY. The short story belongs to the same general type as the novel, but it is not simply a short novel. It differs primarily in two respects. It is usually concerned with a single crisis, whereas the novel will present many facets of the characters and events; and it is limited in its analysis of character. Faulkner, for instance, gives a complete picture of all the family in his novel *The Sound and Fury*, whereas in the short story "Barn Burning" we have only the incidents that resulted in the burning of a barn.

ANECDOTE AND NOVELLA. The anecdote and the novella are sometimes distinguished as types separate from the short story and are sometimes put under that heading.

The *anecdote* is a short narrative giving particulars of some interesting episode or event. Often the anecdote gives details of the life of some one person, as when we repeat an anecdote of the life of Abraham Lincoln or of Thomas Jefferson. The anecdote differs from the short story in that it lacks both the plot and the characterization of that form. The *Lives* of Plutarch are now classed as anecdotal.

The *novella* is identified in two ways. The term is most commonly used to designate a narrative that is longer than the short story though it lacks the characteristics of the novel. Many of the stories of Katherine Anne Porter are classed as novella. Historically the term is applied to narratives such as we find in the *Decameron* of Boccaccio.

DRAMA

The novel, the short story, and the drama are now the outstanding forms of narrative. They are alike in following the regular requirements of narrative: in having plot, characters, setting, and theme. They differ also in many ways, the most important being the medium. The short story and the novel use only words: we know the characters only as the narrator tells us about them. The drama also is basically a story in words—a story without words is called a *pantomime*—but the words are in dialogue and are acted out on stage. All information is conveyed to the audience through dialogue except for what can be told through costume, stage set, and the movements and gestures of the actors. In the novel the narrator tells what the hero is doing, whereas in the drama we see and hear him as he does it.

This difference in medium demands difference in presentation. For one thing, a play is relatively short; if it is to be interesting to the audience, it must not be so long as to be tiring. The reading of a novel may spread out over a winter or be finished in a few hours, but a play must be over in a short time. Three hours is the conventional time, though it may be shorter or longer. There have been many experiments with longer plays, but they have not been very popular. The audience wants its play in one package. Shakespeare's plays are much longer than the usual play, but in his time a play was presented continuously without any breaks for change of scene or costume, or other interruption. It could therefore be presented in about the same time as a modern play.

Again, the pace of a play is fast; since the author is limited in time he must get across his ideas quickly; he cannot put in too many details. Only the important and the essential can be brought in. Moreover, a play must always be clear. If one gets mixed up in a novel, he can turn back and see what happened, but in a play there is no turning back. Also, the action on the stage is always in the present. In this respect a play is like a lyric and is in contrast to a novel. Whatever the action, we the audience are always there, we are not thinking of past events. We are concerned with what is happening on the stage.

Drama differs from the novel in yet another way. Since the story is told by the characters, there can be no comment on what is said or done unless it be by the characters, whereas in a novel the narrator can comment directly on the scene or the situation. Jane Austen begins *Pride and Prejudice* with the statement: "It is a truth universally acknowledged, that a single man in possession of a good fortune must be in want of a wife." In a play that statement could not stand; it would of necessity be spoken by one of the characters and would show that person's character and point of view. Dramatic form is limited also in that the author cannot talk directly to his audience. He cannot in his own person explain what has taken place or what kind of people his characters are. At various times attempts have been made to overcome this limitation but with limited success.

A play is customarily divided into acts. An act is part of a larger whole but distinct and independent in so far as it has its own beginning and, after an interval, its own end. In Shakespeare's time a drama regularly had five acts; now it will more often have three. Acts may or may not be divided into scenes, each scene having its own unity and its own place in the act and the entire play. The end of an act usually indicates the passage of time.

In his dialogue the author must provide suggestions which will connect any act with what went before. In *Macbeth*, for instance, we are told about the hero on three different occasions before we meet him. In the opening scene the witches name Macbeth, in the second scene Macbeth is named again, but this time as a great hero in battle. In the third scene Macbeth is heralded by the witches as one who shall "be King hereafter."

Dramatic structure prescribes a single structure to which all plays conform to a greater or less degree. First is the *exposition*, which gives the audience any information it needs to know about the past. Then comes the *complication* or rising action, which involves the hero in a course of action that will materially affect his future. Soon there follows an event which decides the result of the action, whether it be good or bad. This is the *crisis*. From that point the play moves to its inevitable conclusion, known as the *denouement* (unravelling, falling action), or *catastrophe*. This pattern follows the general plan of a pyramid as the action rises to a climax in the crisis and falls to the catastrophe.

It goes without saying that no author would follow such a scheme slavishly yet it is interesting how often this rule holds true. In *Romeo and Juliet* for example we first see Romeo winning Juliet; then after the death of Tybalt we have a falling action (denouement) which brings about the death of both Romeo and Juliet. In *Julius Caesar* also, Brutus increases in power till the death of Caesar; when he gives Mark Antony the right to speak at Caesar's funeral, he sets in motion his fall.

The characters we get to know primarily through what they say and do. And as we look at the characters, what they think and say must seem inevitable

Even the hairdo may tell whether the character is sick or well, whether she is rich or poor. One should study each character for visible elements that display mental or spiritual features, where the physical features conceal the mental and spiritual. In occasions when the apparent is just the opposite of the truth, we have, of course, irony.

Normally a writer of plays has such visible evidence of character in mind that we often accept costume, action, movement, scenery, placement of people on the stage, gesture, and sound without realizing how we got them. The accent with which one speaks may give status, as in Shaw's *Pygmalion.* Physical appearance may be significant. Shakespeare makes Falstaff large and fat; Richard II is a hunchback. Details of dress can be expressive of character. For example, Tennessee Williams in *A Streetcar Named Desire* shows Blanche's desires in the bright colors of her clothes; other characteristics are seen in her use of cosmetics, her false furs, costume jewelry. They all show her longing to get away from the painful facts of life.

The setting is one means of emphasizing what is said in the play. First we notice the number of sets. An inside scene naturally and inevitably portrays the world inside, whereas an outside scene is not limited. A play that has all the action take place in one room has necessarily a limited scene, one of limited social context, whereas one that is enacted in many places is more rigorous and has many more approaches to life as it is lived. In the set, we notice the kind of furniture: is it in good or bad taste, old or new, primly proper or poorly kept, in order or disorder? And there are always evidences of the special scene. A law court gives sense of law and order, of tradition. Rich and fertile fields make one think of wealth and leisure, a crowded tenement makes for all the disadvantages of the poor.

Stage directions give the author's plan for any matter that is not told in the dialogue, and of course they cover all types of information. Recent authors have often used them very exactly. In Sean O'Casey's *Juno and the Paycock* an entire page is given to a description of the room in which the action takes place; it is followed after one short sentence by a description of Juno, the heroine. Such descriptions are very telling to those who read the play but run into the danger of making statements that can hardly be put into action on the stage, as when in *Juno and the Paycock* again we are told that Juno had "that look which ultimately settles down upon the faces of the women of the working class."

Shakespeare and the Greeks were much more chary in their directions for the stage. *Macbeth* has only the direction "Scotland—An open place" before the entrance of the three witches. The classic Greek play was performed before the palace; for the opening of *Oedipus the King* the steps of the palace are crowded with suppliants in various attitudes of despair. And in every case the setting contributes to the mood of the play. Witches and ghosts prepare us for the mysterious, the spiritual, the ghostly, but the witches in *Macbeth* have a tone of the wicked, whereas the ghost in *Hamlet* is only mysterious.

● THE DANCE

There are three main reasons for organized dancing: (1) purposes of magic or religious ritual—ethnic dances; (2) social dances; (3) dancing for the entertainment of an audience—spectacular dances.[9]

ETHNIC DANCES

This term is used to distinguish religious dances, dances that are hymns of praise to a god, or are designed to bring on good fortunes in peace or war. Probably the common picture of the dances of the American Indian, such as the prayer for rain or for crops, are the best known examples. The royal ballets of Cambodia and India are excellent examples. In early days the Christian mysteries were danced by the clergy. And as late as the eighteenth century the Shakers in America engaged in dances as a form of worship. Usually such dances are traditional; often no one knows exactly how they came into being or where they came from. They are subtle and symbolic in meaning, and can hardly be understood by a person not of that ethnic group. "It is far easier to speak a foreign language without a trace of accent than it is to dance in a foreign idiom with complete purity of style."[10]

One of the best known and most important examples of ethnic dancing is found in the *Noh* play of Japan. Though known as the Noh play, it is actually a composite of dance, song, and music. The Noh play is generally considered one of the highest expressions of Japanese art, if not the highest. It is about six hundred years old. Usually there are only five or six characters in a play, the principal character and those who play opposite him. This principal character is always masked; some of the others may also be masked; but whether they are masked or not, the performance is always dignified and reserved, never realistic. Weeping, for example, is indicated only by a hand at the eye.

The making of masks is considered an important art in Japan. The masks and the gorgeous costumes worn by the characters add greatly to the beauty

---

[9] Arnold Haskell, *Ballet* (annual),
[10] John Martin, *Introduction to the Dance*, p. 106.

of the play. The stage is very small, with a raised passageway leading to it from the actors' dressing room through the audience. The stage is decorated only with branches of pine.

Traditionally a Noh play consists of a series of short plays arranged according to an established order. The first is about the gods, the second about warriors, the third about young and beautiful women, the fourth about madmen, and the fifth about devils or gods. To relieve the suspense, farces are introduced; often the farce imitates the scene just performed.

SOCIAL DANCES

Social, or recreational, dancing is dancing for one's own pleasure; it is usually performed by groups of people who follow definite patterns. Recreational dancing is found primarily in two forms: folk dance and ballroom dancing. The folk dance is often derived from ethnic dances. Recently there has been a revival of interest in folk dancing. Many of the dances are still identified with different countries: the reel, jig, and hornpipe are Irish, the sword and morris dances, English, and the Cossack dances, Russian.

Social, or ballroom, dancing is formal, as fitting the dancing floor. It was originally made up largely of square dances until they gave way to such round dances as the "wicked waltz." The waltz, however, has not been able to keep its place of preeminence; it has been followed by a series of dances each of which was disapproved of when it appeared—the bunny hug, turkey trot, shimmy, Charleston, and so on. In some of these changes, we have been strongly influenced by two sources, the American Negro and Latin American dances. The cakewalk and the tango are two obvious examples.

SPECTACULAR DANCE

Besides the recreational dances which are always participated in by the crowd, there are certain dances called *spectacular* because they are only viewed. The acrobatic dance and the tap dance need only be mentioned as the less honored members of this school. The really important spectaculars are the ballet and the modern dance.

THE CLASSICAL BALLET. The classical ballet was for many years the supreme expression of art in the dance. More than any other dance it was and is subject to a definite and prescribed discipline of body, head, legs, hands, arms, and there are set positions for each. There are, for example, five positions or movements of the head: (1) turn, (2) incline, (3) erect, (4) back, and (5) lowered.

Organization

The language of the ballet is always French.

    Pas de deux—a dance of two
    Pas de trois—a dance of three
    Pas de bourrée—running on points

The female, to gain lightness, works on her toes (*pointes*), whereas the man jumps and turns in the air (*entrechat*). The male supports the female when she is on points; in that way she has become the main figure of the ballet. The ballerina usually wears the familiar short skirt (*tutu*).

The subject of the ballet is most often a story, though in recent years abstract subjects have been used, as when the ballet uses a symphony for the accompanying music. The ideal of the ballet is beauty of line, grace, and purity of execution rather than literary concept.

"MODERN" DANCE. Modern dance, sometimes called the *impressional* dance, was in its origin primarily a revolt against the strict laws and regulations governing other dance forms, especially the classical ballet. Its leader was the American girl, Isadora Duncan. She wanted art to be "free" and thought of her dancing as a "return to nature." As an artist she felt that she had only to "express herself," and that the function of art is to make a supernatural world, not to imitate the natural.[11] The "ideal of the dance that she saw was 'the divine expression of the human spirit through the medium of the body's movement.'"

The people who followed her are less strident in their utterance and less demanding in their claims, and in this way they have produced a new purpose in the dance. Its major emphasis is on the expression of emotion through the dance.

The expressionist dance uses the dance as a basis for direct communication between dancer and spectator, it is concerned not so much with form as such as with the meaning of life and his relation to it. "Its only aim is to impart the sensation of living, to energize the spectator into keener awareness of the vigor, of the mystery, the humor, the variety and the wonder of life."[12]

As yet there is no standard vocabulary, or compositional approach, for the modern dance as there is for the ballet and for music; but modern dance has had great influence over all phases of the dance.

---

[11] William Boletha, and Isadora Duncan, quoted in Magriel, *Chronicles of the American Dance*, p. 196.
[12] Martin, *op. cit.*, p. 253.

17
STYLE

● DEFINITION OF STYLE

. . . I remember myself, years ago, sketching with two well-known men, artists who were great friends, great cronies, asking each other all the time, how to do this and how to do that; but absolutely different in the texture of their minds and in the result that they wished to obtain, so far as the pictures and drawings by which they were well known to the public were concerned.

What we made, or rather, I should say, what we wished to note, was merely a memorandum of a passing effect upon the hills that lay before us. We had no idea of expressing ourselves, or of studying in any way the subject for any future use. We merely had the intention to note this affair rapidly, and we had all used the same words to express to each other what we liked in it. There were big clouds rolling over hills, sky clearing above, dots of trees and water and meadow-land below, and the ground fell away suddenly before us. Well, our three sketches were, in the first place, different in shape; either from our physical differences, or from a habit of drawing certain shapes of a picture, which itself usually indicates—as you know, or ought to know—whether we are looking far or near. Two were oblong, but of different proportions; one was more nearly a square; the distance taken in to the right and left was smaller in the latter case, and on the contrary, the height up and down —that is to say the portion of land beneath and the portion of sky above—was greater. In each picture the distance bore a different relation to the foreground. In each picture the clouds were treated with different precision and different attention. In one picture the open sky above was the main intention of the picture. In two pictures the upper sky was of no consequence—it was the clouds and the mountains that were insisted upon. The drawing was the same, that is to say, the general make of things; but each man had involuntarily looked upon what was most interesting to him in the whole sight; and though the whole sight was what he meant to represent, he had unconsciously preferred a beauty or an interest of things different from what his neighbor liked.

The colour of each painting was different—the vivacity of colour and tone, the distinctness of each part in relation to the whole; and each picture would have been recognized anywhere as a specimen of work by each one of us, characteristic of our names. And we spent on the whole affair perhaps twenty minutes.

I wish you to understand, again, that we each thought and felt as if we had been photographing the matter before us. We had not the first desire of expressing *ourselves,* and I think would have been very much worried had we not felt that each one was true to nature. And we were each one true to nature.

—JOHN LA FARGE (1855–1910, American artist), *Considerations on Painting,* pp. 71–73[1]

This account of a sketching expedition as told by the artist John La Farge is dramatic because of the wide variety in the results. La Farge and his friends had decided together what they wanted to accomplish and how they expected to get it done. Each felt he was merely carrying out the assignment agreed on, and yet each painting showed clearly the individuality of the painter. The fact underlying this experience, however, is familiar to everyone: no two people do anything in the same way. No matter what they are doing or how carefully they plan, the results are different.

We find similar differences if we compare two paintings of nudes. Giorgione made a beautiful study of a reclining figure in his *Sleeping Venus* (Figure 195). Two centuries later Manet tried his hand at the same figure, in *Olympia* (Figure 196). Giorgione puts his figure out of doors and presents her sleeping. Manet opens her eyes and makes her more erect in posture. The effect of the paintings is very different. Giorgione's is calm and idyllic, whereas Manet's is realistic, a frank picture of a courtesan, hard and cold-blooded.

And of course we find the same thing in music. Saint-Saëns and Sibelius each have compositions which describe the grace and beauty of the swan. Both have used the cello as the instrument best fitted to its majestic movements, but again each composition reflects its composer. The work of Saint-Saëns shows the characteristics of Saint-Saëns and that of Sibelius the mood and character of Sibelius.

The differences which we have been talking about are known as differences in style. Each artist has the tools of his own art in subject, medium, and

[1] Reprinted by permission of the Macmillan Company, publishers.

FIGURE 195. GIORGIONE; landscape by TITIAN. *Sleeping Venus* (ca. 1505). (Oil on canvas. Height: 3 feet, 6¾ inches. Dresden, Museum. Photograph by Alinari.)

FIGURE 196. EDOUARD MANET (1832–1883), French painter. *Olympia* (1863). (Oil on canvas. Height: 4 feet, 2 inches. Paris, Louvre. Photograph by Stoedtner.)

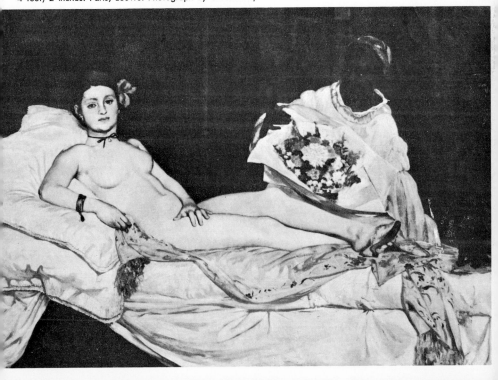

organization, and the student who wants to know what is style will do well to study them in detail. Just what is the subject? How has the artist treated it? Why did he choose it? What are the characteristics of his use of medium? What elements does he prefer? Is the structure clear? Do all the parts fit together to make a whole? If he does this, he will soon come to feel that style is not the use of medium, subject, and organization as such, but is the personality of the artist showing through them. La Farge said that he and his fellow artists were "different in the texture of their minds." Wölfflin, talking of the paintings of two women, says of one that it is "not . . . less skilfully drawn, but . . . it is felt differently." The best definitions of style identify it with personality. This is essentially the famous definition of Buffon: "The style is the man."

● SOME CHARACTERISTICS OF STYLE

When we say that style is personality we do not mean that the artist obtrudes himself. The work is personal and it shows the artist's personality, but it does so because every work necessarily shows personality and not because the artist has tried to show what kind of person he is. In the two paintings of nudes we get a clear impression of Giorgione and an equally clear one of Manet, but not because they have tried to show us what they are; they were interested in what they had to say about the subject, and because they expressed themselves honestly, we learn what they are. Paradoxically, impersonal art is personal.

Since style is a reflection of personality, it follows that when the personality changes, the style changes. An individual does not have the same personality at all times. His personality as a young man is different from his personality as a middle-aged man or an old man. And so it is with style. The style of Beethoven is different from the style of Mozart, and the style of Beethoven as a young man is different from his style in his middle period or his style in his last period. The style of Shakespeare is not the same as that of Marlowe or Beaumont, and Shakespeare's early style is different from his later style.

Often we hear that a young artist is working in the style of another. We hear, for instance, that the early symphonies of Beethoven are in the style of Mozart, or that the early plays of Shakespeare are in the style of Marlowe. Mozart and Marlowe were the models whom the young artists followed just as a child follows the tone and the pronunciation of his father and mother. But even though Beethoven and Shakespeare were working in the style of the older men, theirs is still the style of Beethoven and Shakespeare.

FIGURE 197. BERNARDINO LUINI (ca. 1465–1532), Italian painter. *Holy Family* (undated). (Oil on wood panel. Size: 27⅝ by 24¾ inches. Milan, Pinacoteca Ambrosiana. Photograph, Biblioteca Ambrosiana.)

School work is similar in many respects. An artist creates something that is good; it is recognized as good, and it has an influence over other artists of the time. Soon there arises a school of artists who are carrying on the tradition of the master. Especially is this true in the visual arts. We have a school of Botticelli, a school of Scopas, a school of Cézanne. The work of the school has all the obvious manifestations of the master; at first glance it is mistaken for his work, and it is only on careful study that one can distinguish the work of the school from that of the master. Because "schools" pick up the obvious characteristics of the master the work is simpler, and it is at first glance easier and more attractive than the original. Many a person likes the winsome Madonnas of Luini (Figure 197) and later learns to like the greater Madonnas of Luini's master Leonardo (Figure 198).

FIGURE 198. LEONARDO DA VINCI. *Madonna and St. Anne* (1506–1510). (Oil on canvas. Size: 4 feet, 7 inches by 4 feet, 2 inches. Paris, Louvre. Photograph by Anderson.)

● STYLE AND STYLES

So far we have talked of style as individual, and in the last analysis it is always individual. It is the way some one person living at some one time does that thing by which he is known. And just as no one person is ever an exact duplicate of any other person, the style of any one person is not exactly like that of any other person.

At the same time people are alike in a great many respects, and we soon begin grouping them together under certain headings to show their kinship one with the other. And so we have the various styles. And we speak of a British style or an American style, a humorous style or a poetic style, a journalistic or a scientific style, a medieval or a Renaissance style. A style in this sense is a recognition of certain qualities in which the work of this individual is like that of others.

THE HISTORICAL STYLES. The historical styles rise from the similarities of people living in the same place at the same time. They speak the same language, they dress alike, they have the same manners and customs, they share the same ideas, and their work reflects this community of interests. And so we have a style of Elizabethan England, a style of the Italian Renaissance, a Chinese style, an early Greek style, a late Greek style, and so on.

STYLES BASED ON ATTITUDES AND IDEAS. Besides the historical styles there are also styles based not on history but on similar attitudes and ideas. There are many styles in this category: naturalism, realism, impressionism, expressionism, abstract expressionism, surrealism, cubism, the picaresque novel, the problem novel, Puritanism, the Imagists, and others. Many of them have not lasted very long because the ideas they reflect, the problems they deal with, have ceased to be of importance. There are, however, two categories of style which have been of importance for centuries. We will consider them now. They are: (1) the classic and the romantic, and (2) the tragic and the comic.

● CLASSICISM AND ROMANTICISM

The distinction between classicism and romanticism, though one of the clearest and most basic distinctions in art and one almost unerringly recognizable, does not lend itself easily to exact description or definition. The confusion is made worse by the fact that the words themselves have shifted in meaning a great deal. Classic should mean nothing more than "belonging to a certain class." But by a process analogous to that whereby we say that a person has taste when we mean he has good taste, *classic* came to mean " belonging to the first class of excellence, the best." And the word is still used in that sense when we speak of the *classics* of English literature. Then, since for many years Graeco-Roman culture was considered the best, the word *classic* came to be associated only with Greek and Latin authors, so that even today in the schools the "classics" are Greek and Latin works. When, however, we use the word *classic* or *classicism* as opposed to *romantic* or *romanticism,* we do not mean any of these definitions but a fourth, as the word came to connote the qualities that were supposed to characterize Greek and Latin authors. These qualities were commonly accepted to be clarity, simplicity, restraint, objectivity, and balance.

The word *romantic* is also used in various ways. It should mean nothing more than pertaining to or descended from things Roman or Latin, a usage that survives in the term *Romance languages*—French, Spanish, Italian, Portuguese. The word came into use in the Middle Ages to distinguish the vernacular from the literary Latin. And, by a process of change very similar to that of the word *classic,* the words *romance* and *romantic* came to mean the literature of those countries at that time. The most outstanding type of literature was the tale of chivalry that is still known as the romance, and the word is kept for all narratives with emphasis on plot, as when we speak of Scott's novels as romances. And, in the same way, *romantic* came to mean the qualities found in the medieval romance, which are taken to be love of the remote and indefinite, escape from reality, lack of restraint in form and emotions, the preference for picturesqueness, or grandeur, or passion, to finish and proportion.

Classicism and romanticism are thus fundamentally in opposition; what is classic is not romantic, and what is romantic is not in that respect classic. The classic is restrained, the romantic is not restrained. The classic is real; it is concerned with the life of every day; the romantic is unreal, concerned with the fantastic, the strange, the unusual. The classic is finished, perfect; it has great beauty of form; the romantic is unfinished, imperfect, and is often careless of form. The classic is simple, the romantic is complex; the classic is objective, the romantic is subjective; the classic is finite, concerned only with projects that can be realized and accomplished; the romantic is infinite, concerned with plans that can never be realized, affecting "thoughts co-equal with the clouds." The classic is like an arrow shot from the bow that goes straight to the mark; the romantic is like a sailboat that tacks to one side and then to the other, reaching its destination by heading always away from the mark.

The difference between the two can be seen most clearly in the great art of each type. The Greek temple is classic and the medieval cathedral is romantic. Both are religious edifices, but they show an infinite difference in the attitudes that created them, a difference far deeper than the dissimilarities of mere construction and mechanics. The Greek temple is hard, bright, exact, calm, and complete; the walls and the columns are no higher than will stand of their own strength; the lintels and the roof are simple, sane, and sensible. Nothing more is attempted than can be accomplished, and the result is a perfect building, finished and finite. Anyone can understand its main construction at a glance.

The Gothic cathedral, on the other hand, is not self-contained but is built on the principle of balance. The openings are not made with lintels but are arched. One stone holds in place only by its relation to the other stones. The walls will not stand alone; they must be buttressed. As the walls go higher the arches become more pointed, the roof becomes more pointed, and the buttresses are strengthened with pinnacles and flying buttresses, the whole so carefully and cleverly balanced that a fault in one stone might cause a side or even the entire building to collapse. And the whole cannot be grasped at a glance; one is conscious only of its great complexity, its infinite variety, its striving upward and beyond.

The Greek temple might be as solid as a statue, for all the feeling we have of its interior; the inside does not matter; it has no more character than the inside of a box. But with the cathedral, on the other hand, the outside sends us inevitably within. And inside we find a mystery in light and dark, a spiritual experience of unlimited space which is of the essence both of Gothic and of romanticism (Figure 199). Compare the Greek temple (Figure 158).

The difference between the two can also be seen clearly in music. Mozart is

FIGURE 199. CHARTRES CATHEDRAL, view of ambulatory from south transept. (Photograph, Harry H. Hillberry.)

a typical composer of the classic school. His music is calm, restrained, reasonable; the melodies and harmonies are clear and perfect. The emotions are subordinated to the forms used. Beethoven followed Mozart in his early works; and his early symphonies, notably the second and the fourth, are classic. But his more characteristic symphonies, such as the fifth and ninth, are romantic. The music is personal and emotional; it expresses the struggles of the composer as he sought to find peace and calm. It is not contained and perfect, but exuberant, exultant, and free.

The difference, again, is clearly demonstrated if we take two pieces of sculpture, the Greek *Hegeso Stele* (Figure 51) and the American *Adams Memorial* by Saint-Gaudens (Figure 52). Both are tombstones. The Greek stele shows us Hegeso with her servant; the two are watching intently as Hegeso lifts a jewel from the box. It is a simple scene of everyday life, quiet and impersonal in its treatment. On the other hand, the Adams monument wraps us at once in mystery and questioning. A robed and hooded figure is seated before a severe granite slab. Is it man or woman? What does it mean? Is it supposed to symbolize Death? Or Grief? Moreover, our attention is no longer centered on the object itself, as it was with the stele of Hegeso; the object now serves as a point of departure for our emotions and questionings.

In literature we see the same thing if we compare a great classic play, such as *Oedipus the King* by Sophocles, with a great romantic play, such as *King Lear* by Shakespeare. In *Oedipus the King*, Oedipus has been on the throne for a long time, his reign has been a good one, his daughters are grown, and all has been for the best; but there breaks out a terrible pestilence. Oedipus has sent to the oracle to learn the cause and the means of relief. When the play opens he is waiting for the return of his servant, who comes with the message of the gods that they must get rid of the unclean thing in their midst. Then, as the play develops and Oedipus tries to learn what this unclean thing is, we are told that Oedipus is the son of Laius and Jocasta, whom they exposed as a baby because of the oracle that their son would kill his father and marry his mother; that he ran away from his foster parents in Corinth because the oracle there had said that he was doomed to kill his father and marry his mother; that the man he killed as he first entered the city was Laius, the King; and that hence he had killed his father and married his mother, the queen. Jocasta anticipates the outcome before Oedipus has put all the threads together, and when Oedipus finally realizes that he has unwittingly fulfilled the oracle of the gods, he finds that she has hanged herself. Saying that he is too vile to look upon the earth any longer, he blinds himself with her brooch and, as the play closes, is led off the stage, an outcast. There is no relief, no comedy, no subplot; everything in the play bears directly on the unraveling of the clues that lead to the conclusion that Oedipus is himself the unclean thing that has brought disaster to Thebes.

In *King Lear*, on the other hand, the main plot is buttressed by a subplot very much like it. The main plot tells how Lear cast off Cordelia, the daughter who loved him and was true to him, and gave his all to Goneril and Regan, who had no love for him and were untrue to him, only to be himself cast off by Goneril and Regan and rescued by Cordelia. The subplot parallels the main plot almost to a detail. Gloucester, who cast off his legitimate son Edgar to give everything to his illegitimate son Edward, is thrown out by Edward and saved by Edgar. The seriousness of the two plots is relieved by the humor of the fool, whose songs and dances are designed to cheer up the old king and bring him back to his senses. The contrasts are carried even further in the mad scenes, for Lear goes mad, and in a single scene we have the real madness of the king, the professional madness of the fool, and the pretended madness of Edgar. One scene is balanced against another like the stones of the cathedral, and the whole is fantastic, grotesque, wild, undisciplined, whereas *Oedipus the King* is calm and self-contained like the Greek temple. We cannot say one play is greater than the other; both reach the greatest heights of emotion, but their methods are opposite.

The difference is fundamentally a difference of attitude, which may be found in all types of art. We have it illustrated in two love poems, the first, which is classic, by Landor, and the second, which is romantic, by Shelley.

> Ah, what avails the sceptred race,
> > Ah, what the form divine!
> What every virtue, every grace!
> > Rose Aylmer, all were thine.
> Rose Aylmer, whom these wakeful eyes
> > May weep, but never see,
> A night of memories and of sighs
> > I consecrate to thee.
>
> > —WALTER SAVAGE LANDOR (1775–1864) British poet,
> > > "Rose Aylmer"

> I arise from dreams of thee
> In the first sweet sleep of night,
> When the winds are breathing low,
> And the stars are shining bright:
> I arise from dreams of thee,
> And a spirit in my feet
> Hath led me—who knows how?
> To thy chamber window, Sweet!

The wandering airs they faint
On the dark, the silent stream—
The Champak odours fail
Like sweet thoughts in a dream;
The nightingale's complaint,
It dies upon her heart;—
As I must on thine,
Oh! beloved as thou art!

Oh lift me from the grass!
I die! I faint! I fail!
Let thy love in kisses rain
On my lips and eyelids pale.
My cheek is cold and white, alas!
My heart beats loud and fast;—
Oh! press it to thine own again,
Where it will break at last.

    —PERCY BYSSHE SHELLEY (1792–1822, British poet),

      "The Indian Serenade"

We find the difference also in acting. Many years ago Sarah Bernhardt was starring in Racine's *Phèdre*. The story tells how Theseus, in his old age, married Phaedra, the sister of Ariadne, the daughter of Minos. She fell in love with his son Hippolytus, who combined all the virtues of his father with youth and beauty that matched her own. Hippolytus, though he returned the love of Phaedra, would have nothing to do with his father's wife. In one scene Phaedra makes passionate love to Hippolytus. In the production by Sarah Bernhardt and her company Hippolytus stood apparently unmoved through the time that Phaedra was wooing him; at last she turned away in desperation, and as she turned Hippolytus took one step forward, with his arms outstretched, showing in this one movement all the love that was in his own heart but which honor had kept him from making known. If this gesture of Hippolytus is compared with what we may call the usual cinema portrayal of love, with its emphasis on the embrace, we see again the difference between the classic and the romantic. It is not a difference in the amount of feeling that is expressed but in the manner of expression.

Between the two extremities of classicism and romanticism there are, as always, many gradations. We can never say that any work of art is entirely classic or romantic, but it usually tends toward one or the other, and the work of any artist is apt to be predominantly classic or romantic, though almost any artist will show both tendencies. Shakespeare is unabashedly romantic in most of his plays but severely classic in *Othello*, where every scene is focused on the jealousy of the hero, its arousal, and its consequences.

Classicism and romanticism are an opposition that is ever-present in all art of all ages. But, although it is a mistake to say that any period is exclusively classic or romantic, we may discern times when either classicism or romanticism is distinctly ascendant, such as classicism in fifth-century Greece and eighteenth-century Europe and romanticism in the Gothic period and the nineteenth century.

It may be noted also that, just as some periods lean toward classicism or toward romanticism, so, of the various arts, some are more essentially classic or romantic than others. Figure painting may be either classic or romantic, but landscape painting tends to the romantic. The distant view is necessarily vague and mysterious, and even when a composition concentrates on a nearby scene it is not limited and self-contained; landscape, by its nature, leads one on and on; one wants to know what is over the river, beyond the tree, on the other side of the hill. Poussin is known as a classic painter, but his landscapes are classic only in the sense that they are intellectually conceived and planned; in other respects they are romantic. El Greco, in his *View of Toledo*, has heightened the romantic aspects of the scene by his use of light and cloud; the landscape is gloomy and menacing as well as mysterious and romantic (Figure 200).

FIGURE 200. EL GRECO. *View of Toledo* (ca. 1610). (Oil on canvas. Size: 48 by 42¾ inches. New York, courtesy Metropolitan Museum of Art; bequest of Mrs. H. O. Havemeyer, 1929. H. O. Havemeyer Collection.)

Sculpture is by nature exact, precise, well defined, and balanced. The effects most natural to it are therefore classic, and a people of marked classic tendencies, like the Greeks, find in sculpture one of their best means of expression. It can, however, be romantic, as we have seen in the *Adams Memorial*. Nevertheless the classic seems the more appropriate style for sculpture, and most sculpture tends to be classic in feeling. Music, on the other hand, is by nature vague, elusive, evocative, emotional. The effects most natural for it are therefore romantic, and music can express in a few bars all the yearning and poignancy that it takes the profoundest efforts of the other arts to express. We often hear it said that the truest or best music is the "absolute" music of the eighteenth century, which is objective and without emotion, devoted to purely formal beauty. This is not at all the case; music is essentially emotional, and such objective music as that of Mozart and Scarlatti is the rarest kind.

Finally, we should perhaps insert a word of warning that classicism and romanticism are not in themselves good or bad; they are merely different points of view and must be judged on their own merits. The good in the classic is poised, serene, and balanced; the bad in the classic is cold, overformal, and lifeless. The good in the romantic is rich and full of emotion; the bad in the romantic is gushing and undisciplined. Either can be a complete approach to art; neither without the other is a complete approach to reality.

18
THE TRAGIC AND
THE COMIC

● **THE KINSHIP OF TRAGEDY AND COMEDY**

It has been said that tragedy is life viewed close at hand, and comedy is life viewed at a distance. It has also been said that life is comedy to the man who thinks and tragedy to the one who feels. In other words, the same situation may seem tragic to one and comic to another, or tragic at one time and comic at another. Pieter Brueghel has painted a picture illustrating the parable of Jesus: "Can the blind lead the blind? Shall they not both fall into the ditch?" The old men in this picture might be inmates of any workhouse or poor farm. Each is trying to keep in touch with the one in front of him by holding to his shoulder or by touching him with his stick. But the one in front has stumbled and the others are falling. To some the grotesque positions they assume as they try to keep balance are comic; to others they are tragic.

The close connection between the comic and the tragic is very well illustrated in characters that formerly were considered comic but now are counted tragic. There is no question but that Shylock, in *The Merchant of Venice,* was originally considered a comic character; now he is tragic. We feel only sympathy for the old man when we hear him say:

In the Rialto you have rated me
About my moneys and my usances.
Still have I borne it with a patient shrug,
For suff'rance is the badge of all our tribe.
You call me misbeliever, cut-throat dog,
And spit upon my Jewish gaberdine,
And all for use of that which is mine own.
Well then, it now appears you need my help.
Go to, then! You come to me, and you say,
"Shylock, we would have moneys;" you say so—
You, that did void your rheum upon my beard
And foot me as you spurn a stranger cur
Over your threshold; moneys is your suit.
What should I say to you? Should I not say,
"Hath a dog money? Is it possible
A cur can lend three thousand ducats?" Or
Shall I bend low and in a bondsman's key,
With bated breath and whisp'ring humbleness,
Say this:
"Fair sir, you spat on me on Wednesday last;
You spurn'd me such a day; another time
You call'd me dog; and for these courtesies
I'll lend you thus much moneys"?

> —WILLIAM SHAKESPEARE (1564–1616, British poet and dramatist), *The Merchant of Venice*, I, iii, 108–130 (ca. 1595)

● THE FUNDAMENTAL TYPES

The fundamental types of comedy and tragedy are seen in the attitudes toward the old joke in which a person about to sit down has the chair pulled out from under him. There are, in general, four possibilities: (1) The person sits on the floor, and we laugh. It is comic, but it is a comedy of situation only; we are amused because the person on the floor is in a situation in which he did not expect to be. (2) The person sitting on the floor breaks his back. This is obviously not comedy but tragedy, but again it is a tragedy of situation because the person is in an unfortunate situation. It does not matter in either of these cases who the person is; it is the situation that gives the scene its character. (3) We laugh when the chair is pulled out from under someone, but we laugh not at the person who sits on the floor but at the man who pulls out the chair. We are amused that anyone should think such a thing is funny. We are laughing, in this case, not at a situation but at a man; in other words, this is comedy of character rather than of situation. (4) From comedy of character to tragedy of character is only a step. Instead of laughing at the person who has such a depraved sense of humor we feel it is tragic that anyone who is living in a civilized community should find such a trick amusing.

Comedy and tragedy of situation are also called *low comedy* and *low tragedy*; comedy and tragedy of character, *high comedy* and *high tragedy*. Low comedy is the basis for slapstick comedy and farce—the comedy that results from the throwing of custard pies or from the big feet of Charlie Chaplin. Low tragedy is the essence of melodrama. One is interested in the events that occur because they are exciting—a train wreck, an explosion, a race, the hunt for a criminal. In low comedy and low tragedy the characters are not individuals but types—the hero, the heroine, the villain, etc. In high comedy and high tragedy the people are individuals.

Shakespeare's *Comedy of Errors* is comedy of situation. As everyone knows, the play deals with twin masters who have twins for their servants. To make the confusion worse both the masters are named Antipholus and both the servants are named Dromio. The masters, who have been separated since birth, find themselves in Ephesus, and naturally there are many amusing situations as masters and servants are mixed up, until at last their identity is discovered and their relationship established. There is nothing comic in the twin masters or in the twin servants as such. The comedy lies in the situations which arise because they are confused one with the other.

The French comedy of Molière and the English comedy of Ben Jonson present comedy of character almost without comedy of situation. For example, the miser Volpone, in Ben Jonson's play of that name, pretends to be very ill; his miserly friends bring rich gifts, each one hoping to ingratiate himself so as to be the sick man's heir. When Volpone has got all their gifts, he resumes his usual state of health. There is nothing comic in this situation; we are amused only by the characters.

Ordinarily a dramatist uses elements of both high and low drama; the preponderance of one or the other determines the character of the play. In *Hamlet*, for instance, many elements of the plot are frankly melodramatic. To enumerate: the guards are watching at midnight when they see a ghost; the hero kills a man through a curtain; there is a fight in an open grave; drinks are poisoned and the wrong person gets the poison; swords are exchanged and a man is killed with his own poisoned sword. All this is melodrama. The real tragedy is concerned with what takes place in the minds of the people. But so great is this interest that we are surprised when we realize how much melodrama the play contains.

Shakespeare's comedies, in general, are not comedies in the strict sense of the word; the plot is not itself a comic plot. The plot is a pleasant, gay story which does not take life too seriously. In *Twelfth Night,* for instance, the plot tells how Viola, learning that she is near the estate of a duke (Orsino) of whom she has heard much, decides to assume the guise of a boy, and enter the duke's service in the hope that she may win him and marry him. She does both. It is a pleasant tale, not a comic one. In the development of the story, however, Shakespeare uses both comedy of character and comedy of situation.

● THE BASIS OF COMEDY

The chief source of the comic is the incongruous, the unexpected. We expect one thing and we find another. If one man pulls a chair out from under another, the joke lies in the fact that the second sits on the floor when he expected to sit on the chair.

It is the unexpectedness of the speech that makes for comedy in the reply of the nurse in *Romeo and Juliet:*

> Your love says, like an honest gentleman, and a courteous, and a kind, and a handsome,
> and I warrant, a virtuous,—Where is your Mother?
> —II, v, 56–59

Juliet has sent the nurse to find out from Romeo whether she is to be married that day. The nurse has returned with the news, and Juliet wants to know. But the nurse is hot and tired and out of humor because of the long trip she has had. At last she begins to tell the message from Romeo, but when she comes to the word *virtuous,* she is reminded of the nature of the alliance she is promoting and she breaks off with the question "Where is your mother?" It is the contrast between what we expect and what we receive that is comic.

In comedy of character it is the difference between what a person thinks he is and the person we think him to be that is funny. In the famous passage from *Much Ado about Nothing* when Dogberry is swearing in the watch, there is nothing funny in the situation. The comedy comes from the fact that Dogberry is pompous; he thinks he is better than he is.

> DOGBERRY: Are you good men and true?
> VERGES: Yea, or else it were pity but they should suffer salvation, body and soul.
> DOGBERRY: Nay, that were a punishment too good for them, if they should have any allegiance in them, being chosen for the Prince's watch.
> VERGES: Well, give them their charge, neighbour Dogberry.

DOGBERRY: First, who think you the most desartless man to be constable?

FIRST WATCH: Hugh Oatcake, sir, or George Seacole; for they can write and read.

DOGBERRY: Come hither, neighbour Seacole. God hath bless'd you with a good name. To be a well-favoured man is the gift of fortune, but to write and read comes by nature.

—SHAKESPEARE, *Much Ado about Nothing*, III, iii, 1–22 (ca. 1599)

Comedy thus implies a norm or a standard; the actual is measured by this norm, and the comic arises in the difference between the actual and the norm. It is normal for a man to be taller than a woman, for a person to sit in a chair rather than on the floor, for a girl to get an intelligible answer when her messenger returns from an important errand. It is in this sense that the unexpected is comic. The unexpected is not, as such, comic; there is nothing comic in having an unexpected attack of ptomaine poisoning, or in getting a letter one has not expected; but if one is expecting to learn whether she is to be married, and hears the question "Where is your mother?" the difference between what one expects and what one hears *is* comic. Sometimes the standard is given; more often it is implied; but in any case we expect a standard, and we find it amusing when the actual deviates from it.

It is this measurement against a standard which has induced us to think of the abnormal as funny. Deformity, insanity, and pain used to be considered comic and were regularly used for low comedy effects. The fool, the hunchback, and the midget were accepted as comic characters of the court; as such they are prominent in Velázquez's paintings of court scenes. In the Elizabethan drama choruses of madmen were sometimes introduced for comic effects. Drunkenness, until a few years ago, was considered a cause of laughter and is still so considered in many cases. Children laugh if they see a cat having fits. In these cases the abnormal is measured against the standard of the normal and found funny.

● CHARACTERISTICS OF THE COMIC

Comedy is primarily intellectual. The perception of the comic depends on the recognition of the difference between the normal and the actual. If one does not know the standard, or if he does not perceive the deviation from the standard, he does not find it funny. It is for this reason that jokes are tricky and that there are so many limitations on them. For comedy is highly specialized in its appeal. The people of one country do not like the jokes of another country. There is the American joke, the English joke, the French joke, the German joke. Even the sexes differ in their appreciation of comedy; women do not appreciate all the jokes of men, nor do men appreciate all the jokes appealing to women.

Comedy, moreover, is detached. No one can laugh at anything that is very close to him. Even when one laughs at himself he must, as it were, get away from himself in order to laugh. When one is suffering from puppy love he cannot laugh at himself, but when he has recovered from the attack he can join with others in the laugh. There is thus something impersonal about the comic. And it implies a degree of insensibility on the part of the audience; we cannot sympathize too much if we are going to laugh. If we are distressed about the nurse's fatigue or her concern over Romeo's being a virtuous young man, we cannot laugh when she interrupts her tale, "Your love says, . . . Where is your mother?"

Because comedy is detached, we laugh at all sorts of things in the world of comedy that we do not find funny in everyday life: the man who does not pay his bills, the woman who deceives her husband, the young boy suffering from puppy love. In *Arsenic and Old Lace,* one of the most delightful of recent comedies, two gentle old ladies are in the habit of administering arsenic in elderberry wine to the lonely old men they meet, because they feel sorry for them. The men are then buried in the basement by a brother who thinks he is Teddy Roosevelt and counts this digging as part of the work on the Panama Canal. In real life we would demand that something be done; it would be no excuse that the old ladies are insane. Nor would it be possible to keep the whole thing quiet as is done in the play. In short there would be consequences. In the play there are none; the situations are hilariously funny, but the plot takes place, as it were, in a vacuum. Evil in comedy is not evil but something to be laughed at.

Because comedy is intellectual and depends on perception, the comic always has in it a feeling of superiority. The person who sees the joke feels superior to the one who does not, and frequently he is patronizing. There is a bond of union between people who like the same joke. But feeling superior is a tight-rope to walk on. The artist usually veers to one side or the other; and he takes sides for or against the people who are the subject of his comedy. He is either sympathetic or critical. If he is sympathetic, his writing becomes humorous; if he is critical, it becomes satirical.

● HUMOR AND SATIRE

Humor is a matter of spirit rather than of words. It is kindly; it is sympathetic. Usually it has in it something of extravagance, and the author, looking at the extravagant person, smiles with tolerant indulgence. In this way we love Falstaff while we smile at the extravagance of his statements:

Bardolph, am I not fallen away vilely since this last action? do I not bate? do I not dwindle? Why, my skin hangs about me like an old lady's loose gown; I am withered like an old apple-john. Well, I'll repent, and that suddenly, while I am in some liking; I shall be out of heart shortly, and then I shall have no strength to repent. An I have not forgotten what the inside of a church is made of, I am a peppercorn, a brewer's horse. The inside of a church! Company, villainous company, hath been the spoil of me.

—SHAKESPEARE, *Henry IV*, Part I, III, iii, 1–11 (1592)

When Orlando, in *As You Like It*, protests that he will die if he does not win Rosalind, she reminds him of famous lovers, none of whom died of love: the brains of Troilus were beaten out with a club; Leander died of a cramp while swimming the Hellespont, and so on. She ends with a summary for all time:

But these are all lies: men have died from time to time, and worms have eaten them, but not for love.

—IV, i, 106–108

Because we know Rosalind, and realize how much she is in love with Orlando, and how gallantly and cleverly she is carrying on her game with him, we find the words humorous, but had they been spoken by another we might have found them cynical.

Satire aims, or at least pretends to aim, at improvement. The satirist sees the vices and faults of the human race, and exposes them in a comic manner in order to call the matter to attention. To this end, the satirist may use any device. Swift uses allegory in *Gulliver's Travels*, where he is satirizing the littleness of men. On his first voyage Gulliver goes into the land of the Lilliputians, a people who are only a few inches in height. Here he is amazed at the cunning and the foolishness of the little people. The test of the politician's ability to hold office is his skill in walking a rope. The Lilliputians are in a great agony of disagreement and even fight a war to decide at which end an egg should be broken. Some who believe it should be broken at the big end are called the Big-endians; others, who are just as strong in their faith that it should be broken at the little end, are called the Little-endians.

● WIT

Wit is a general name for those forms of the comic which have to do with words. Like all other forms of the comic, it is based on incongruity. We expect one word and we hear another.

Under the heading of wit come spoonerisms, malapropisms, puns, epigrams, and parody.

The *spoonerism,* named from one of its most distinguished makers, the Reverend W. A. Spooner of Oxford, is the accidental transposition of the initial letters of two or more words. One says he has just received a "blushing crow," when he means a "crushing blow." The English poets Keats and Shelley become, by juxtaposition, Sheets and Kelly.

The *malapropism,* named for Mrs. Malaprop in *The Rivals,* is the ludicrous misuse of a word for one resembling it, for example, "contagious countries" for "contiguous countries."

> Observe me, Sir Anthony, I would by no means wish a daughter of mine to be a progeny of learning; I don't think so much learning becomes a young woman. For instance, I would never let her meddle with Greek, or Hebrew, or Algebra, or simony, or fluxions, or paradoxes, or such inflammatory branches of learning—neither would it be necessary for her to handle any of your mathematical, astronomical, diabolical instruments.—But Sir Anthony, I would send her, at nine years old, to a boarding-school in order to learn a little ingenuity and artifice. Then, sir, she should have supercilious knowledge in accounts; and as she grew up, I would have her instructed in geometry, that she might know something of the contagious countries;—but above all, Sir Anthony, she should be mistress of orthodoxy, that she might not misspell and mispronounce words so shamefully as girls usually do; and likewise that she might reprehend the true meaning of what she is saying.—This, Sir Anthony, is what I would have a woman know; and I don't think there is a superstitious article in it.
>
> —RICHARD SHERIDAN (1751–1816, Irish-born British playwright), *The Rivals* (1775)

A *pun* is a play on words which have the same sound or similar sounds but different meanings. One of the more serious puns is that on "grave" in Mercutio's speech in *Romeo and Juliet:*

> ROMEO: Courage, man; the hurt cannot be much.
> MERCUTIO: No, 'tis not so deep as a well, nor so wide as a church-door; but 'tis enough, 'twill serve. Ask for me tomorrow, and you shall find me a grave man. I am pepper'd, I warrant, for this world.
>
> —SHAKESPEARE, *Romeo and Juliet,* III, i, 99–102 (ca. 1593)

James Joyce made a delightful pun in "Lawn Tennyson" with definite reference to lawn tennis—[1]

The *epigram* is a condensed, pithy statement, like that of the young man in Wilde's *Lady Windemere's Fan:* "I can resist everything except temptation." Martial is one of the most famous writers of epigrams:

[1] David Daiches, *A Study of Literature for Readers and Critics,* p. 44.

I do not love thee, Doctor Fell,
The reason why I cannot tell;
But this alone I know full well,
I do not love thee, Doctor Fell.

> —MARTIAL (ca. A.D. 40–104, Roman poet),
> *"Non Amo Te,"* trans. Tom Brown (1663–1704)

And there is always the famous epigram of John Wilmot on Charles II:

Here lies our Sovereign Lord the King,
Whose word no man relies on,
Who never said a foolish thing,
Nor ever did a wise one.

> —JOHN WILMOT, EARL OF ROCHESTER (1648–1680, British courtier and poet),
> *Epitaph on Charles II* (ca. 1675).

A *parody* is an imitation of a piece of writing, usually a very well-known work. The parody imitates the model very closely but turns the serious sense of the original into ridicule.

Lewis Carroll was a great writer of parodies. He made nonsense of "How Doth the Little Busy Bee."

How doth the little crocodile
  Improve his shining tail,
And pour the waters of the Nile
  On every golden scale!

> —LEWIS CARROLL (1832–1898, British mathematician and writer), *Alice in Wonderland*

And "Twinkle, Twinkle, Little Star" becomes:

Twinkle, twinkle, little bat!
How I wonder what you're at!
Up above the world you fly,
Like a tea-tray in the sky.[2]

● THE NATURE OF THE TRAGIC

Tragedy implies an unhappy or unfortunate ending to a series of events; usually it means death. But it is not just any kind of death; if an old man of eighty

[2] *Ibid.*, p. 205.

dies after an illness of months or years, his death is not called tragic. Tragedy implies a sudden reversal in prospects, a drop from a high estate to a low one. In the great tragedies the hero is usually one of royal, or at least noble, blood, so as to make the change in his position all the more apparent. Lear is king, Hamlet is prince, Agamemnon is king and leader of all the Greek armies in the Trojan War. Moreover, he is not just any king or prince; he is an exceptionally fine man. Othello came from "men of royal siege," and he is cherished by all the people of Venice. Macbeth is no average general; he is an unusual person in bravery, courage, devotion; he is "brave Macbeth," "Valour's minion." The tragic hero is always a person of merit, usually of outstanding merit. We admire and respect him for virtues that are above the ordinary. When, therefore, we see his fall, there is something catastrophic about it. We cannot believe that a person so great or fine could come to such an end.

Yet at the same time the hero's fall seems inevitable. In high tragedy the ending must be a necessary consequence from the events and the hero's character.

The necessity for the hero's death is clearly defined and distinguished in the two great types of tragedy, the Greek and Shakespearean. With the Greeks, the necessity was primarily religious in character. The hero does something that is against the law, and so he must suffer. In the play called by her name, Antigone heard the decree of the ruler, Creon, that her brother should not be buried. This decree pronounced a horrible sentence, since according to the Greek religion the funeral rites determined the position of the dead in the next world. Therefore she refused to obey the decree, and buried her brother. By doing so she violated the law and incurred death.

With Shakespeare, the necessity is found not in the law of religion, but in character; because the hero is the kind of person he is, he must fail. Othello sins innocently, but the reason is in the man. His personality, his background, his idealism, his ignorance of Venice, even the secrecy and hurry of the wedding make the murder of Desdemona inevitable. The real cause of the tragedy is in Othello.

But even though the hero fails, tragedy is never fatalistic or pessimistic, nor does it leave one with a sense of frustration. We know that the hero has failed, we realize that he had to fail, but there is not any sense of despair or desolation. We feel even more strongly the essential values of life: love, justice, truth, goodness. In *Othello*, Iago is the only one of the important characters left alive when the play is over, but we do not admire him as a clever schemer; we hate him with all the power we have, and we love and admire even more the goodness we saw in the lives of Othello, Desdemona, and Emilia. When Antigone tells her sister she has planned to bury her brother and asks for her help, Ismene objects: it is against the law, they are but women, it is no use to attempt the impossible. But Antigone goes right on:

> I'll neither urge thee, nor, if now thou'dst help
> My doing, should I thank thee for thine aid.
> Do thou after thy kind; thy choice is made;
> I'll bury him; doing this, so let me die.

> But leave me, and the folly that is mine,
> This worst to suffer—not the worst—since still
> A worse remains, no noble death to die.

> —SOPHOCLES (495–406 B.C., Greek dramatist), *Antigone*, 74–77, 102–104 (ca. 442 B.C.), trans. Robert Whitelaw

Antigone is killed, as she knew she would be, but there is no question but that she has played the nobler part, and that it is better to die for what is right than to live knowing that wrong is being done.

In tragedy we know that the hero will not be saved, he cannot be saved. There is no possibility of a happy ending. And at the same time we know that the values with which these men were identified are not lost, and we feel triumphant in that assurance. Tragedy leaves one in a state not only of grief and sorrow but of positive exaltation. It is a strange combination, and if we add the fact that in tragedy these emotions are felt keenly, we have the reason why tragedy is counted the greatest of all literary forms. The pain of tragedy is great, so great it can hardly be endured. And the heroes of tragedy suffer. Othello, Antigone, Oedipus, and Lear are great because they suffer. "It is by our power to suffer, above all," says Edith Hamilton, "that we are of more value than the sparrows."[3] And because we have the power to suffer, we can feel both the pain of the hero and the joy and exaltation that follow.

Tragedy is thus almost an exact opposite of comedy. Comedy is intellectual; tragedy is emotional. Comedy depends on the unexpected, the incongruous; tragedy demands a sense of inevitability. Comedy lives in a world of trivial values where there are no consequences, tragedy in a real world where every deed brings its consequences, and values are triumphant.

● TRAGEDY IN THE PRESENT DAY

Tragedy as written by the Greeks and by Shakespeare is generally recognized as the highest phase of literary art, but it is not common today. Aside from the

---

[3] Edith Hamilton, *The Greek Way to Western Civilization*, p. 130.

pat assertion that the greatest examples of art are not found easily or in abundance, there are several reasons to which we may call attention.

One has to do with the sense of inevitability in the fall of the tragic hero. With the rise of our concern for all men we do not care to recognize that man is responsible. Today we are apt to see man as the pathetic victim, the worm that crawls on the pavement for a half hour in the sunlight and then is squashed under the heel of some person or thing. It is not his fault, he is the helpless sufferer. Because of this attitude toward man, there has grown up a new type of play which is often called the serious drama, and which tries to fix the blame for man's inadequacy. The fault is that of labor or capital, as in Galsworthy's *Strife;* or it is religion and society which force a woman to live with a diseased man and bring diseased children into the world, as in Ibsen's *Ghosts*. It is anything and everything except a man's responsibility for his own soul.

Another cause of our lack of tragedy is the confusion of values and consequent negative view of life. Before the failure of the hero we tend to feel cynical or frustrated. The different viewpoints can be seen in comparing two novels, *Madame Bovary* and *Anna Karenina*. The former leaves one without hope or philosophy. There is little in Emma Bovary or in any of the other characters that one can admire; this is the way it is, a sorry mess. The latter novel, *Anna Karenina*, has more nearly the tragic point of view. There is much that is wrong, but the good is still good.

A third influence on our judgment may be mentioned, though it is a question as to how much emphasis it deserves—the cheap solution, the idea that all will come out all right anyway. We associate this attitude with Hollywood, but the film is not the only medium that reflects it.

● COMEDY AND TRAGEDY IN THE OTHER ARTS

Literature can deal with the intellectual more completely and more exactly than the other arts because its medium is the language of the intellect, the language of philosophy; therefore, the comic finds itself at home in literature more than in any of the other arts. This does not mean, however, that there is no comedy in music and the visual arts. In the visual arts there are paintings of comic situations. In these, however, the problem of interpretation is ever present. The scene or the character that is intended as comic may not seem comic once it is painted; the picture intended to be tragic may seem comic, as we saw in Brueghel's *Parable of the Blind*. For pictures or statues of happy people having a good time there is no difficulty of interpretation, but neither is there anything comic found in them.

There is a great deal of comedy in program music and in vocal music, but the comedy lies primarily in the story or in the words, not in the music. The music of Haydn is friendly and genial, and we are tempted to call it witty because of the way one theme or one voice repeats and answers another, but it is not really comic. A superb example is the Rondo from the Sonata in E minor. We laugh aloud when listening to it, but it is a laugh of pleasure, of joy and excitement from following the garrulous repetitions; the music is not itself comic.

The tragic, like the comic, is primarily in the realm of literature, though it, too, is found in the other arts. Music can and does portray tragic conflict and the resolution of the conflict. Most of Beethoven's sonatas and symphonies show conflict, and one feels the exultation of the ending. But, as always, music is disembodied unless it is associated with a story. Wagner's music dramas are superb examples of the way music may interpret and resolve the conflict of a story.

Painting and sculpture are limited by the fact that they can present only a single moment of time. Hence they can show either the struggle or the peace attained after the struggle is ended, but they cannot show both. The so-called *Medusa Ludovisi* (Figure 201) from the Terme Museum at Rome shows the struggle but not the peace that follows.

FIGURE 201. MEDUSA LUDOVISI, or *Sleeping Fury*, copy of a late Hellenistic original. (Pentelic marble. Size: about 14½ inches. Rome, Terme Museum. Photograph by Alinari.)

FIGURE 202. PIERO DELLA FRANCESCA (ca. 1410–1492), Italian painter. *The Resurrection of Christ* (1460). (Fresco. Figures life size. Borgo San Sepolcro, Palazzo del Comune. Photograph by Alinari.)

The painting of *The Resurrection* by Piero della Francesca (Figure 202) shows the solution. It is as nearly tragic as can be found in the visual arts. Many have found on the face of the Christ the suffering and the horror of the time in hell, the sympathy that he had felt for those whom he met, and his final victory over death. Painting and sculpture at their greatest show the elements of the conflict after the conflict is ended, when the warring elements are no longer in collision but at peace.

19
JUDGMENT

POETRY

I, too, dislike it: there are things that are important beyond all this fiddle.
    Reading it, however, with a perfect contempt for it, one discovers in
        it after all, a place for the genuine.
        Hands that can grasp, eyes
        that can dilate, hair that can rise
            if it must, these things are important not because a

high-sounding interpretation can be put upon them but because they are
    useful. When they become so derivative as to become unintelligible,
        the same thing may be said for all of us, that we
            do not admire what
            we cannot understand: the bat
                holding on upside down or in quest of something to

eat, elephants pushing, a wild horse taking a roll, a tireless wolf under
    a tree, the immovable critic twitching his skin like a horse that feels
                        a flea, the base-

ball fan, the statistician--
   nor is it valid
      to discriminate against 'business documents and

school-books'; all these phenomena are important. One must make a distinction
   however: when dragged into prominence by half poets, the result is not
                                                      poetry,

nor till the poets among us can be
   'literalists of
   the imagination'--above
      insolence and triviality and can present

for inspection, imaginary gardens with real toads in them, shall we have
   it. In the meantime, if you demand on the one hand,
   the raw material of poetry in
      all its rawness and
      that which is on the other hand
         genuine, then you are interested in poetry.

   —MARIANNE MOORE (1887–   , American poet)[1]

● THE PROBLEM OF JUDGMENT

With the study of style we have completed our formal analysis of art and turn
to our last question about art, that of judgment. We ask of any example, how
good is it? What has the artist tried to do? How far has he succeeded in accom-
plishing his purpose?

This does not imply that we can in a short time check off opinions of individual works which will be permanent and lasting. The great scholars and
critics have not succeeded at that game; what is liked in one year or one dec-
ade may be considered worthless in the one following. The only real test of
value in art is that of time. The really good, the truly great artists are those
that have survived the centuries: Shakespeare, Sophocles, Bach, Beethoven,
Michelangelo, Phidias, Rembrandt.

On the other hand, if we have pursued the analysis of art according to the
plan of this book, we have consciously or unconsciously been making judgments
of individual qualities in specific works of art, and to that extent have been

---

[1] From *Poems* by Marianne Moore. Copyright 1935 by Marianne Moore. Used by permission of The
Macmillan Company, New York.

answering the questions of judgment. Not that our analysis has said, "This is good," or "That is bad," but through the better understanding that comes from analysis we have learned to know details, and as a result we have instinctively judged them interesting or dull, superficial or significant. What remains now is to assemble such partial judgments into a comprehensive evaluation. To the questions already discussed, however, we must add others which deal with judgment alone. They are assembled here under three headings:

1. Sincerity
2. Depth of meaning
3. Magnitude

SINCERITY

One of the important demands in making a judgment has to do with the sincerity of the artist, or, as we say more often, the honesty of his work. We want a work of art to be a serious expression of the author's thoughts and ideas. As Marianne Moore says, we want the genuine, and we do not care for those things "so derivative as to become unintelligible," or those other phenomena "dragged into prominence by half poets" or other half artists. We want in a work of art an honest, genuine piece of work.

Honesty is extremely difficult to judge; judging sincerity in art is like judging sincerity in people. Which of our friends are sincere? Which can we trust to give us their honest opinions? What do our friends really think? It is impossible to have any final or fixed judgment of sincerity, but it is nevertheless a matter of the greatest importance. Once we suspect a man or an artist is not being sincere, we judge his work inferior. The Laocoön, for instance, seems theatrical; for all its vividness it is hardly sincere; there is a deliberate striving for effect. Is the cathedral of Milan quite honest? (Figure 203) Is there too much decoration "like a wedding cake"? Is Lawrence Ferlinghetti truly sincere in his reiterated "I am waiting"? Is he genuine in his concern for the lack of values in America? It sometimes happens that we label a work sentimental when we do not agree with the point of view of the author.

SENTIMENTALITY

The form in which insincerity is most often found in art is sentimentality. Sentimentality may be defined as an insincere emotion; it is interest in the effect of an action rather than in the action itself. Sentimentality is not to be confused with sentiment, which is a genuine feeling. We are all sentimental when we are

FIGURE 203. CATHEDRAL AT MILAN (mostly 1386–1522; West Façade seventeenth to nineteenth centuries; most of the pinnacles nineteenth century). (White marble. Length: about 490 feet; width: about 200 feet. Milan. Photograph, courtesy Italian State Tourist Office.)

young; we love to think how good and noble we are and how we are not appreciated, how sorry our parents will be when we die and they recognize us as the wonderful people we really are. This is essentially the point of view in the little poem by Christina Rossetti.

When I am dead, my dearest,
  Sing no sad songs for me;
Plant thou no roses at my head,
  Nor shady cypress-tree:
Be the green grass above me
  With showers and dewdrops wet;
And if thou wilt, remember,
  And if thou wilt, forget.

I shall not see the shadows,
  I shall not feel the rain;
I shall not hear the nightingale
  Sing on, as if in pain:
And dreaming through the twilight
  That doth not rise nor set,
Haply I may remember,
  And haply may forget.

   —CHRISTINA ROSSETTI (1830–1894, British poet of Italian parentage),
    " Song" (1862)

Miss Rossetti is interested in the effect of her death, and she is enjoying the melancholy prospects of being in the grave. It is essentially a romantic pose, but it is a pose nevertheless.

Similarly, in the "Good Night" from the first canto of *Childe Harold's Pilgrimage*, Byron is not so much lonely and deserted as he is enjoying the thought of being lonely and deserted.

> And now I'm in the world alone,
>   Upon the wide, wide sea;
> But why should I for others groan,
>   When none will sigh for me?
> Perchance my dog will whine in vain,
>   Till fed by stranger hands;
> But long ere I come back again
>   He'd tear me where he stands.
>
>   —LORD BYRON (1788–1824, British poet), *Childe Harold's Pilgrimage*, Canto I (1812)

For comparison, read the lyric "She Walks in Beauty," where Byron has his mind on the woman, not on himself; in other words, he is not sentimental.

> She walks in beauty, like the night
>   Of cloudless climes and starry skies;
> And all that's best of dark and bright
>   Meet in her aspect and her eyes:
> Thus mellow'd to that tender light
>   Which heaven to gaudy day denies.
>
>   —"She Walks in Beauty" (1814)

It is harder to be sincere about oneself than about other people, but in his later years, Byron was sincere even about himself.

> And I have loved thee, Ocean! and my joy
> Of youthful sports was on thy breast to be
> Borne, like thy bubbles, onward. From a boy
> I wanton'd with thy breakers—they to me
> Were a delight; and if the freshening sea
> Made them a terror—'twas a pleasing fear,
> For I was as it were a child of thee,
> And trusted to thy billows far and near,
> And laid my hand upon thy mane—as I do here.
>
>   —*Childe Harold's Pilgrimage*, Canto IV (1818)

The examples of the sentimental given so far have been from literature, but sentimentality is found in all the arts. We are especially conscious of it in music, though we cannot explain how we know it any better than we can in literature. Beethoven's Sonata in C minor has in it something of self-pity, something of the spirit that finds itself an abused and sorrowful object; in short, something of sentimentality. This character is evidenced in the title by which it is usually known, the *Pathétique,* "pathetic." In comparison, Beethoven's Symphony in C minor is entirely lacking in sentimentality; it is open, frank, direct. It shows suffering but it does not enjoy the suffering.

Painting, like literature and music, is an open field for the sentimental; and sweet, sentimental creatures are almost as common in painting as in life. In the *Virgin of Consolation* by Bouguereau (Figure 204) the figures are artificially posed; the Virgin, the mother on her knee, and the child lying at her feet are all designed primarily to produce a certain effect. There is no truth; it is not genuine. If this is compared with any of the great paintings of the Madonna, the difference is clear; in Giotto's *Madonna Enthroned* (Figure 205), for example, the artist is expressing an emotion he feels—he is not striving to show one that he does not feel.

FIGURE 204. ADOLPHE WILLIAM BOU-
GUEREAU (1825–1905), French painter. *Virgin of Consolation* (1877). (Oil on canvas. Size: about 14 feet by 11 feet, 3 inches. Paris, Luxembourg. Photograph, Braun, Inc.)

FIGURE 205. GIOTTO (1266–1336). *Madonna Enthroned* (ca. 1304). (Tempera on wood. Height: 10 feet, 8½ inches. Florence, Uffizi Gallery. Photograph by Anderson.)

DEPTH OF MEANING

Another question to ask of a work of art has to do with its depth of meaning. How much is the artist trying to do? What has he attempted? A single daffodil may be just as beautiful as the Grand Canyon, and will probably be more perfect, but there is something of greatness in the Grand Canyon that we do not find in a daffodil.

Consider two works by Brahms. The "Lullaby" we love to sing: "Hushabye and goodnight, with roses bedight" is beautiful. But compare it with the magnificent last movement of Brahms's Symphony No. 1. The "Lullaby" remains true and fine, but it lacks the breadth of design of the symphony. Each is supreme of its kind, but Brahms has attempted more in the symphony than in the "Lullaby."

Or take the subject of war. Hardy has a short poem in which a peasant is thinking back on his experiences when he was in the army.

"Had he and I but met
　By some old ancient inn,
We should have sat us down to wet
　Right many a nipperkin!

"But ranged as infantry,
　And staring face to face,
I shot at him as he at me,
　And killed him in his place.

"I shot him dead because—
　Because he was my foe,
Just so: my foe of course he was;
　That's clear enough; although

"He thought he'd list, perhaps,
　Off-hand like—just as I—
Was out of work—had sold his traps—
　No other reason why.

"Yes, quaint and curious war is!
　You shoot a fellow down
You'd treat if met where any bar is,
　Or help to half-a-crown!"
　　　—THOMAS HARDY (1840–1928, British novelist, short-story writer, and poet),
　　　"The Man He Killed" (1902)[2]

Tolstoi's novel *War and Peace* comes to conclusions that are not radically different from Hardy's poem so far as the real value and meaning of war are concerned, but its scope is much greater. Tolstoi makes us see the horrors of war year in and year out, the hopes, dreads, uncertainties, and dangers as they are stretched out for years, until it seems man can take no more.

One of the reliefs from the Temple of Athena Niké in Athens is known by the title *Niké Loosening Her Sandal* (Figure 206). The goddess rests her entire weight on her left leg; the right leg is raised as she leans over to loosen the cord of her sandal. Her costume is of a soft material, which falls in soft folds across her body, curve after curve all falling in the same general lines but with no two exactly alike.

[2] From *Collected Poems* of Thomas Hardy. Copyright 1925 by The Macmillan Company. Used by permission of The Macmillan Company.

FIGURE 206. *NIKÉ LOOSENING HER SANDAL* (end of fifth century B.C.), from Temple of Athena Niké. (Pentelic marble. Height: 3 feet, 2 inches. Athens, Acropolis Museum. Photograph, courtesy Royal Greek Embassy.)

We have already studied a Greek vase which shows two women putting away their clothes (Figure 153). The figures, their clothes, are balanced perfectly, the space is filled but is not crowded, the bodies of the women are very graceful, and each seems to complement the other though there is little exact repetition. It is not a picture to make one think or ponder. One is not concerned as to who washed the clothes, where they are being put, or why. As in the *Niké*, one simply rejoices in the grace of the shapes in the design.

There is the same sense of untroubled enjoyment when one reads a little poem like Yeats's "The Fiddler of Dooney:"

When I play on my fiddle in Dooney
Folk dance like a wave of the sea;
My cousin is priest in Kilvarnet,
My brother in Mocharabuiee.

I passed my brother and cousin;
They read in their books of prayer;
I read in my book of songs
I bought at the Sligo fair.

When we come at the end of time
To Peter sitting in state,
He will smile on the three old spirits,
But call me first through the gate;

For the good are always the merry,
Save by an evil chance,
And the merry love the fiddle,
And the merry love to dance:

And when the folk there spy me,
They will all come up to me,
With 'Here is the fiddler of Dooney!'
And dance like a wave of the sea.

—W. B. YEATS (1865–1939, Irish poet and playwright),
"The Fiddler of Dooney" (1899)[3]

It is very pleasant. We don't stop to ask if the Catholic church puts the work of the fiddler above that of the priest. We just like it; it makes the heart dance "like a wave of the sea."

These examples are simple, clear, direct, finished, and perfect. We know them at once and we feel we know them well. There is no hidden meaning. But often a work of art has more than one level of meaning. To start with an obvious instance, let us look at a poem by Robert Frost. It has only two lines:

The old dog barks backward without getting up,
I can remember when he was a pup.

—ROBERT FROST (1875–1963, American poet)[4]

It is a short simple piece like the ones we have just studied, but with a difference. Change the second line to

He was frisky and lively when he was a pup

and our poem is like the three first pieces, pleasant, final. But go back to the line as Frost wrote it, "I can remember when he was a pup"; the meaning is changed entirely. It gives sudden realization of the weakness of age, the eager-

[3] From *The Collected Poems* of W. B. Yeats. Copyright 1903 by The Macmillan Company; rev. ed., 1956. Used by permission of The Macmillan Company.
[4] From *A Further Range* by Robert Frost, Copyright 1936, by Robert Frost. By permission of Henry Holt and Company, Inc.

ness of youth, and the shortness of life. In spite of the use of the pronoun *I*, it seems far away and abstract. It fits the title, "The Span of Life."

From a small and simple and obvious particular object the poet can and does draw philosophical conclusions of depth. John Ciardi in his poem "Credibility" looks at an ant and sees in it universal significance.

> Who could believe an ant in theory?
> a giraffe in blueprint?
> Ten thousand doctors of what's possible
> could reason half the jungle out of being.
> I speak of love, and something more,
> to say we are the thing that proves itself
> not against reason, but impossibly true,
> and therefore to teach reason reason.
>
>   —JOHN CIARDI (1916– , American poet),
>   "Credibility"[5]

Muriel Rukeyser interviews a Zen Buddhist and captures the essence of an obscure philosophy in her poem "Fragile."

> I think of the image brought into my room
> Of the sage and the thin young man who flickers and asks.
> He is asking about the moment when the Buddha
> Offers the lotus, a flower held out as declaration.
> "Isn't that fragile?" he asks. The sage answers:
> "I speak to you. You speak to me. Is that fragile?"
>
>   —MURIEL RUKEYSER (1913– , American poet),
>   "Waterlily Fire," Part IV "Fragile"[6]

We find the same in two short poems by Robert Browning, "Meeting at Night" and "Parting at Morning." The first is a vivid description of the meeting of two lovers, the eagerness hardly to be borne as the lover makes his way to the house where his loved one is awaiting him. The images are very clear: gray sea, long black land, yellow half-moon large and low, tap on pane, scratch of match, warm sea-scented beach.

---

[5] From *In Fact.* Copyright 1962, Rutgers, the State University. Reprinted by permission of the author.
[6] From *Poems* by Muriel Rukeyser, 1935–1962. Copyright 1962. Reprinted with permission of The Macmillan Company.

The gray sea and the long black land;
And the yellow half-moon large and low;
And the startled little waves that leap
In fiery ringlets from their sleep,
As I gain the cove with pushing prow,
And quench its speed i' the slushy sand.

Then a mile of warm sea-scented beach;
Three fields to cross till a farm appears;
A tap at the pane, the quick sharp scratch
And blue spurt of a lighted match,
And a voice less loud, through its joys and fears,
Than the two hearts beating each to each!
    —ROBERT BROWNING (1812–1889, British poet),
      "Meeting at Night"

In the second poem, the *him* in the third line refers to the sun.

Round the cape of a sudden came the sea,
And the sun looked over the mountain's rim:
And straight was a path of gold for him,
And the need of a world of men for me.

    —ROBERT BROWNING,
      "Parting at Morning"

Each of the two poems has its own meaning, clear and exact when taken by itself. Each describes a situation. But the meaning changes when they are taken together, and Browning is our authority for considering them together. Together, they say that the "need of a world of men" is a greater, higher appeal than that of "two hearts beating each to each."

    "Ozymandias" is nothing if it is only a description of a ruined monument.

I met a traveller from an antique land
Who said: Two vast and trunkless legs of stone
Stand in the desert . . . Near them, on the sand,
Half sunk, a shattered visage lies, whose frown,
And wrinkled lip, and sneer of cold command,
Tell that its sculptor well those passions read
Which yet survive, stamped on these lifeless things,
The hand that mocked them, and the heart that fed:
And on the pedestal these words appear:

"My name is Ozymandias, king of kings:
Look on my works, ye Mighty, and despair!"
Nothing beside remains. Round the decay
Of that colossal wreck, boundless and bare
The lone and level sands stretch far away.

—PERCY BYSSHE SHELLEY (1792–1822, British poet),
   "Ozymandias" (1817)

In the visual arts, we find differences in the levels of meaning illustrated very neatly in the photograph and the portrait. The photograph rarely goes beyond the first level: it shows what can be seen at any time and by anyone. The portrait shows more. It shows the man inside the face, as it were; looking at it, we know what the man hoped and feared, and to what he was true.

In Rembrandt's *Man in the Gold Helmet* (Figure 207) we see first the beauty of the helmet, its rich chasing; then we notice the rich garments. The exterior details show a man who has apparently all that money and power can bring him. The face is a great contrast to the rich garments. It is tired, stern,

FIGURE 207. REMBRANDT HARMENSZ VAN RIJN (1606–1669). *Man in the Gold Helmet.* (Oil on canvas. Height: 2 feet, 2½ inches. Berlin, State Museums. Photograph by Stoedtner.)

FIGURE 208. EDWARD HOPPER (1882–   ), American painter. *Early Sunday Morning* (ca. 1930). (Oil on canvas. Size: 35 by 60 inches. New York, Whitney Museum of American Art.)

kind; it is the face of a man who has known hard work, who has had to make hard decisions and take the consequences; a man who has had so much wealth it means nothing to him; a man who can be trusted to see truth and deal fairly with it.

In *Early Sunday Morning* (Figure 208) Hopper has given us more than a painting of a street. There is a sense of loneliness that prevades the street, and we are conscious of its meager resources and its spiritual poverty. The scene is an indictment of our civilization.

What El Greco has put into his *View of Toledo* could never be caught in a photograph. It is a painting of a city, a city where a storm is about to break. But beyond the natural appearance, the scene is ominous and foreboding; it is one of emotional intensity, mystery, and passion.

MAGNITUDE

Magnitude is concerned with the impact of a work as a whole, whether it be shallow or deep, important or unimportant, great or trivial—in short, with the quality of greatness felt in it. By common consent the greatest art is called the *sublime.*

The source of the sublime is always a greatness of power. One feels the sublime in the ocean, in a fierce storm, in a mighty waterfall, whereas there is no sense of greatness in a small pond or a trickling stream in a pleasant meadow. But even greater than the sublimity of physical power is the sublimity of spiritual power, the power of the Mass in B minor by Bach, or the book of Job.

The sublime ordinarily demands a great protagonist in the sense of a person who is noble or powerful; it seems more natural to think of great emotions in great persons—kings, queens, and people in authority; hence the tradition that heroes and heroines must be of noble birth. But greatness of rank is not essential; the highest emotions can be found even in the simplest subjects. Professor Bradley quotes this passage from Turgenev as an example of sublimity in so little a thing as a sparrow.

> I was on my way home from hunting, and was walking up the garden avenue. My dog was running in front of me.
>
> Suddenly he slackened his pace, and began to steal forward as though he scented game ahead.
>
> I looked along the avenue; and I saw on the ground a young sparrow, its beak edged with yellow, and its head covered with soft brown. It had fallen from the nest (a strong wind was blowing, and shaking the birches of the avenue); and there it sat and never stirred, except to stretch out its little half-grown wings in a helpless flutter.
>
> My dog was slowly approaching it, when suddenly, darting from the tree overhead, an old black-throated sparrow dropped like a stone right before his nose, and, all rumpled and flustered, with a plaintive desperate cry flung itself, once, twice, at his open jaws with their great teeth.
>
> It would save its young one; it screened it with its own body; the tiny frame quivered with terror; the little cries grew wild and hoarse; it sank and died. It had sacrificed itself.
>
> What a huge monster the dog must have seemed to it! And yet it could not stay up there on its safe bough. A power stronger that its own will tore it away.
>
> My dog stood still, and then slunk back disconcerted. Plainly he too had to recognize that power. I called him to me; and a feeling of reverence came over me as I passed on.
>
> Yes, do not laugh, It was really reverence I felt before that little heroic bird and the passionate outburst of its love.
>
> Love, I thought, is verily stronger than death and the terror of death. By love, only by love, is life sustained and moved.[7]

Below the sublime are many other degrees of magnitude, such as the pretty, graceful, beautiful, and grand. By common consent the pretty is the opposite of the sublime; it is pleasant, but it arouses no strong emotions. The grand and the sublime both have the quality of greatness; the pretty and the graceful have not. The beautiful may or may not be great.

These terms will become more meaningful if we try to apply them to definite works. Differences can be seen most easily if we contrast two subjects that are alike or two works by the same artist.

[7] A. C. Bradley, "The Sublime," *Oxford Lectures on Poetry*, p. 44. With permission of Macmillan & Co., Ltd., St. Martin's Press, Inc.

The *Humoresque* of Dvořák is pretty or graceful, but the same composer's *New World Symphony* is beautiful or even great. Yeats's poem "The Second Coming" is great or beautiful, whereas his "Fiddler of Dooney" is no more than pretty or graceful.

Turning and turning in the widening gyre
The falcon cannot hear the falconer;
Things fall apart; the center cannot hold;
Mere anarchy is loosed upon the world,
The blood-dimmed tide is loosed, and everywhere
The ceremony of innocence is drowned;
The best lack all conviction, while the worst
Are full of passionate intensity.

Surely some revelation is at hand;
Surely the Second Coming is at hand.
The Second Coming! Hardly are those words out
When a vast image out of *Spiritus Mundi*
Troubles my sight: somewhere in sands of the desert
A shape with lion body and the head of a man,
A gaze blank and pitiless as the sun,
Is moving its slow thighs, while all about it
Reel shadows of the indignant desert birds.
The darkness drops again; but now I know
That twenty centuries of stony sleep
Were vexed to nightmare by a rocking cradle,
And what rough beast, its hour come round at last,
Slouches towards Bethlehem to be born?

      —W. B. YEATS (1865–1939, Irish poet and playwright),
        "The Second Coming." 1921[8]

Compare two great figure compositions by Michelangelo: the *Pietà* (Figure 209) at St. Peter's in Rome, which was done when Michelangelo was a young man, and his *Entombment* (Figure 210) in the cathedral at Florence, some fifty years later. Both are sincere, both are complete. In the *Pietà*, the Madonna is young, her face sweetly serious, her head bent forward as she tries to comprehend the thing that has happened. One hand is holding the body of Jesus, the other is left free in a youthful gesture. In the *Entombment*, youth has been left behind, and all is serious. The greatest change is in the face of Jesus, for

[8] From *The Collected Poems* of W. B. Yeats. Copyright 1903 by The Macmillan Company; rev. ed., 1956. Used by permission of The Macmillan Company.

FIGURE 209. MICHELANGELO. Pietà (1498–1502). (Marble. Height: about 6 feet, 3 inches. Rome, St. Peter's. Photograph by Anderson.)

FIGURE 210. MICHELANGELO. The Entombment (ca. 1550). (Marble. Height: about 7 feet. Florence, Cathedral. Photograph by Anderson.)

he is now the Christ who has died to save the world. This statue has elements of sublimity, whereas the *Pietà* lacks them.

The sublime arouses in one a feeling of astonishment, rapture, and awe. In comparison with its greatness one feels his own littleness but, paradoxically, the attempt to share the sublime makes one greater than he was before. Confronted with the greatness of Socrates as we see him in Plato's account, we feel petty, and yet our attempt to understand him makes us greater than we were.

Crito, when he heard this, made a sign to the servant; and the servant went in, and remained for some time, and then returned with the jailer carrying the cup of poison. Socrates said: "You, my good friend, who are experienced in these matters, shall give me directions how I am to proceed." The man answered: "You have only to walk about until your legs are heavy, and then to lie down, and the poison will act." At the same time he handed the cup to Socrates, who in the easiest and gentlest manner, without the least fear or change of color or feature, looking at the man with all his eyes . . . as his manner was, took the cup and said: "What do you say about making a libation out of this cup to any god? May I, or not?" The man answered: "We only prepare, Socrates, just so much as we deem enough." "I understand," he said: "yet I may and must pray to the gods to prosper my journey from this to that other world—may this then, which is my prayer, be granted to me." Then holding the cup to his lips, quite readily and cheerfully he drank off the poison. And hitherto most of us had been able to control our sorrow; but now when we saw him drinking, and saw too that he had finished the draught, we could no longer forbear, and in spite of myself my own tears were flowing fast; so that I covered my face and wept over myself, for certainly I was not weeping over him, but at the thought of my own calamity in having lost such a companion. Nor was I the first, for Crito, when he found himself unable to restrain his tears, had got up and moved away, and I followed; and at that moment, Apollodorus, who had been weeping all the time, broke out into a loud cry which made cowards of us all. Socrates alone retained his calmness. "What is this strange outcry?" he said. "I sent away the women mainly in order that they might not offend in this way, for I have heard that a man should die in peace. Be quiet then, and have patience." When we heard that, we were ashamed, and refrained our tears; and he walked about until, as he said, his legs began to fail, and then he lay on his back, according to the directions, and the man who gave him the poison now and then looked at his feet and legs; and after a while he pressed his foot hard and asked him if he could feel; and he said, "No"; and then his leg, and so upwards and upwards, and showed us that he was cold and stiff. And he felt then himself, and said: "When the poison reaches the heart, that will be the end." He was beginning to grow cold about the groin, when he uncovered his face, for he had covered himself up, and said (they were his last words)—he said: "Crito, I owe a cock to Asclepius; will you remember to pay the debt?" "The debt shall be paid," said Crito; "is there anything else?" There was no answer to this question; but in a minute or two a movement was heard, and the attendants uncovered him; his eyes were set, and Crito closed his eyes and mouth.

—PLATO (427?–347 B.C., Greek philosopher), *The Phaedo*, trans. Benjamin Jowett (1817–1893, British scholar)

● GROWTH IN JUDGMENT

The judgment each person makes of a work of art is individual and personal, just as the experience itself was individual and personal. And since one person is never exactly like any other, his judgment of art will never be exactly like that of another. Moreover, no person's judgment of any work of art will remain exactly the same. With each new experience he tends to like it more or less well, to find it more or less rewarding. In short, there is never one judgment which can be embalmed and put away as a final evaluation.

Not only does judgment change with each new experience, but it changes as one learns to know the judgments of others. Both history and criticism can help us to see and hear what we have not seen and heard for ourselves, and so our experience becomes richer and deeper.

This is the greatest contribution history and criticism can make to us, but there is a secondary influence which is also of importance. History and criticism can help us in the selection of works we want to become acquainted with. No one can possibly know all the art in the world; he cannot read all the books that are printed or hear all the music that is composed and played in any one year; he can hardly know all the pictures and statues in any one of the great galleries, much less in all of them. Therefore, we use the opinions of others to help us decide what is worth looking at and listening to, to tell what has been thought good and what poor, what has been reckoned great and what mediocre.

This is especially important in the case of those artists who have become known through the ages as the very great: Dante, Homer, Rembrandt, Shakespeare, Phidias, Bach, Beethoven, Michelangelo. They cannot be known easily or at once. Therefore we do not get the immediate satisfaction we get from lesser works; we are perhaps repulsed, and we put them aside. The very great in art, as in everything else, is difficult; almost anything worth doing is difficult; it cannot be attained easily or without hard work. The prophecies of Isaiah and the book of Job in the Old Testament are among the supreme examples of literature, but it is doubtful if anyone can get very great pleasure from them without study. No one can ever appreciate the Mass in B minor or the *Divine Comedy* on a casual hearing or a superficial reading; they need concentrated attention. But knowing that these are considered among the world's great masterpieces, we can prepare to give them the necessary study. The person who gives them this study will not necessarily like them; in art, as in life, one must count on a certain number of failures. But no one can know if he will like the great works of art until he has given them the necessary attention.

Fortunately, there is little difference of opinion with regard to the very great. About the lesser works there are many and various judgments; one person prefers this and another that, but as we approach those few masterpieces that can be called supremely great, the differences melt away. Hence we may approach them with greater assurance, understanding that though they demand work, they will bring their reward, the work will not be in vain. Fortunately, also, the rewards of art, like the rewards of goodness, are open to everyone. Appreciation of art, like virtue, is not reserved for the learned but is free to the honest and sincere.

20
A FINAL WORD

In the preceding chapters we have attempted to guide you in experiencing some of the great art of the past, our artistic heritage, and in experiencing selected examples of our recent past. What of the art of our time and the future? How does the way of looking at art, of listening to music, and of reading literature which has been presented in these chapters apply to these newer and yet-to-be-developed schools and styles? What of "aleatory music," "electronic music," "musique concrête"? What about "happenings," "the theater of the absurd," "the drama of the imagination"? What of "aleatory painting," "chimpanzee art," "light sculpture," "op art," "pop art," "found objects"?

The present chapter attempts to provide a context for dealing with these and similar questions. It does so not by analysis of specific examples, styles, or schools. You have by this time been sufficiently exercised in that. It insists, rather, that now that your eyes have been opened and your senses sharpened—one really wants to say: Now that they have been given back to you—as the ultimate authority, as the only tools necessary for experiencing the contemporary arts *or* the arts which are yet to come, you can with confidence produce your own "talk about" the arts, and expand still further your horizons of awareness.

As guides to your continued growth beyond the exercises in experiencing and the "talking about" experiencing, we suggest here some broad perspectives which will be helpful on the way.

● **PERSPECTIVE ONE**

All art comes before the theories which explain it, the terminology which enables us to point to various aspects of it, the name which classifies it. This fact is especially important to remember as we consider the newer art forms and styles. Often we tend to approach them with the expectancies built into us from all our previous experiencing of art. When these do not correspond to what we see or hear, we are prone to reject the new art completely or to judge it harshly. To give the new a chance, however, we must go beyond the *sensing that it is different* to asking what the "differences" sensed are expressing. Sometimes we may conclude that the "difference" is no more than deliberate perversity. More often we shall discover that it evokes in us new ranges of response, that it extends our frame of awareness, that it awakens new areas of sensitivity.

● **PERSPECTIVE TWO**

In looking at any new or unfamiliar work of art, we should interpret the terms we have been using to point to various aspects in their broadest sense. Organization, order, whatever term one uses, should be thought of not as an entity but as a continuum running from chaos at one end to geometric, mathematical forms at the other. Art always seeks some reconciliation of these opposites. The reconciliation may be toward one end of the continuum or toward the other. Style is the part of art which gets into it unconsciously. In all periods there are the great individualists whose personal stamp is so strong that it becomes recognizable in everything they produce. Sometimes it is so distinctive and powerful that it is copied by lesser artists and creates a "school" or "movement." At other times the style may break so completely with prevailing ones that the works of the artist when seen in the perspective of history do not seem to belong. That is, they do not fit into the academic generalizations about a period. Medium, too, should be broadly interpreted. In contemporary art the traditional compartmentalization of mediums has yielded to experimentation with various "intermediums," for example, art which is between music and theater, between sculpture and painting, between sculpture and architecture. There is no right or wrong medium nor any known limit to appropriate mediums. Mediums are always being found, and artists are always exploiting them to their maximum expressive potential.

● PERSPECTIVE THREE

It is helpful to look at new art from the point of view of the artist as he slowly creates it step by step. From this point of view, from the way in which it came into being, one can consider art on a homogeneous-heterogeneous scale. "From the moment work starts on a picture it begins to shift slowly along a scale from extreme homogeneity (blank space) toward ever-increasing heterogeneity. Maximum heterogeneity (a mass of fuzzy detail) is not apparently visually desirable and so somewhere along this homogeneous-heterogeneous scale there is for each picture a point of optimum heterogeneity. This is the point at which the picture is considered finished."[1] Similarly, into utter silence the musician puts a sound, a succession of sounds, a harmony. He leaves more or less of the homogeneous silence in his composition. By including greater amounts of silence he can focus attention on a single sound which would otherwise be "lost" in the din of maximum heterogeneity.

● PERSPECTIVE FOUR

New art frequently strikes us as a bit shocking. It has always been so; much of what is now accepted as standard repertoire in music, as well as the accepted pieces for inclusion in anthologies of literature, was at one time considered odd, strange, or incomprehensible. This will continue to be so, because one of the functions of art is to help us bring again into our perceptual systems things which we have been conditioned to exclude. Each of us has his own personal orientation which "keeps us from seeing reality, locks us into the illusory embrace of given orientations," but "art . . . by breaking up those orientations releases us to see aspects of reality which orientations conceal from us."[2] Thus, while it is correct to think of art as an ordering and extending of relationship, it is also important to remember that it is a disordering of our usual ways of seeing; it omits things commonly emphasized and includes those not commonly emphasized. A function of art, therefore, is to read back into life the complexities which our orientations, our systems and abstractions, have

[1] Desmond Morris, *The Biology of Art*, Alfred A. Knopf, New York, 1962, p. 165.
[2] Morse Peckham, *Beyond the Tragic Vision*, George Braziller, Inc., New York, 1962, p. 150.

tended to obscure and omit. The simplifications and systems necessary to functioning in our social structure tend to impoverish our full functioning as organisms. By reincluding into the consciousness the excluded, art can give back to us some sense of our wholeness. It is, therefore, in the strict sense of the word psychedelic—consciousness-expanding—in its nature.

● PERSPECTIVE FIVE

One thing the new art forms say is simple. They are saying that the old forms are too constricting to hold our view of the world or to hold the personal experience of the artist in our world or to accommodate to our perceptual patterns. They are saying that the same courageous freedom which produced the older art is a continuing right of the artist and that this freedom must be exercised and is necessary for art to fulfill its cultural function. The established conventions, traditions, and forms constrict. And artists who begin to sense themselves trapped by them often resort to somewhat violent means to escape them. Serendipity processes, the planned accident, chance art, and other ways of achieving random relationships have throughout history been used by artists in their search for immediacy, freshness, and individual expression. It is, however, only in our time that they have gained status as a significant phase of the creative process.

● PERSPECTIVE SIX

The arts should be viewed as continuous with other human activities contemporary with them. A new invention, medium, world view, way of seeing things, reflects the changes in science, psychology, and philosophy that have been taking place in ways frequently unnoticed by the public at large. Art is a way of making visible these changes in our thinking and feeling. It is a way of making them a part of our sensory and conscious experience. It explores their echoes and eddies in our psychic life and gives expression to them. Advances in our understanding of how we think, new insights into our ways of perceiving, have in the past influenced the arts. A question always worth asking, therefore, is: How does what is being done in the arts relate to the other human activities in which the culture is engaging? The discoveries of the past twenty years and the consequent revisions of what we know have confirmed the observation that "Knowledge does not keep any better than fish." To continue as participants in our culture, therefore, it is imperative that we become competent in fishing, that is, in the attitudes of open inquiry which will continue to add to and replace our present knowledge. Already we have come to see that logic frequently leads us to go wrong with a sense of certainty, that myth is as true as history, that the world is a letter addressed *To Whom It May Concern,* and that the answers it gives depend upon the questions we ask of it. If one looks for a single word to characterize the attitude toward knowing in our time, he might well choose "tentativeness," for we have come to entertain the possibility that all knowledge is tentative and partial and personal.

It is quite possible that these new insights have contributed to an insecurity in our time. In fact, it has been argued that one of the reasons we have clung with such desperateness, persistence, and inflexibility to the vision of an ordered, certain universe is that we cannot tolerate such uncertainty. To the extent that you, however, can entertain this broader view, it should be liberating, for it makes you an authority along with whatever other authorities you know. It should give you confidence and freedom in your own observing and perceiving. Whose eyes but yours can see the world you see?

While these developments may appear to move in the direction of feeling that one is adrift in chaos, they can and do, after the initial shock, function to expand one's sense of his own presence in a cosmos which always seems to be breaking out of our little contrived systems and orderly thought forms.

● ART IS A ROAD BACK

If it is true, as many people are saying, that we have become caught in our own thinking, that in making the machine the model of perfection and measuring our achievements in terms of it we have become automatons dissociated from our feelings and autonomous responses, that we have relinquished ourselves so completely that we are willing, conspiring victims of authoritarianism, it is time that we asked: Is there no alternative for us? Is there no road back? Art is a road back; and, like all roads back, it is a road forward, for it leads not to a past, accomplished somewhere back there, but to the past within us. It offers a road back to experiencing, to a quickening of the senses, to a fuller realization of our humanity, and to a wholeness, our "real heritage."

TEACHING MATERIALS

ILLUSTRATIONS OF ART SUBJECTS

UNESCO WORLD ART SERIES (NEW YORK GRAPHIC SOCIETY)
The following volumes have been issued: Spain, India, Egypt, Australia, Yugoslavia, Norway, Iran, Ceylon, U.S.S.R., Mexico, Japan, Czechoslovakia, Greece, Israel, Ethiopia, Turkey, Bulgaria, Tunisia, Rumania, Cyprus, Poland, Austria, Masaccio (Italy).

SKIRA
Skira Inc., Publishers, New York, have brought out a number of books of art with excellent illustrations in color. Some deal with a single artist, some with a movement or a period.

PHAIDON PRESS
A series of volumes brought out by the Oxford University Press, Fair Lawn, N.J., exceptionally high in quality. Each volume is devoted to a single artist, or more rarely a period or group of artists.

UNIVERSITY PRINTS (CAMBRIDGE, MASS.)
Photographs of the major art works of the world. The price (only a few cents) makes reproductions easily available.

ARTEXT PRINTS (WESTPORT, CONN.)
A large collection of colored prints, very inexpensive.

TEACHING PORTFOLIOS (MUSEUM OF MODERN ART, NEW YORK)
Large illustrations suitable for mounting on a wall, one on *Modern Sculpture*, one on *Textures*, one on *Structure and Space in Contemporary Architecture*.

THREE SMALLER SERIES
Form and Color (Harper & Row, Publishers, Inc., New York)
Hyperion (Duell, Sloan & Pearce, Inc., New York)
Iris (Oxford University Press, Fair Lawn, N.J.)

Form and Color devotes a volume to many reproductions of a single masterpiece. *Hyperion* is a collection of modern painters, one artist to a volume. Some volumes are excellent. *Iris* is an excellent set of very thin volumes devoted to subjects of restricted interest, e.g., *Art of the Far East, French Cathedral Windows, Persian Painting.*

PITKIN, PRIDE OF BRITAIN BOOKS
Cathedrals and churches, famous cities and places, royal history.

MUSIC

SKELETON SCORES. A skeleton score shows the melodic line of a composition, with annotations which give indications of form (first theme, development, etc.), timbre, tempo, and dynamics.

The series of *Symphonic Skeleton Scores* is edited and annotated by Violet Katzner (Theodore Presser Company, Bryn Mawr, Pa.). The series at present contains these six symphonies:

Beethoven, Symphony No. 5 in C minor
Brahms, Symphony No. 1 in C minor
Brahms, Symphony No. 3 in F major
Franck, Symphony in D minor
Mozart, Symphony in G minor
Schubert, Symphony in B minor (*Unfinished*)
Tchaikowsky, Symphony No. 4 in F minor
Tchaikowsky, Symphony No. 6 in B minor (*Pathétique*)

Scored for Listening, by Bockman and Starr (Harcourt, Brace & World, Inc., New York, 1959) contains skeleton scores for many of the compositions referred to in this volume.

MINIATURE SCORES. As the name implies, the miniature score gives the entire score, but in miniature; collections of miniature scores are published by E. F. Kalmus Orchestra Scores, Inc., New York, and by Penguin Books, Inc., Baltimore, Md.

LIBRETTOS. The complete words of operas, often with one or two musical excerpts, can be obtained from the Metropolitan Opera Association or Fred Rullman, Inc., in New York City, and Oliver Ditson Co., Boston.

III. FILMS

Henry Moore (British contemporary sculptor), British Information Service (1947)
Rodin (French sculptor, 1840–1947), United World (1950)
Steps of the Ballet, Encyclopedia Britannica Films (1949)
Four Films on Design, Young America (1950)
How to Make an Etching, Almanac Films (1951)
Frank Lloyd Wright, Encyclopedia Britannica Films (1960)
Boundary Lines, McGraw-Hill (1947)
What Is a Painting? Metropolitan Museum (n.d.)
The Making of a Mural (Thomas Hart Benton), Encyclopedia Britannica Films (1947)
Orpheus and Eurydice, Stephens College (1960)

BIBLIOGRAPHY

This bibliography is divided into five groups. The first contains the dictionaries and other volumes needed for factual reference or allusion. The second contains those volumes, such as the ones on aesthetics, which are concerned with more than one art. The third, fourth, and fifth groups are the regular classifications of the individual arts—literature, drama, and film; the visual arts; and music and the dance. Biographies and collections of illustrations are kept to a minimum.

I. DICTIONARIES AND REFERENCES

Avery, Catherine B., ed.: *The New Century Classical Handbook*, New York, 1962.

Catholic Encyclopedia, New York, 1907–1922.

Cirlot, J. E.: *A Dictionary of Symbols*, trans. from the Spanish by Jack Sage, New York, 1962.

Cruden, Alexander: *Complete Concordance to the Old and New Testament . . . with . . . a Concordance to the Apocrypha*, London, 1769.

Encyclopedia of World Art, New York, 1959.

Ferguson, George: *Signs and Symbols in Christian Art*, New York, 1954.

Frazer, Sir James George: *The Golden Bough: A Study in Magic and Religion*, 3rd ed., London, 1907–1915, 12 vols.

Gayley, Charles Mills: *Classic Myths in English Literature and in Art*, rev. ed., New York, 1939.

Gray, L. H., ed.: *Mythology of All Races*, Boston, 1916–1932, 13 vols.

Grove, George: *Grove's Dictionary of Music and Musicians*, 5th ed., New York, 1954, 10 vols.

Guirand, F., ed.: *Larousse Encyclopedia of Mythology*, London, 1959.

Hackin, J.: *Asiatic Mythology: A Detailed Description and Explanation of the Mythologies of All the Great Nations of Asia*, New York, 1963.

Hamilton, Edith: *Mythology*, New York, 1961.

Harmon, N. B., ed.: *The Interpreter's Bible*, New York, 1951–1957, 12 vols.

Hastings, James, ed.: *Encyclopedia of Religion and Ethics*, Edinburgh and New York, 1908–1927, 12 vols. and index.

The Interpreter's Dictionary of the Bible, New York, 1962, 4 vols.

Jacobs, Arthur: *A New Dictionary of Music*, rev. ed., Baltimore, 1960.

Lehner, Ernst: *The Picture Book of Symbols*, New York, 1956.

Maillard, Robert: *Dictionary of Modern Sculpture*, New York, 1960.

Nelson's Complete Concordance of the Revised Standard Version Bible, New York, 1957.

Standard Dictionary of Folklore, Mythology, and Legend, New York, 1949.

Whittick, Arnold: *Symbols, Signs, and Their Meaning*, Newton, Mass., 1961.

II. AESTHETICS

Berenson, Bernard: *Aesthetics and History in the Visual Arts*, New York, 1954.

Bonnard, André: *Greek Civilization—From the Iliad to the Parthenon*, London, 1957, 3 vols.

Bosanquet, Bernard: *Three Lectures on Aesthetics*, New York, 1963.

Coomaraswamy, Ananda K.: *The Transformation of Nature in Art*, New York, 1934.

Fleming, William: *Arts and Ideas*, New York, 1963.

Hamilton, Edith: *The Greek Way to Western Civilization*, New York, 1942.

Hauser, Arnold: *The Philosophy of Art History*, Cleveland and New York, 1963.

Langer, Susanne K.: *Feeling and Form*, New York, 1956.

———— *Philosophy in a New Key,* 3rd ed., Baltimore, 1957.

———— *Problems of Art: Ten Philosophical Lectures,* New York, 1957.

Larkin, Oliver: *Art and Life in America,* New York, 1960.

Margolis, Joseph Z.: *The Language of Art and Art Criticism: Analytic Questions in Aesthetics,* Detroit, 1965.

Maritain, Jacques: *Creative Intuition in Art and Poetry,* New York, 1955.

Miller, William Hugh: *Introduction to Music Appreciation: An Objective Approach to Listening,* Rahway, N.J., 1961.

Murry, John M.: *The Problem of Style,* London, 1960.

Rader, Melvin: *A Modern Book of Aesthetics: An Anthology,* 3rd ed., New York, 1960.

Read, Sir Herbert: *The Meaning of Art,* Baltimore, 1959.

Seldes, Gilbert: *Seven Lively Arts,* New York, 1962.

Sypher, Wylie, ed.: *Rococo to Cubism in Art and Literature,* New York, 1960.

———— *Art History: An Anthology of Modern Criticism,* New York, 1963.

III. LITERATURE, DRAMA, AND FILM

Barnet, Sylvan, and others: *A Dictionary of Literary Terms,* Boston, 1962.

Baugh, Albert C., ed.: *A Literary History of England,* New York, 1958.

Beardsley, Monroe, Robert Daniel, and Glenn Leggett: *Theme and Form,* 2nd ed., Englewood Cliffs, N.J., 1962.

Benét, William Rose, ed.: *The Reader's Encyclopedia,* 2nd ed., New York, 1965.

Booth, Wayne C.: *The Rhetoric of Fiction,* Chicago, 1961.

Bradley, A. C.: *Shakespearean Tragedy,* London, 1956.

———— *Oxford Lectures on Poetry,* 2nd ed., Bloomington, Ind., 1961.

Butcher, S. H.: *Aristotle's Theory of Poetry and Fine Art,* 4th rev. ed., New York, 1955.

Chase, Richard: *The American Novel and Its Tradition,* Garden City, New York, 1964.

Daiches, David: *A Study of Literature for Readers and Critics,* New York, 1964.

———— *The Present Age in British Literature,* Bloomington, Ind., 1958.

———— *English Literature,* Englewood Cliffs, N.J., 1964.

Eisenstein, Sergei M.: *Film Form (and) Film Sense,* New York, 1957. 2 vols. in one.

Eliot, T. S.: *On Poetry and Poets,* New York, 1957.

Forster, E. M.: *Aspects of the Novel,* New York, 1956.

Fowler, H. W.: *A Dictionary of Modern English Usage,* 2nd rev. ed. by E. Gowers, New York, 1965.

Harvey, P.: *Oxford Companion to English Literature,* 3rd ed., New York, 1946.

———— *Oxford Companion to Classical Literature,* 2nd ed., New York, 1937.

Isaacs, J.: *Background of Modern Poetry,* New York, 1952.

Jesperson, Otto: *Growth and Structure of the English Language,* 9th ed., New York, 1955.

Keene, Donald: *Anthology of Japanese Literature,* New York, 1956.

Kernan, Alvin B.: *Character and Conflict: An Introduction to Drama,* New York, 1963.

Kettle, Arnold: *An Introduction to the English Novel,* New York, 1951, 2 vol.

Kronenberger, Louis, *The Thread of Laughter,* New York, 1952.

Lattimore, Richmond: *The Poetry of Greek Tragedy,* Baltimore, 1958.

Lawson, John H.: *Film: The Creative Process: The Search for an Audio-Visual Language and Structure,* New York, 1964.

Leavis, F. R.: *The Great Tradition: A Study of the English Novel,* New York, 1963.

Legouis, E., and L. Cazamian: *A History of English Literature, 630–1914,* trans. by H. D. Irvine and W. D. MacInnes, 2 vols., rev. ed., New York, 1957.

Mandel, Oscar: *A Definition of Tragedy,* New York, 1961.

Manvell, Roger: *Film,* rev. ed., Baltimore, 1946.

McCollom, William G.: *Tragedy,* New York, 1957.

Nilsen, Vladimir S.: *The Cinema as a Graphic Art,* New York, 1959.

Preminger, Alex: *Encyclopedia of Poetry and Poetics*, Princeton, N.J., 1965.
Quiller-Couch, Sir Arthur: *On the Art of Writing*, New York, 1961.
Reinert, Otto: *Drama: An Introductory Anthology*, alt. ed., Boston, 1964.
Sapir, Edward: *Language: An Introduction to the Study of Speech*, New York, 1949.
Shapiro, Karl, and Robert Beum: *A Prosody Handbook*, New York, 1965.
Spurgeon, Caroline: *Shakespeare's Imagery*, Cambridge, 1952.
Thrall, William Flint, and Addison Hibbard: *A Handbook to Literature*, rev. ed., New York, 1960.
Tyler, Parker: *The Three Faces of the Film*, New York, 1960.
Van Ghent, Dorothy: *The English Novel: Form and Function*, New York, 1961.
Watt, Ian: *The Rise of the Novel*, Berkeley, Calif., 1964.
Wellek, René, and Austin Warren: *Theory of Literature*, 2nd ed., New York, 1956.

IV. THE VISUAL ARTS

Arnheim, Rudolf: *Art and Visual Perception: A Psychology of the Creative Eye*, Berkeley, Calif., 1954.
Barr, Alfred H., Jr., ed.: *Masters of Modern Art*, New York, 1954.
Berenson, Bernard: *The Italian Painters of the Renaissance*, New York, 1957.
Boardman, John: *Greek Art*, New York, 1964.
Canaday, John: *Keys to Art*, New York, 1963.
Christ-Janer, Albert, and Mary Mix Foley: *Modern Church Architecture*, New York, 1962.
Clark, Kenneth: *The Nude: A Study in Ideal Form*, Garden City, New York, 1956.
Drexler, Arthur: *The Architecture of Japan*, New York, 1955.
Faulkner, Ray, Edwin Ziegfeld, and Gerald Hill: *Art Today*, 4th ed., New York, 1963.
Fletcher, Bannister: *A History of Architecture on the Comparative Method*, 17th ed., New York, 1961.
Gardner, Ernest A.: *A Handbook of Greek Sculpture*, 2nd ed., New York, 1929.
Gardner, Helen: *Art Through the Ages*, 4th ed., revised by the Department of the History of Art, Yale University, New York, 1959.
Giedion, S.: *Architecture, You and Me*, Cambridge, Mass., 1958.
———— *Space, Time and Architecture*, 4th ed., Cambridge, Mass., 1962.
Gombrich, E. H.: *The Story of Art*, 10th ed., Greenwich, Conn., 1960.
Heller, Jules: *Printmaking Today: An Introduction to the Graphic Arts*, New York, 1958.
Hitchcock, Henry-Russell: *In the Nature of Materials: The Buildings of Frank Lloyd Wright*, New York, 1942.
———— and Arthur Drexler: *Built in U.S.A.: Post-War Architecture*, New York, 1953.
———— *Architecture: Nineteenth and Twentieth Centuries*, Baltimore, 1963.
Huyghe, René: *Ideas and Images in World Art (Dialogue with the Visible)*. New York, 1959.
Illinois, University of: *Contemporary American Painting and Sculpture*, 1965.
Janson, H. W., with Dora Jane Janson: *The Picture History of Painting*. New York, 1957.
———— *A History of Art*, New York, 1962.
———— ed.: *Key Monuments of the History of Art (A Visual Survey)*, New York, 1962.
Lavedan, Pierre: *French Architecture*, Baltimore, 1957.
Lawrence, A. W.: *Greek Architecture*, Baltimore, 1957.
Le Corbusier (pseud. of Charles E. Jeanneret-Gris): *Towards a New Architecture*, trans. from the 13th French ed., with an introduction by Frederick Etchells, New York, 1959.
Loran, Erle: *Cézanne's Composition: Analysis of His Form with Diagrams and Photographs of His Motifs*, 3rd ed., Berkeley, Calif., 1963.
Mâle, Emile: *Religious Art from the Twelfth to the Eighteenth Century*, New York, 1963.
Mumford, Lewis: *The Culture of Cities*, New York, 1938.
———— *Sticks and Stones*, 2nd rev. ed., New York, 1955.
Myers, Bernard S.: *Art and Civilization*, New York, 1957.
———— *Modern Art in the Making*, 2nd ed., New York, 1959.
———— *Understanding the Arts*, rev. ed., New York, 1963.

Newton, Eric: *European Painting and Sculpture*, 4th ed., Baltimore, 1960.
Paine, Robert Treat, and Alexander Soper: *The Art and Architecture of Japan*, Baltimore, 1955.
Panofsky, Erwin: *Meaning in the Visual Arts*, New York, 1955.
Peterdi, Gabor: *Printmaking: Methods Old and New*, New York, 1959.
Pevsner, Nikolaus: *Outline of European Architecture*, 5th ed., Baltimore, 1960.
Pope, Arthur: *The Language of Drawing and Painting*, Cambridge, Mass., 1949.
Read, Sir Herbert: *A Concise History of Modern Painting*, New York, 1959.
Rewald, John: *Post-Impressionism: From Van Gogh to Gauguin*, New York, 1958.
Richards, J. M., and Elizabeth B. Mock: *An Introduction to Modern Architecture*, Baltimore, 1956.
Richter, Gisela M. A.: *The Sculpture and Sculptors of the Ancient Greeks*, rev. ed., New Haven, Conn., 1950.
Robb, David M., and J. J. Garrison: *Art in the Western World*, 4th ed., New York, 1963.
Scott, Geoffrey: *The Architecture of Humanism*, New York, 1954.
Seiberling, Frank: *Looking into Art*, New York, 1959.
Seuphor, Michel: *Dictionary of Abstract Painting*, New York, 1957.
Sewall, John Ives: *A History of Western Art*, rev. ed., New York, 1962.
Tapié, Victor L.: *The Age of Grandeur: Baroque Art and Architecture*, trans. from the French by A. Ross Williamson, New York, 1960.
Upjohn, Everard M., Paul S. Wingert, and Jane Gaston Mahler: *History of World Art*, 2nd ed., New York, 1958.
Venturi, Lionello: *Painting and Painters: How to Look at a Picture from Giotto to Chagall*, New York, 1945.
Warner, Langdon: *The Enduring Art of Japan*, New York, 1958.
Woelfflin, H.: *Principles of Art History*, trans. from the 7th German ed. by M. D. Hottinger, New York, 1949.
Wright, Frank Lloyd: *The Living City*, New York, 1958.
Zigrosser, Carl: *Prints: Thirteen Illustrated Essays on the Art of the Print*, New York, 1962.

V. MUSIC AND THE DANCE

Abraham, Gerald: *Design in Music*, New York, 1949.
Apel, Willi: *Harvard Dictionary of Music*, Cambridge, Mass., 1944.
———— *Gregorian Chant*, Bloomington, Ind., 1958.
Barlow, Wayne: *Foundations of Music*, New York, 1953.
Bauman, Alvin, and Charles W. Walton: *Elementary Musicianship*, 2nd ed., Englewood Cliffs, N.J., 1959.
Bernstein, Martin: *An Introduction to Music*, 2nd ed., Englewood Cliffs, N.J., 1951.
Boyden, David Dodge: *An Introduction to Music*, New York, 1956.
Chujoy, Anatole: *The New York City Ballet*, New York, 1953.
Cooper, Grosvenor: *Learning to Listen: A Handbook for Music*, Chicago, 1957.
    Prepared with the humanities staff of the College at the University of Chicago.
Copland, Aaron: *Music and Imagination*, Cambridge, Mass., 1953.
———— *What to Listen for in Music*, rev. ed., New York, 1957.
Dallin, Leon: *Listener's Guide to Musical Understanding*, Dubuque, Iowa, 1959.
DeMille, Agnes: *The Book of the Dance*, New York, 1963.
Dent, Edward J.: *Opera*, Baltimore, 1940.
Ewen, David, ed.: *From Bach to Stravinsky: The History of Music by Its Foremost Critics*, New York, 1933.
Finney, Theodore M.: *A History of Music*, rev. ed., New York, 1947.
Forsyth, Cecil: *Orchestration*, 2nd ed., New York, 1942.
Geiringer, Karl: *Musical Instruments*, New York, 1945.
Green, Douglass M.: *Form in Tonal Music*, New York, 1965.

Grout, Donald J.: *A History of Western Music,* New York, 1960.

———— *A Short History of Opera,* 2 vols., 2nd. ed., New York, 1965.

Grove, George: *Beethoven and His Nine Symphonies,* London, 1898.

Hadow, Sir W. H., ed.: *The Oxford History of Music,* 6 vols., 2nd ed., New York, 1929.

Hansen, Peter S.: *An Introduction to Twentieth Century Music,* Boston, 1961.

Harman, Alec: *Man and his Music: the Story of Musical Experience in the West,* New York, 1962.

Haskell, Arnold, ed.: *Ballet* (annual), nos. 16 and 17, New York, 1962 and 1963.

Hill, Ralph: *The Symphony,* Baltimore, 1949.

Hindemith, Paul: *The Craft of Musical Composition, Part I,* New York, 1942.

———— *A Composer's World: Horizons and Limitations,* Cambridge, Mass., 1952.

Howard, John Tasker, and James Lyons: *Modern Music: A Popular Guide to Greater Musical Enjoyment,* rev. ed., New York, 1957.

Humphrey, Doris: *The Art of Making Dances,* ed. by Barbara Pollack, New York, 1959.

Hutchinson, Ann: *Labanotation,* New York, 1954.

Lang, Paul Henry: *Music in Western Civilization,* New York, 1941.

Lawson, Joan: *A History of Ballet and Its Makers,* New York, 1964.

Liepmann, Klaus: *The Language of Music,* New York, 1953.

Mann, Alfred: *The Study of Fugue,* New Brunswick, N.J., 1958.

Marek, George R., ed.: *The World Treasury of Grand Opera,* New York, 1957.

Martin, John: *Introduction to the Dance,* New York, 1939.

———— *The Modern Dance,* New York, 1933.

———— *The Dance,* New York, 1946.

Meyer, Leonard B.: *Emotion and Meaning in Music,* Chicago, 1956.

———— and Grosvenor W. Cooper: *The Rhythmic Structure of Music,* Chicago, 1960.

Mitchell, Donald: *The Language of Modern Music,* New York, 1963.

Morris, R. O.: *The Structure of Music: An Outline for Students,* New York, 1935.

Murphy, Howard A.: *Form in Music for the Listener,* Camden, N.J., 1945.

New Oxford History of Music, New York, 1963.

Newman, Ernest: *Wagner Operas,* New York, 1949.

Piston, Walter: *Harmony,* 3rd rev. ed., New York, 1962.

Portnoy, Julius: *Music in the Life of Man,* New York, 1963.

Raffe, Walter G.: *Dictionary of the Dance,* New York, 1965.

Ratner, Leonard G.: *Music, The Listener's Art,* New York, 1957.

Rufer, Joseph: *Composition with Twelve Notes,* trans. by Humphrey Searle, New York, 1954.

Sachs, Curt: *The Wellsprings of Music,* ed. by Jaap Kunst, The Hague, Netherlands, 1962.

———— *World History of the Dance,* New York, 1963.

Salazar, Adolfo: *Music in Our Time: Trends in Music since the Romantic Era,* trans. by Isabel Pope, New York, 1946.

Scholes, Percy A.: *Listener's Guide to Music,* with a concertgoer's glossary and an introduction by Sir W. Henry Hadow, 10th ed., New York, 1948.

———— *Oxford Companion to Music,* 9th ed., New York, 1955.

Stearns, Marshall W.: *The Story of Jazz,* New York, 1956.

Stringham, Edwin John: *Listening to Music Creatively,* 2nd ed., New York, n.d.

Toch, Ernst: *The Shaping Forces in Music,* New York, 1948.

Tovey, Donald Francis: *Essays in Musical Analysis,* 6 vols., New York, 1935–1939.

———— *Musical Articles from the Encyclopaedia Britannica,* with an editorial preface by Hubert J. Foss, New York, 1944.

———— *Beethoven,* with an editorial preface by Hubert J. Foss, New York, 1945.

———— *The Main Stream of Music and Other Essays,* collected with an introduction by Hubert J. Foss, New York, 1949.

Tyndall, Robert E.: *Musical Form,* Rockleigh, N.J., 1964.

Zuckerkandl, Victor: *The Sense of Music,* Princeton, N.J., 1959.

INDEX

Boldface type indicates pages with illustrations or quotations

426

Index

430

Index

432

Index